思维导图

English

在小学英语教学中的应用

韩丽萍 李军荣 / 主编

东北师范大学出版社

长 春

图书在版编目（CIP）数据

思维导图在小学英语教学中的应用／韩丽萍，李军荣主编. — 长春：东北师范大学出版社，2020.11
ISBN 978-7-5681-7390-2

Ⅰ. ①思… Ⅱ. ①韩… ②李… Ⅲ. ①英语课—教学研究—小学 Ⅳ. ①G623.312

中国版本图书馆CIP数据核字（2020）第220707号

□责任编辑：邓江英　　　　　　　□封面设计：言之凿
□责任校对：刘彦妮　张小娅　　　□责任印制：许　冰

东北师范大学出版社出版发行
长春净月经济开发区金宝街 118 号（邮政编码：130117）
电话：0431-84568115
网址：http://www.nenup.com
北京言之凿文化发展有限公司设计部制版
北京政采印刷服务有限公司印装
北京市中关村科技园区通州园金桥科技产业基地环科中路 17 号（邮编：101102）
2022年6月第1版　2022年6月第1次印刷
幅面尺寸：170mm×240mm　印张：14.25　字数：226千

定价：59.90元

惠州市中小学和中等职业技术学校教育科研课题研究项目"思维导图在小学英语教学中的应用"（2013kt209）研究成果

惠州市第九届教育科研成果一等奖，证书编号：HZJYKY（HC47）

让思维在课堂绽放光彩

时间进入21世纪，英语不仅已成为小学义务教育中的必修课程，教育部还明确要求各学科的教师要加强对学生核心素养的培养，英语学科也不例外。核心素养下的英语课堂不再只是单纯的教学几个单词、几个句子、一些语法和一些应试技巧，而是要培养学生的语言能力、学习能力、思维品质和文化品格。因此要求广大英语教师们必须大胆尝试各种教学方法的改革，勇于闯出教学新路，让我们学生能在快乐中学习英语，在英语学习中不断完善自我。思维导图在课堂教学上的应用，不仅能够有助于学生的学习，提升注意力和记忆力，还能启发学生的想象力和创造力，这与当前提出的英语学科核心素养是高度一致的。

"思维导图在小学英语教学中的应用"是广东省名师工作室主持人韩丽萍老师和广东省惠州市惠城区教育局教研室小学英语教研员李军荣老师研修的主题，团队由锐意进取，勇于研究与实践的市、区骨干教师组成。他们率领的团队踏踏实实开展了理论学习、课例研讨与展示、论文撰写，又不遗余力地向省、市、区推广，指导教师参赛，培养了一大批青年教师走向专业成才的快车道。他们不仅完成了课题的所有研究工作，而且把课题研究取得的丰硕成果编撰成书。本书紧扣义务教育教科书英语PEP（三年级起点）八册教材46个单元，基于英语学科核心素养和单元整体教学的理念，利用思维导图工具把教材内容整合为词汇（Vocabulary）、话题（Topics）、读写（Read and Write）、写作（Writing）4个方面。这无疑是对合理使用教材，创造性使用教材的勇敢尝试，对广大小学英语教师开展课堂教学具有可操作性和借鉴性。我衷心希望本书的出版能够为广大教师奉献启迪课堂教学的价值。

以此为序，祝贺本书的出版！

2020年10月

（孟庆玲，吉林省教学名师，南粤优秀教师，广东省粤北中小学英语教师培训专家，广东韶关学院外国语学院英语系主任、教授）

走在思维导图探索路上

　　我时常听老师们说，"教材不好教，学生教不动"。在教学中，学生往往出现教了这个单元内容忘了上个单元内容，学了这册书知识丢了上册书知识的现象。特别是学习能力较弱的学生，有时连几个单词都记不住，更别说阅读、写作与语法的学习了。英语是外语，对于大部分学生来说，学习缺乏语言环境，因此对所学的知识也只是以单纯性的背诵、机械性的操练为主，知识之间缺乏联系，更谈不上发展思维的层面。面对这些问题，我一直在思索教学中如何可以"授之以鱼"，也"授之以渔"，这时思维导图的概念在我的脑海里出现了。

　　恰逢2013年市级课题申报，我与几位志同道合的老师希望通过课题研究的路径，探讨如何利用思维导图来优化课堂教学策略，从而发展学生的思维。思维导图在小学英语教学中的应用研究课题就这样产生了。课题实施了两年，又经过了多年的应用与推广，均得到专家、一线教师和学生的好评。本书的编写主要把课题研究的过程和研究的成果与各位读者交流探讨。

　　本书由报告、案例、绘制三部分组成。报告分为开题报告、中期报告、结题报告及成果公报。报告主要阐述了为什么要选这项课题进行研究、这项课题是怎样进行研究的、课题研究取得了哪些研究成果，从根本上论证了选题的实用性与可操作性。

　　案例部分紧扣义务教育教科书英语PEP（三年级起点）八册教材46个单

元，基于英语学科核心素养和单元整体教学的理念，利用思维导图工具把教材内容整合为词汇（Vocabulary）、话题（Topic）、读写（Read and write）、写作（Writing）4个方面，让学生在话题情境中进行有意义、有目的的输入和输出。全书共绘制了超过200幅思维导图呈现给读者。书中每幅思维导图的中心主题是教材单元话题，一级分支是思维的维度，二级及以下分支是思维的广度和深度。

绘制部分主要阐述了思维导图绘制的规则与步骤。这里首先要感谢思维导图的发明人东尼·博赞先生，是他把思维导图带到这个世界并使其得以广泛地推广运用。在课题研究和编写此书过程中我们大量地阅读东尼·博赞先生关于思维导图论述的系列丛书，从理论高度上认识思维导图的精髓。操作类的书籍得益于阅读了赵国庆博士的专著《别说你懂思维导图》，让我们进一步深入了解了思维导图的操作与应用。特别是关于思维导图的读图与绘制这两章内容让我们受益匪浅，这里也一并与读者们分享。

思维导图是思维可视化的有效工具，是基于大脑神经元工作原理而设计的。思维导图的正确使用可以训练学生的结构化思维、发散思维、逻辑思维以及可视化思维等。思维导图的作用是提供思考问题、分析问题和解决问题的工具。

"苔花如米小，也学牡丹开"，这本书承载着全体编委的殷切期待，希望不久的将来会有更多的老师把思维导图应用于课堂教学，让课堂成为启迪学生思维的摇篮。

是为序！

2019年10月于惠州

关于使用本书的两点建议：

一、阅读和学习有关思维导图的书籍，了解思维导图的基本理论及精髓，不能把思维导图简单地用于复述文本。

二、本书使用的对象主要是面向教师。书中所呈现的思维导图是我们在课堂教学实践中的一个样式，但并不是一成不变的。老师们可以基于学情，合理地删减、丰富或重构，创造性地使用本书，达到图为我用、提高课堂教学的效果。

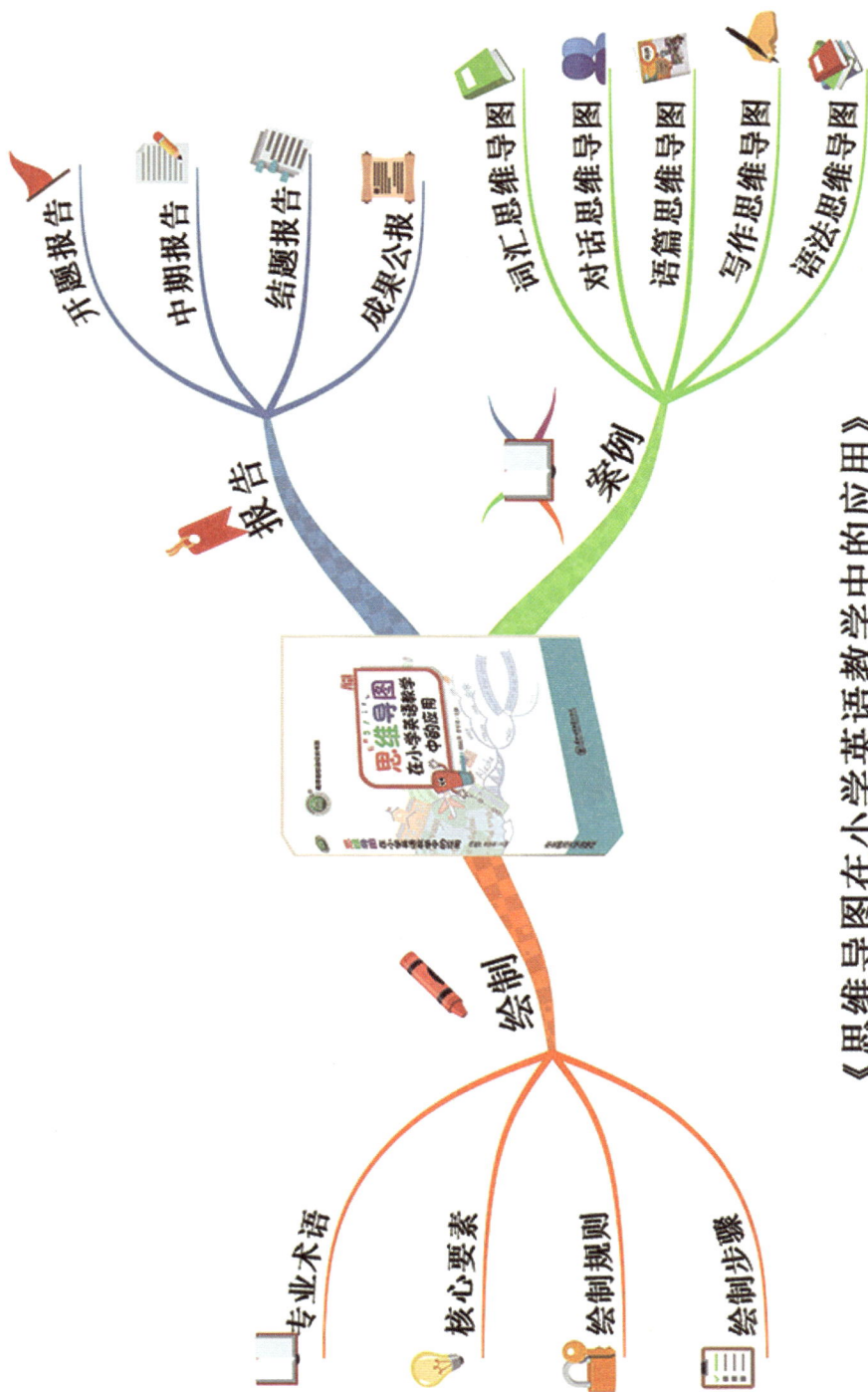

《思维导图在小学英语教学中的应用》
目录概览图

绘制
- 专业术语
- 核心要素
- 绘制规则
- 绘制步骤

报告
- 开题报告
- 中期报告
- 结题报告
- 成果公报

案例
- 词汇思维导图
- 对话思维导图
- 语篇思维导图
- 写作思维导图
- 语法思维导图

目 录
CONTENTS

下 篇　思维导图绘制方法 \ 199

上 篇
思维导图研究报告

中期
报告

结题
报告

开题
报告

成果
公报

报告

开题报告

一、课题研究的背景和意义

（一）课题研究的背景

思维导图又称心智图、心灵图、脑图等。最早由英国心理学家东尼·博赞（Tony Buzan）提出。他在《思维导图》一书中对思维导图是这样定义的："思维导图是放射性思维的表达，因此也是人类思维的自然功能。它是一种非常有用的图形技术，是打开大脑潜力的万能钥匙。思维导图可以用于生活的各个方面，其改进后的学习能力和清晰的思维方式会改善人的行为表现。"

在国外，思维导图在教育领域的研究与应用已经相当成熟。如英国、美国、新加坡、日本、韩国、德国、瑞士、澳大利亚等国家的教育教学机构已经对该课题进行了深入地研究和探索。在英国和新加坡思维导图早已列入国民中小学的必修课程中。在许多知名学府，如哈佛大学、剑桥大学等，教授们热衷于使用思维导图来提高他们的教学效率。

在国内，开始对思维导图的学习和研究不是很早。美国珍妮特·沃斯的著作《学习的革命》于1998年出版发行以来，从那时起，思维导图才漂洋过海进入中国，从此国内的研究者和教师才开始对其进行探索和钻研。2000年，王功玲首次介绍了思维导图使用的方法，并在教案编写以及课堂教学中应用思维导图做笔记。2004年，赵国庆、陆志坚等人对思维导图的概念、来源等进行了深入地剖析，拉开了思维导图在中国研究的序幕，并奠定了坚实的基础。此后，陆续涌现出很多学者和专家对思维导图进行研究。

思维导图应用于英语教学的研究主要集中在英语词汇、阅读、写作教学中。例如，2005年，辽宁师范大学的张丹从英语阅读教学中存在的问题出发，介绍了思维导图的特点和绘制方法，并分析了如何将其应用到英语阅读的课前、课中和课后，最后总结了其实验过程。2005年，陈敏细致分析了外语教学中运用思维导图的优势，并且探讨了该学习策略的认识理论基础。2008年，曾燕燕结合相应的理论，提出了根据不同的教学内容可绘制不同类型的思维导图，为笔者的研究提供了实践上的参考。

通过以上综述得知：思维导图是一种新的思维模式和学习方法。由此可见将思维导图应用于小学英语教学实践中是一个值得研究的课题。

（二）研究的意义

《义务教育英语课程标准（2011年版）》提出，英语课程承担着培养学生基本英语素养和发展学生思维能力的任务。语言既是交流的工具，又是思维的工具。英语课堂应成为学生在教师指导下构建知识、发展技能、拓宽视野、活跃思维、展现个性的过程。思维导图作为一种可视化的教学和学习策略，能使语言表征重点突出、条理清晰、层次分明。它能够帮助学生加深对知识的理解，提高学生的自学能力和创造性思维能力。因此，思维导图作为一种新的思维模式和学习方法具有强大的优势。

1. 突出重点，有效助记

思维导图一方面把学习者的主要精力集中在关键知识点上，不把时间浪费在无关重要的内容上，从而节省了宝贵的学习时间。另一方面，思维导图通过有效的概念意义的组织和概念框架的建立成为一个有力的助记工具。

2. 改善学生的信息加工方式，建立合理的知识网络

思维导图促进学习者对新旧知识的整合，提升思维能力，对思维导图节点的增加或对概念结构的修改都体现了学习者个性化的、主动的信息加工和知识构建过程。

3. 提高综合信息的能力，激发联想与创意

思维导图有利于开发学习者的创造力，它能把各种零散的智慧、观点等融会贯通成为一个系统，允许学习者自由联想。

4. 促使学生形成系统学习和思维的习惯

本课题的研究立足于小学英语教学实践，从课堂教学实际入手，根据教学内容探讨词汇（Vocabulary）、话题（Topic）、读写（Read and write）、写作（Writing）4个方面的思维导图样式，帮助学生根据一定的逻辑顺序建构知识网络，

从整体上把握所学的英语知识，为学生的可持续学习和发展奠定基础。

二、课题概念的界定

思维导图又名心智图，是由英国著名心理学家和教育家东尼·博赞创造的一种有效记笔记的方法。它是充分利用右脑的形象思维和左脑的抽象思维，采用图文并茂的方式来表征、组织、阐述知识，展现人们获取知识、解决问题时的思维过程。通俗地说，思维导图是一个简单、有效的思维工具。它依据全脑的概念，按照大脑自身的规律进行思考，使大脑潜能得到最充分的开发，从而极大地发掘人的记忆、创造、语言等各方面的潜能。

三、课题研究的理论基础

（一）脑科学理论

解剖学的研究表明，人的大脑分左脑和右脑两个半球，左右脑通过胼胝体连接起来。20世纪60年代，美国心理生物学家罗杰·斯佩里对裂脑人进行了深入的研究，提出了"左右脑分工理论"，并因此荣获1981年诺贝尔生理学或医学奖。该理论认为左脑主要负责责词汇、逻辑、数字、次序、线性、分析、序列等，右脑主要负责节奏、空间知觉、维度、想象、色彩、整体意识等。虽然左右脑在功能上不对称，存在偏侧化现象，但它们并不是单独工作，而是通过左右脑的协作来完成的。因此，"左脑+右脑"的"全脑"思维模式是一种创造性思维模式。脑科学研究发现，人类大脑的各种技巧如果能被和谐而巧妙地加以运用，将比彼此分开工作产生更高的效率。思维导图利用"左脑+右脑"的"全脑"思维模式，有利于激发大脑的潜能，并使大脑平衡协调发展。无论是在效率、效果还是效益上，思维导图都比传统学习方法更有效。

（二）认知心理学理论

1. 可视化学习理论

可视化是一种使复杂信息能够容易和快速被人理解的手段，是一种聚焦信息重要特征的信息压缩语言，是可以放大人类感知的图形化表示方法。可视化就是把数据、信息和知识转化为可视的表现形式，并获得对数据更深层次认识的过程。从可视化的表示中人们可以发现新的线索、新的关联、新的结构、新的知识，促使系统整合，促进科学决策。可视化技术以人们惯于接受的表格图形、图像等形式并辅以信息处理技术将客观事物及其内在的联系进行表现，使可视化结果便于人们记忆和理解。

思维导图是将知识可视化的一种工具，它将隐性知识显性化、言语信息图像化。除了传达事实信息之外，还将所学内容转换成可被人的感官领悟的知识表征形式，有效地帮助学生对抽象文字的理解、记忆，加快认知活动，以这种方式帮助他人正确地重构、记忆和应用这些知识，从而促进知识的获取、共享与创新。

2. 格式塔理论

格式塔心理学主要研究人们怎样理解整体和构成整体的部分之间的关系。格式塔理论认为如果对构成部分有恰当的认识，将有助于形成整体的认知，了解各构成部分之间的联系。思维导图从整体上表现了某个较为广域概念中的各个组成部分。学习变化的实质在于使内在逻辑结构的教材与学生原有的认知结构产生联系，新旧知识相互渗透，使新材料在学习者头脑中获得新意义。从某种程度上讲，思维导图就是从整体上表现为某个广泛意义上的各个组成部分。

3. 建构主义学习理论

建构主义学习理论的一个重要的概念是图式。图式是组织、描述和解释我们经验的概念网络，是人们在认知过程中对同类客体或活动的基本结构的抽象概括，是一种知识框架、组织结构和分类系统。建构主义的学习理论认为，每个学习者都具有不同的知识和经验，这些是存在学习者头脑中原有的图式。图式的形成和变化反映了认知的发展。学习者在外界的刺激下，通过同化或顺应，把它们纳入到原有的图式内，或修改重建原有图式，形成新的认知结构，使认知发展从旧的平衡向新的平衡过渡，获得新的知识与能力。思维导图将思维过程和知识结构用图像的形式展示出来，可以更好地把握思维过程和知识的整体架构，以便于将新知识整合到已有的知识体系中。因此，思维导图在教学中的应用也体现了建构主义学习理论的观点。

4. 最近发展区理论

最近发展区理论的主要特征有两点：一是学生承担的任务必须略高于个人当前能力水平，任务应该拓展其能力，但又不能超出其能力范围；二是必须有一个成年人或能力更强的同伴在学生要处理的任务或问题之间起中介作用。教学的目的就是要通过教师或同伴的帮助消除实际发展水平和潜在发展水平之间的差距，使潜在发展水平变成实际发展水平。随着教学要求的不断提高以及知识的进一步深化，为今后的教学创造出一个个新的最近发展区，从而形成一种良性循环，不断推动学生发展水平向更高层次发展。

最近发展区存在于学生已知与未知、能够胜任和不能胜任之间，教师需要为学生提供一种概念框架，这种框架中的概念正为发展学生对问题的进一步理解所需要。思维导图恰恰就是这样的工具。它既能够表示知识体系中概念以及概念之间已有的联系，又能够体现学生认知结构中已有的概念以及相互的关系，并在教与学之间建立互通的桥梁和架构。应用思维导图的教学实际上就是最近发展区内的教与学。其中，学生的"学"是在思维导图的扶持下，力图跨越最近发展区的学习；教师的"教"则是在最近发展区内提供支架，帮助学生跨越最近发展区的教学，思维导图是在强调以学生为中心的文化背景中提出的。通过思维导图的帮助，管理学习的任务能逐渐由教师转移给学生，即学习过程被内化，最后达到撤去支架，无须教师引导，学生自己能在概念框架中继续攀爬的目的，从而使学生思维的实际发展水平与潜在发展水平得到最大限度的发挥。[①]

四、课题研究的国内外现状

（一）国外研究现状

思维导图最早是英国著名心理学家和教育家东尼·博赞提出的。他在《思维导图》一书中对思维导图是这样定义的："思维导图是放射性思维的表达，因此也是人类思维的自然功能。它是一种非常有用的图形技术，是打开大脑潜力的万用钥匙。思维导图可以用于生活的各个方面，其改进后的学习能力和清晰的思维方式会改善人的行为表现。"

东尼·博赞发明思维导图后，很快在各国企业培训和教育推广中运用。思维导图在教育、医学、农业、工业、气象、管理等各个领域，都发挥过巨大作用，尤其在欧美发达国家。国外教育界关于思维导图在学科教学中的应用研究已有一

---

① 吉桂凤.思维导图与小学英语教学［M］.北京：教育科学出版社，2015.

定的理论、实践的积淀。

思维导图作为一种思维发散和导向的工具，在中小学教育改革实验项目中得到广泛应用。英国、新加坡已经把思维导图作为国民中小学的必修课程，韩国、日本、德国等国家的教育教学机构也已经开始对该课题进行研究和探索。在美国的《美国国家教育技术标准》所提供的教案范例和软件资源目录中也可以看到许多优秀教案都使用了思维导图。

（二）国内研究现状

相对于国外的发展来说，国内思维导图的应用还刚刚起步，教育界的很多教师和研究人员也对此进行了积极的探索，在一些小学、中学、大学进行了思维导图与学科教学的尝试，使思维导图的应用无论在理论上还是实践上都有了很大的发展。目前国内研究思维导图和英语学科结合的尚不多见，思维导图在课堂教学中的应用研究还处在理念的推广阶段，实践操作层面的理论及经验还较为缺乏，小学阶段尤为明显。思维导图形象直观的方式有助于提高学生英语学习的兴趣，让学生感受到英语学习带来的快乐，有助于帮助学生养成良好的英语学习习惯，逐步培养其独立学习英语的能力。我国有不少学校都在推行思维导图教学，已经有众多教育界的先行者在关注并积极探讨它的应用。可以肯定的是，思维导图必将有更加广泛的应用，也必将更加深入到教学的各个环节中去。

五、课题的基本内容和总体目标

（一）基本内容

本课题研究将立足于小学英语教学实践，从课堂教学实际入手，根据教学内容探讨词汇、话题、读写、写作4个方面的思维导图案例，帮助学生根据一定的逻辑顺序建构知识网络，从整体上把握所学的英语知识，为学生的可持续学习和发展奠定基础。本课题的基本内容为：

（1）小学英语词汇、话题、读写、写作等思维导图的案例。

（2）指导教师和学生绘制简单的思维导图，并运用思维导图整合所学的知识形成知识链，从而完成对知识的整体建构。

（二）拟达到的目标

1. 总体目标

（1）通过研究和实践，从课堂教学实际入手，根据教学内容探讨出词汇、话题、读写、写作4个方面的思维导图案例，帮助学生更好地理解和记忆所学的英语知识，从而有效地提高教学质量。

（2）通过研究和实践，培养学生的逻辑思维能力、发散思维能力和创新能力。

（3）通过研究和实践，进一步更新教师的教育观念，促使课题组成员在研究中实现专业成长，从而提升教师的理论水平和研究能力。

2. 年度目标

（1）2013年5月至9月，确定选题，申请立项。组建课题小组，学习相关理论知识。

（2）2013年10至2014年10月，组织课题组成员制订研究实施方案，明确研究的内容、目的、要求及思路。学习思维导图的基本理论，并掌握绘制思维导图的基本方法。以实验班为单位，由教师向学生讲解思维导图的知识及绘制方法。课题组成员完成"小学英语词汇思维导图"和"小学英语人教版教材三至六年级单元核心词句思维导图"的案例汇编。

（3）2014年11月至2015年2月，课题组完成"小学英语人教版教材三至六年级单元话题教学思维导图""小学英语人教版教材四至六年级单元读写教学思维导图""小学英语人教版教材五至六年级单元写作教学思维导图""小学英语人教版教材语法教学思维导图"的案例汇编。

（4）2015年3月至2015年5月，收集整理研究实施过程的教学案例、影像资料、论文、课例等相关材料，完成撰写课题研究总结和结题报告，邀请专家指导，向有关部门申请结题。

六、课题拟突破的重点、拟解决的关键问题及创新之处

（1）以改变目前学生词汇、对话、阅读、写作学习能力偏低的状况作为课题的"突破点"。

（2）以培养学生的逻辑思维能力、发散思维能力和创新能力作为"关键问题"。

（3）以形成小学英语词汇、话题、读写、写作等思维导图的案例作为"创新点"。

七、课题研究的方法和手段、研究计划

（一）研究方法和手段

1. 案例研究法

对典型的课堂教学案例进行分析研究，归纳整理出有效的思维导图案例。

2. 行动研究法

在教与学的过程中，通过"专家引领—合作探究—总结完善—形成特色"，把研究与实践紧密地结合起来，最终编制出一套较为完善的有利于教与学的思维导图案例。

3. 课堂观察法

一方面是观察学生的课堂行为，包括学生的学习行为、思考能力、对老师授课的反应等。另一方面是观察教师，包括思维导图的应用、引导技巧等。

4. 实验总结法

根据教学实践的研究，挖掘现有的经验材料，并上升到理论的高度，以便更好地指导新的教学案例。这一研究方法有利于教师撰写课题论文，出版课题研究成果专著等。

（二）研究计划

本课题整个研究步骤大致分为：确定方案—开题论证—研究实施—总结提炼—成果鉴定。研究计划用两年时间完成，即2013年5月至2015年5月。本研究计划分为三个阶段：

第一阶段：课题准备阶段（2013年5月—9月）

（1）确定选题，申请立项。

（2）组建课题小组，学习相关理论知识。

第二阶段：课题实施阶段（2013年10月—2015年2月）

（1）制订研究实施方案，明确研究的内容、目的、要求及思路。

（2）课题开题论证。

（3）定期开展课题研讨、课例教学。

（4）课题组成员撰写教学设计、论文、教学反思等。

（5）撰写中期报告，接受课题中期检查。

（6）积极反思，探索总结不同年级不同教学内容的思维导图案例。

第三阶段：成果总结与鉴定阶段（2015年3月—5月）

收集整理研究实施过程中的教学案例、影像资料、论文、课例等相关材料，撰写课题研究总结和结题报告，邀请专家指导，向有关部门申请结题。

八、预期的成果与表现形式

1. 阶段性成果

（1）开题报告、实施方案、教案、教学反思、研究论文等。

（2）课堂教学案例、师生设计的思维导图作品、阶段性研究总结、中期研究报告等。

2. 最终研究成果

（1）具有代表性的思维导图教学展示课。

（2）形成主题词汇思维导图、对话思维导图、语篇思维导图、写作思维导图、语法思维导图案例集、学生思维导图设计作品集、结题报告及各种获奖证书等。

九、经费使用预算

经费使用预算表

预算内容	预算金额	用　途
图书资料费	4000元	课题组成员理论学习的依据
国内调研差旅费	3000元	课题组成员外出研修
小型会议费	500元	课题组成员召开研讨会
计算机使用费	500元	借用学校、其他单位或个人电脑设备
印刷补助费	1000元	印刷课题资料
咨询费	500元	用于通过电话咨询课题研究
其他	2000元	宣传、推广课题成果等
合计	11500元	

十、项目组成员

韩丽萍　李军荣　李深婷　胡小娥　陈秀连　石斯婷　伍嘉敏　吴珊珊
郭东梅

一、研究工作进展情况

本课题组从2013年5月申报课题起，课题组成员便积极准备，收集课题研究所需要的资料。2013年9月收到立项通知后，课题组马上制订研究实施方案，明确研究的内容、目的、要求及思路，同年10月邀请专家进行课题开题论证。到2014年11月止，课题组取得了阶段性成果，汇编了课题成果集《小学英语词汇思维导图》和《小学英语人教版教材三至六年级单元核心词句思维导图》。

1. 工作方案

（1）理论学习：课题组购买了思维导图的相关应用书籍，网上收集了学习资料，在学科教研活动、集体备课等时间开展理论学习，采用集体学习和自主学习相结合的方式，学习后撰写读书笔记。

（2）实践研究：思维导图作为帮助学生学习的工具，也作为教师一种辅助教学手段，如何架构及应用是我们研究的首要内容。实际教学中采用丰富的课型，有词汇课、对话课、阅读课等，如何应用思维导图使各种课型的课都能高效地开展教学是我们研究的重点。所以，课题组结合学校的教研课、校际联动课、专家指导课等一系列活动开展课例研究。

（3）过程管理：课题组注重研究过程性管理。每学期初制订研究计划，期末进行学期总结。学期内定期开展课题组会议，课题组成员理一理课题研究的进展情况，谈一谈研究过程中碰到的问题，安排好下阶段的研究内容。

（4）教会课题组成员制作正确、有效的思维导图。

（5）教会学生制作正确、有效的思维导图。

（6）将小学英语人教版教材46个单元的核心词句制作成一个或多个思维导图，并将绘制的思维导图汇编成册。

（7）将优秀的论文发表。

（8）完成年度研究报告。

2. 调研计划

（1）2013年6月至2013年7月，先请专家对课题组成员进行思维导图理论的培训，让课题组成员对思维导图的理论有一个较为全面的了解。

（2）2013年8月，在对思维导图理论了解的基础上，请绘制思维导图的专家培训课题组成员。

（3）2013年9月至2013年10月，以实验班为单位，由实验教师向实验学生讲解思维导图的一系列知识及绘制方法等。

（4）2013年11月至2014年10月，课题组成员完成《小学英语词汇思维导图》和《小学英语人教版教材三至六年级单元核心词句思维导图》，收集课题组成员的课题论文。

（5）2014年6月至8月，收集学生的思维导图作品。

（6）2014年9月，召开课题中期工作汇报会议，阐述前半段研究的进展、成果及下阶段研究任务的安排。

（7）2014年10月，接受中期检查。

3. 实施情况

（1）2013年举办了两场关于思维导图的专题讲座。

（2）收集了几百份实验教师关于主题与单元核心词汇类的思维导图作品，并从中筛选出优秀作品结集成册。

（3）收集了30多篇教师课题论文，并将优秀的论文发表。

（4）2014年举行了学生思维导图作品比赛，涌现出一批优秀的学生作品。

（5）汇编了课题阶段性成果——《小学英语词汇思维导图》和《小学英语人教版教材三至六年级单元核心词句思维导图》。

4. 后期拟开展的工作

（1）汇编《小学英语人教版教材三至六年级单元话题教学思维导图》。

（2）汇编《小学英语人教版教材四至六年级单元读写教学思维导图》。

（3）汇编《小学英语人教版教材五至六年级单元写作教学思维导图》。

（4）汇编《小学英语人教版教材语法教学思维导图》。

5. 存在问题

（1）课题主持人及成员在思维导图研究方面仍然欠缺经验，需要专家的引领、务实地思索和大胆地实践。

（2）实验教师教学任务重，时间不充裕，造成对思维导图的绘制上还不够精细。

（3）如何把思维导图作品与课堂教学高效地结合仍需课题组成员深入实践。

6. 完成情况

（1）实验教师撰写论文30多篇。

（2）课题组成员和学生都掌握了绘制思维导图的方法。

（3）课题组成功举办了教师和学生的思维导图绘制比赛。

（4）课题组汇编了课题阶段性成果——《小学英语词汇思维导图》和《小学英语人教版教材三至六年级单元核心词句思维导图》。

（5）课题组深入开展实践并推广阶段性成果，将其应用于课堂教学。

7. 经费使用

购买图书资料约3000元，国内调研差旅费约2000元，印刷费600元，其他1000元，合计6600元。

二、1—2项代表性成果简介

《小学英语词汇思维导图》和《小学英语人教版教材三至六年级单元核心词句思维导图》是课题"思维导图在小学英语教学中的应用"的研究阶段性成果——词汇教学的思维导图内容丰富新颖，实用性强，学术价值高，对词汇教学改革影响深远。

1. 用思维导图整合话题词汇，内容丰富新颖，实用性强

现行的小学教材由于既没有系统地学习音标，也没有学习构词法，所以学生学习新单词往往是靠死记硬背，不但学得累，忘得快，更重要的是没有形成系统的学习词汇的思维。合理地设计思维导图，利用图标、线条、色彩，可以帮助学生形成词汇学习的网络，提高学习词汇的效率，达到事半功倍的效果。而且课题组用思维导图把主题词汇、核心词汇进行整合，整合后的主题词汇和单元核心词汇具有形象化、系统化的特点，有利于新旧知识的联系，很好地帮助学生对所学

的词汇进行梳理和运用，实用性很强。

2. 用思维导图支撑小学英语词汇教学活动，学术价值高

词汇学习是小学英语学习的重要组成部分，它始终贯穿于英语学习的全过程，掌握一定数量的词汇是学好英语的重要保证。根据《义务教育英语课程标准（2011年版）》，对小学词汇的语言技能目标是要求学生能根据图文说出单词或短语，能围绕周围熟悉的环境和话题进行简单的交流。词汇教学的目的是培养学生的语言技能，并发展学生的说和写的能力。人教版小学英语课程的编排与设计都是以某一个话题为单元模块，即知识的学习是围绕某一主题而展开的。鉴于此，教师在课堂教学中借助思维导图帮助学生形成词汇网络，发展学生的思维能力，就一定能有效地提高学生对词汇的学习与运用能力。同时不管是教师还是学生，也不管是电脑绘制还是手绘的思维导图，都具有色彩鲜明、简洁明了、条理清晰、想象丰富的特点，把词汇思维导图应用于课堂教学，学术价值很高。

3. 用思维导图开发学生的大脑潜能，意义深远

教师在词汇教学中利用思维导图把与主题相关的词汇呈现给学生，这样不仅有利于学生对词汇的理解，也有利于他们进行自主学习，并提高他们的学习效率。在思维导图的指引下，学生能够形成发散思维，联想到更多的知识，学会将新旧知识进行联系，并进行思考和总结，进而更加牢固地记忆。这与当今英语学科的核心素养提出的充分发展学生的思维能力、提高学生的思维品质是一致的。用思维导图的方式去开发学生的智力，挖掘学生的潜能，具有深远的意义。

一、课题研究的背景和意义

（一）课题研究的背景

思维导图又称为心智图、心灵图、脑图等。最早是由英国心理学家东尼·博赞（Tony Buzan）提出的。他在《思维导图》一书中对思维导图是这样定义的："思维导图是放射性思维的表达，因此也是人类思维的自然功能。它是一种非常有用的图形技术，是打开大脑潜力的万用钥匙。思维导图可以用于生活的各个方面，其改进后的学习能力和清晰的思维方式会改善人的行为表现。"

在国外，思维导图在教育领域的研究与应用已经相当成熟。如英国、美国、新加坡、日本、韩国、德国、瑞士、澳大利亚等国家的教育教学机构已经开始对该课题进行了深入地研究和探索。在英国和新加坡思维导图早已列入国民中小学的必修课程中。在许多知名学府，如哈佛大学、剑桥大学等，教授们热衷于使用思维导图来提高他们的教学效率。

在国内，开始对思维导图的学习和研究不是很早。美国珍妮特·沃斯的著作《学习的革命》于1998年出版发行以来，思维导图才漂洋过海进入中国，从此国内的研究者和教师才开始对其进行探索和钻研。2000年，王功玲首次介绍了思维导图使用的方法，并在教案编写以及课堂教学中应用思维导图记笔记。2004年，赵国庆、陆志坚等人对思维导图的概念、来源等进行了深入地剖析，拉开了思维导图在中国研究的序幕，并奠定了坚实的基础。此后，陆续涌现出很多学者和专家对思维导图进行研究。

思维导图应用于英语教学的研究主要集中在英语词汇、阅读、写作教学中。例如，2005年，辽宁师范大学的张丹从英语阅读教学中存在的问题出发，介绍了思维导图的特点和绘制方法并分析了如何将其应用到英语阅读的课前、课中和课后，最后总结了其实验过程。2005年，陈敏细致分析了外语教学中运用思维导图的优势，并且探讨了该学习策略的认识理论基础。2008年，曾燕燕结合相应的理论，提出了根据不同的教学内容可绘制不同类型的思维导图，为笔者的研究提供了实践的参考。

通过以上对国内外思维导图的研究现状分析可以看，思维导图是一种新的思维模式和学习方法，如何将思维导图深入应用到英语教学的各个环节中去是我们研究者关注的问题。

（二）研究的意义

《义务教育英语课程标准（2011年版）》提出，英语课程承担着培养学生基本英语素养和发展学生思维能力的任务。语言既是交流的工具，也是思维的工具。英语课堂应成为学生在教师指导下构建知识、发展技能、拓宽视野、活跃思维、展现个性的过程。思维导图作为一种可视化的教学和学习策略，能使语言表征重点突出、条理清晰、层次分明。它能够帮助学生加深对知识的理解，提高学生的自学能力和创造性思维能力。因此，思维导图作为一种新的思维模式和学习方法具有强大的优势。

1. 突出重点，有效助记

思维导图一方面把学习者的主要精力集中在关键知识点上，不把时间浪费在无关重要的内容上，从而节省了宝贵的学习时间。另一方面，思维导图通过有效的概念意义的组织和概念框架的建立成为一个有力的助记工具。

2. 改善学生的信息加工方式，建立合理的知识网络

思维导图促进学习者对新旧知识的整合，提升思维能力，对思维导图节点的增加或对概念结构的修改都体现了学习者个性化的、主动的信息加工和知识构建过程。

3. 提高综合信息的能力，激发联想与创意

思维导图有利于开发学习者的创造力，它能把各种零散的智慧、观点等融会贯通成为一个系统，允许学习者自由联想。

4. 促使学生形成系统学习和思维的习惯

本课题研究将立足于小学英语教学实践，从课堂教学实际入手，根据教学

内容探讨词汇（Vocabulary）、话题（Topics）、读写（Read and write）、写作（Writing）4个方面的思维导图样式，帮助学生根据一定的逻辑顺序建构知识网络，从整体上把握所学的英语知识，为学生的可持续学习和发展奠定基础。

二、课题概念的界定和理论依据

（一）课题概念的界定

思维导图又名心智图，是由英国著名心理学家和教育家东尼·博赞创造的一种有效记笔记的方法。它充分利用右脑的形象思维和左脑的抽象思维，采用图文并茂的方式来表征、组织、阐述知识，展现人们获取知识、解决问题时的思维过程。通俗地说，思维导图是一个简单、有效的思维工具。它依据全脑的概念，按照大脑自身的规律进行思考，使大脑潜能得到最充分的开发，从而极大地发掘人的记忆、创造、语言等各方面的潜能。

（二）课题研究的理论基础

1. 脑科学理论

解剖学的研究表明，人的大脑分左脑和右脑两个半球，左右脑通过胼胝体连接起来。20世纪60年代，美国心理生物学家罗杰·斯佩里对裂脑人进行了深入的研究，提出了"左右脑分工理论"，并因此荣获1981年诺贝尔生理学或医学奖。该理论认为左脑主要负责词汇、逻辑、数字、次序、线性、分析、序列等，右脑主要负责节奏、空间知觉、维度、想象、色彩、整体意识等。虽然左右脑在功能上不对称，存在偏侧化现象，但它们并不是单独工作，而是通过左右脑的协作来完成的。因此，"左脑+右脑"的"全脑"思维模式是一种创造性思维模式。脑科学研究发现，人类大脑的各种技巧如果能被和谐而巧妙地加以运用，将比彼此分开工作产生更大的效率。思维导图利用"左脑+右脑"的"全脑"思维模式，有利于激发大脑的潜能，并使大脑平衡协调发展。无论是在效率、效果还是效益上，思维导图都比传统学习方法更有效。

2. 认知心理学理论

（1）可视化学习理论

可视化是一种使复杂信息能够容易和快速被人理解的手段，是一种聚焦信息重要特征的信息压缩语言，是可以放大人类感知的图形化表示方法。可视化就是把数据、信息和知识转化为可视的表现形式，并获得对数据更深层次认识的过程。从可视化的表示中人们可以发现新的线索、新的关联、新的结构、新的知识，促使系统整合，促进科学决策。可视化技术以人们惯于接受的表格图形、图像等形式并辅以信息处理技术将客观事物及其内在的联系进行表现，使可视化结果便于人们记忆和理解。

思维导图是将知识可视化的一种工具，它将隐性知识显性化、将言语信息图像化。除了传达事实信息之外，还将所学内容转换成可被人的感官领悟的知识表征形式，有效地帮助学生对抽象文字的理解、记忆，加快认知活动，以这种方式帮助他人正确地重构、记忆和应用这些知识，从而促进知识的获取、共享与创新。

（2）格式塔理论

格式塔心理学主要研究人们怎样理解整体和构成整体的部分之间的关系。格式塔理论认为如果对构成部分有恰当的认识，将有助于形成整体的意义，了解各构成部分之间的联系。思维导图从整体上表现了某个较为广域概念中的各个组成部分。学习变化的实质在于使内在逻辑结构的教材与学生原有的认知结构产生联系，新旧知识相互渗透，新材料在学习者头脑中获得新意义。

（3）建构主义学习理论

建构主义学习理论中一个重要的概念是图式。图式是组织、描述和解释我们经验的概念网络，是人们在认知过程中对同类客体或活动的基本结构的抽象概括，是一种知识框架、组织结构和分类系统。建构主义的学习理论认为，每个学习者都具有不同的知识和经验，这些是存在学习者头脑中原有的图式。图式的形成和变化反映了认知的发展。学习者在外界的刺激下，通过同化或顺应，把它们纳入到原有的图式内，或修改重建原有图式，形成新的认知结构，使认知发展从旧的平衡向新的平衡过渡，获得新的知识与能力。思维导图将思维过程和知识结构用图像的形式展示出来，可以更好地把握思维过程和知识的整体架构，以便于将新知识整合到已有的知识体系中。因此，思维导图在教学中的应用也体现了建构主义学习理论的观点。

（4）最近发展区理论

最近发展区理论的主要特征有两点：一是学生承担的任务必须略高于个人

当前能力水平，任务应该拓展其能力，但又不能超出其能力范围；二是必须有一个成年人或能力更强的同伴在学生要处理的任务或问题之间起中介作用。教学的目的就是要通过教师或同伴的帮助消除实际发展水平和潜在发展水平的差距，使潜在发展水平变成实际发展水平，随着教学要求的不断提高以及知识的进一步深化，为今后的教学创造出一个个新的最近发展区，从而形成一种良性循环，不断推动学生发展水平向更高层次发展。

最近发展区存在于学生已知与未知、能够胜任和不能胜任之间，教师需要为学生提供一种概念框架，这种框架中的概念正为发展学生对问题的进一步理解所需要。思维导图恰恰就是这样的工具。它既能够表示知识体系中概念以及概念之间已有的联系，又能够体现学生认知结构中已有的概念以及相互的关系，并在教与学之间建立互通的桥梁和架构。应用思维导图的教学实际上就是最近发展区内的教与学。其中，学生的"学"是在思维导图的扶持下，力图跨越最近发展区的学习；教师的"教"则是在最近发展区内提供支架，帮助学生跨越最近发展区的教学，思维导图是在强调学生中心的文化背景中提出的。通过思维导图的帮助，能逐渐将管理学习的任务由教师转移给学生，即学习过程被内化，最后达到撤去支架，无须教师引导，学生自己能在概念框架中继续攀爬的目的，从而使学生思维的实际发展水平与潜在发展水平得到最大限度的发挥。[①]

三、课题的基本内容和总体目标

（一）基本内容

本课题研究将立足于小学英语教学实践，从课堂教学实际入手，根据教学内容探讨词汇、话题、读写、写作4个方面的思维导图样式，帮助学生根据一定的逻辑顺序建构知识网络，从整体上把握所学的英语知识，为学生的可持续学习和发展奠定基础。本课题的基本内容为：

（1）小学英语词汇、话题、读写、写作等思维导图的案例。

（2）指导教师和学生绘制简单的思维导图，并运用思维导图整合所学的知

---

① 吉桂凤.思维导图与小学英语教学［M］.北京：教育科学出版社，2015.

识形成知识链，从而完成对知识的整体建构。

（二）拟达到的目标

1. 总体目标

（1）通过研究和实践，从课堂教学实际入手，根据教学内容探讨词汇、话题、读写、写作4个方面的思维导图样式，帮助学生更好地理解和记忆所学的英语知识，从而有效地提高教学质量。

（2）通过研究和实践，培养学生的逻辑思维能力、发散思维能力和创新能力。

（3）通过研究和实践，进一步更新教师的教育观念，促使课题组成员在研究中实现专业成长，从而提升教师的理论水平和研究能力。

2. 年度目标

（1）2013年5月至9月，确定选题，申请立项。组建课题小组，学习相关理论知识。

（2）2013年10至2014年10月，组织课题组成员制订研究实施方案，明确研究的内容、目的、要求及思路。学习思维导图的基本理论，并掌握绘制思维导图的基本方法。以实验班为单位，由教师向学生讲解思维导图的知识及绘制方法。课题组成员完成《小学英语词汇思维导图》和《小学英语人教版教材三至六年级单元核心词句思维导图》的案例汇编。

（3）2014年11月至2015年2月，课题组完成《小学英语人教版教材三至六年级单元话题教学思维导图》《小学英语人教版教材四至六年级单元读写教学思维导图》《小学英语人教版教材五至六年级单元写作教学思维导图》《小学英语人教版教材语法教学思维导图》的案例汇编。

（4）2015年3月至2015年5月，收集整理研究实施过程的教学案例、影像资料、论文、课例等相关材料，撰写完成课题研究总结和结题报告，邀请专家指导，向有关部门申请结题。

四、研究方法和途径

（一）研究方法和手段

1. 案例研究法

对典型的课堂教学案例进行分析研究，归纳整理出有效的思维导图案例。

2. 行动研究法

在教与学的过程中，通过"专家引领—合作探究—总结完善—形成特色"，把研究与实践紧密地结合起来，最终编制一套较为完善的有利于教与学的思维导图案例。

3. 课堂观察法

一方面是观察学生的课堂行为，包括学生的学习行为、思考能力、对老师授课的反应等。另一方面是观察教师，包括思维导图的应用、引导技巧等。

4. 实验总结法

根据教学实践的研究，挖掘现有的经验材料，并上升到理论的高度，以便更好地指导新的教学案例。这一研究方法有利于教师撰写课题论文，出版课题研究成果专著等。

（二）研究途径

（1）购买有关思维导图的书籍，让课题组成员大量阅读，深入了解学习思维导图的理论。

（2）通过"专家引领—合作探究—总结完善—形成特色"，把研究与实践紧密地结合起来。

（3）聘请专业电脑老师指导课题组成员学习使用制作思维导图的软件，掌握绘制思维导图的要领。

（4）边研究，边实践，边推广，边完善，把实验成果与推广结合起来。

五、研究成果和效果

（一）研究成果

（1）实验教师的教科研水平大大提升，教师撰写了30多篇课题论文，部分优秀的论文已发表。

（2）实验教师学会了用电脑软件制作思维导图。

（3）学生学会了手绘思维导图，部分学生还会用电脑软件制作思维导图。

（4）汇编《小学英语词汇思维导图》和《小学英语人教版教材三至六年级单元核心词句思维导图》。

（5）汇编《小学英语人教版教材三至六年级单元话题教学思维导图》。

（6）汇编《小学英语人教版教材四至六年级单元读写教学思维导图》。

（7）汇编《小学英语人教版教材五至六年级单元写作教学思维导图》。

（8）汇编《小学英语人教版教材语法教学思维导图》。

（二）研究效果

1. 学生方面

（1）小图像，大兴趣。我们在教学实践中发现，学生对于图像、线条、颜色的兴趣远比单纯的单词和句子的兴趣要浓得多。思维导图从视觉上吸引了小学生对英语的注意力，既活跃了课堂学习英语的氛围，也激发了学生乐于开口的意愿，增强了学生语言组织能力和综合运用能力。

（2）小图像，大改变。大部分学生的学习方式只是被动地接受教师所传授的知识，这种接受式的学习方式存在着重知识轻能力、重考试轻应用、重书本轻实践、重接受轻探究、重模仿轻创新的诸多弊端。通过思维导图的教学，学生对知识理解的过程可视化，便于对知识整理归类。而制作思维导图的过程本身也是一种思维的过程，学生学会把与学习内容有关的资料整合到图中来，学生开始由接受式学习变为探究式学习，能自主地构建自己的知识体系，并在此基础上提高自己的记忆能力、表达能力、空间想象能力和创造性思维能力。

2. 教师方面

（1）有助于教师加强理论与实践的结合，提高教科研能力。在进行研究初始阶段，课题组全体成员查阅了大量的文献，学习了大量关于思维导图的理论知识。结合所学理论知识和实际教学，大家都在自己的英语教学中进行了大胆的尝试，积极运用思维导图来架构授课内容，开设研讨课；指导学生运用思维导图帮助自己更好地进行英语学习；结合实践经验，积极撰写相关的教学论文等等。通过本课题研究，促使课题组成员在探索小学英语思维导图的研究中实现专业成长，从而提升教师的理论水平和教科研能力。

（2）有助于进一步更新教学观念，转变教学方式。思维导图应用于小学英语教学可以改变教师的教育观、教学观等。在使用思维导图教学过程中，教师可以更有效地进行知识的传授，让整个教学过程和流程设计更加系统、科学，形成互动的教学过程，促进学生与教师之间的交流，打破传统的"一言堂"。让学生成为教学过程中的主体，引导学生来充分发挥主观能动性和创造力，使得课堂的落脚点真正从"教"转变到了"学"和"用"，使得学生真正成为学习的主体。

六、课题研究结论和思考

（一）研究结论

1. 科研促进教师的发展

教师的专业发展指教师在专业理论、专业知识、专业能力等方面的成长。教师开展课题研究首先要寻找自己教育教学上的困惑，把问题上升为课题。在课题研究全过程中，教师一定会以先进的理念来指导自己的研究活动和实践过程。研究、实践、反思、总结到结题论证的整个过程其实就是教师不断实验、验证、成长的过程。同时在实施课题的过程中教师也积累了一些有价值的论文、课例、案例、教学反思，形成了教学主张、教学风格等。

2. 科研促进教学的改革

作为一线教师，我们经常会发现：学生缺乏英语学习的环境，英语学习效率低，尽管老师费了九牛二虎之力把教材内容教完了，但仍有部分学生学不懂、学不好。再细看教材，虽然教材编写以"话题—功能—结构—任务"为思路，但实际上教材中单元与单元之间的联系有时并不是特别紧凑。曾有一位特级教师说过："教学艺术来自于执教者对教材的把握度，大到一册书，小到一个单元，一句话，一个单词都要了然于心，否则就不能教，也无法教。"我个人很认同这个说法。因此通过课题研究促使我们教师去研究教材、合理使用教材、创新教材，在这个过程中通过对理论的思考、对课例的探讨、对学生的研究，从而促进教学的改革。

3. 要做有生命力的课题

我们从狭义上常说，问题即是课题。课题"思维导图在小学英语教学中的应用"就是基于过去我们的英语课堂以教师为主，学生被动学习，造成学习兴趣不浓，学习效果不佳的困境而提出的。如何通过优化课堂教学策略来发展学生的发散思维从而培养学生自主学习的能力无疑是本课题提出的基础。这些年我们把课题的研究成果应用于一线课堂教学，并广泛地推广应用验证，可以说所到之处皆为赞之、学之和用之。这让我深刻地认识到只有把一线教学中遇到的问题上升为课题研究，然后把研究的成果反馈回一线教学实践并对教学改革有促进作用的课题才是有生命力的课题。

（二）研究思考

1. 从事教科研工作，选题要"实"

（1）研究内容真实。课题研究应该是发生在教育教学前线的、真实的、有生命力的课题。

（2）研究过程实在。要从实践中来，为实践服务。"做真研究、开展真讨论、进行真实践、写真文章。"

2. 从事教科研工作，选题要"小"

（1）研究规模小。课题研究常常以教师小团体为主体，从身边的实际问题出发开展研究。

（2）研究切入点要小，内容单一。就是从小事、小现象、小问题入手，以小见大。

3. 从事教科研工作，选题要"活"

（1）研究过程方式灵活。可以是行动研究、个案研究、调查研究、经验总结式研究等，方式灵活。研究存在于教师日常的工作生活中，时时都可以开招，处处都可以进行，在兴趣中生根，在实践中开花，在过程中结果。

（2）研究成果形式简单。一个问题解决了，就可以得到一点收获。教师们可进行个性化的研究，甚至得出个性化的结论。关键是要让自己体会到"眼前一亮""心头一喜"的愉悦。

4. 从事教科研工作，选题要"行"

课题研究的目的是改进自己的教学实践，促进自己的专业发展，所以选题一定要来自日常教育教学实际，要具有可操作性、可借鉴性。

课题批准号：2013kt209

课题类别：一般课题

学科分类：小学英语

课题负责人：韩丽萍　小学一级教师　惠州市上排小学

主要成员：

1. 课题实验成员

李军荣　李深婷　胡小娥　陈秀连　石斯婷　伍嘉敏　吴珊珊　郭东梅

2. 课题推广成员

董智慧　叶思通　李华春　林敏如　陈春颜　温娉婷　陈嘉莉　陈懿　黄慧敏
潘诗琦　黄小慧　温玉雪　吴爱苗　杨育枚　林奕玲　潘艺思

一、课题研究的指导思想、理论基础

《义务教育英语课程标准（2011年版）》提出，英语课程承担着培养学生基本英语素养和发展学生思维能力的任务。语言既是交流的工具，也是思维的工具。英语课堂应成为学生在教师指导下构建知识、发展技能、拓宽视野、活跃思维、展现个性的过程。

我们现行的小学英语教材每个单元都有新单词和句式的教学，怎样使这些知识在学生的头脑中形成一个整体的概念，帮助学生系统地建构这个单元的知识是一个值得研究的课题。另外，每个单元都有一个主题，而单元之间的关联性不大，不利于学生产生联想和单元间的信息交流。如何使各单元之间的知识形成一个知识链，使学生能综合运用所学的语言也是值得研究的一个方面。思维导图作为一种可视化的教学和学习策略，能使语言表征重点突出，条理清晰，层次分明。它能够帮助学生加深对知识的理解，提高学生的自学能力和创造性思维能力。

皮亚杰的建构主义发展观的核心是：以学生为中心，强调学生对知识的主动探索、主动发现和对所学知识意义的主动建构。思维导图的使用能有效地促进学生的知识建构。首先，思维导图以结构化的形式表征知识，有助于学习者把握某个知识领域的全貌，将知识融会贯通。其次，思维导图的分支结构能够形象地展示和说明知识间的关联，能够促进学生以一种全新的认知方式去建构知识。

由此可见，思维导图在小学英语教学中的应用是一个值得研究的课题。

二、课题研究的主要内容和研究方法

（一）主要内容

本课题研究将立足于小学英语教学实践，从课堂教学实际入手，根据教学内容探讨词汇（Vocabulary）、话题（Topics）、读写（Read and write）、写作（Writing）4个方面的思维导图案例，帮助学生根据一定的逻辑顺序建构知识网络，从整体上把握所学的英语知识，为学生的可持续学习和发展奠定基础。该课题研究的主要内容为：

（1）小学英语词汇、话题、读写、写作等思维导图的案例。

（2）指导教师和学生绘制简单的思维导图，并运用思维导图整合所学的知识形成知识链，从而完成对知识的整体建构。

（二）研究方法

1. 案例研究法

对典型的课堂教学案例进行分析研究，归纳整理出有效的思维导图案例。

2. 行动研究法

在教与学的过程中，通过"专家引领—合作探究—总结完善—形成特色"，把研究与实践紧密地结合起来，最终编制一套较为完善的有利于教与学的思维导图案例。

3. 课堂观察法

一方面是观察学生的课堂行为，包括学生的学习行为、思考能力、对老师授课的反映等。另一方面是观察教师，包括思维导图的应用、引导技巧等。

4. 实验总结法

根据教学实践的研究，挖掘现有的经验材料并上升到理论的高度，以便更好地指导新的教学案例。这一研究方法有利于教师撰写课题论文，出版课题研究成果专著等。

三、课题研究取得的主要成果

（一）主要成果

（1）实验教师的教科研水平大大提升，教师撰写了30多篇课题论文，部分优秀的论文已发表。

（2）实验教师学会了用电脑软件制作思维导图。

（3）学生学会了手绘思维导图，部分学生还会用电脑软件制作。

（4）汇编《小学英语人教版词汇思维导图》和《小学英语人教版教材三至六年级单元核心词句思维导图》。

（5）汇编《小学英语人教版教材三至六年级单元话题教学思维导图》。

（6）汇编《小学英语人教版教材四至六年级单元读写教学思维导图》。

（7）汇编《小学英语人教版教材五至六年级单元写作教学思维导图》。

（8）汇编《小学英语人教版教材语法教学思维导图》。

（二）新论点

1. 科研促进教师的发展

教师的专业发展指教师在专业理论、专业知识、专业能力等方面的成长。教师开展课题研究首先要寻找自己教育教学上的困惑，把问题上升为课题。在课题研究全过程中，教师一定会以先进的理念来指导自己的研究活动和实践过程。研究、实践、反思、总结到结题论证的整个过程其实就是教师不断实验、验证、成长的过程。同时在实施课题的过程中也可以积累一些有价值的论文、课例、案例、教学反思，形成了教学主张、教学风格等。

2. 科研促进教学的改革

作为一线教师，我们经常会发现：学生缺乏英语学习的环境，英语学习效率低，尽管教师费了九牛二虎之力把教材内容教完了，但仍有部分学生学不懂，学不好。再细看教材，虽然教材编写以"话题—功能—结构—任务"为思路，但实际上教材中单元与单元之间的联系有时并不是特别紧凑。曾有一位特级教师说过："教学艺术来自于执教者对教材的把握度，大到一册书，小到一个单元，一句话，一个单词都要了然于心，否则就不能教，也无法教。"我个人很认同这个说法。因此通过课题研究促使我们教师去研究教材、合理使用教材、创新教材，在这个过程中通过对理论的思考，对课例的探讨，对学生的研究，促进教学的改革。

3. 要做有生命力的课题。

我们从狭义上常说：问题即是课题。课题"思维导图在小学英语教学中的应用"就是基于过去我们的英语课堂以教师为主，学生被动学习，造成学习兴趣不浓，学习效果不佳的困境而提出的。如何通过优化课堂教学策略来发展学生的发散思维从而培养学生自主学习的能力无疑是本课题提出的基础。这些年我们把课题的研究成果应用于一线课堂教学，并广泛地推广应用验证，可以说所到之处皆为赞之、学之和用之。这让我深刻地认识到只有把一线教学中遇到的问题上升为课题研究，然后把研究的成果反馈回一线教学实践并对教学改革有促进作用的课题才是有生命力的课题。

（三）突破性进展

经过课题的实验与推广，无论是课题组教师还是推广学校的教师都意识到培养学生思维能力的重要性，更重要的是意识到研究教材的迫切性，这为下一个课题研究"小学英语单元整体教学设计的实践与研究"打下坚实的基础。

四、研究成果推广的范围

1. 班级的推广范围

由实验班扩大到全校所有班级。

2. 学科的推广范围

由英语学科扩大到各个学科。

3. 区域的推广范围

由实验学校扩大到惠州市各县区。由于课题负责人是广东省名师工作室主持人，伴随着工作室承担全国各地的跟岗任务，研究的成果也相继扩大到西藏林芝、广东湛江、潮州、梅州、汕头、汕尾、清远、肇庆、韶关、揭阳等地。

五、研究成果取得的社会效益

课题"思维导图在小学英语教学中的应用"经过两年的研究和推广，于2016年获得惠州市第九届教育科研成果一等奖。课题负责人于2015年起至今是广东省名师工作室主持人，其研究的课题成果已成为所有跟岗学员必修的学习课程之一，学员跟岗结业回到原单位后也广泛使用课题成果，反响热烈。课题负责人还把成果纳入惠州学院外国语学院嵌入课程内容之中，让广大的大学生受益匪浅。总之，课题研究成果得到教育专家、领导和广大教师的高度评价，引起了积极的反响，社会效应热烈。

六、主要研究成果

主要研究成果表

成果名称	作者姓名	成果形式	字数	完成年月	出版单位或发表刊物名称、刊号	获奖或转载引用情况
《小学英语人教版主题词汇思维导图》	叶思通	汇编	—	2016年5月	校本教材《导图教学》	全部引用
《小学英语人教版三年级单元话题教学思维导图》	陈嘉莉	汇编	—	2016年5月	校本教材《导图教学》	全部引用
《小学英语人教版四年级（上册）单元话题教学思维导图》	陈懿	汇编	—	2016年5月	校本教材《导图教学》	全部引用
《小学英语人教版四年级（下册）单元话题教学思维导图》	黄慧敏	汇编	—	2016年5月	校本教材《导图教学》	全部引用
《小学英语人教版五年级（上册）单元话题教学思维导图》	黄小慧	汇编	—	2016年5月	校本教材《导图教学》	全部引用
《小学英语人教版五年级（下册）单元话题教学思维导图》	潘诗琦	汇编	—	2016年5月	校本教材《导图教学》	全部引用

续 表

成果名称	作者姓名	成果形式	字数	完成年月	出版单位或发表刊物名称、刊号	获奖或转载引用情况
《小学英语人教版六年级（上册）单元话题教学思维导图》	董智慧	汇编	—	2016年5月	校本教材《导图教学》	全部引用
《小学英语人教版六年级（下册）单元话题教学思维导图》	林敏如	汇编	—	2016年5月	校本教材《导图教学》	全部引用
《导图在小学英语教学中的各种运用》	韩丽萍	论文	3084	2013年11月	《基础教育课程》ISSN 1672–6715	广东省论文评比一等奖
《思维导图在小学英语阅读教学中的实践与探索》	李深婷	论文	4793	2013年11月	—	广东省论文评比一等奖
《图式理论在小学英语阅读中的运用及成果》	李军荣	论文	3883	2015年12月	—	惠州市论文评比一等奖
《巧用思维导图，"畅游"小学英语复习课堂》	林奕玲	论文	3541	2018年12月	—	惠州市论文评比一等奖
《巧用思维导图学习英语词汇》	伍嘉敏	论文	1822	2013年11月	—	惠州市论文评比二等奖
《思维导图在英语教学中的应用》	胡小娥	论文	2212	2013年12月	—	惠城区论文评比二等奖
《浅谈如何提高小学高年级英语阅读教学》	陈秀连	论文	2489	2013年12月	—	惠城区论文评比二等奖
《思维导图在小学英语的教与学》	石斯婷	论文	1850	2015年12月	—	惠城区论文评比二等奖
《思维导图在小学英语教学中的运用》	吴珊珊	论文	3155	2013年12月	—	惠城区论文评比二等奖
《巧妙运用思维导图于小学英语单词教学中的实践》	郭东梅	论文	5303	2013年12月	—	惠城区论文评比三等奖
《思维导图在小学英语仿写教学模式的应用》	陈春颜	论文	7082	2018年1月	—	课题组论文评比一等奖

成果名称	作者姓名	成果形式	字数	完成年月	出版单位或发表刊物名称、刊号	获奖或转载引用情况
《思维导图在小学英语写作教学中的应用研究》	温娉婷	论文	2507	2018年1月	—	课题组论文评比一等奖
《巧用思维导图，助力小学英语高年级阅读教学》	李华春	论文	3256	2018年1月	—	课题组论文评比一等奖
《思维导图提高小学英语阅读教学的有效性的研究》	温玉雪	论文	3533	2018年1月	—	课题组论文评比一等奖
《思维导图在小学英语教学的尝试》	吴爱苗	论文	2285	2018年1月	—	课题组论文评比一等奖

七、该研究领域尚待进一步研究的主要理论与实际问题

（1）思维导图用哪种绘制方法好？有人认为思维导图电脑绘制太死板，不如手绘的灵活。

（2）思维导图的读图顺序一定不变吗？有人提出质疑：思维导图读图一定是按从纸张的右上角45°开始，按照顺时针的方向到左上角结束吗？是否还有别的读图规则？

（3）东尼·博赞先生是思维导图与思维可视化教学体系的创建人、学科思维导图概念提出者刘濯源教授提出的学科思维导图，两者之间的共性与不同有多大？

以上理论和实际问题，还需要我们继续研究、探索和实践。

中 篇
思维导图制作案例

subjects

months

week

词汇思维导图

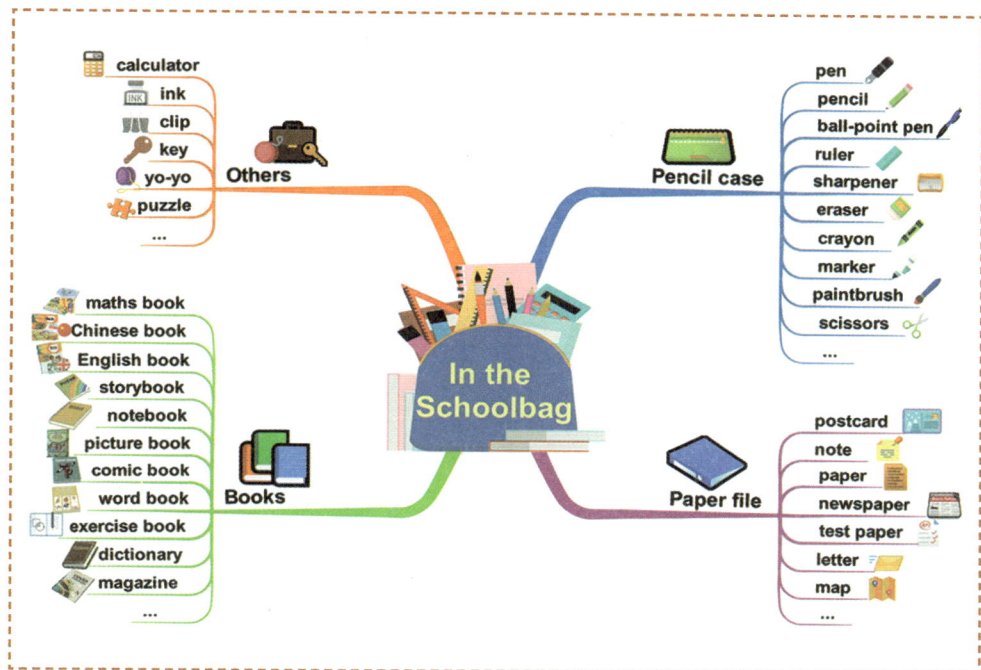

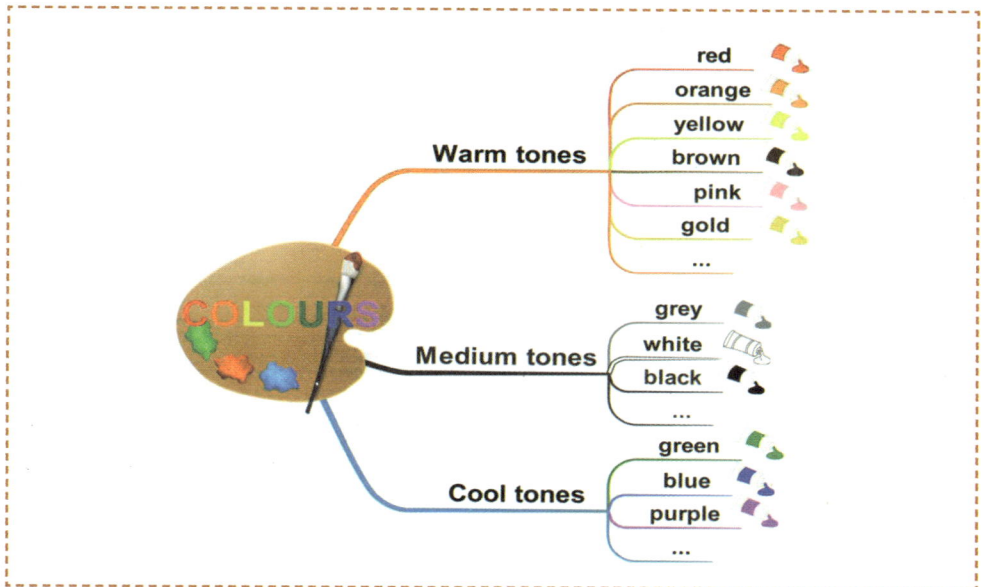

词汇思维导图

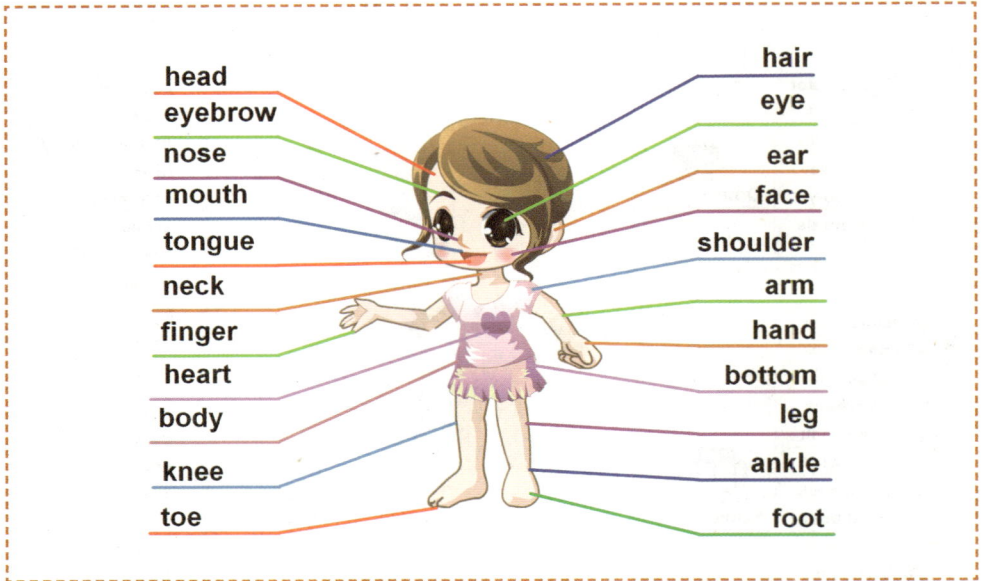

head
eyebrow
nose
mouth
tongue
neck
finger
heart
body
knee
toe

hair
eye
ear
face
shoulder
arm
hand
bottom
leg
ankle
foot

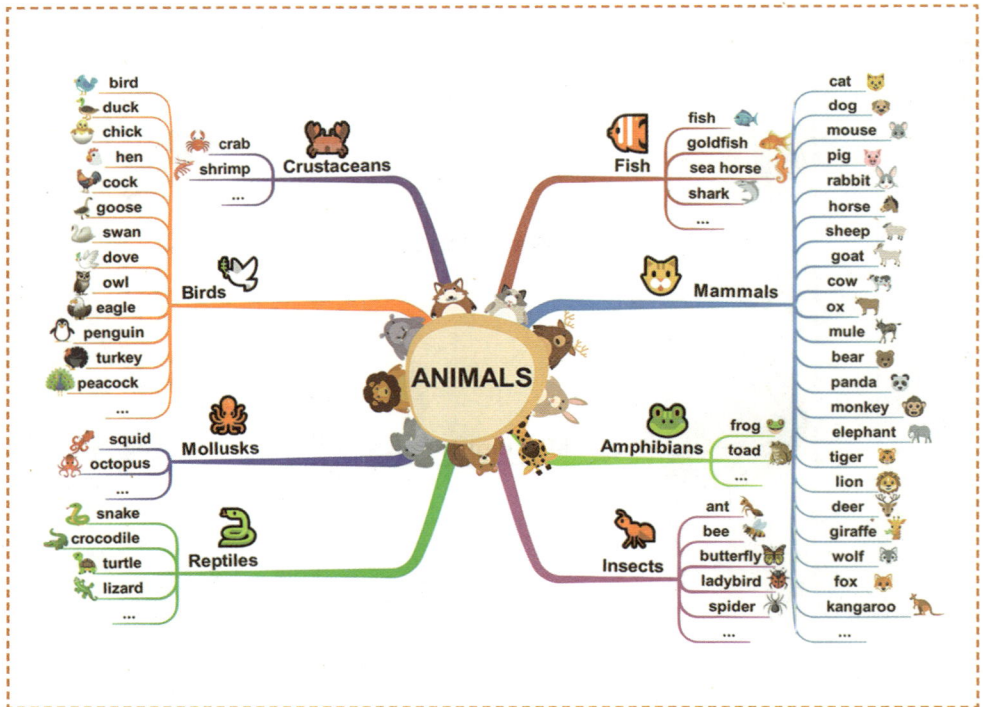

bird
duck
chick
hen
cock
goose
swan
dove
owl
eagle
penguin
turkey
peacock
...

crab
shrimp
...
Crustaceans

fish
goldfish
sea horse
shark
...
Fish

cat
dog
mouse
pig
rabbit
horse
sheep
goat
cow
ox
mule
bear
panda
monkey
elephant
tiger
lion
deer
giraffe
wolf
fox
kangaroo
...

Birds

ANIMALS

Mammals

squid
octopus
...
Mollusks

Amphibians

frog
toad
...

snake
crocodile
turtle
lizard
...
Reptiles

Insects

ant
bee
butterfly
ladybird
spider
...

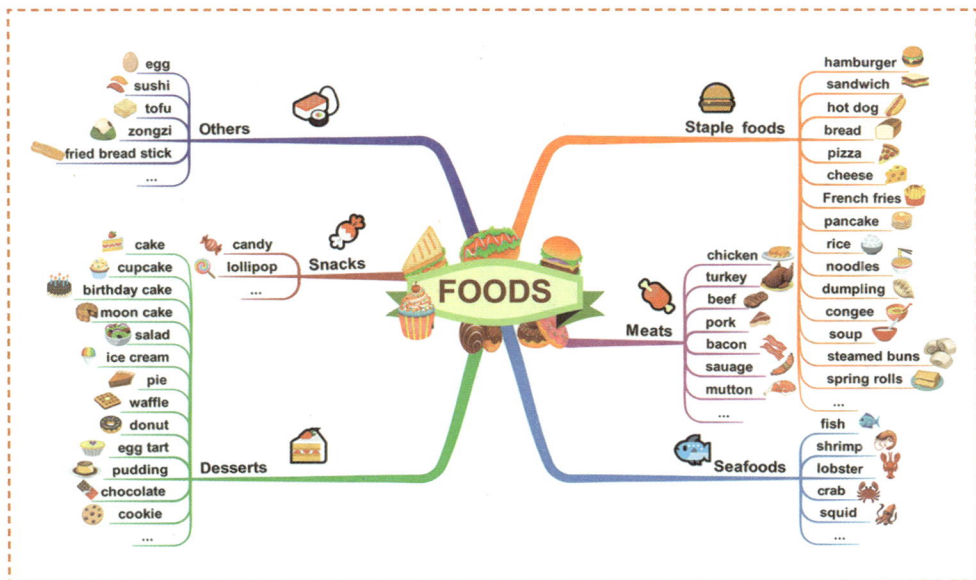

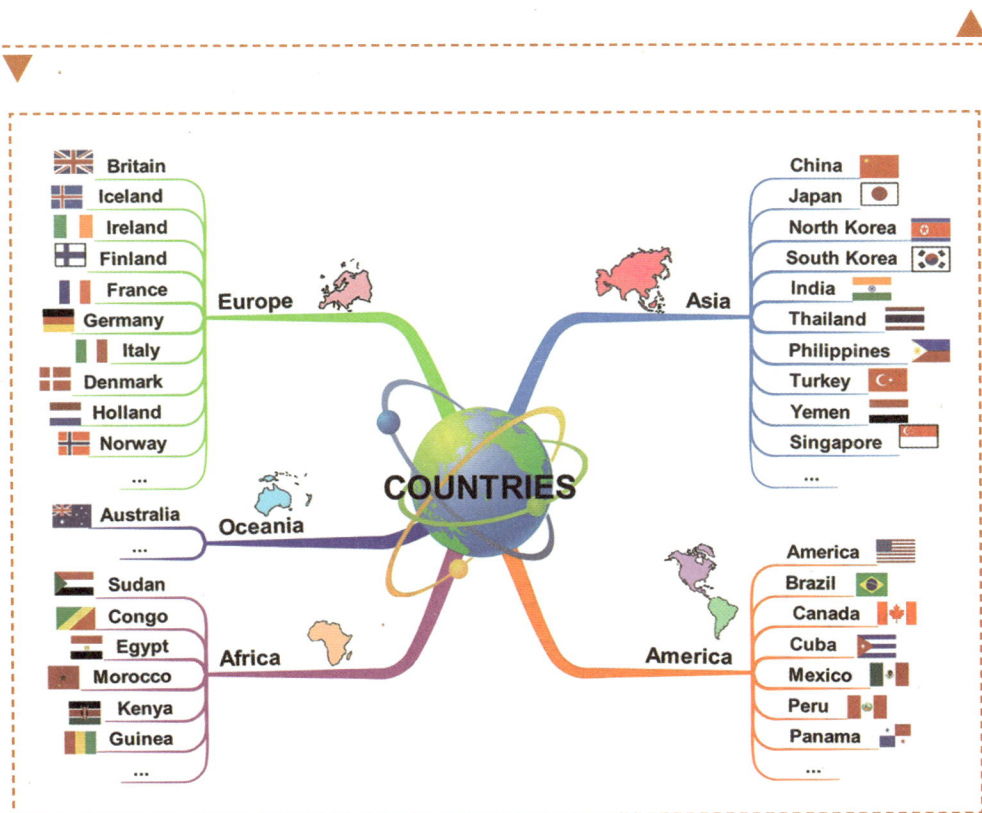

词汇思维导图

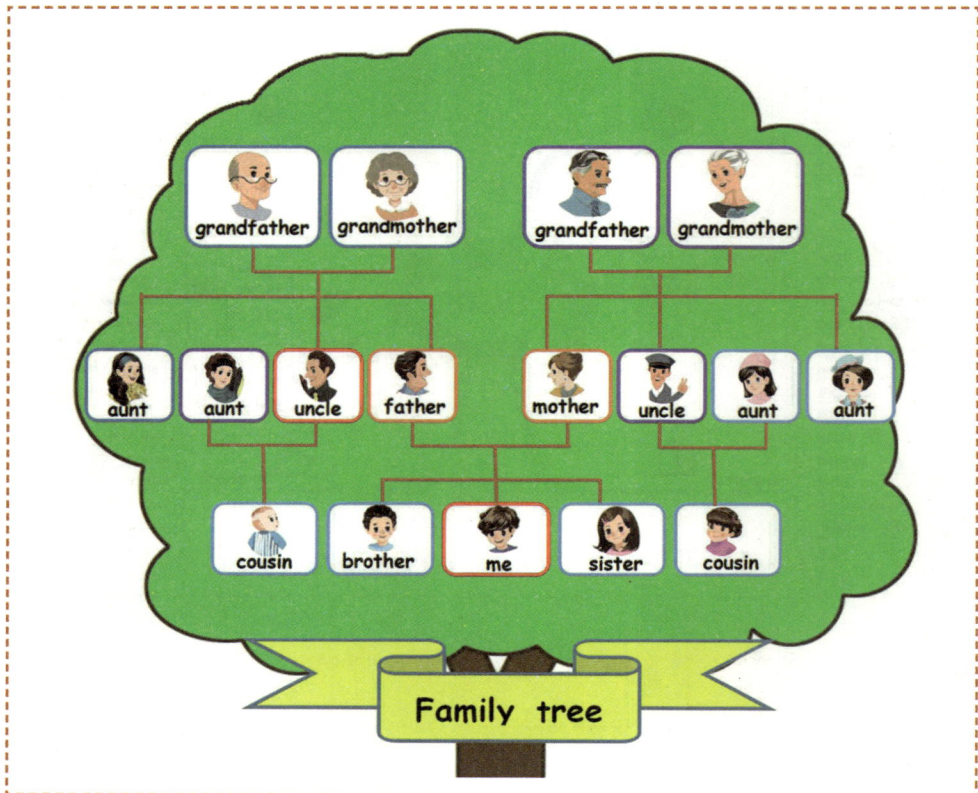

Family tree

grandfather grandmother grandfather grandmother

aunt aunt uncle father mother uncle aunt aunt

cousin brother me sister cousin

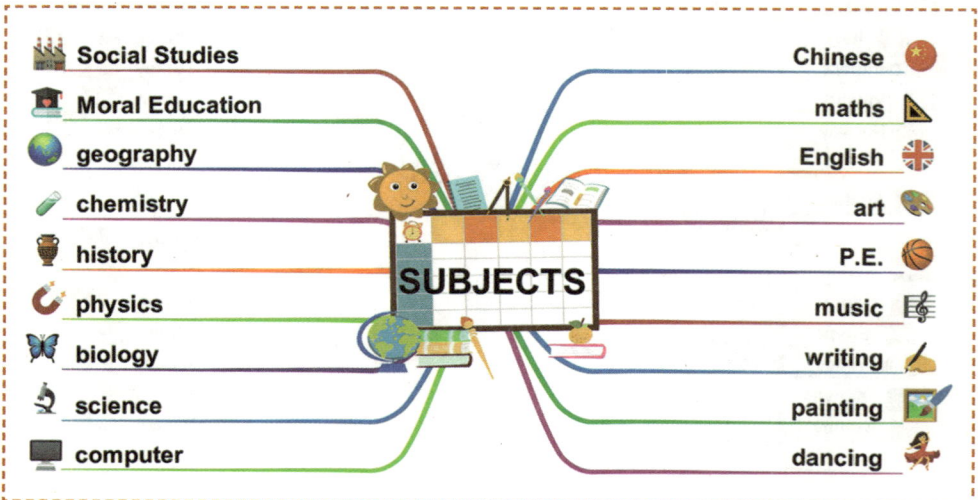

Social Studies

Moral Education

geography

chemistry

history

physics

biology

science

computer

SUBJECTS

Chinese

maths

English

art

P.E.

music

writing

painting

dancing

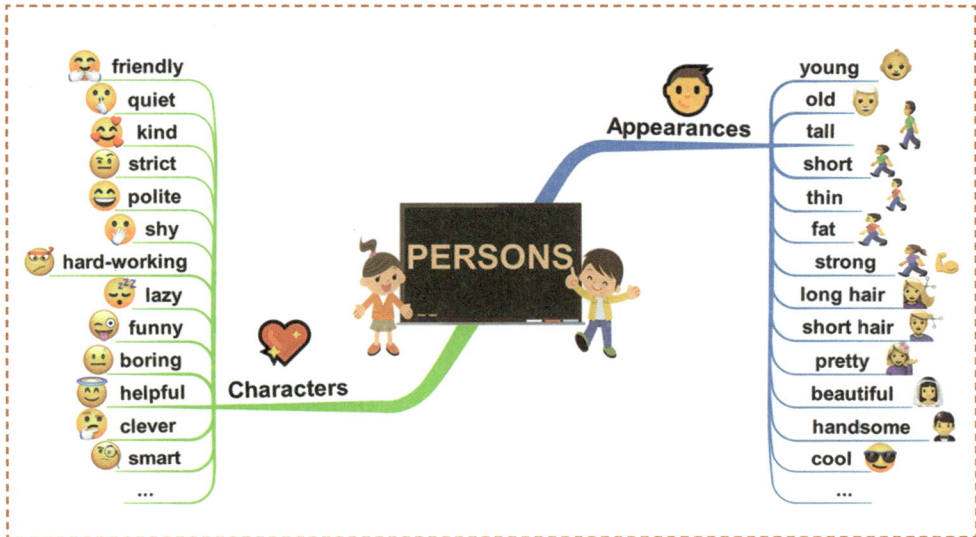

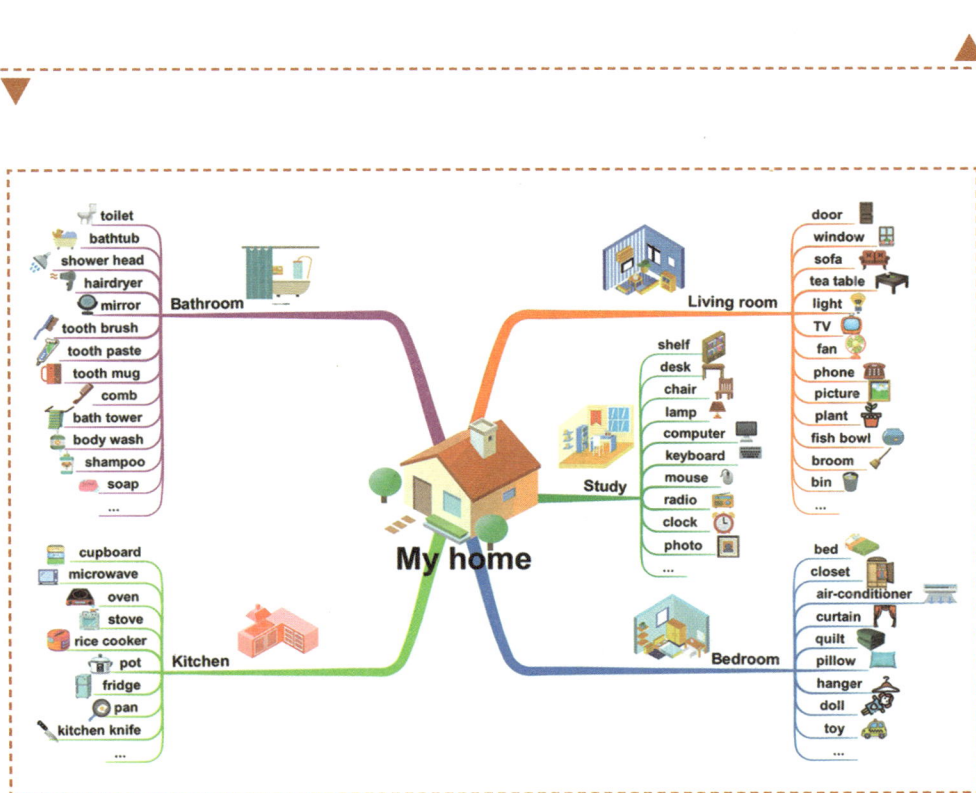

PERSONS

Appearances
- young
- old
- tall
- short
- thin
- fat
- strong
- long hair
- short hair
- pretty
- beautiful
- handsome
- cool
- ...

Characters
- friendly
- quiet
- kind
- strict
- polite
- shy
- hard-working
- lazy
- funny
- boring
- helpful
- clever
- smart
- ...

My home

Bathroom
- toilet
- bathtub
- shower head
- hairdryer
- mirror
- tooth brush
- tooth paste
- tooth mug
- comb
- bath tower
- body wash
- shampoo
- soap
- ...

Kitchen
- cupboard
- microwave
- oven
- stove
- rice cooker
- pot
- fridge
- pan
- kitchen knife
- ...

Living room
- door
- window
- sofa
- tea table
- light
- TV
- fan
- phone
- picture
- plant
- fish bowl
- broom
- bin
- ...

Study
- shelf
- desk
- chair
- lamp
- computer
- keyboard
- mouse
- radio
- clock
- photo
- ...

Bedroom
- bed
- closet
- air-conditioner
- curtain
- quilt
- pillow
- hanger
- doll
- toy
- ...

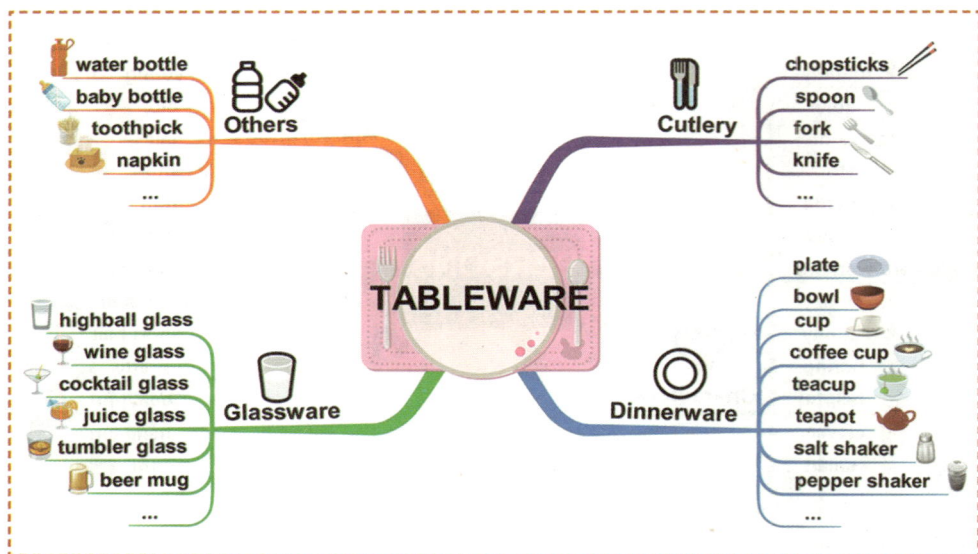

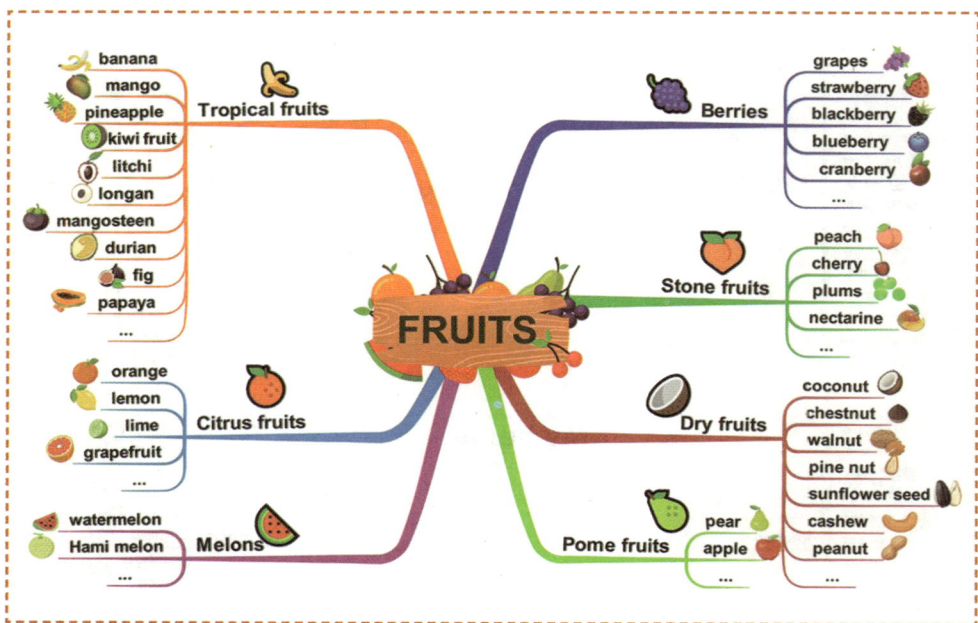

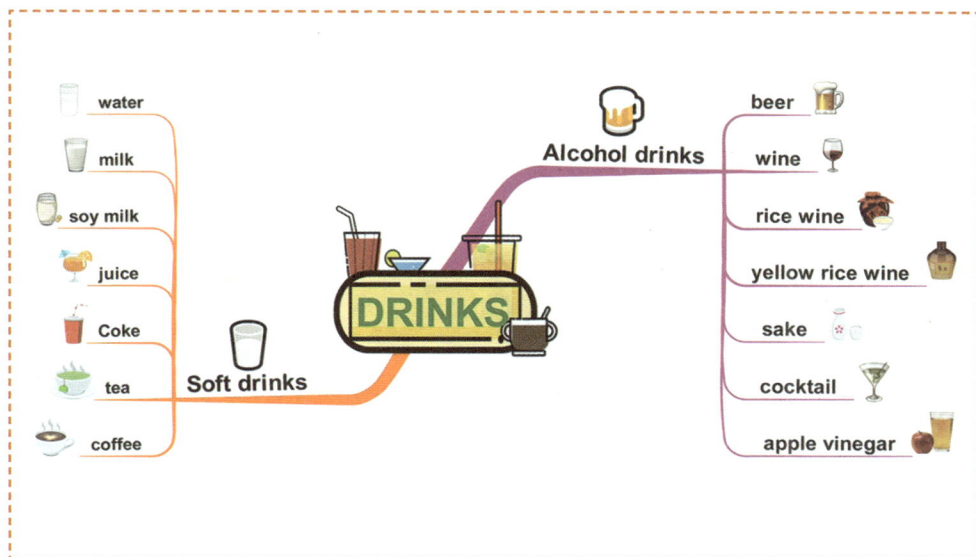

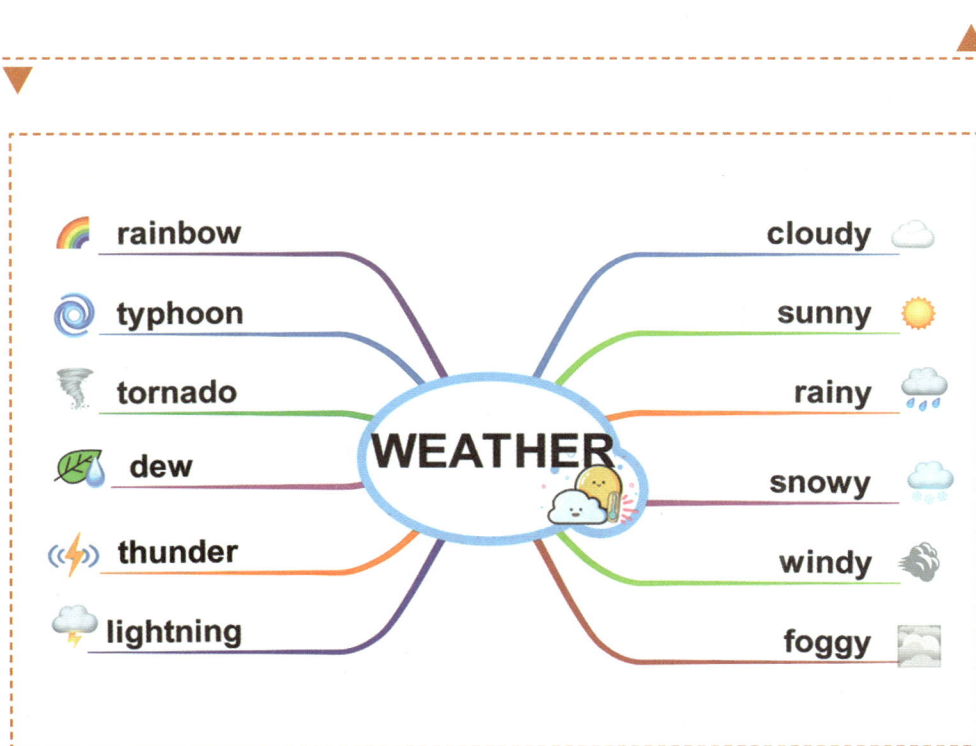

词汇思维导图

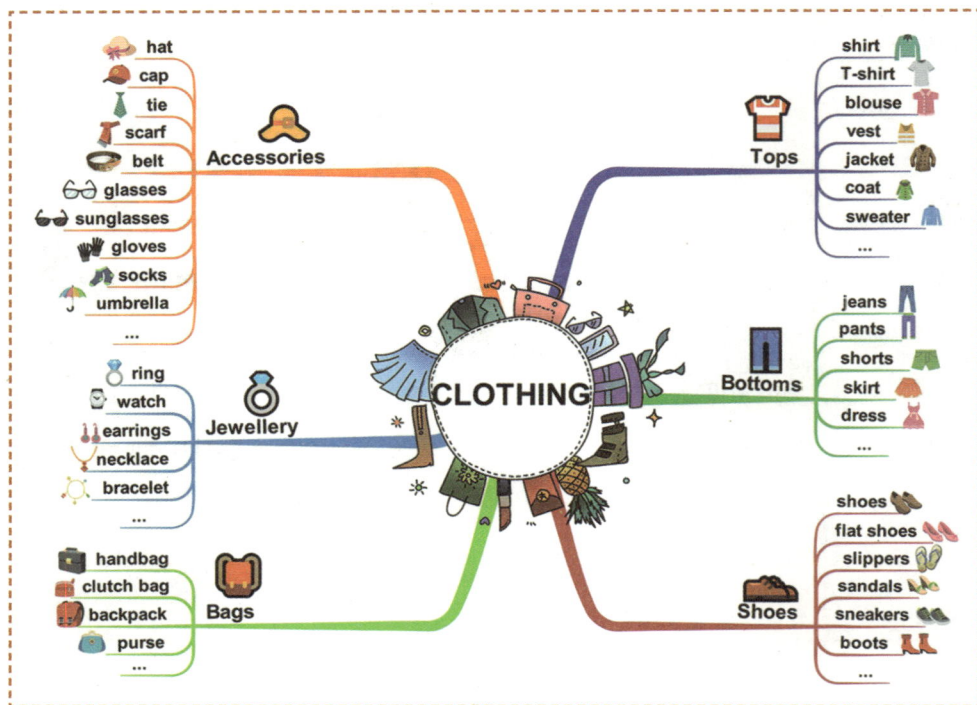

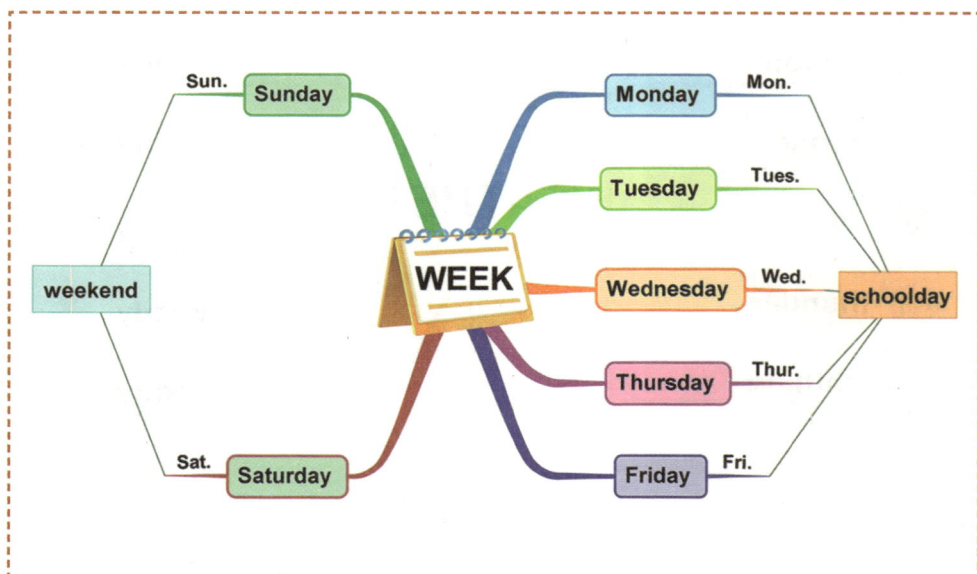

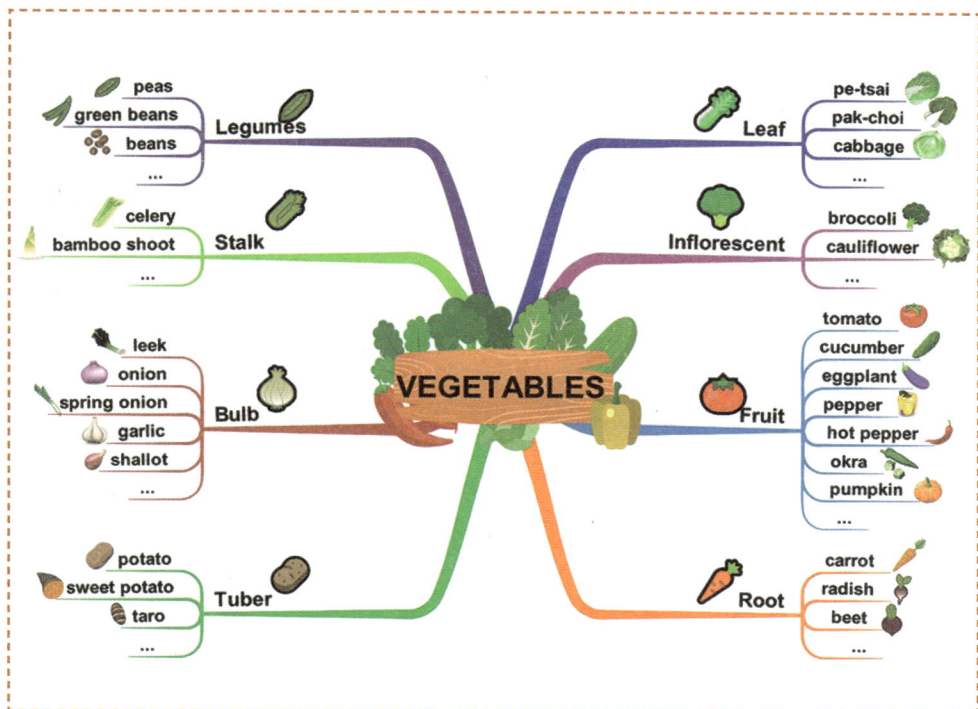

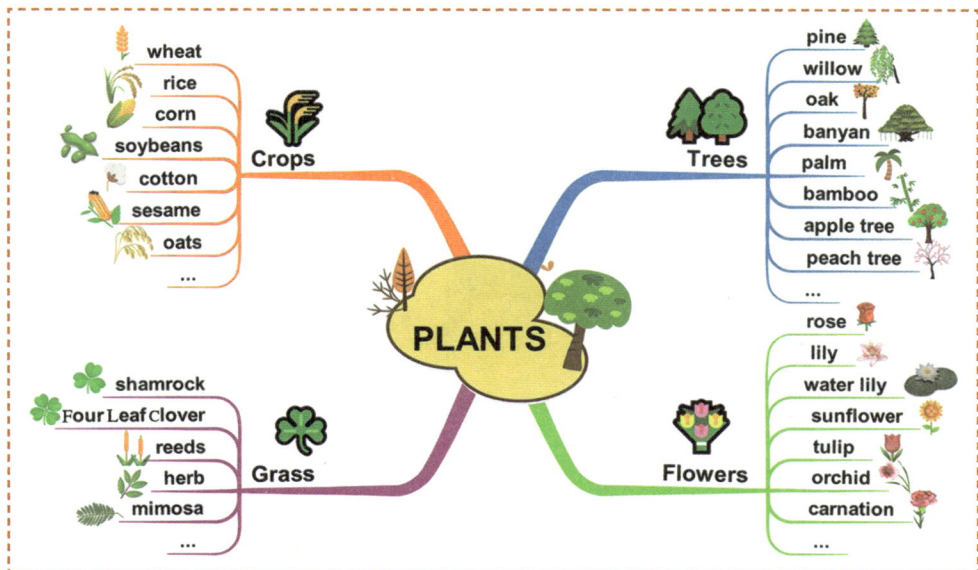

词汇思维导图

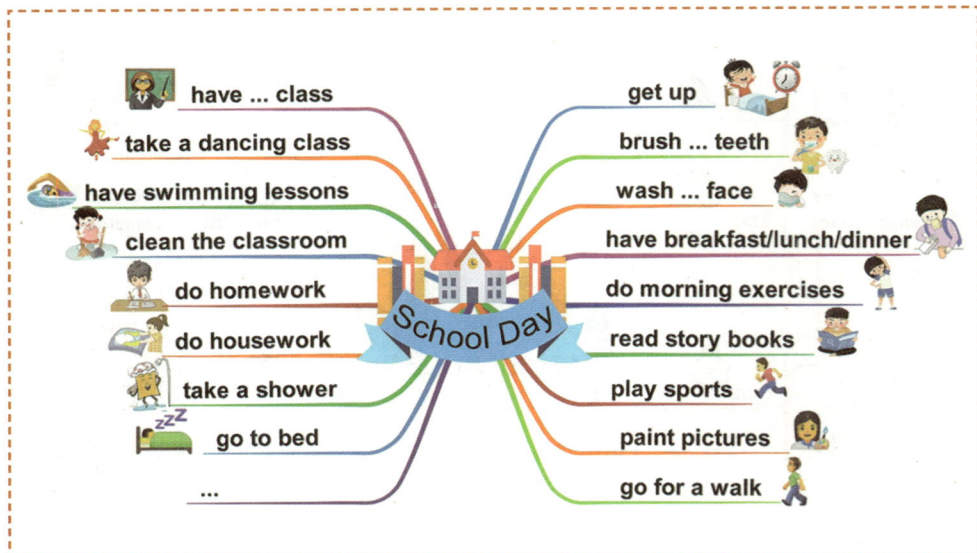

School Day

have ... class
take a dancing class
have swimming lessons
clean the classroom
do homework
do housework
take a shower
go to bed
...

get up
brush ... teeth
wash ... face
have breakfast/lunch/dinner
do morning exercises
read story books
play sports
paint pictures
go for a walk

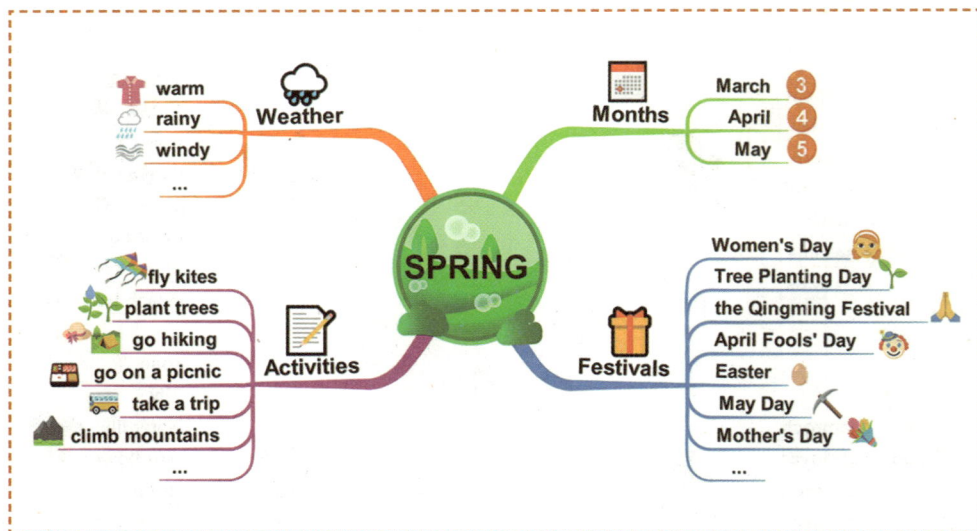

SPRING

Weather
warm
rainy
windy
...

Months
March 3
April 4
May 5

Activities
fly kites
plant trees
go hiking
go on a picnic
take a trip
climb mountains
...

Festivals
Women's Day
Tree Planting Day
the Qingming Festival
April Fools' Day
Easter
May Day
Mother's Day
...

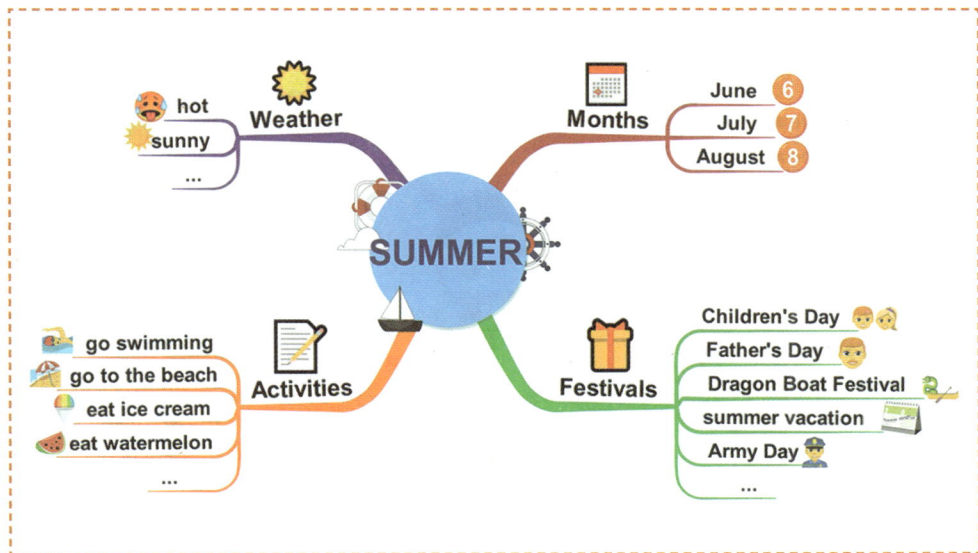

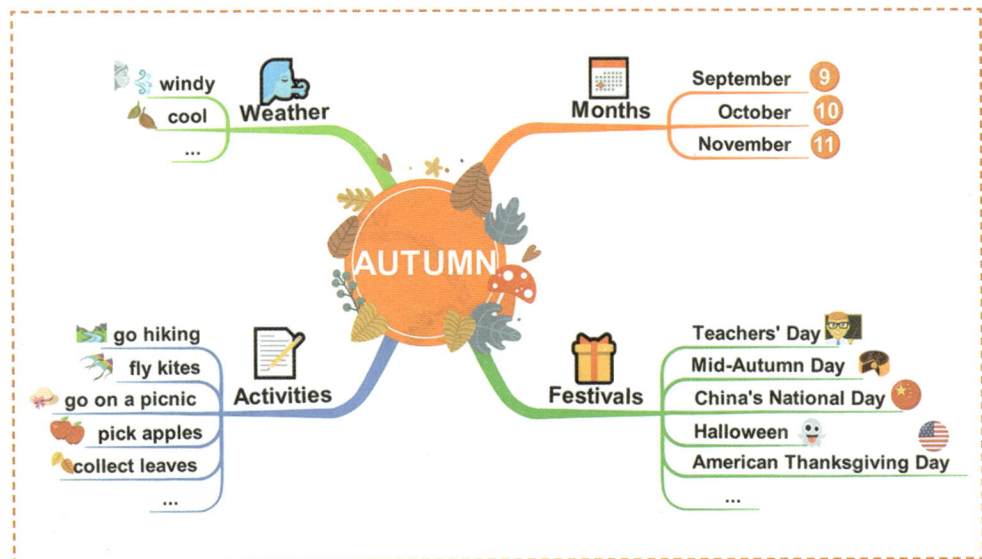

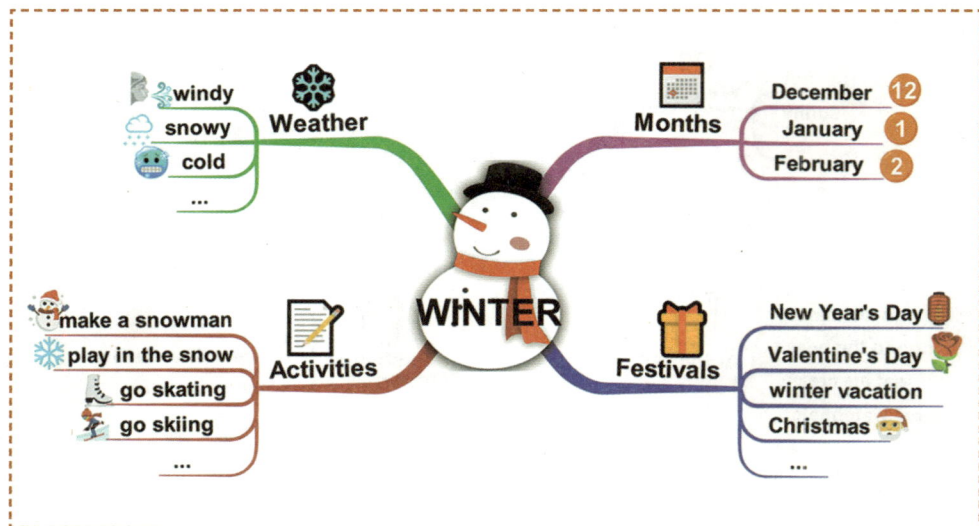

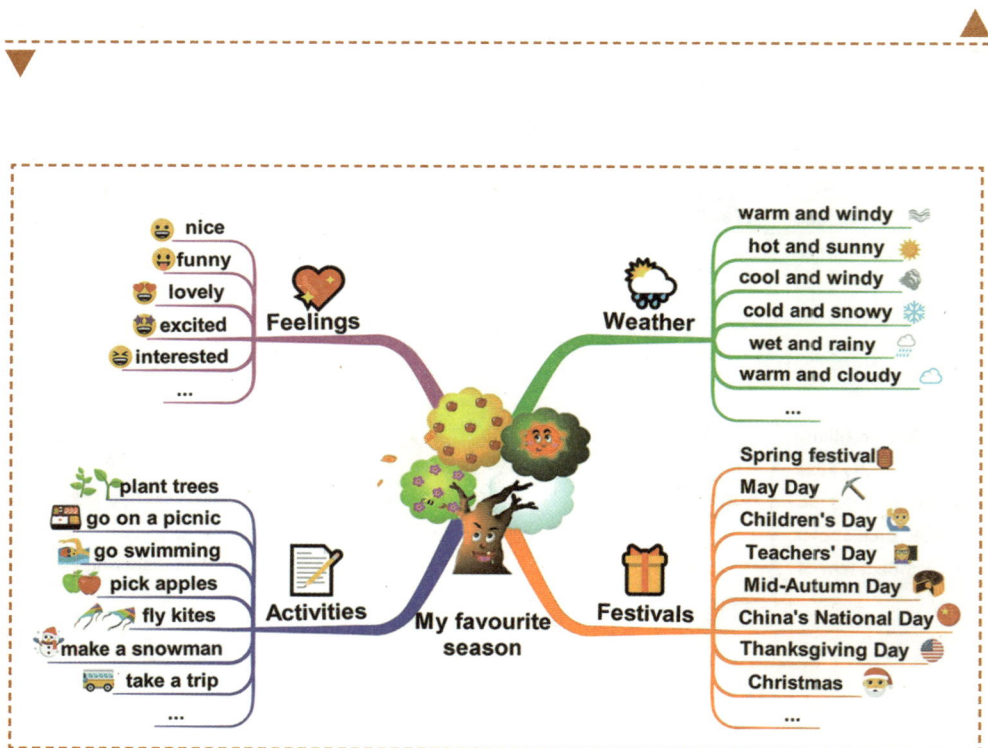

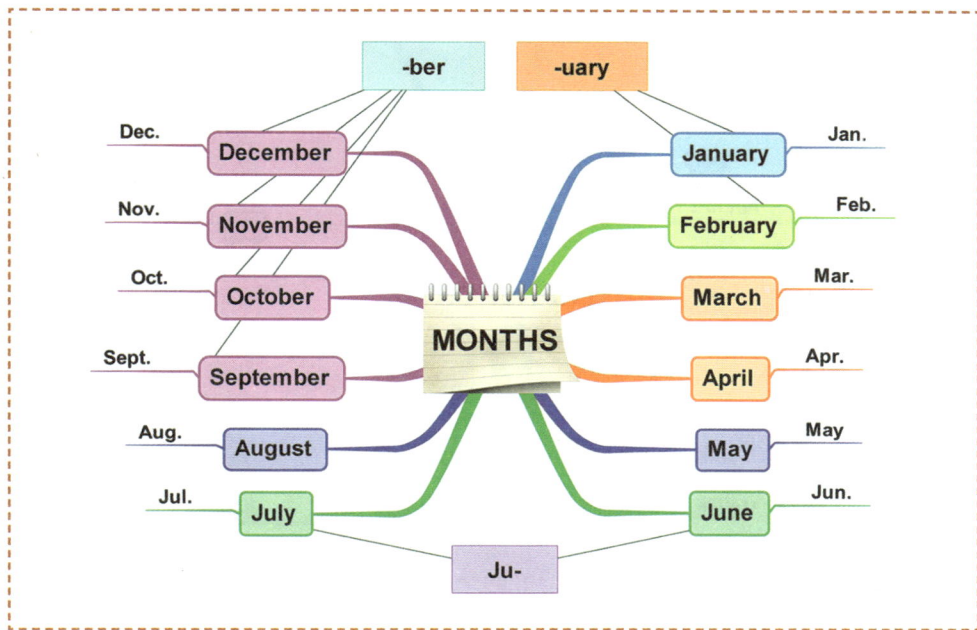

-ber

-uary

Dec. December

Nov. November

Oct. October

Sept. September

Aug. August

Jul. July

MONTHS

January Jan.

February Feb.

March Mar.

April Apr.

May May

June Jun.

Ju-

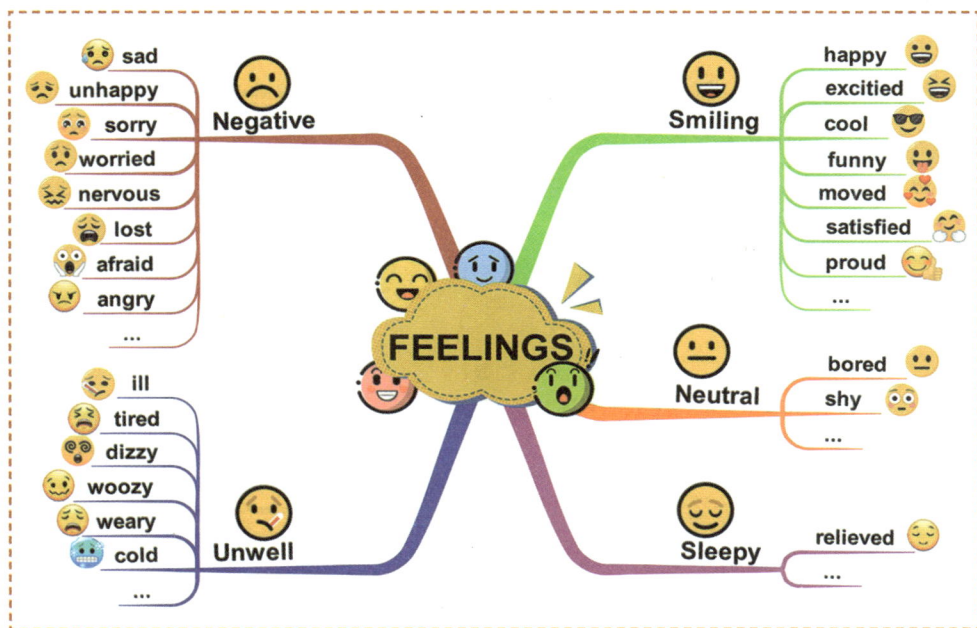

Negative

sad
unhappy
sorry
worried
nervous
lost
afraid
angry
...

Unwell

ill
tired
dizzy
woozy
weary
cold
...

FEELINGS

Smiling

happy
excitied
cool
funny
moved
satisfied
proud
...

Neutral

bored
shy
...

Sleepy

relieved
...

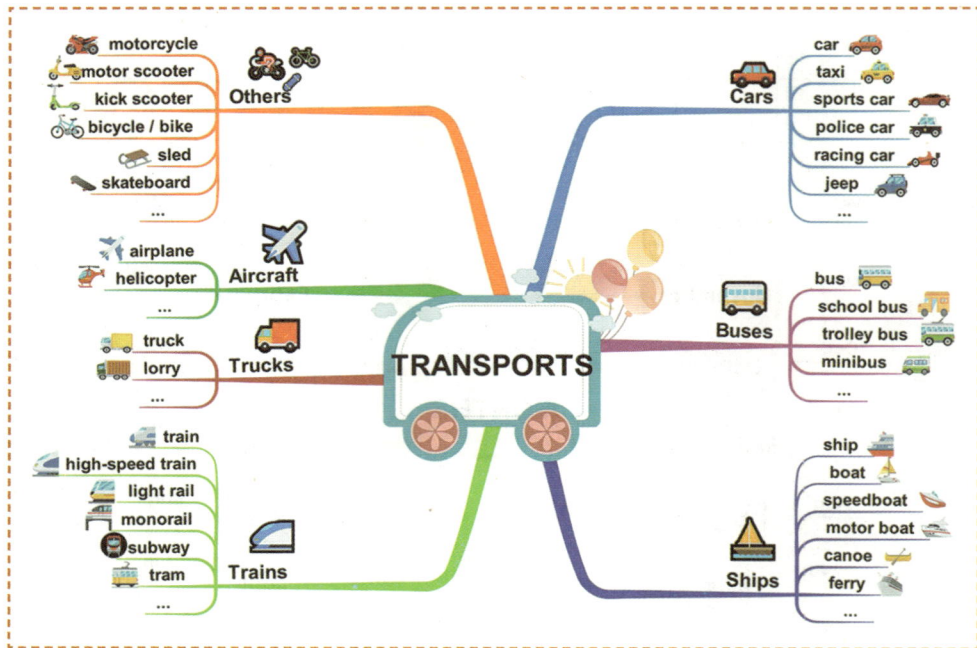

TRANSPORTS

- **Others**
  - motorcycle
  - motor scooter
  - kick scooter
  - bicycle / bike
  - sled
  - skateboard
  - ...
- **Aircraft**
  - airplane
  - helicopter
  - ...
- **Trucks**
  - truck
  - lorry
  - ...
- **Trains**
  - train
  - high-speed train
  - light rail
  - monorail
  - subway
  - tram
  - ...
- **Cars**
  - car
  - taxi
  - sports car
  - police car
  - racing car
  - jeep
  - ...
- **Buses**
  - bus
  - school bus
  - trolley bus
  - minibus
  - ...
- **Ships**
  - ship
  - boat
  - speedboat
  - motor boat
  - canoe
  - ferry
  - ...

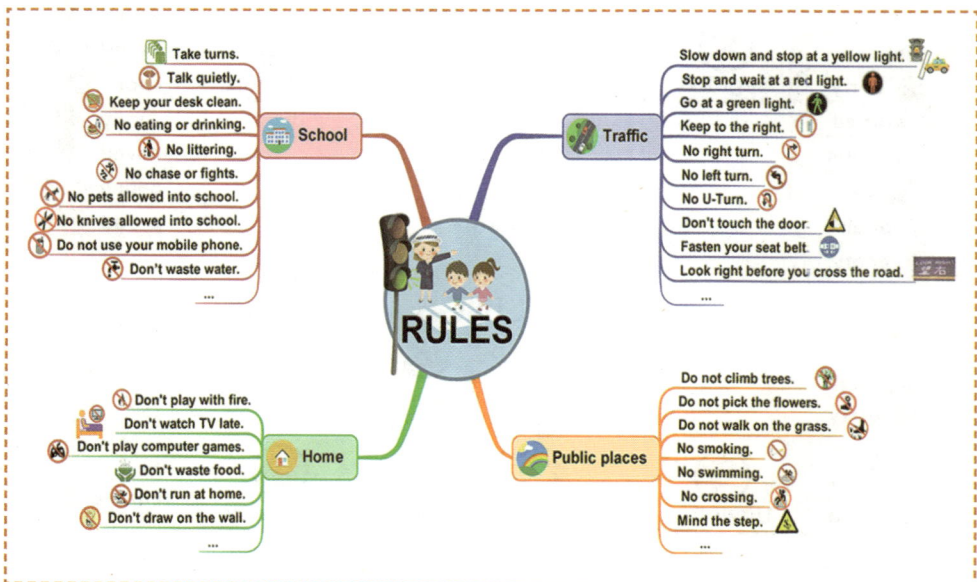

RULES

- **School**
  - Take turns.
  - Talk quietly.
  - Keep your desk clean.
  - No eating or drinking.
  - No littering.
  - No chase or fights.
  - No pets allowed into school.
  - No knives allowed into school.
  - Do not use your mobile phone.
  - Don't waste water.
  - ...
- **Traffic**
  - Slow down and stop at a yellow light.
  - Stop and wait at a red light.
  - Go at a green light.
  - Keep to the right.
  - No right turn.
  - No left turn.
  - No U-Turn.
  - Don't touch the door.
  - Fasten your seat belt.
  - Look right before you cross the road.
  - ...
- **Home**
  - Don't play with fire.
  - Don't watch TV late.
  - Don't play computer games.
  - Don't waste food.
  - Don't run at home.
  - Don't draw on the wall.
  - ...
- **Public places**
  - Do not climb trees.
  - Do not pick the flowers.
  - Do not walk on the grass.
  - No smoking.
  - No swimming.
  - No crossing.
  - Mind the step.
  - ...

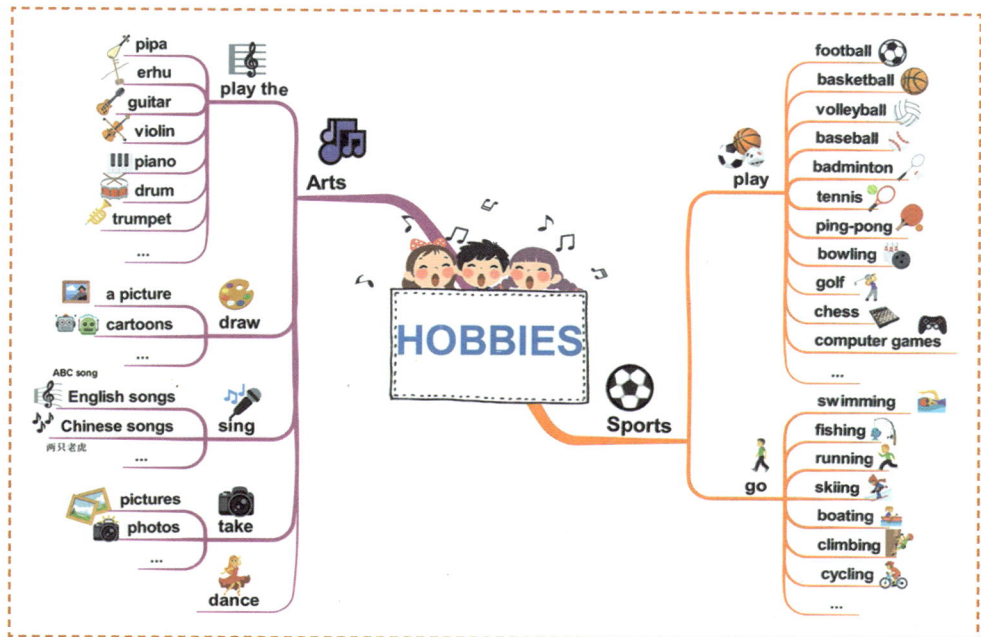

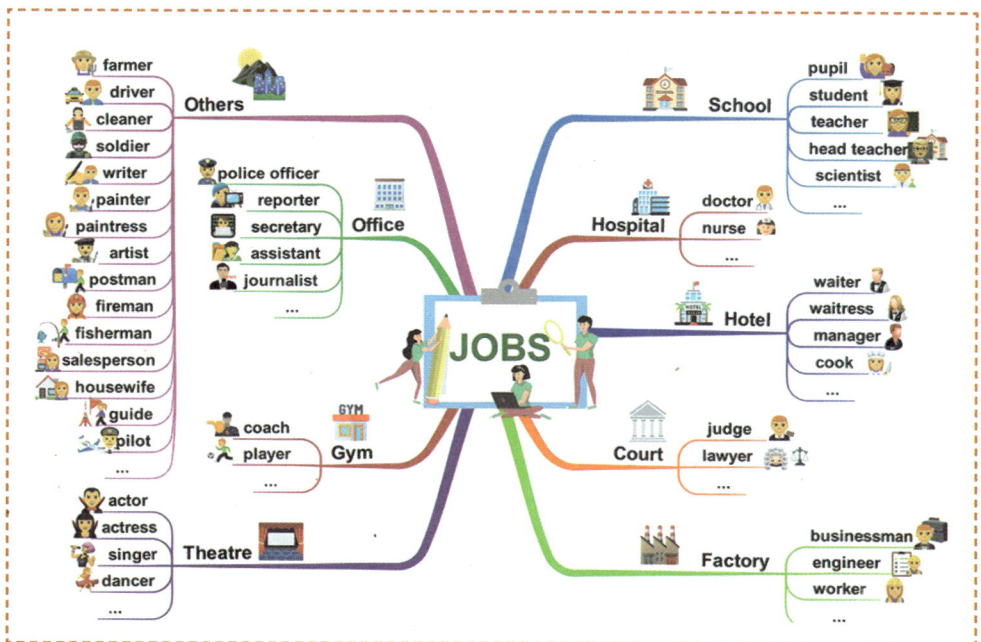

词汇思维导图

教材思维导图

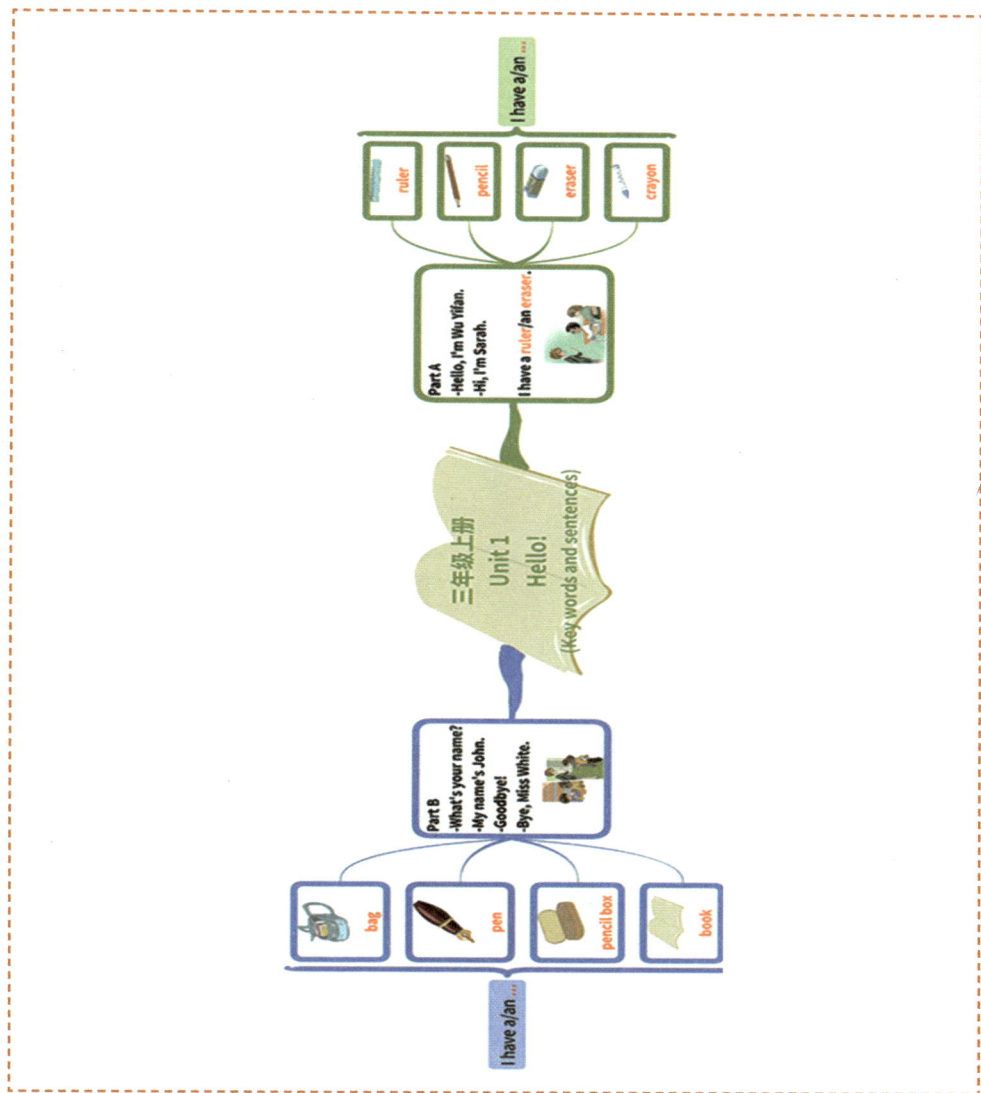

小学英语人教版三年级上册

Unit 1　Hello !

I have a/an ...

ruler	pencil	eraser	crayon

Part A
-Hello, I'm Wu Yifan.
-Hi, I'm Sarah.
-I have a ruler/an eraser.

三年级上册
Unit 1
Hello!
(Key words and sentence(s))

Part B
-What's your name?
-My name's John.
-Goodbye!
-Bye, Miss White.

bag	pen	pencil box	book

I have a/an ...

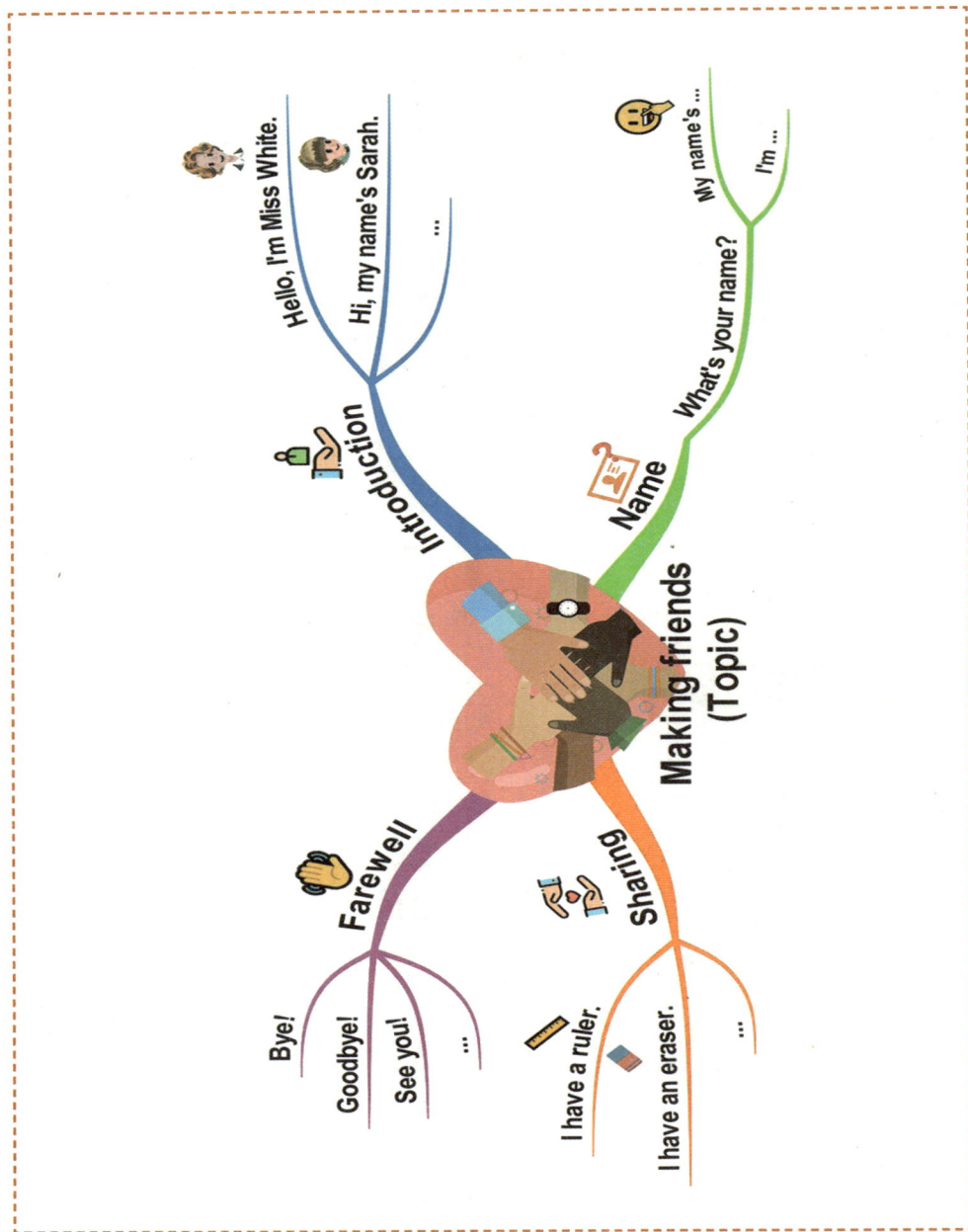

Making friends (Topic)

Introduction
- Hello, I'm Miss White.
- Hi, my name's Sarah.
- ...

Name
- What's your name?
- My name's ...
- I'm ...

Farewell
- Bye!
- Goodbye!
- See you!
- ...

Sharing
- I have a ruler.
- I have an eraser.
- ...

Unit 2　Colours

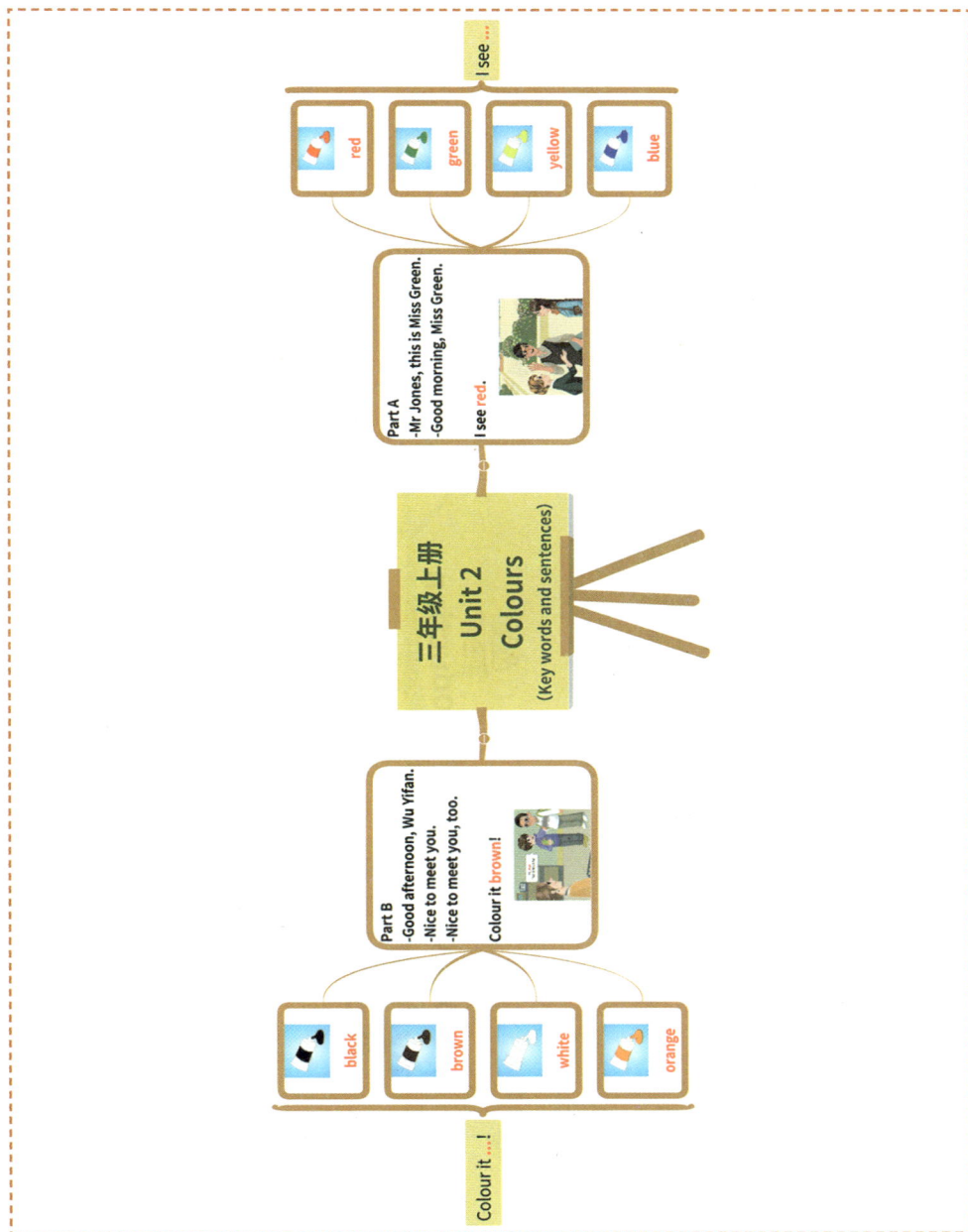

I see ...

red　green　yellow　blue

Part A
-Mr Jones, this is Miss Green.
-Good morning, Miss Green.

I see red.

三年级上册
Unit 2
Colours
(Key words and sentences)

Part B
-Good afternoon, Wu Yifan.
-Nice to meet you.
-Nice to meet you, too.

Colour it brown!

black　brown　white　orange

Colour it ....!

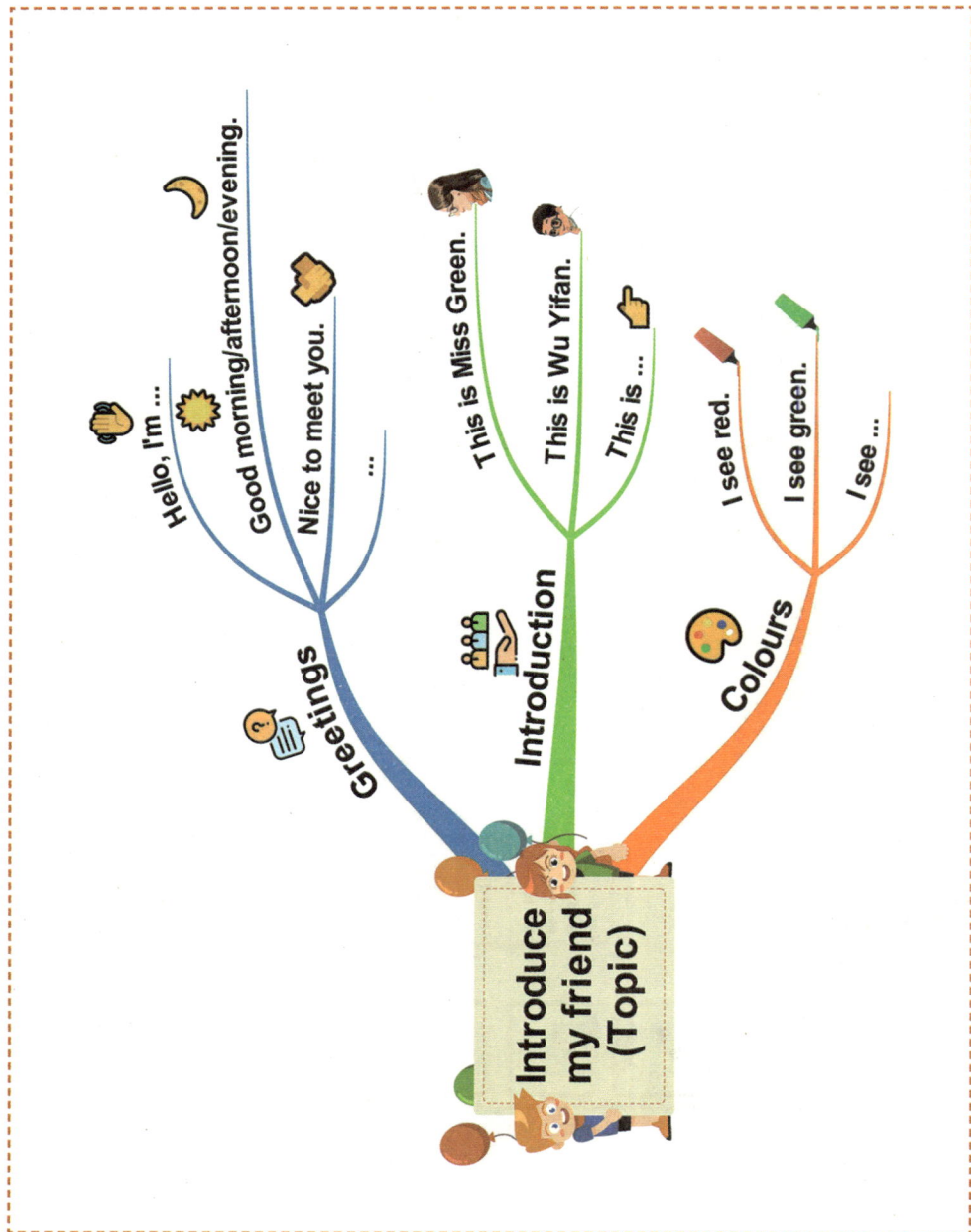

Hello, I'm ...

Good morning/afternoon/evening.

Nice to meet you.

...

This is Miss Green.

This is Wu Yifan.

This is ...

I see red.

I see green.

I see ...

Greetings

Introduction

Colours

Introduce my friend (Topic)

Unit 3 Look at me!

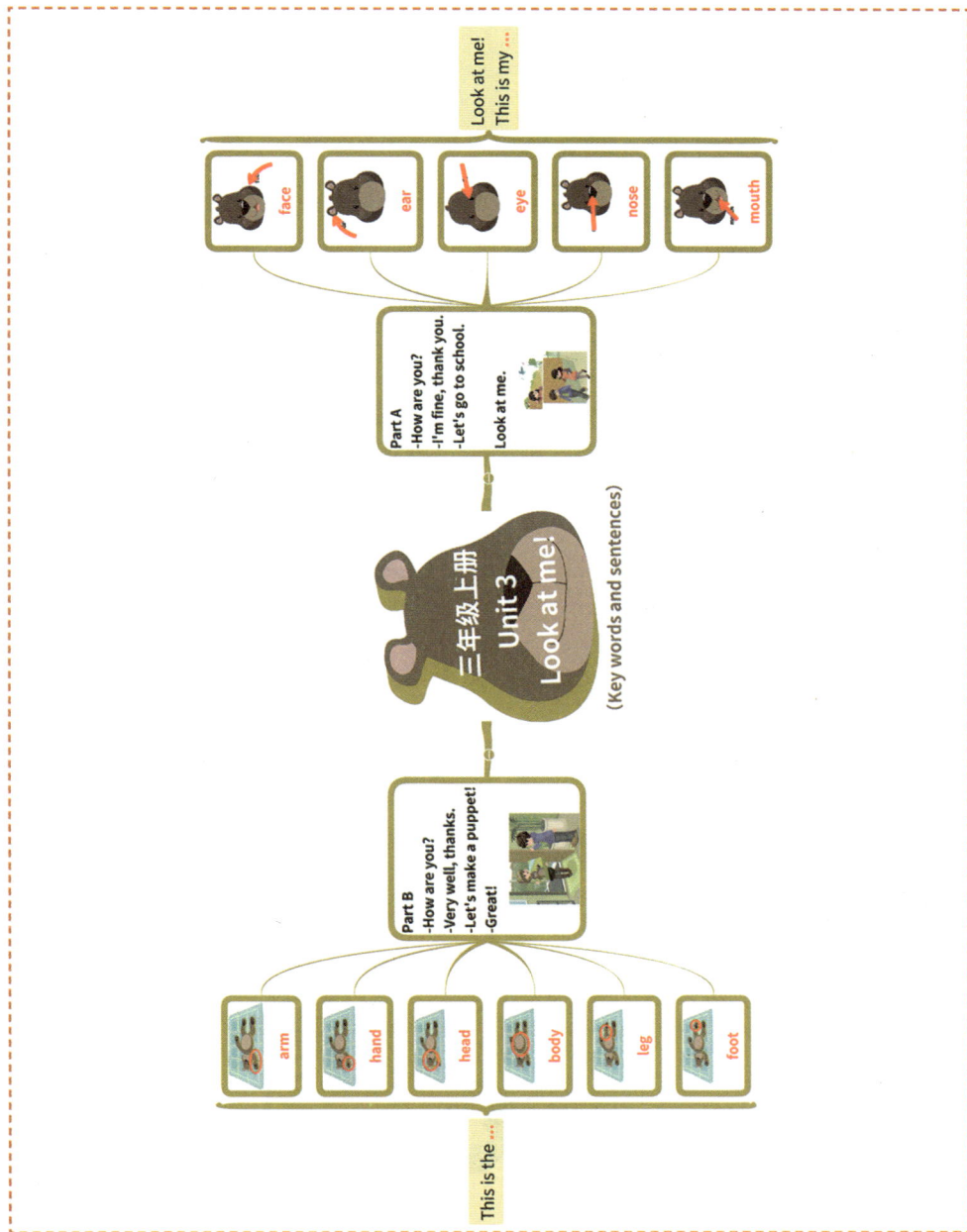

三年级 上册
Unit 3
Look at me!

(Key words and sentences)

Look at me!
This is my ...

face

ear

eye

nose

mouth

Part A
-How are you?
-I'm fine, thank you.
-Let's go to school.

Look at me.

Part B
-How are you?
-Very well, thanks.
-Let's make a puppet!
-Great!

arm

hand

head

body

leg

foot

This is the ...

三年级 上册

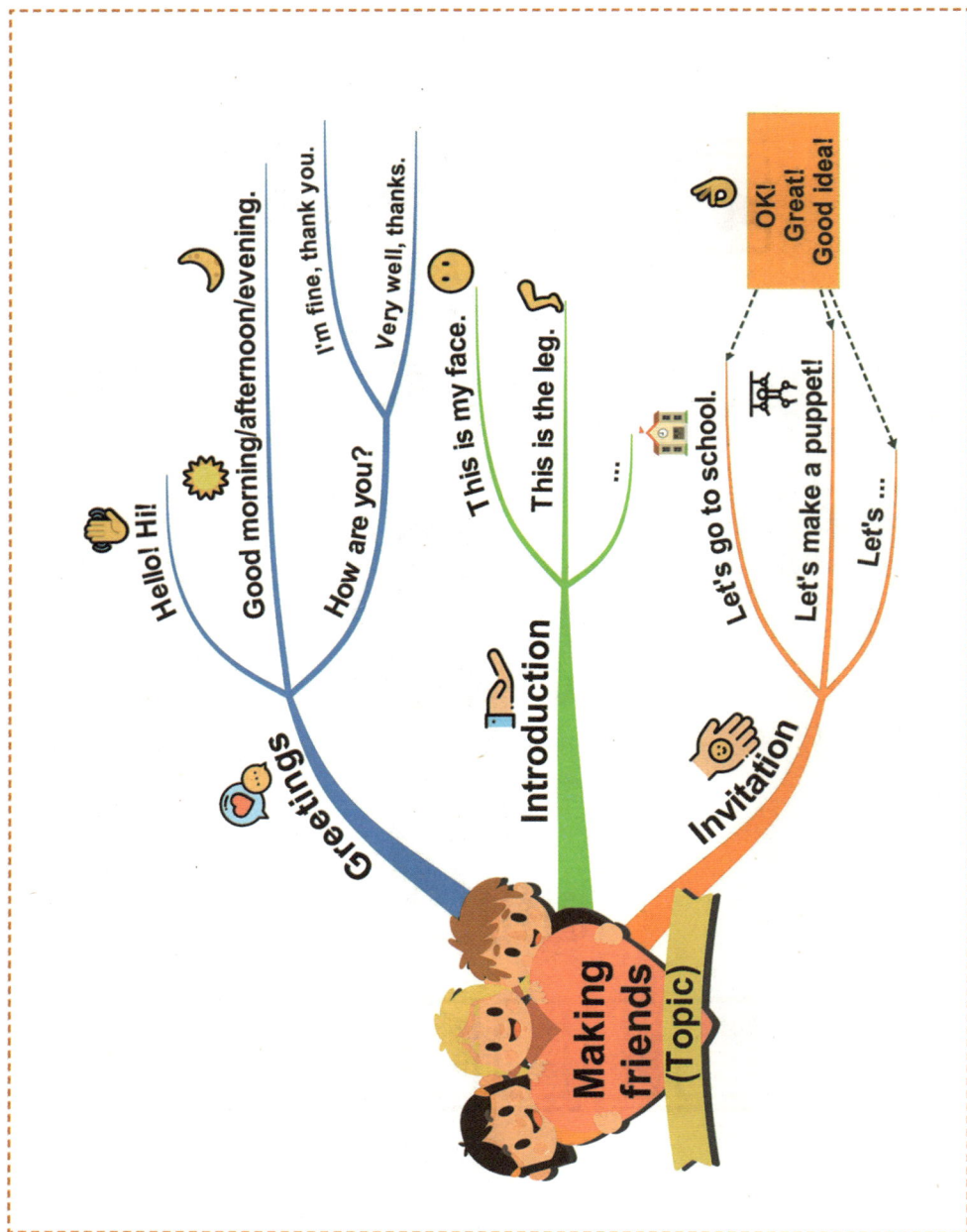

Making friends (Topic)

Greetings
- Hello! Hi!
- Good morning/afternoon/evening.
- How are you?
  - I'm fine, thank you.
  - Very well, thanks.

Introduction
- This is my face.
- This is the leg.
- ...

Invitation
- Let's go to school.
- Let's make a puppet!
- Let's ...
  - OK!
  - Great!
  - Good idea!

Unit 4 We love animals

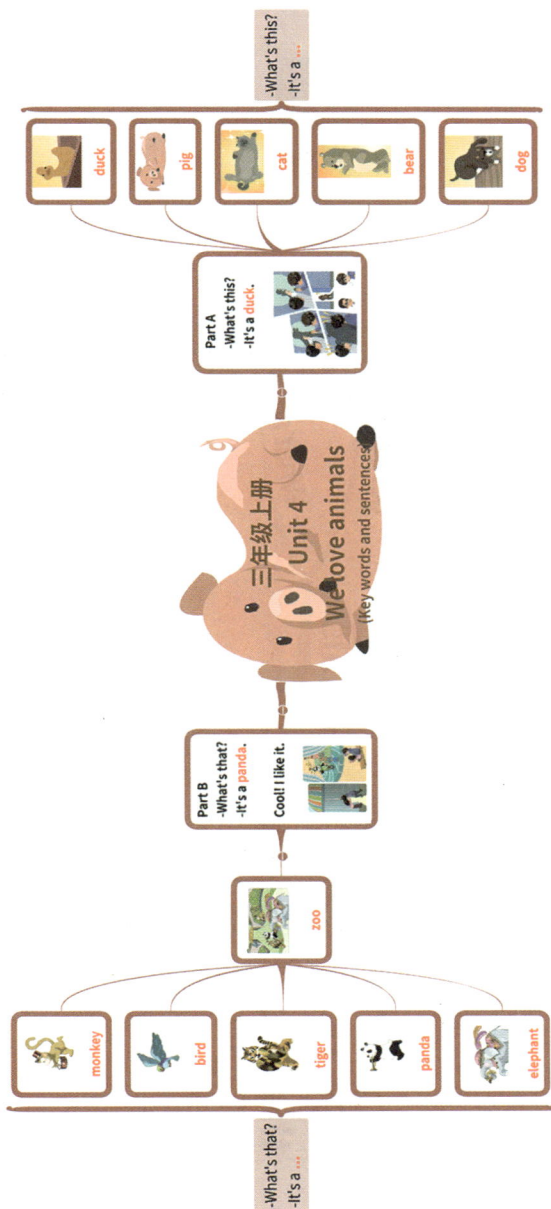

-What's this?
-It's a ...

duck | pig | cat | bear | dog

Part A
-What's this?
-It's a duck.

三年级上册
Unit 4
We love animals
(Key words and sentences)

Part B
-What's that?
-It's a panda.
Cool! I like it.

zoo

monkey | bird | tiger | panda | elephant

-What's that?
-It's a ...

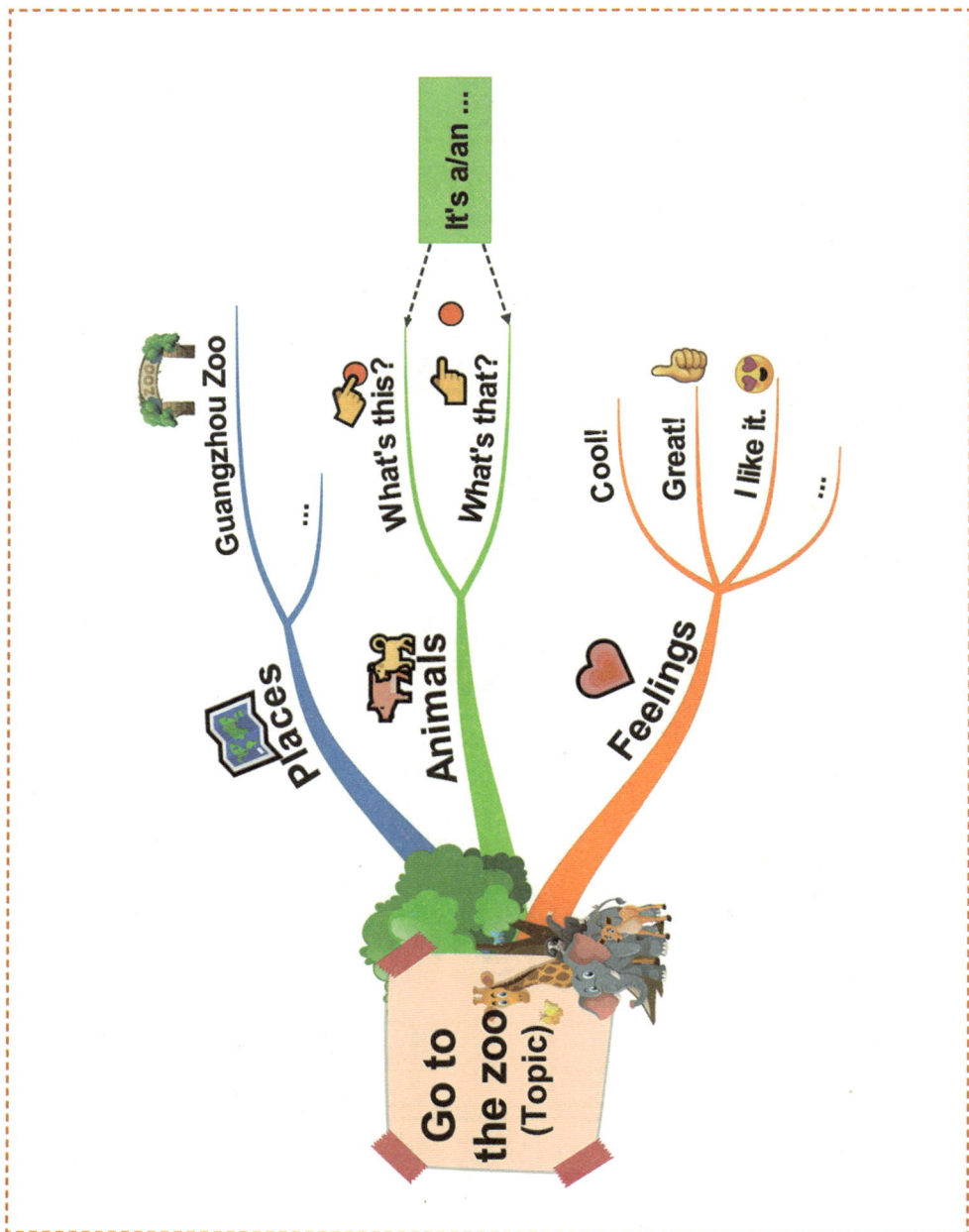

It's a/an …

Guangzhou Zoo

…

What's this?

What's that?

Cool!

Great!

I like it.

…

Places

Animals

Feelings

Go to
the zoo
(Topic)

Unit 5 Let's eat !

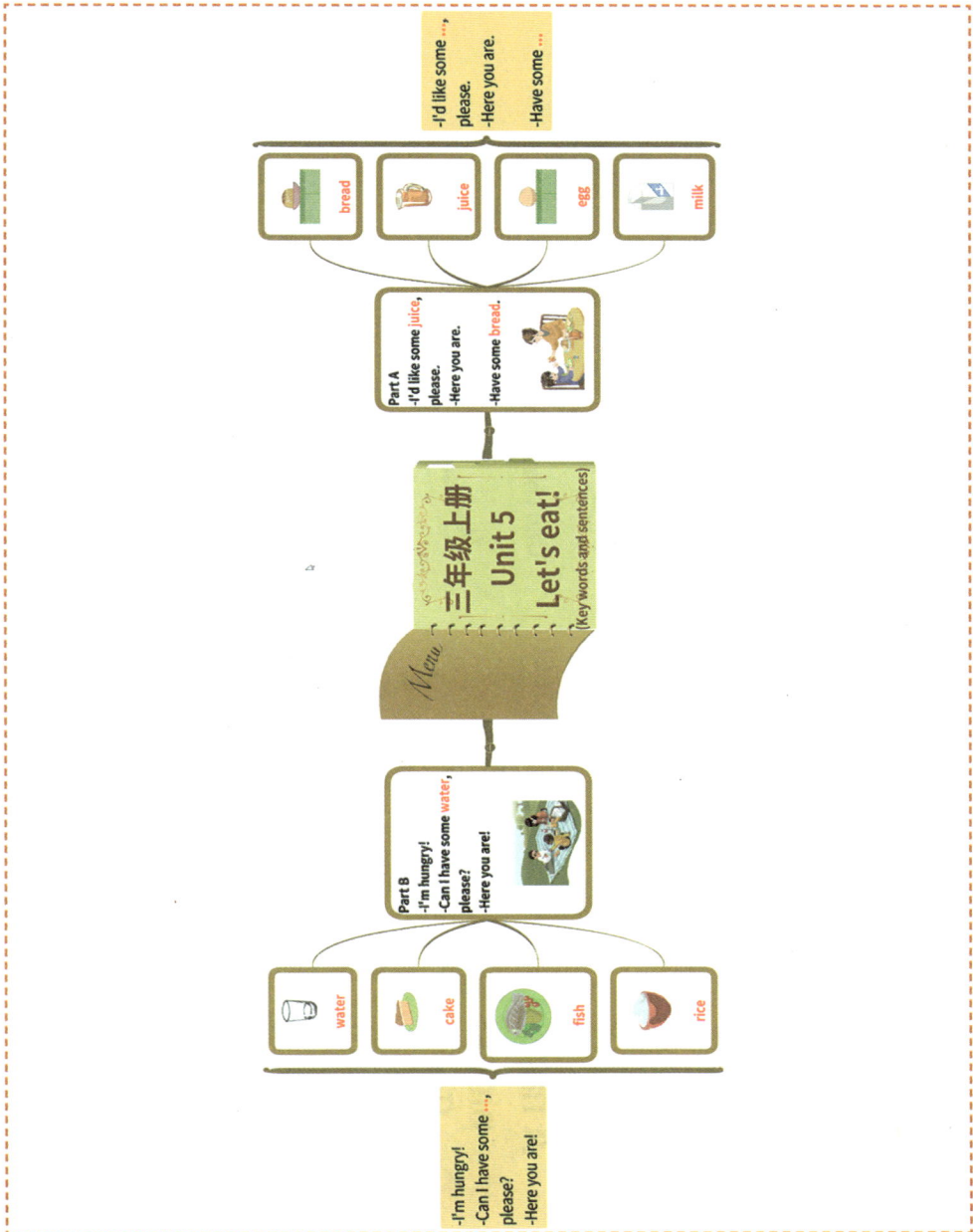

- I'd like some ···, please.
- Here you are.
- Have some ···.

bread juice egg milk

Part A
- I'd like some juice, please.
- Here you are.
- Have some bread.

三年级上册
Unit 5
Let's eat!
(Key words and sentences)

Menu

Part B
- I'm hungry!
- Can I have some water, please?
- Here you are!

water cake fish rice

- I'm hungry!
- Can I have some ···, please?
- Here you are!

三年级 上册

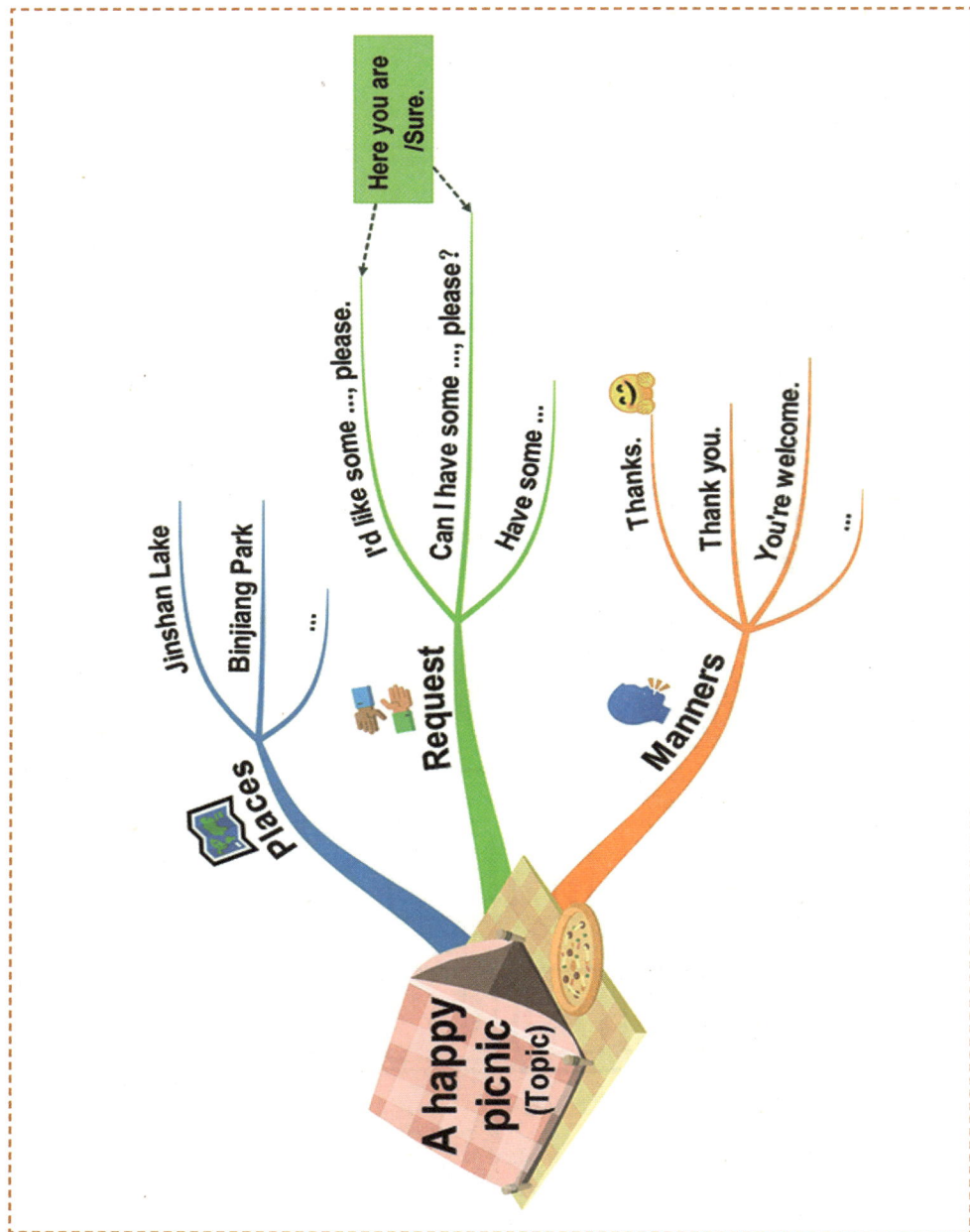

Here you are /Sure.

I'd like some ..., please.

Can I have some ..., please?

Have some ...

Thanks.

Thank you.

You're welcome.

...

Jinshan Lake

Binjiang Park

...

Places

Request

Manners

A happy picnic (Topic)

Unit 6 Happy birthday!

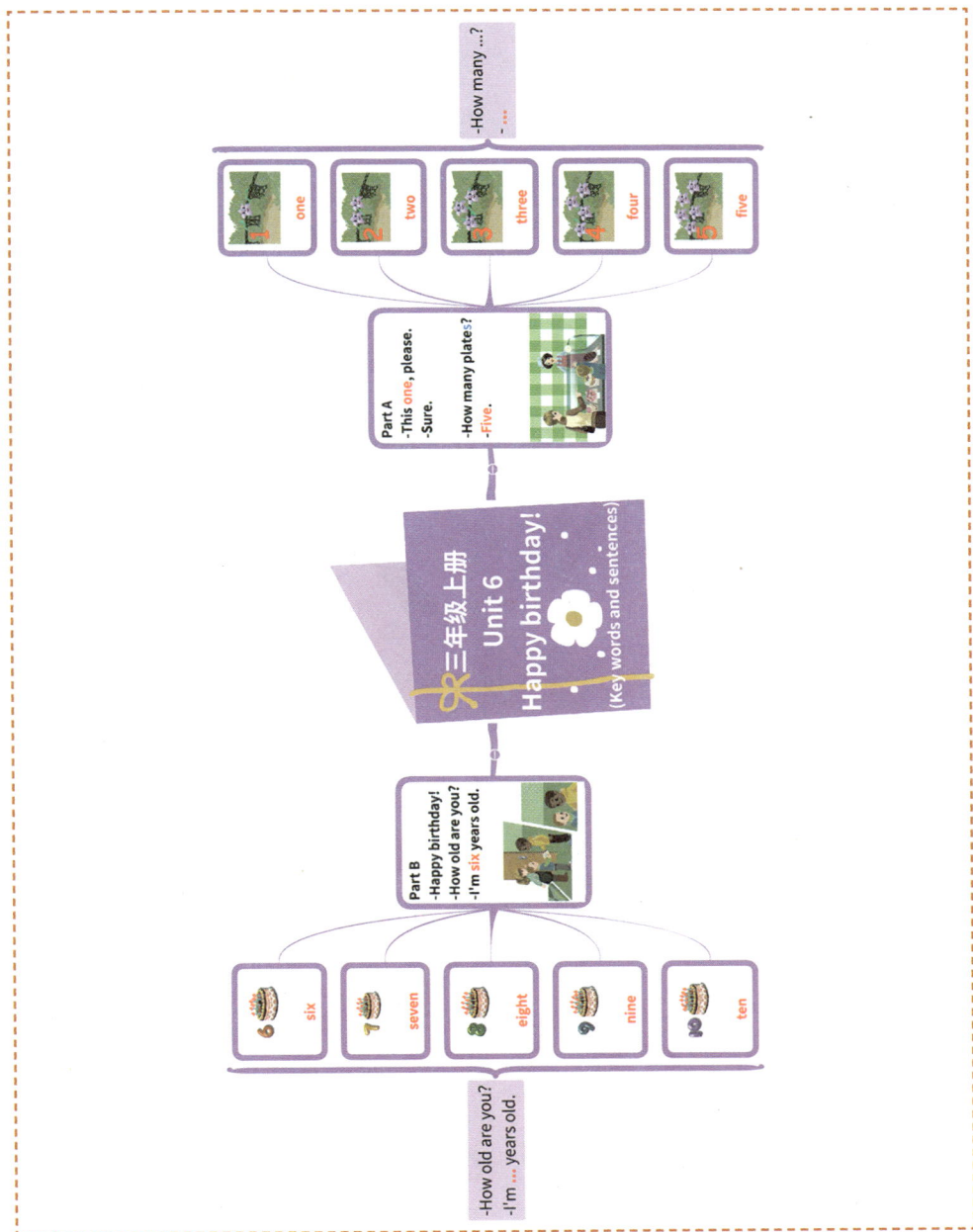

-How many ...?
-It's ...

one
two
three
four
five

Part A
-This one, please.
-Sure.
-How many plates?
-Five.

三年级上册
Unit 6
Happy birthday!
(Key words and sentences)

Part B
-Happy birthday!
-How old are you?
-I'm six years old.

six
seven
eight
nine
ten

-How old are you?
-I'm ... years old.

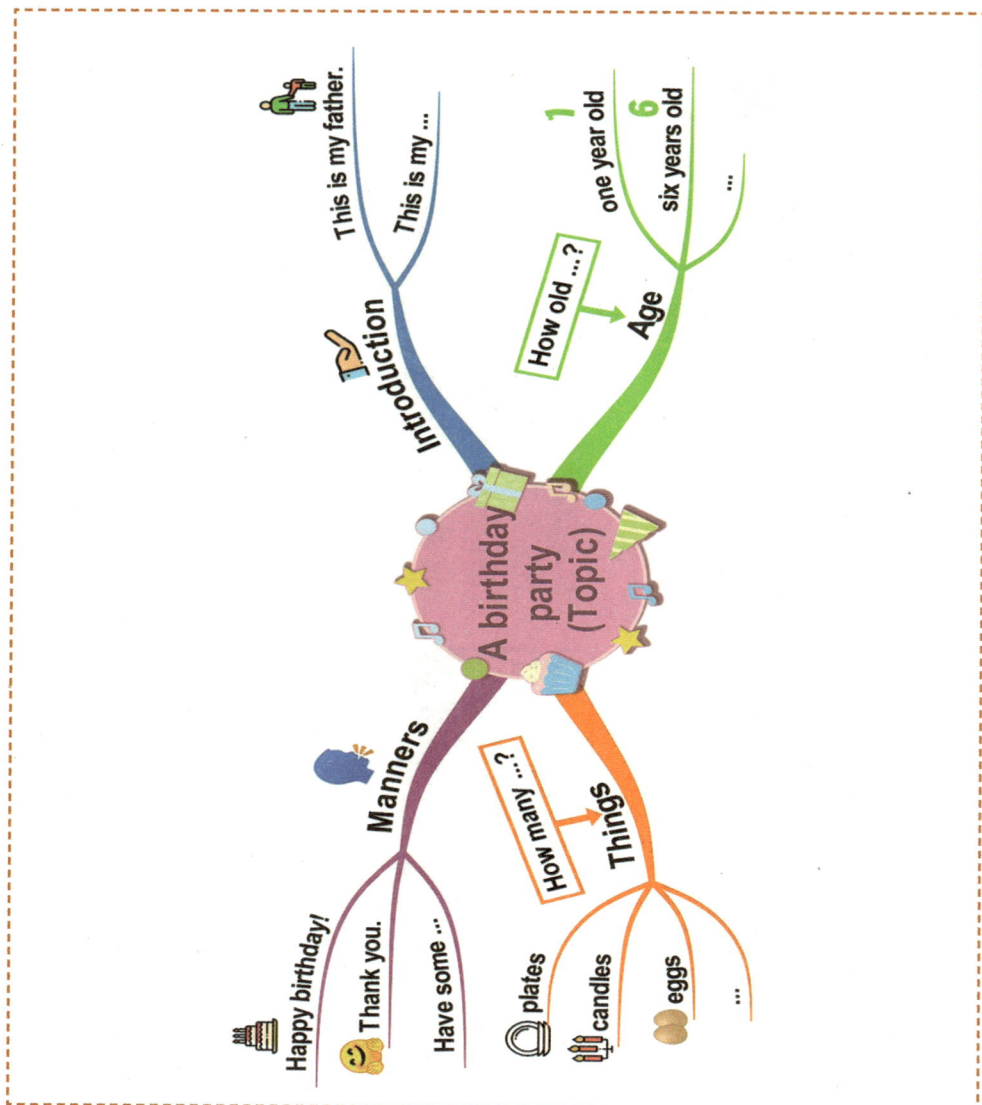

This is my father.

This is my ...

Introduction

How old ...?

Age

1
one year old

6
six years old

...

A birthday party
(Topic)

Manners

Happy birthday!

Thank you.

Have some ...

How many ...?

Things

plates

candles

eggs

...

小学英语人教版三年级下册

Unit 1 Welcome back to school!

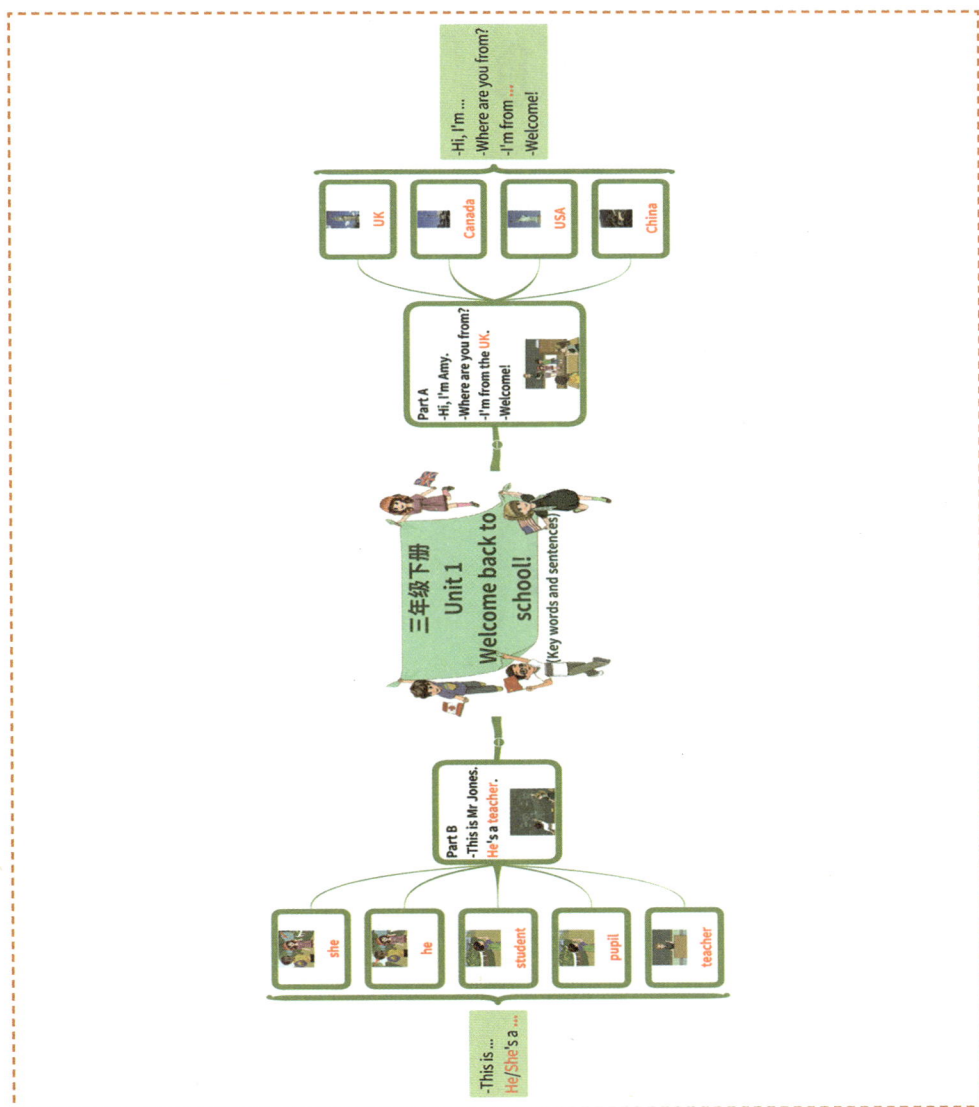

-Hi, I'm ...
-Where are you from?
-I'm from ···
-Welcome!

UK Canada USA China

Part A
-Hi, I'm Amy.
-Where are you from?
-I'm from the UK.
-Welcome!

三年级下册
Unit 1
Welcome back to school!
(Key words and sentences)

Part B
-This is Mr Jones.
-He's a teacher.

she he student pupil teacher

-This is ...
-He/She's a ...

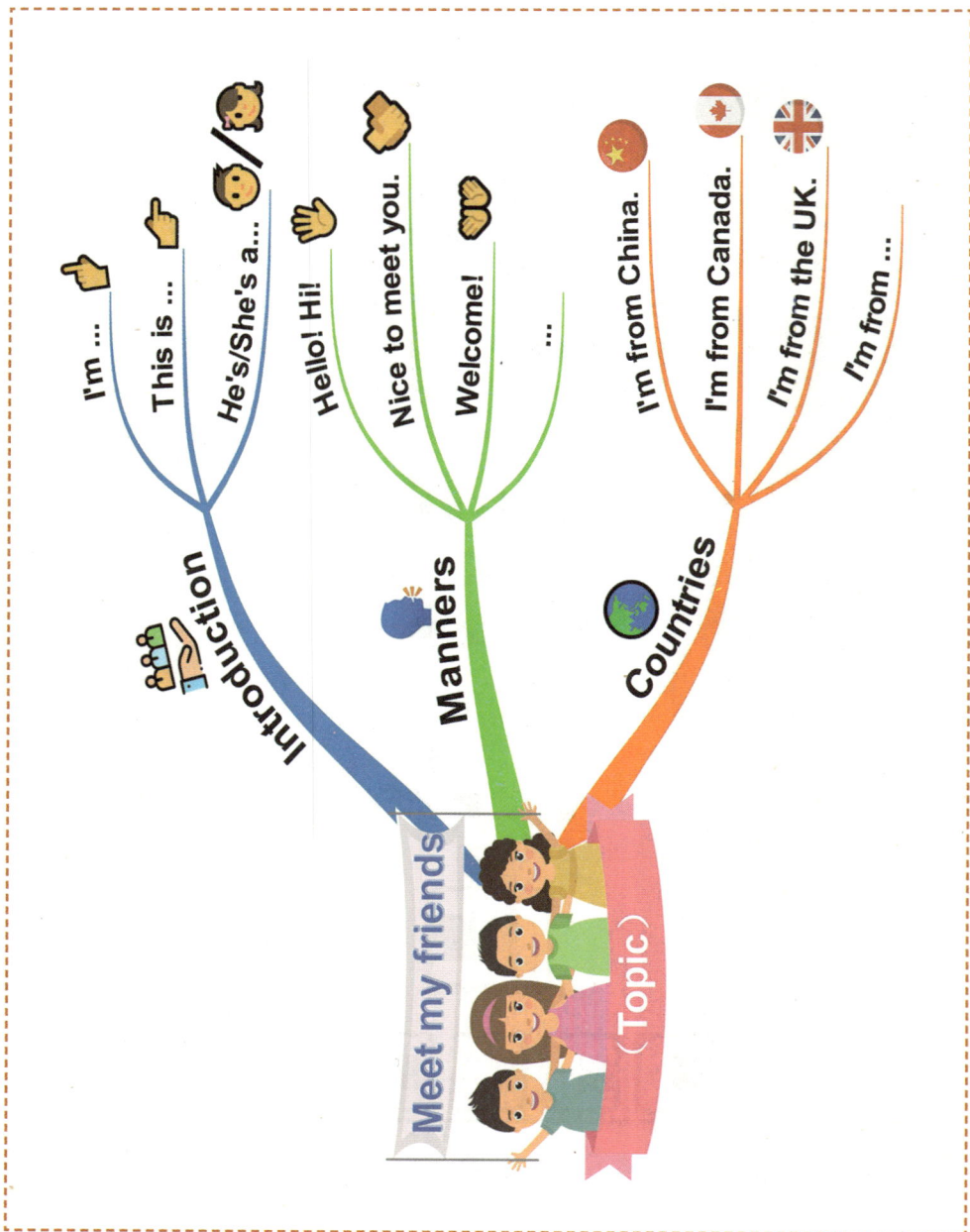

I'm ...

This is ...

He's/She's a...

Hello! Hi!

Nice to meet you.

Welcome!

...

I'm from China.

I'm from Canada.

I'm from the UK.

I'm from ...

Introduction

Manners

Countries

Meet my friends

（Topic）

Unit 2 My family

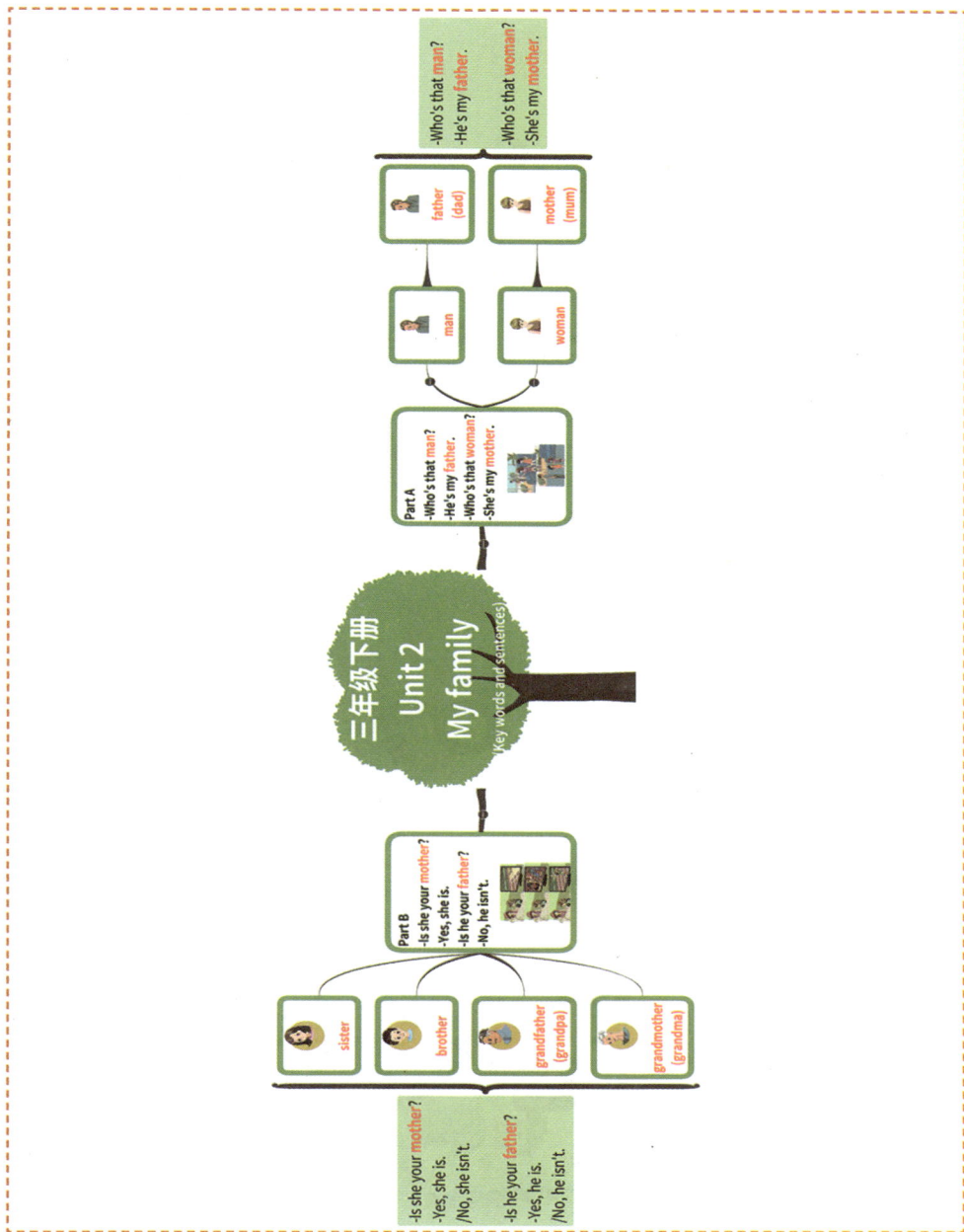

-Who's that man?
-He's my father.
-Who's that woman?
-She's my mother.

father (dad)

mother (mum)

man

woman

Part A
-Who's that man?
-He's my father.
-Who's that woman?
-She's my mother.

三年级下册
Unit 2
My family
(Key words and sentences)

Part B
-Is she your mother?
-Yes, she is.
-Is he your father?
-No, he isn't.

sister

brother

grandfather (grandpa)

grandmother (grandma)

-Is she your mother?
-Yes, she is.
-No, she isn't.
-Is he your father?
-Yes, he is.
-No, he isn't.

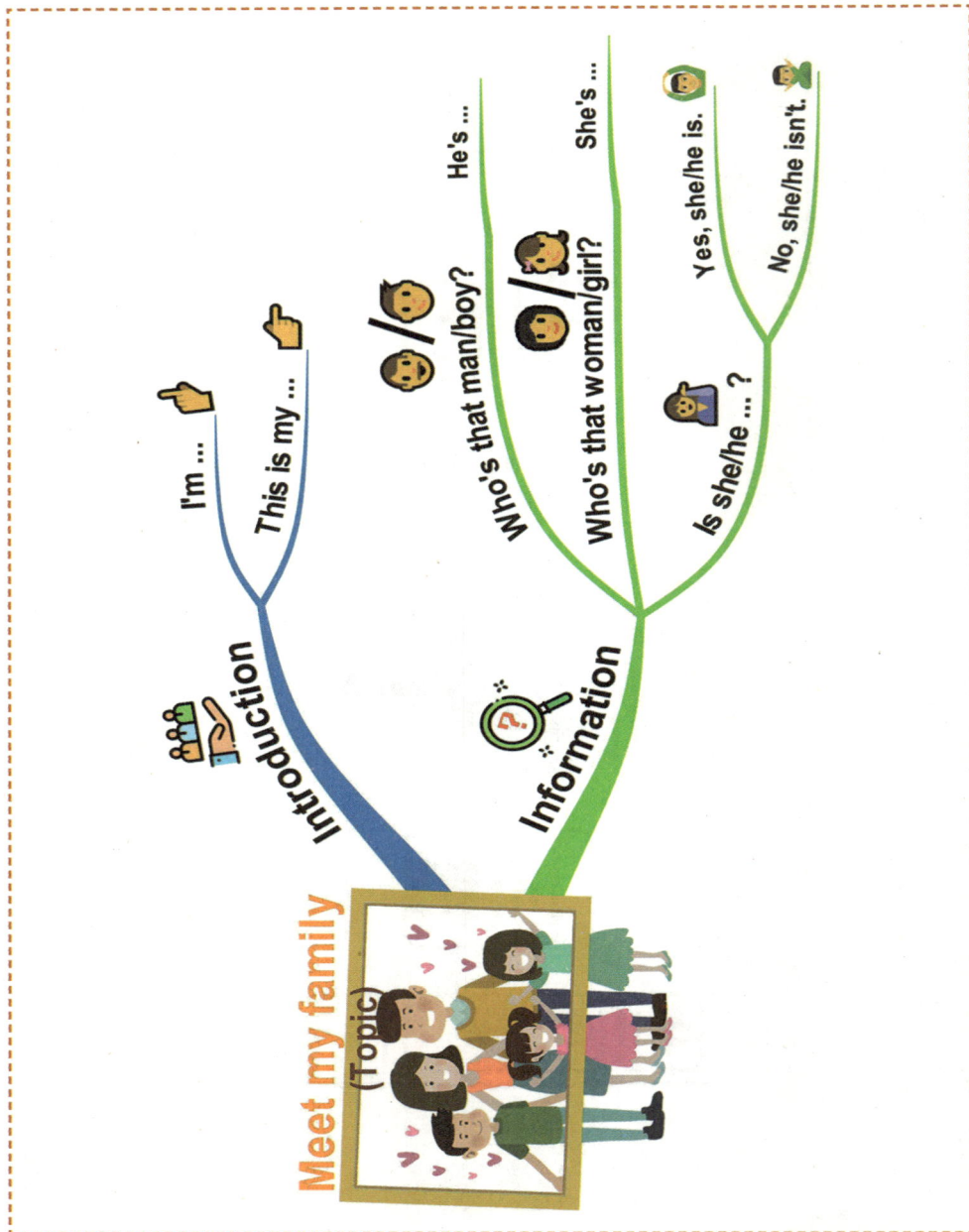

Meet my family
(Topic)

Introduction

I'm ...

This is my ...

Information

Who's that man/boy?

He's ...

Who's that woman/girl?

She's ...

Is she/he ... ?

Yes, she/he is.

No, she/he isn't.

Unit 3 At the zoo

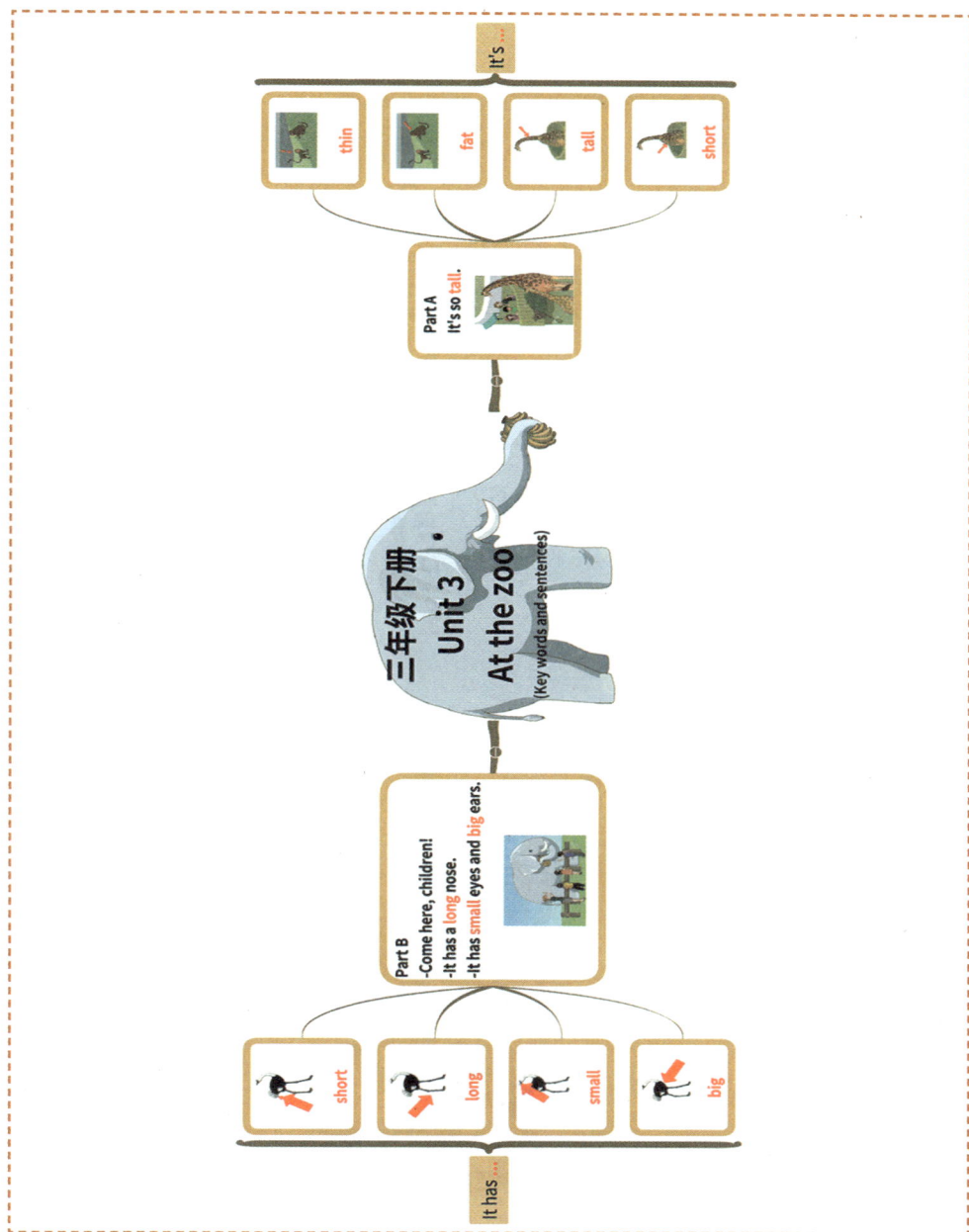

三年级 下册

It's ...

thin

fat

tall

short

Part A
It's so tall.

三年级下册
Unit 3
At the zoo
(Key words and sentences)

Part B
-Come here, children!
-It has a long nose.
-It has small eyes and big ears.

short

long

small

big

It has ...

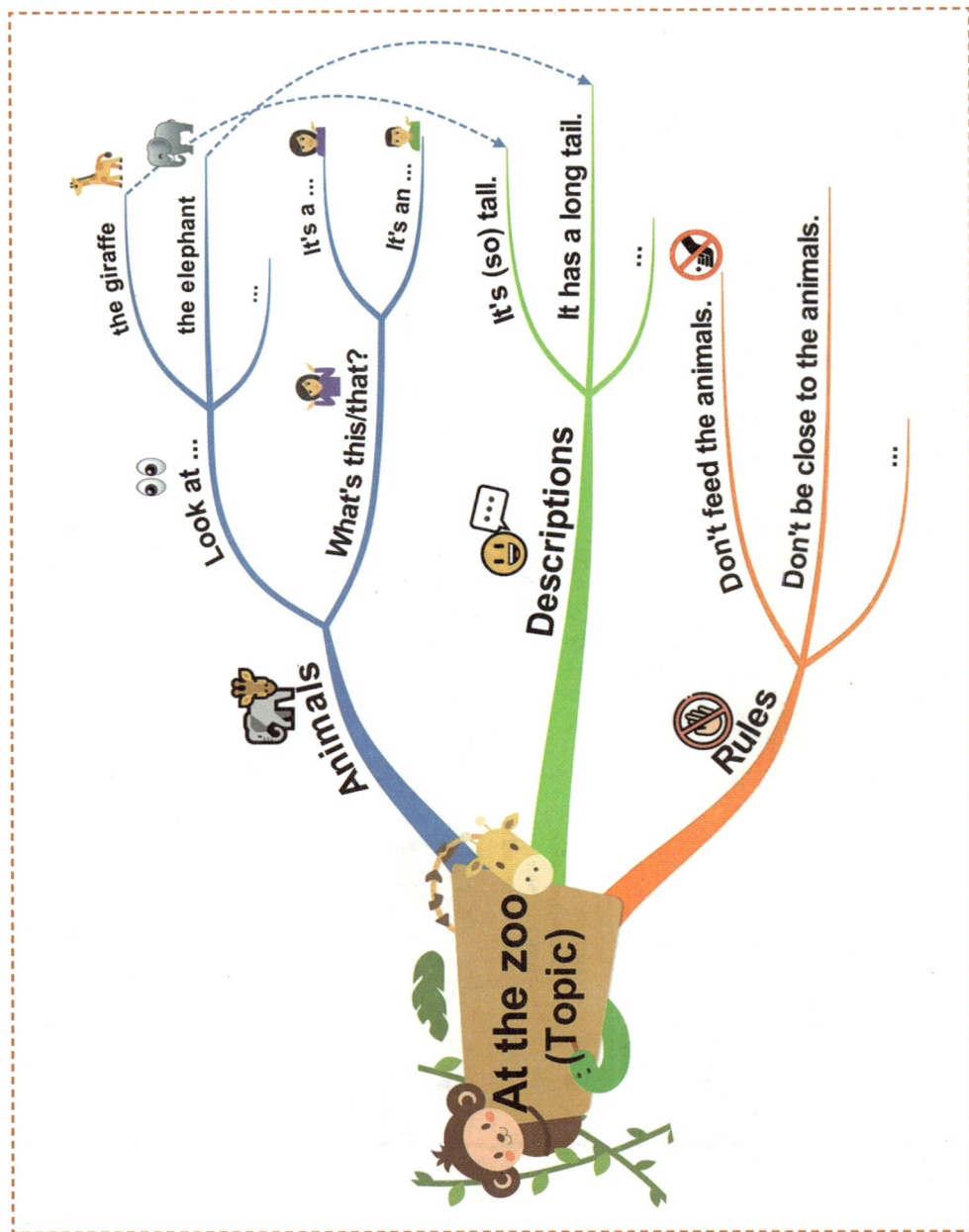

Unit 4 Where is my car?

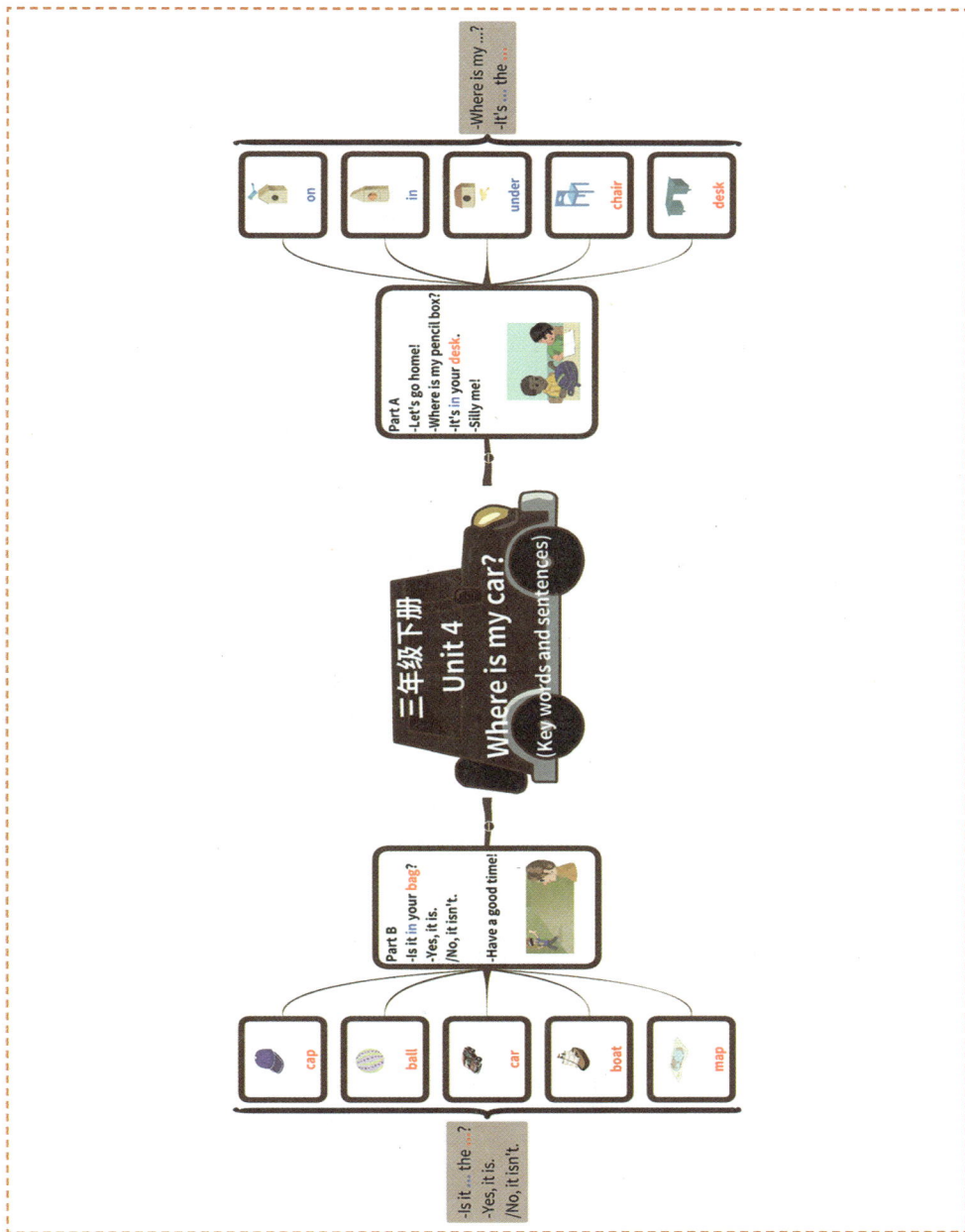

-Where is my ...?
-It's ... the ...

on

in

under

chair

desk

Part A
-Let's go home!
-Where is my pencil box?
-It's in your desk.
-Silly me!

三年级下册
Unit 4
Where is my car?
(Key words and sentences)

Part B
-Is it in your bag?
-Yes, it is.
/No, it isn't.
-Have a good time!

cap

ball

car

boat

map

-Is it ... the ...?
-Yes, it is.
/No, it isn't.

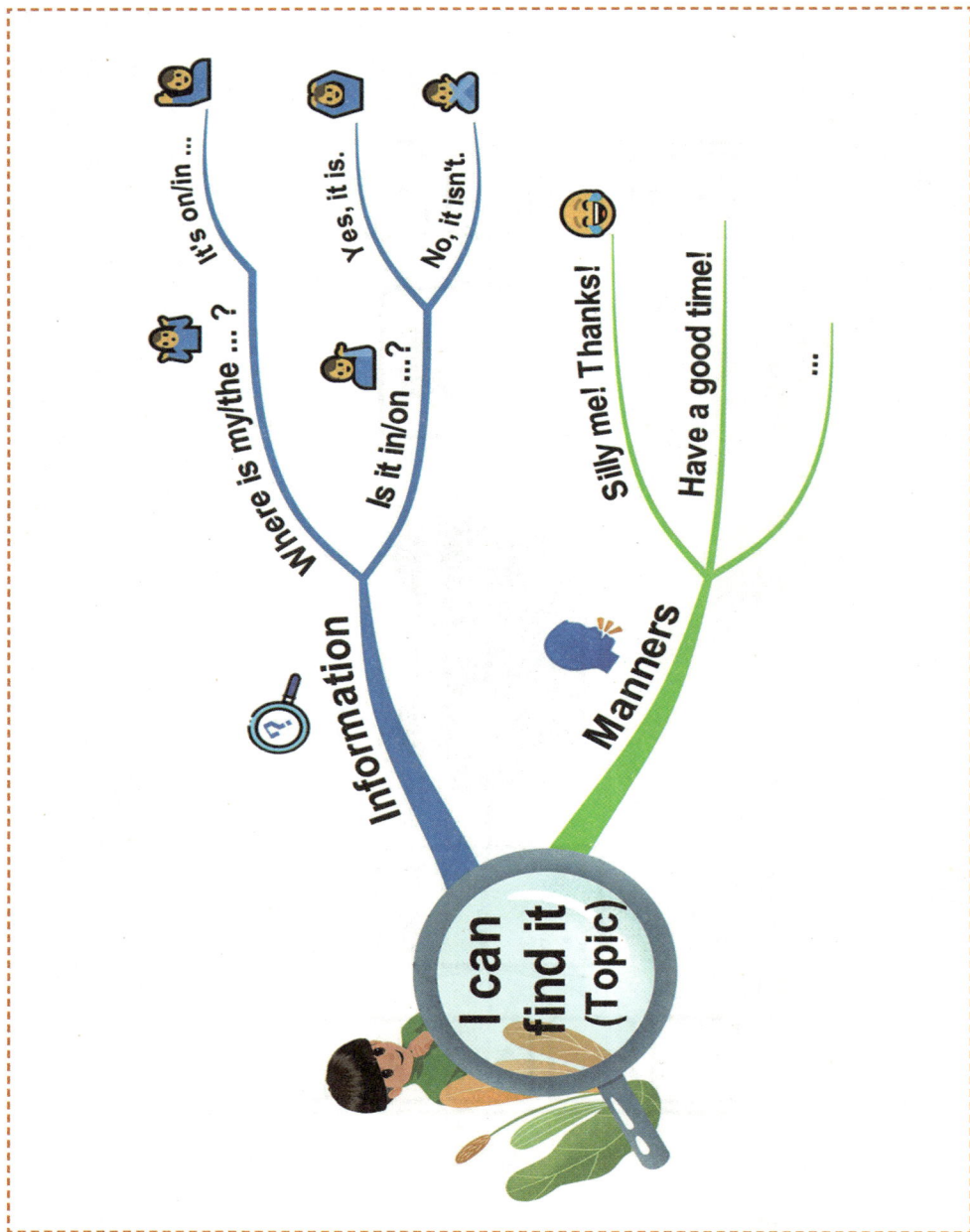

Unit 5 Do you like pears?

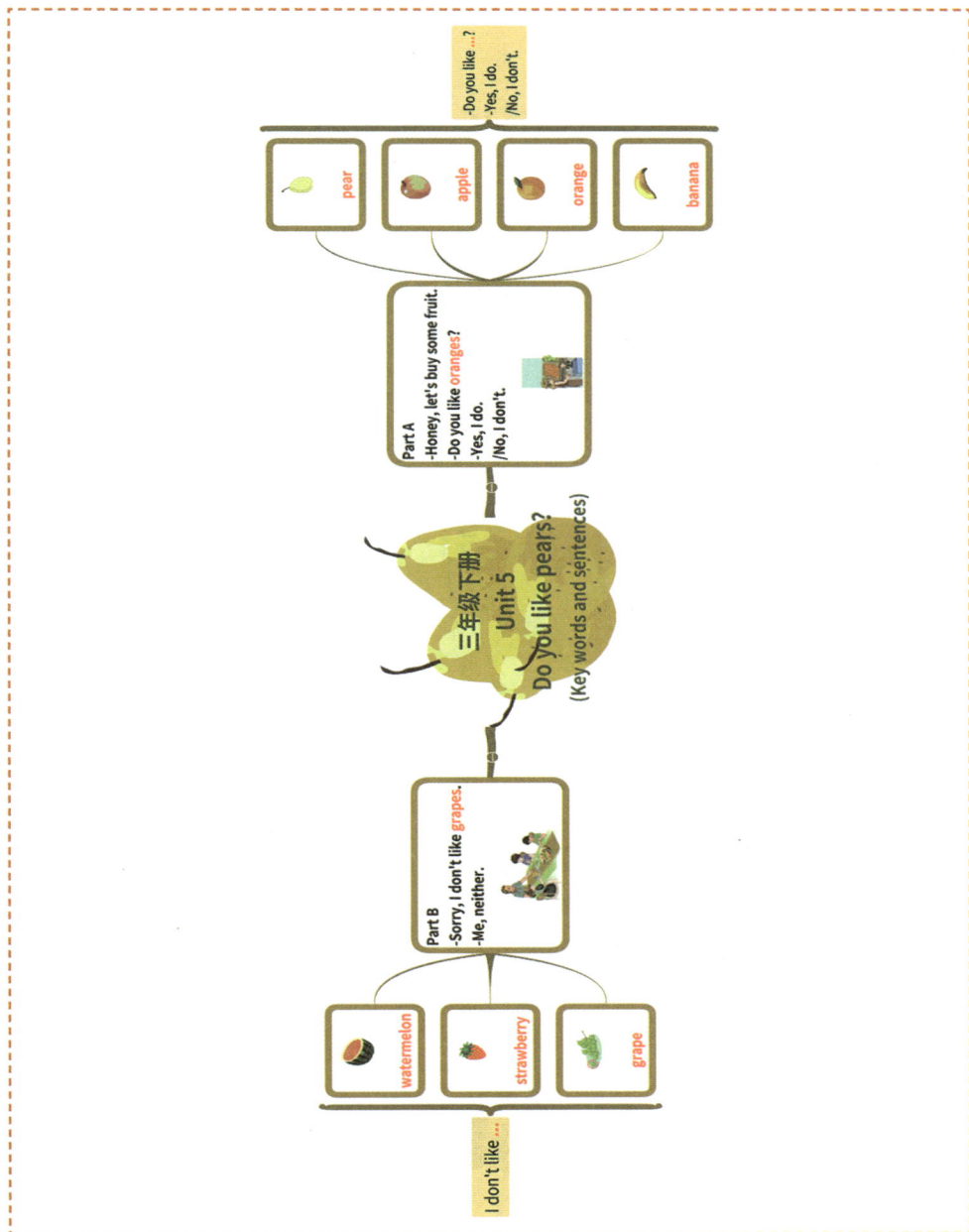

-Do you like .....?
-Yes, I do.
/No, I don't.

pear

apple

orange

banana

Part A
-Honey, let's buy some fruit.
-Do you like oranges?
-Yes, I do.
/No, I don't.

三年级 下册
Unit 5
Do you like pears?
(Key words and sentences)

Part B
-Sorry, I don't like grapes.
-Me, neither.

watermelon

strawberry

grape

I don't like ...

三年级 下册

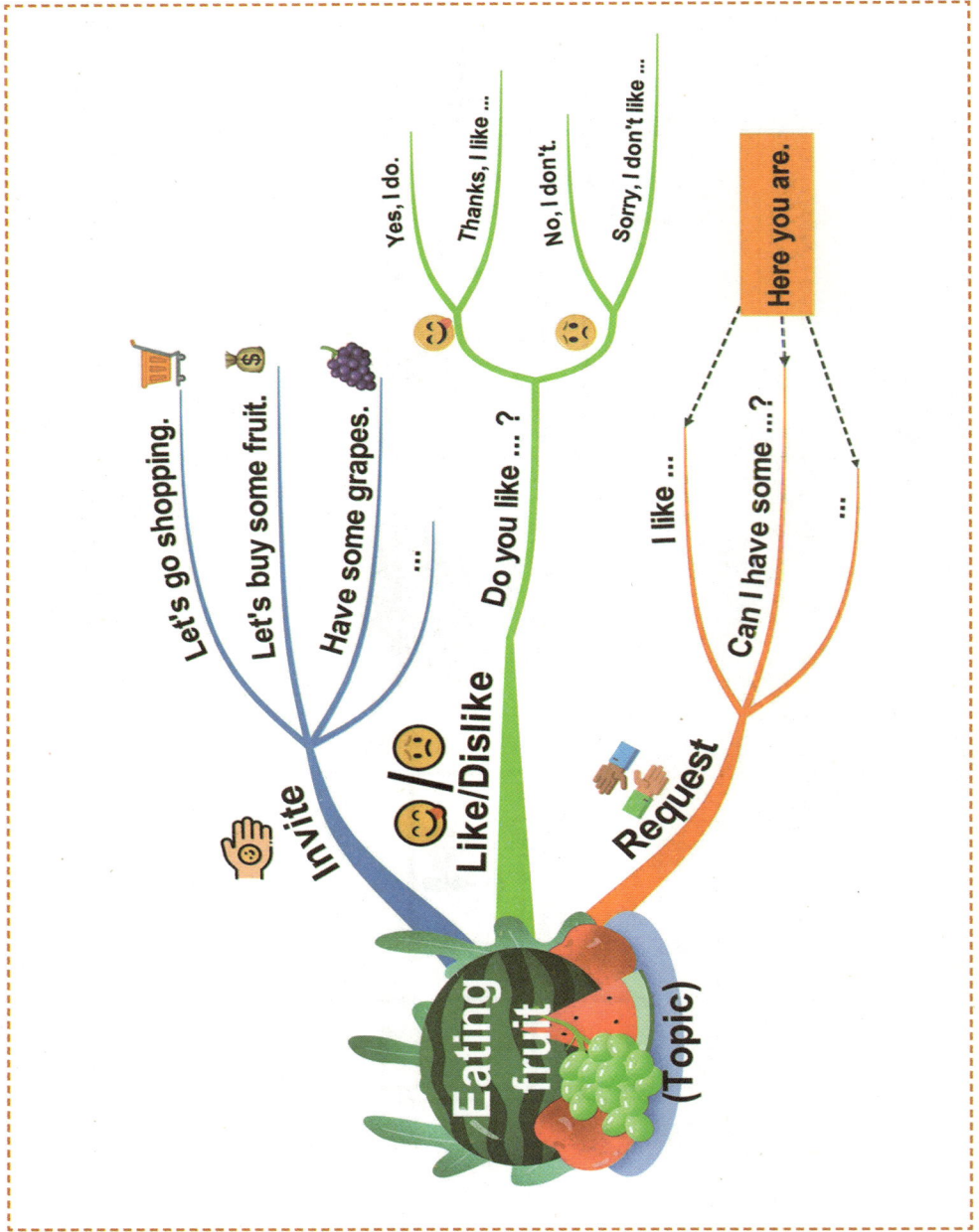

Unit 6 How many...?

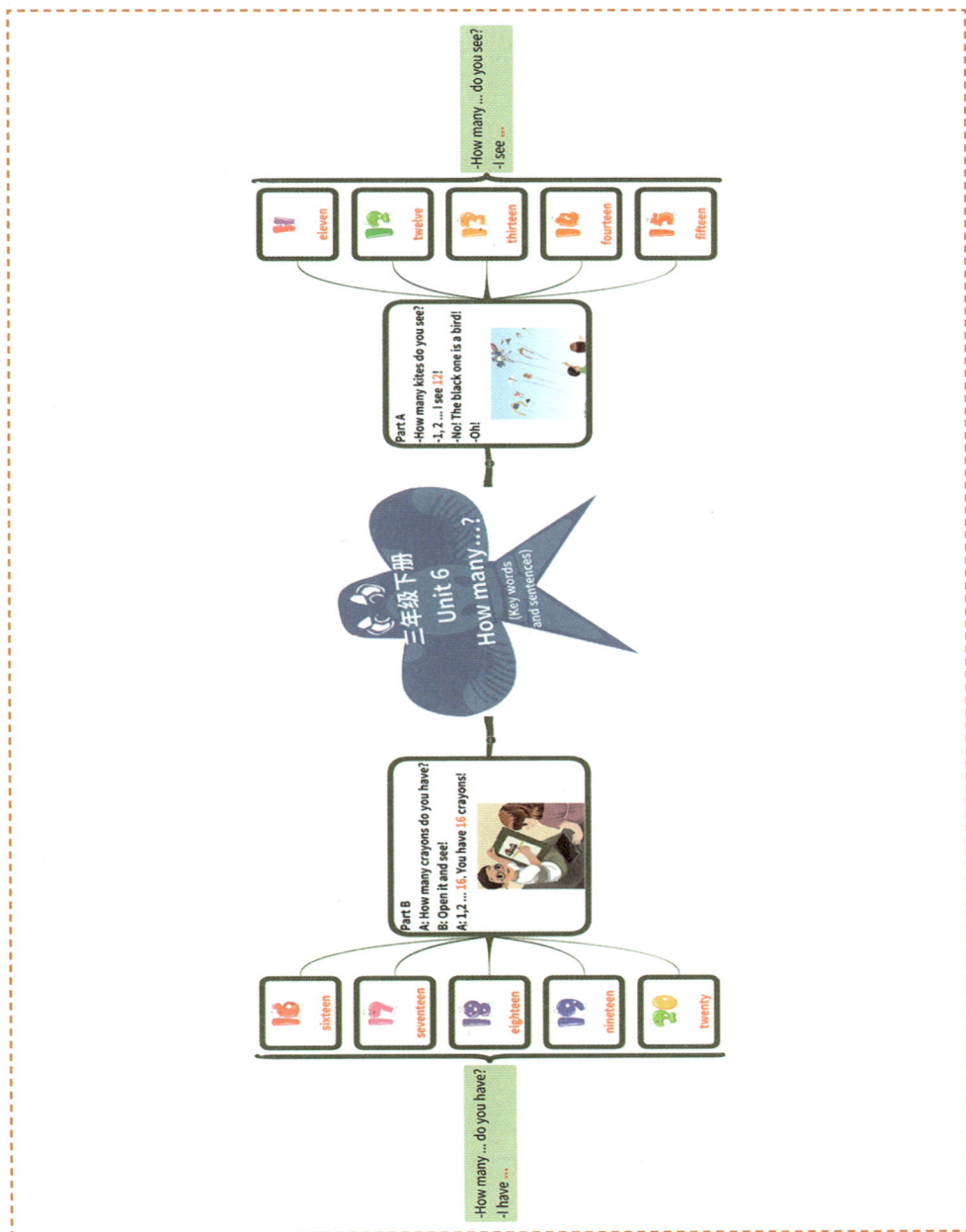

-How many... do you see?
-I see ...

eleven	twelve	thirteen	fourteen	fifteen

Part A
-How many kites do you see?
-1, 2 ... I see 12!
-No! The black one is a bird!
-Oh!

三年级下册
Unit 6
How many...?
(Key words and sentences)

Part B
A: How many crayons do you have?
B: Open it and see!
A: 1, 2 ... 16. You have 16 crayons!

sixteen	seventeen	eighteen	nineteen	twenty

-How many ... do you have?
-I have ...

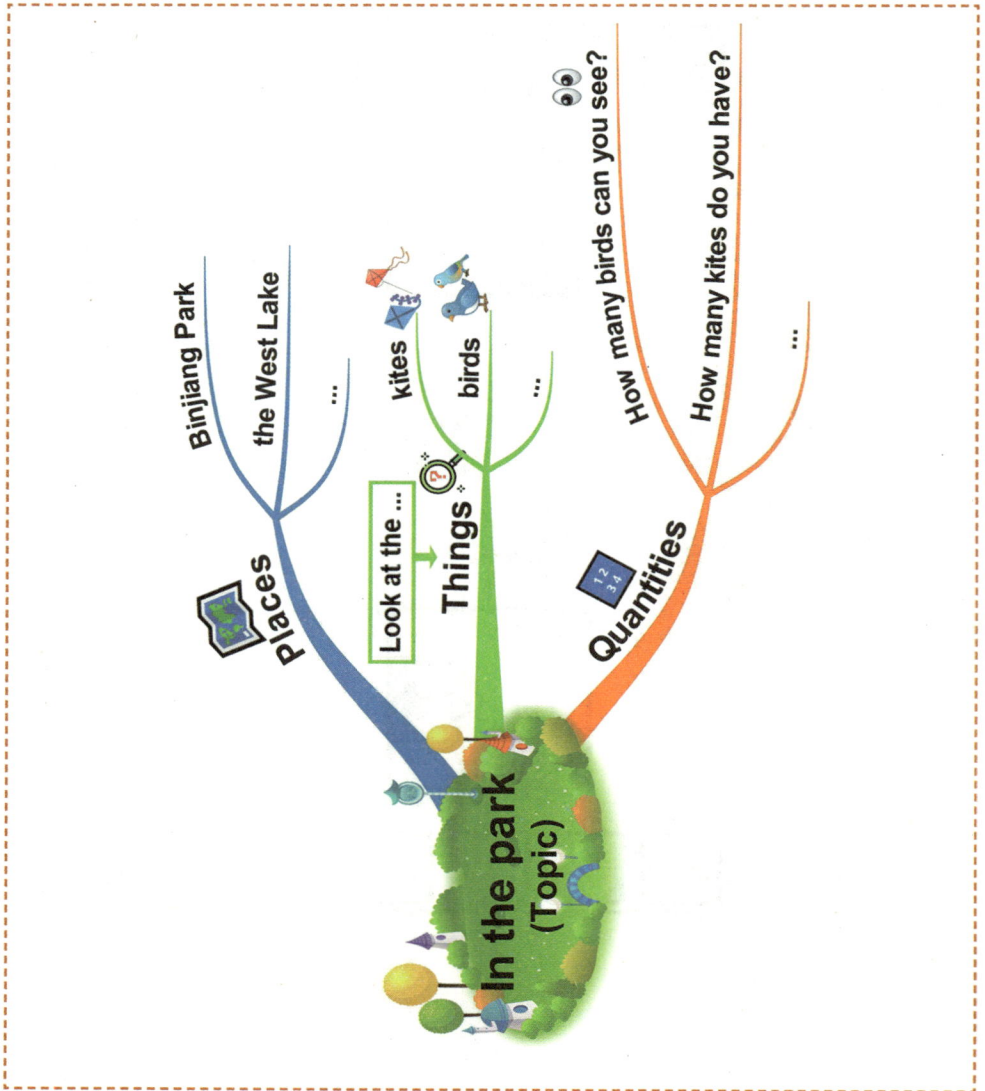

Places
- Binjiang Park
- the West Lake
- ...

Things
Look at the ...
- kites
- birds
- ...

Quantities
- How many birds can you see?
- How many kites do you have?
- ...

In the park
(Topic)

小学英语人教版四年级上册

Unit 1 My classroom

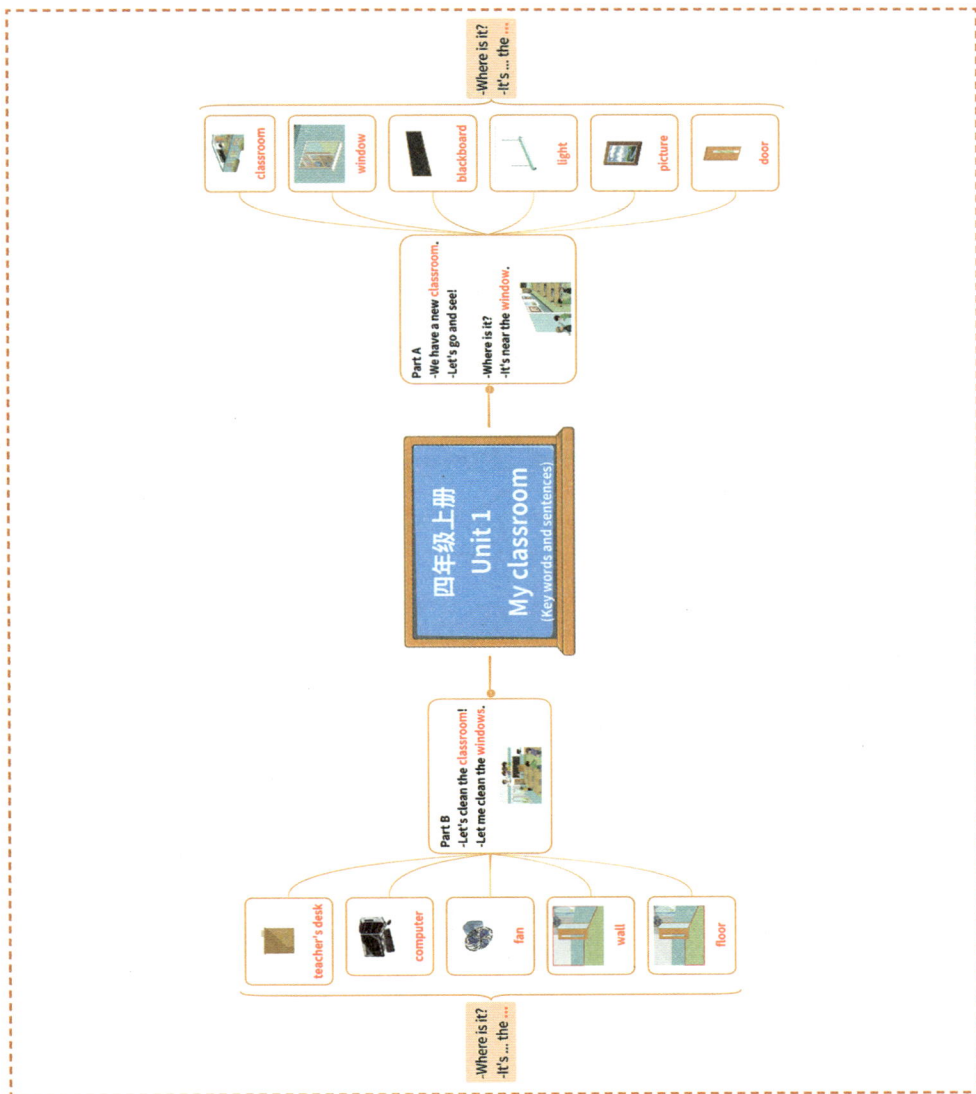

-Where is it?
-It's ... the ...

classroom　window　blackboard　light　picture　door

Part A
-We have a new classroom.
-Let's go and see!

-Where is it?
-It's near the window.

四年级上册
Unit 1
My classroom
(Key words and sentences)

Part B
-Let's clean the classroom!
-Let me clean the windows.

teacher's desk　computer　fan　wall　floor

-Where is it?
-It's ... the

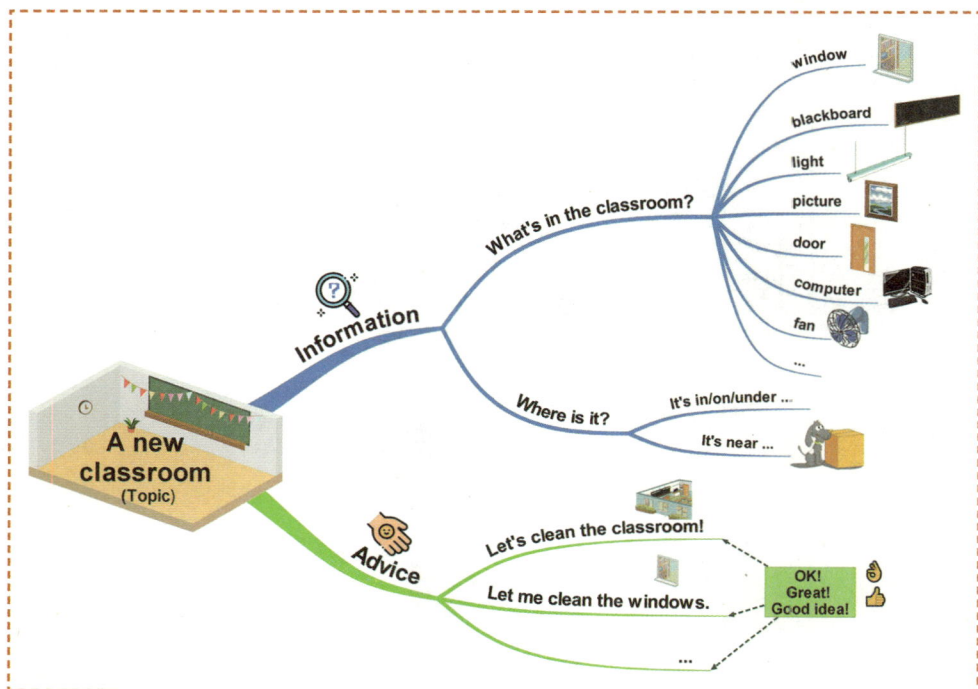

A new classroom (Topic)

Information

What's in the classroom?
- window
- blackboard
- light
- picture
- door
- computer
- fan
- ...

Where is it?
- It's in/on/under ...
- It's near ...

Advice
- Let's clean the classroom!
- Let me clean the windows.
- ...

OK!
Great!
Good idea!

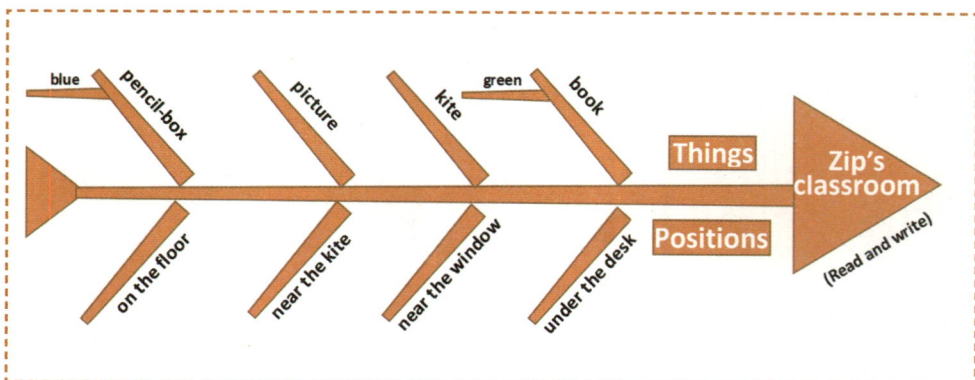

blue　pencil-box　picture　kite　green　book

Things

on the floor　near the kite　near the window　under the desk

Positions

Zip's classroom
(Read and write)

Unit 2 My schoolbag

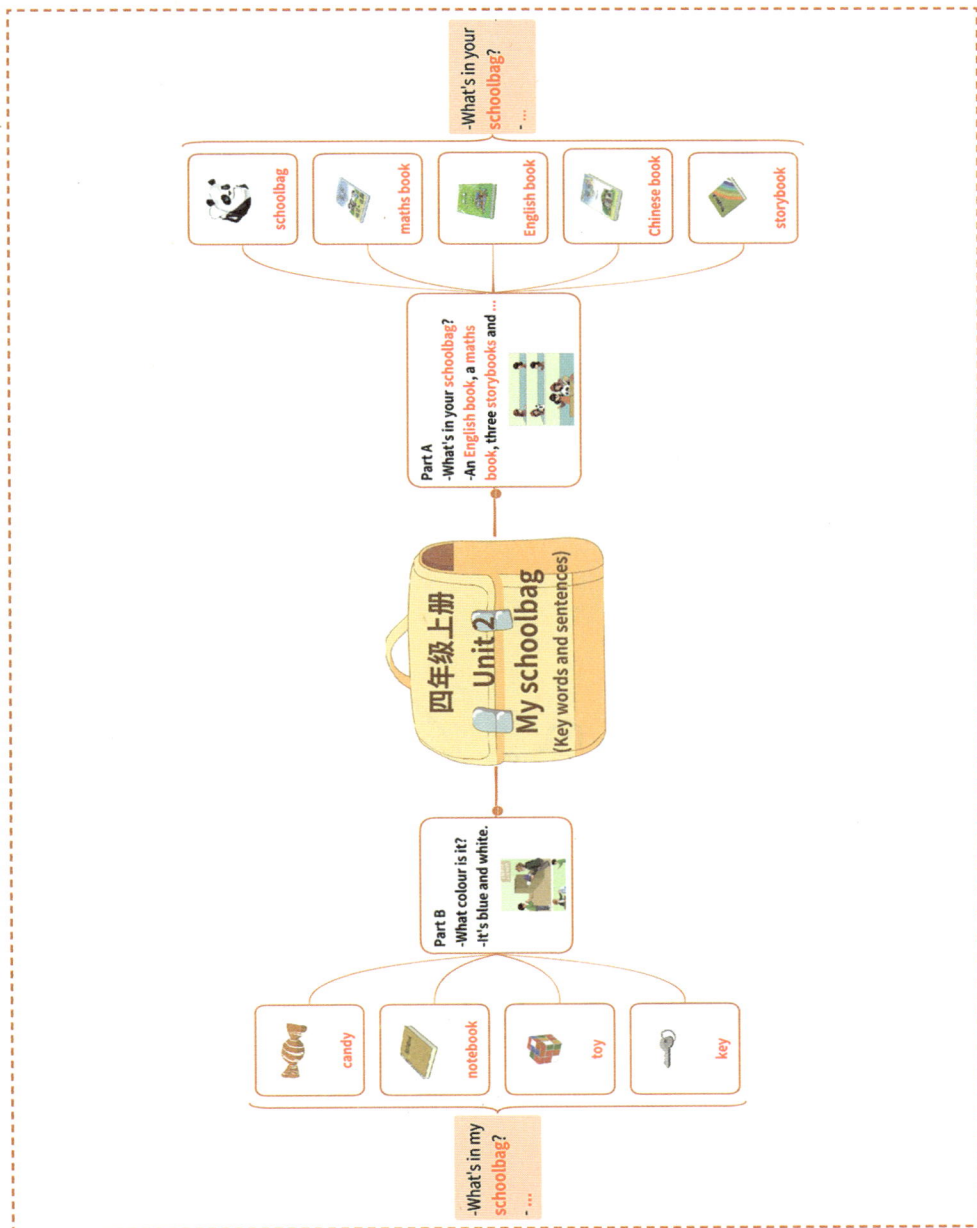

-What's in your schoolbag?

schoolbag

maths book

English book

Chinese book

storybook

Part A
-What's in your schoolbag?
-An English book, a maths book, three storybooks and ...

四年级上册
Unit 2
My schoolbag
(Key words and sentences)

Part B
-What colour is it?
-It's blue and white.

candy

notebook

toy

key

-What's in my schoolbag?
-...

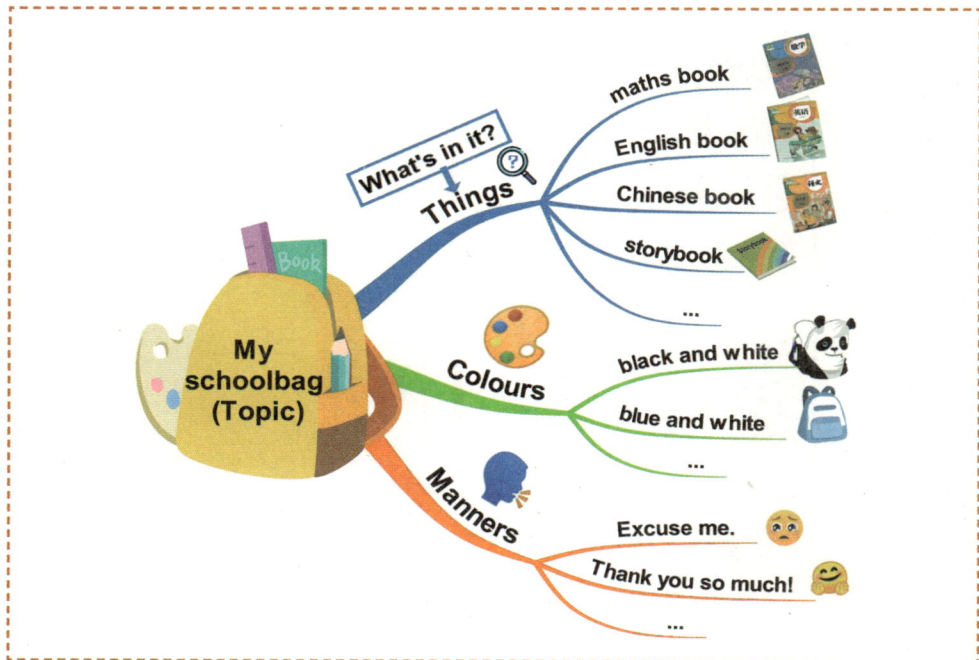

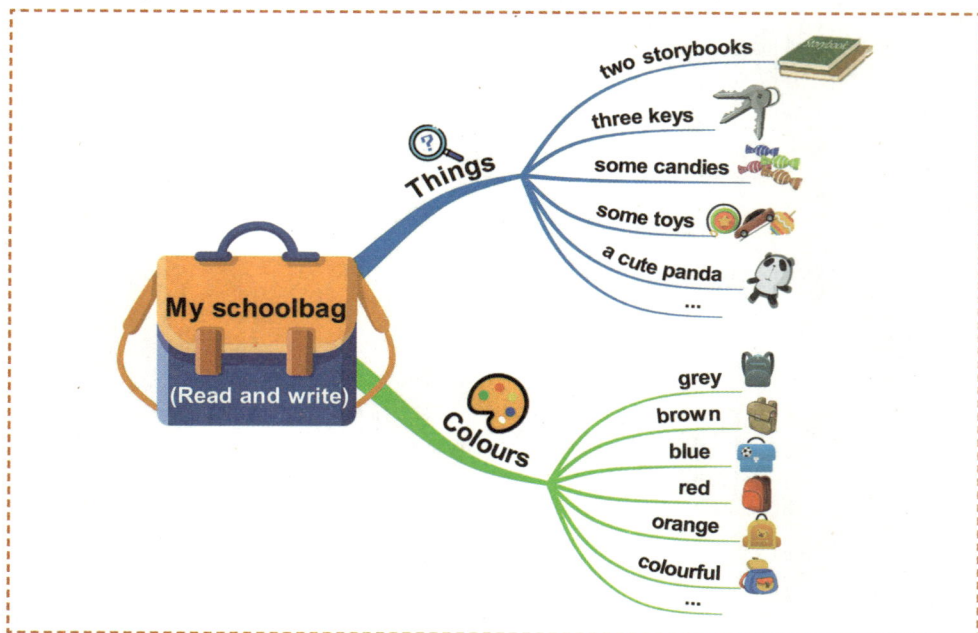

Unit 3 My friends

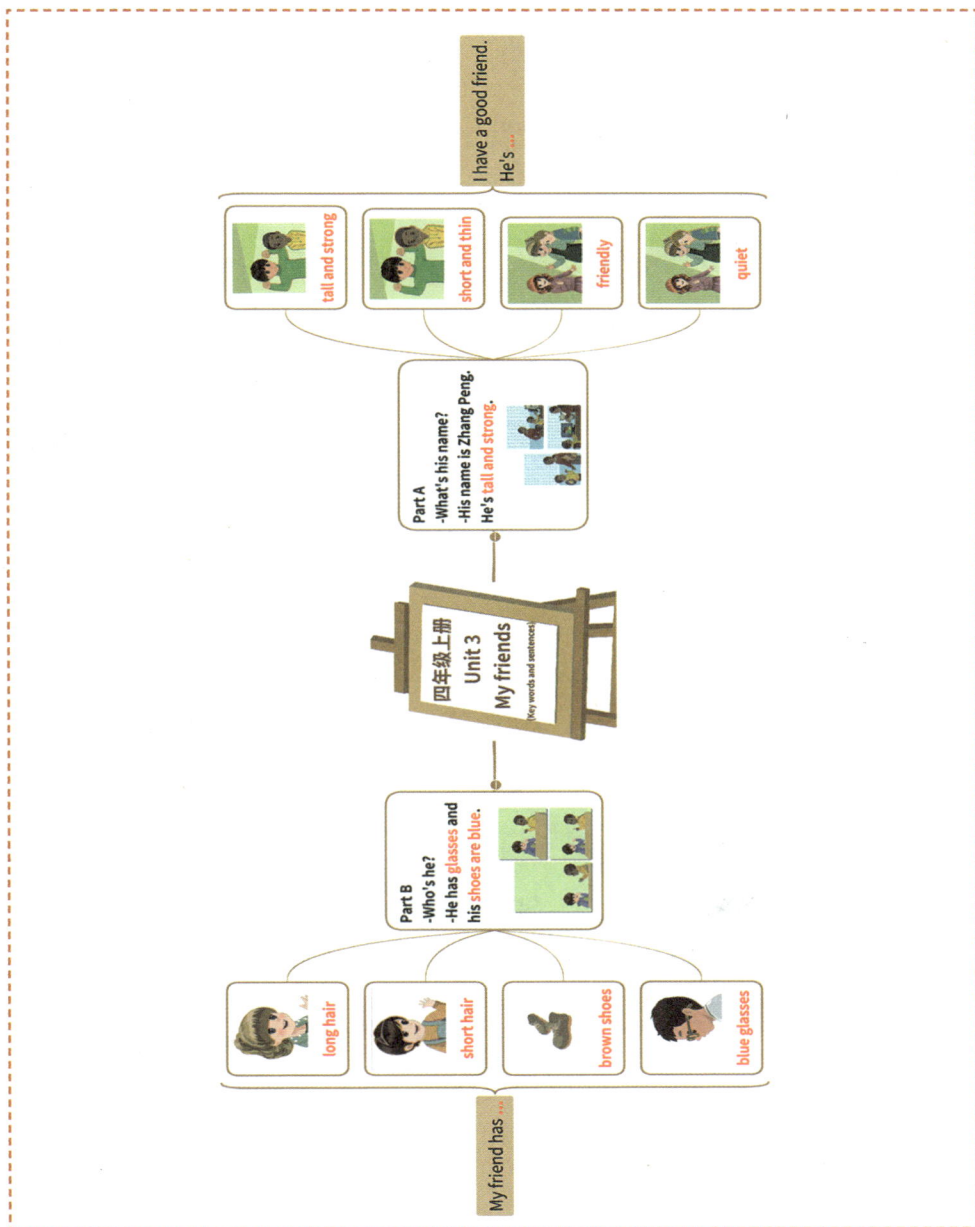

I have a good friend.
He's ...

tall and strong

short and thin

friendly

quiet

Part A
-What's his name?
-His name is Zhang Peng.
He's tall and strong.

四年级 上册
上册

四年级上册
Unit 3
My friends
(Key words and sentences)

Part B
-Who's he?
-He has glasses and
his shoes are blue.

long hair

short hair

brown shoes

blue glasses

My friend has ...

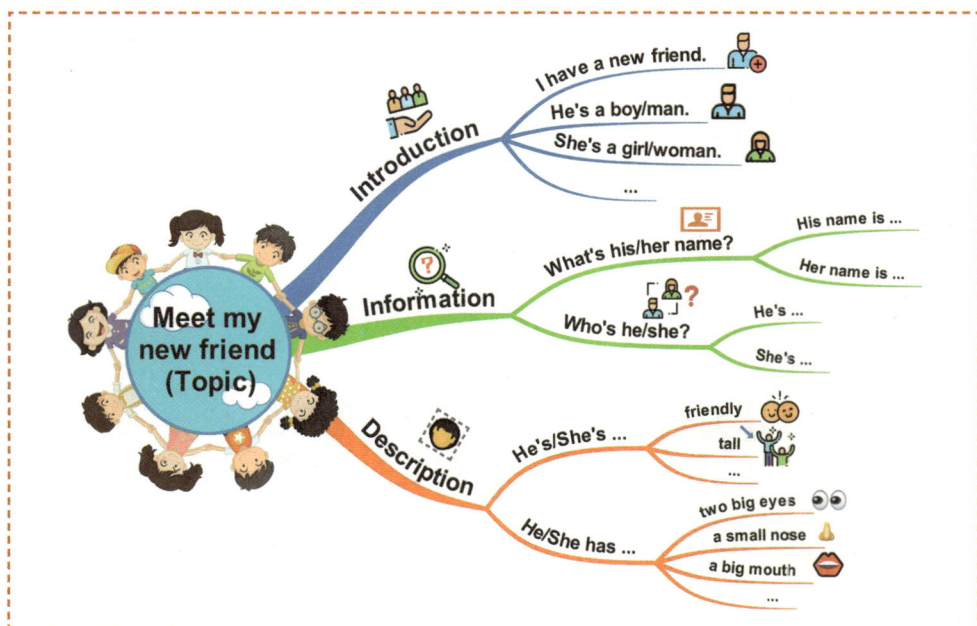

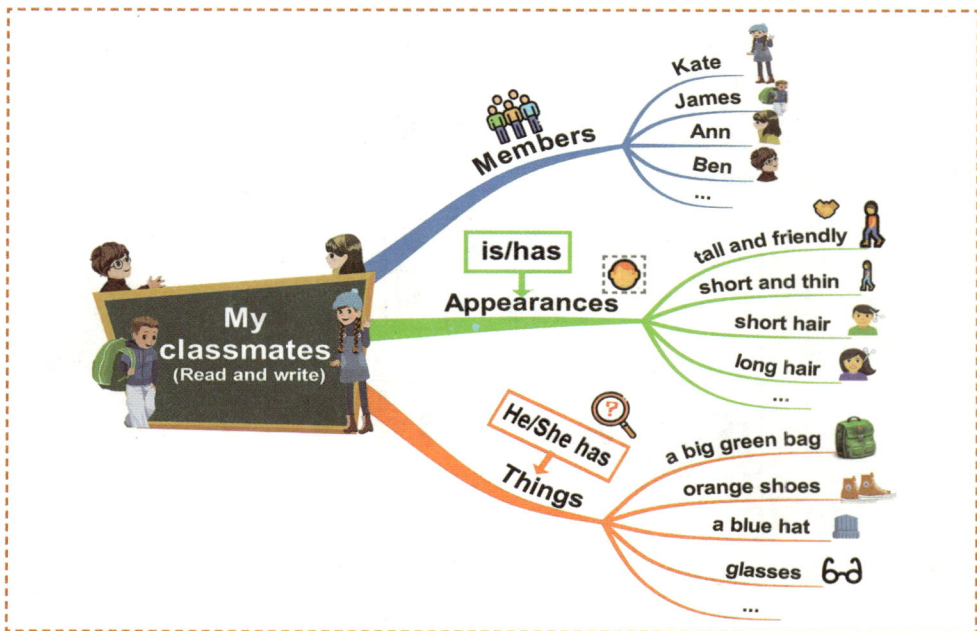

Unit 4 My home

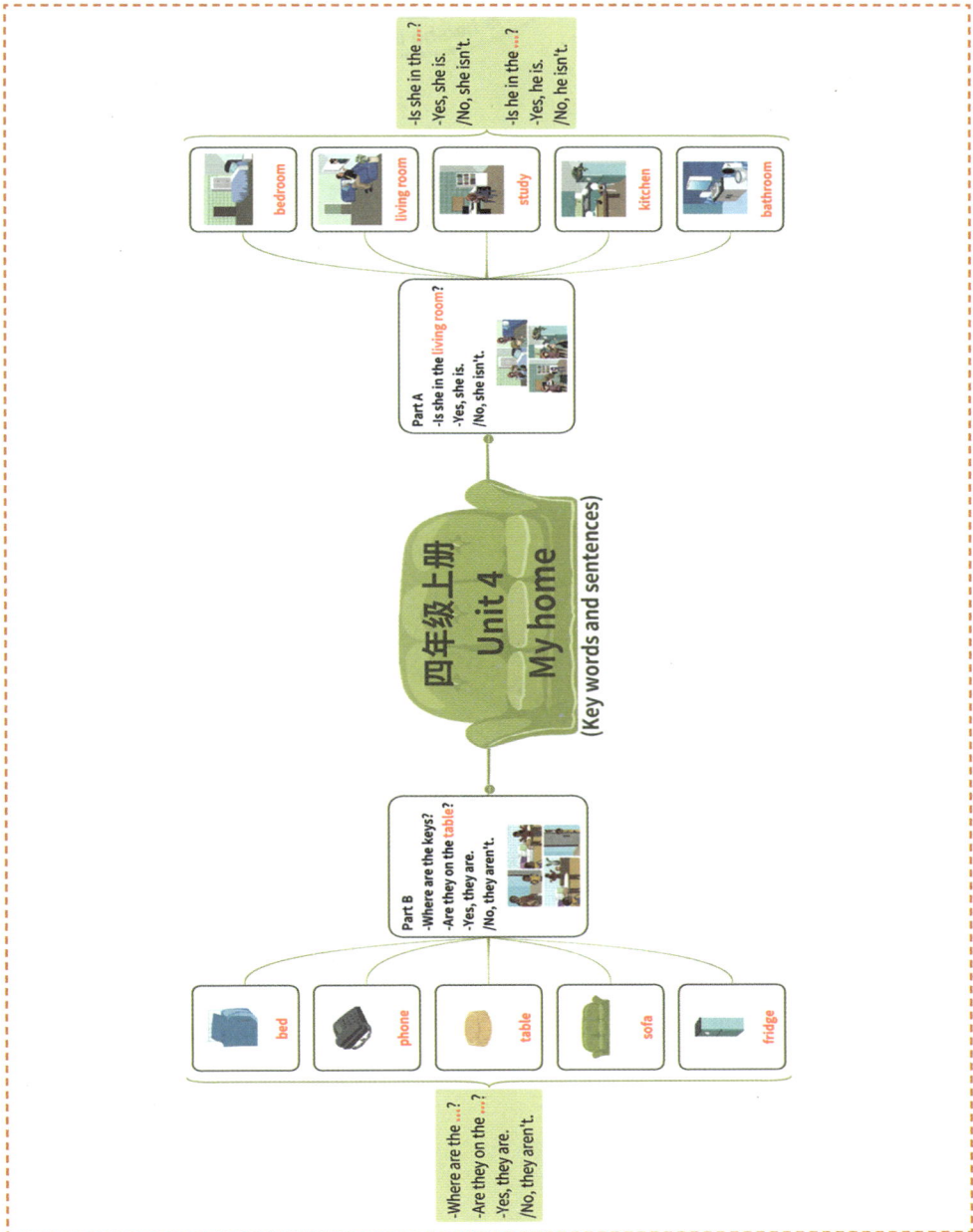

-Is she in the ...?
-Yes, she is.
/No, she isn't.

-Is he in the ...?
-Yes, he is.
/No, he isn't.

bedroom

living room

study

kitchen

bathroom

Part A
-Is she in the living room?
-Yes, she is.
/No, she isn't.

四年级上册
Unit 4
My home
(Key words and sentences)

Part B
-Where are the keys?
-Are they on the table?
-Yes, they are.
/No, they aren't.

bed

phone

table

sofa

fridge

-Where are the ...?
-Are they on the ...?
-Yes, they are.
/No, they aren't.

四年级　上册

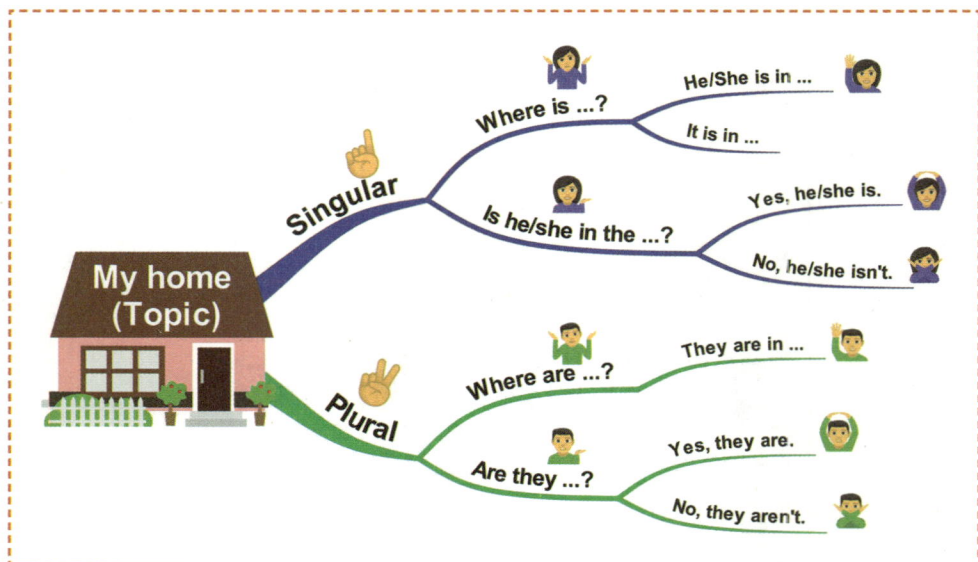

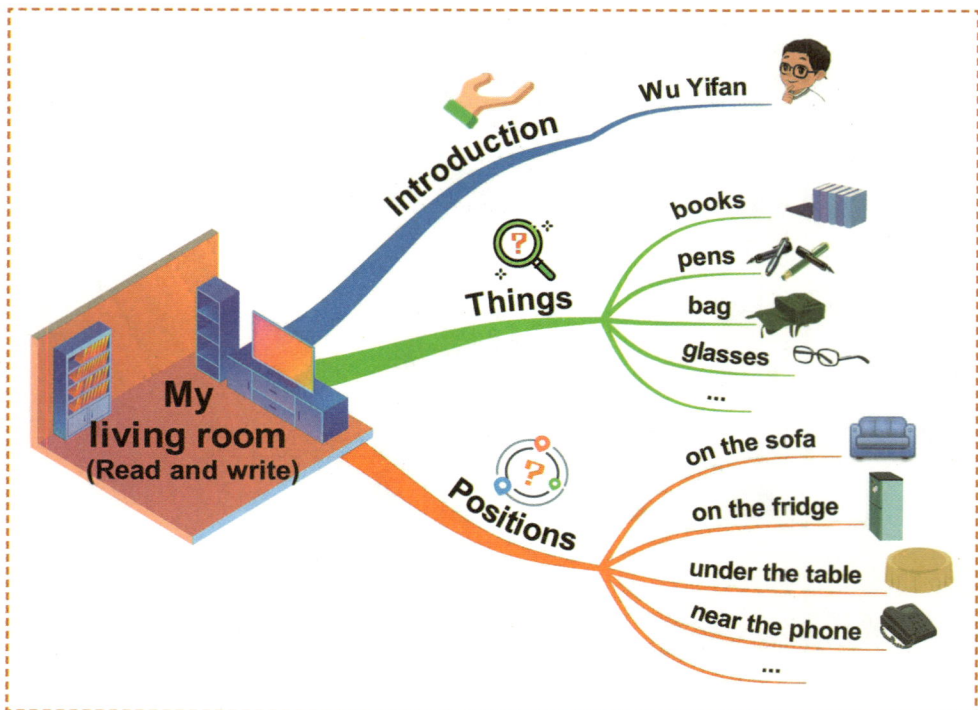

Unit 5 Dinner's ready

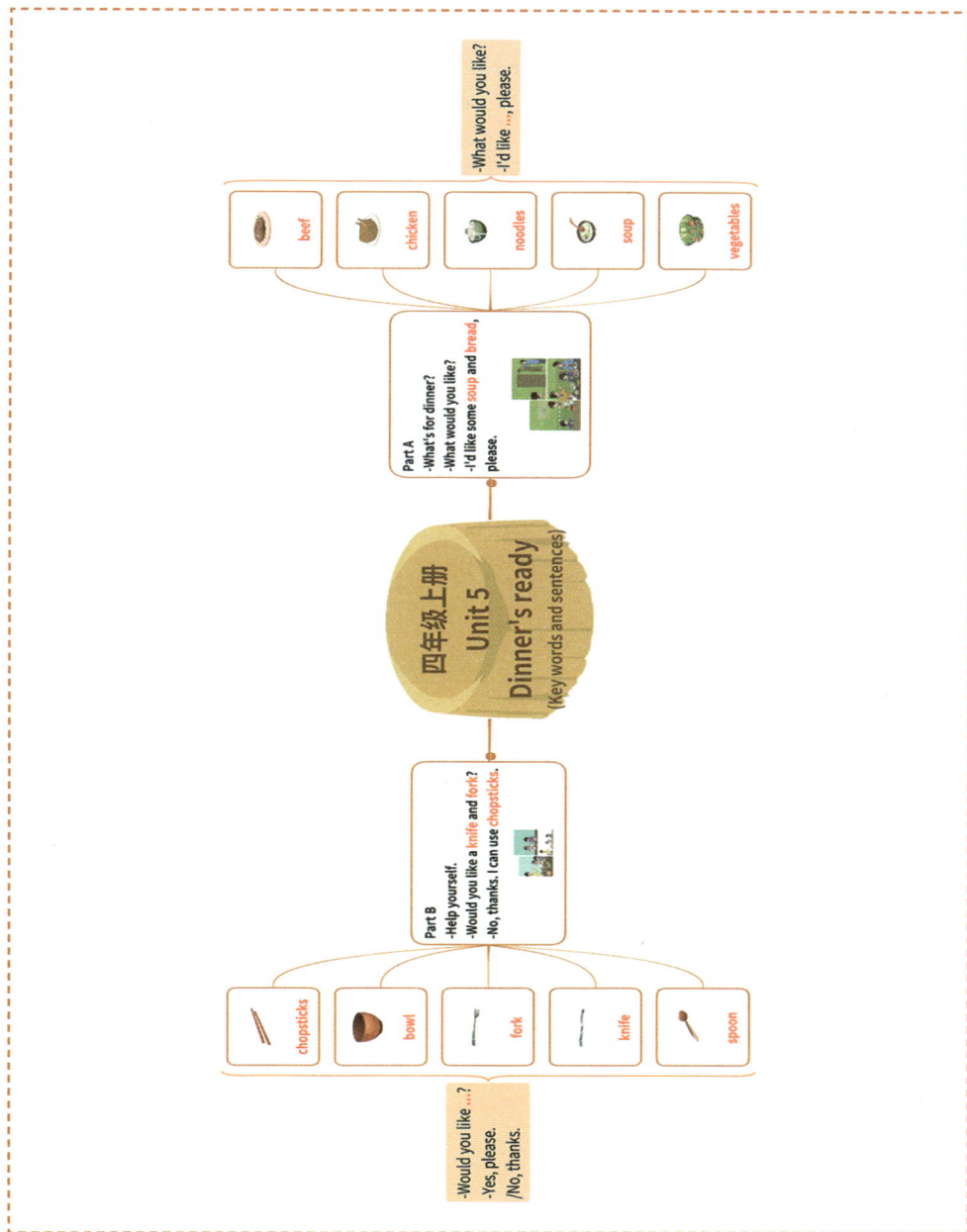

-What would you like?
-I'd like …, please.

beef

chicken

noodles

soup

vegetables

Part A
-What's for dinner?
-What would you like?
-I'd like some soup and bread, please.

四年级上册
Unit 5
Dinner's ready
(Key words and sentences)

Part B
-Help yourself.
-Would you like a knife and fork?
-No, thanks. I can use chopsticks.

chopsticks

bowl

fork

knife

spoon

-Would you like …?
-Yes, please.
/No, thanks.

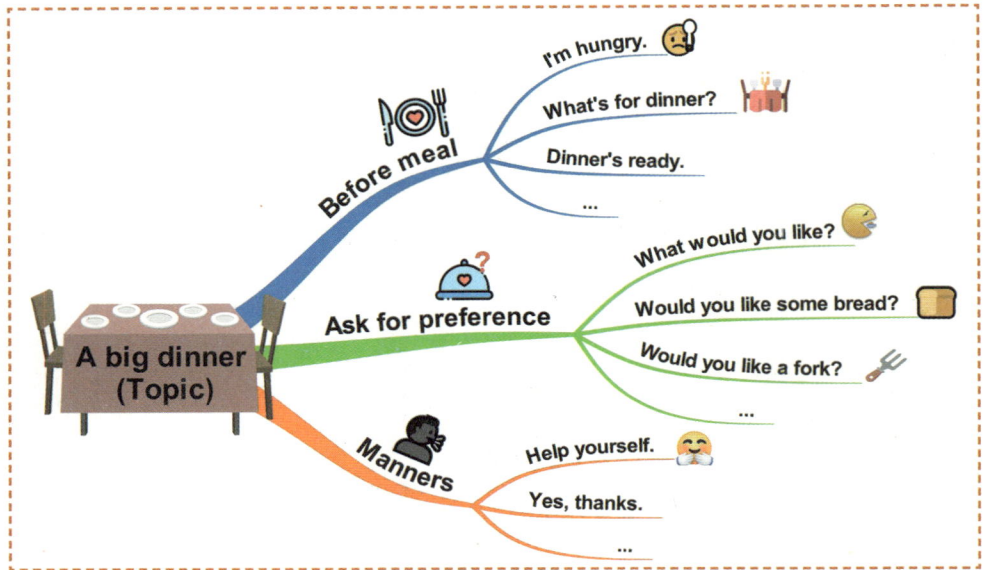

A big dinner (Topic)

Before meal
- I'm hungry.
- What's for dinner?
- Dinner's ready.
- ...

Ask for preference
- What would you like?
- Would you like some bread?
- Would you like a fork?
- ...

Manners
- Help yourself.
- Yes, thanks.
- ...

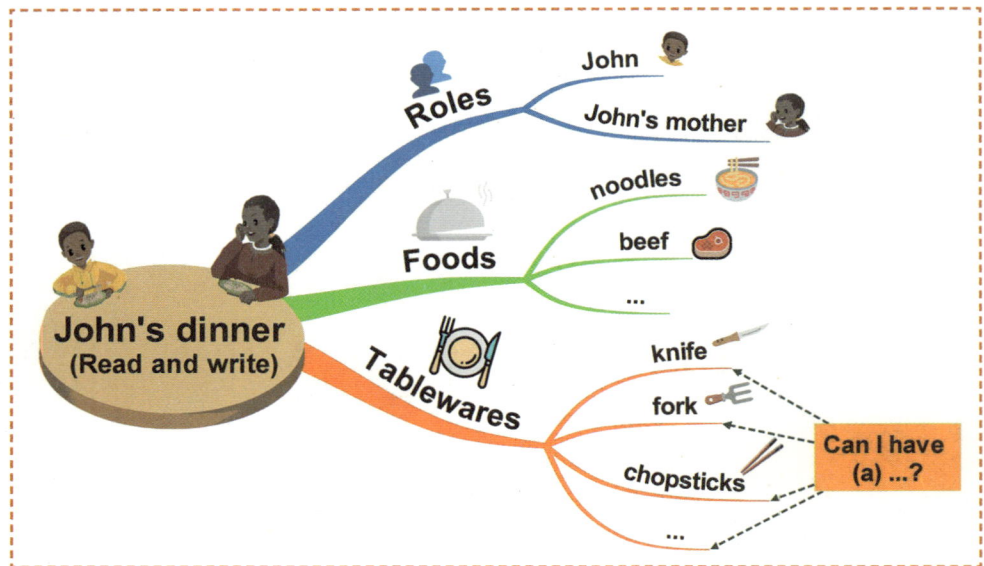

John's dinner (Read and write)

Roles
- John
- John's mother

Foods
- noodles
- beef
- ...

Tablewares
- knife
- fork
- chopsticks
- ...

Can I have (a) ...?

Unit 6 Meet my family

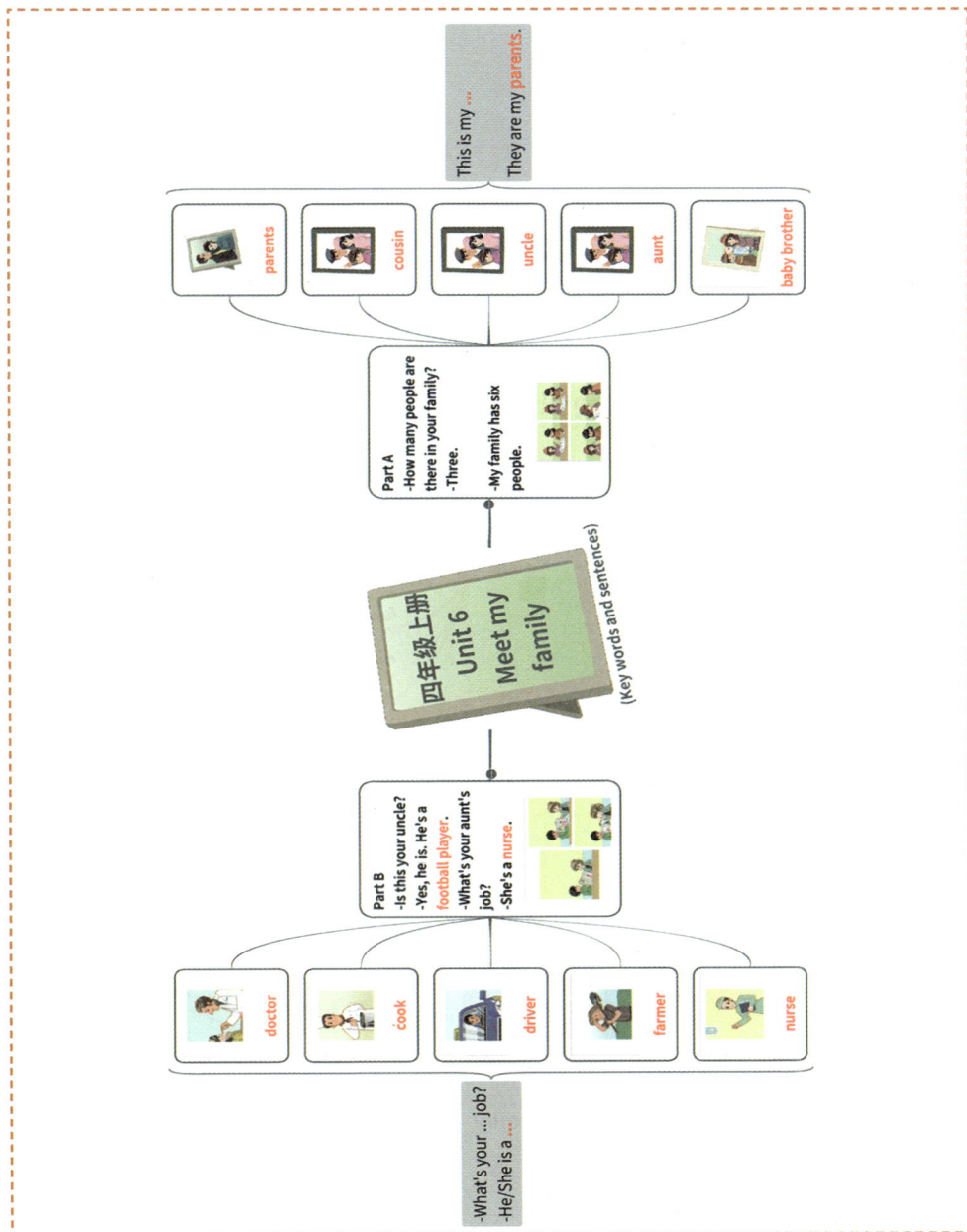

This is my ...

They are my parents.

parents

cousin

uncle

aunt

baby brother

Part A
-How many people are there in your family?
-Three.
-My family has six people.

四年级上册
Unit 6
Meet my family

(Key words and sentences)

Part B
-Is this your uncle?
-Yes, he is. He's a football player.
-What's your aunt's job?
-She's a nurse.

doctor

cook

driver

farmer

nurse

-What's your ...job?
-He/She is a ...

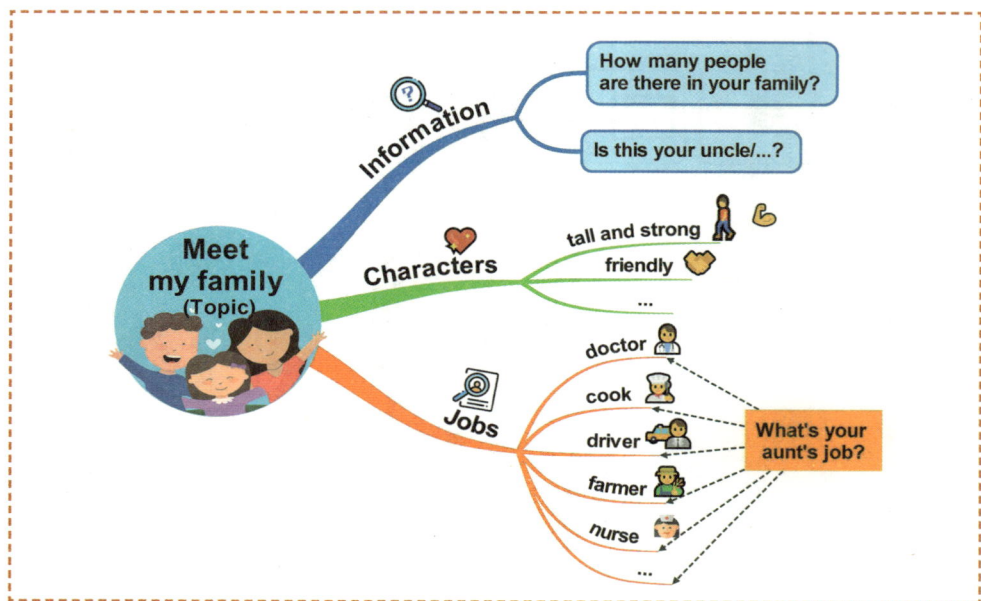

Meet my family (Topic)

Information
- How many people are there in your family?
- Is this your uncle/...?

Characters
- tall and strong
- friendly
- ...

Jobs
- doctor
- cook
- driver
- farmer
- nurse
- ...

What's your aunt's job?

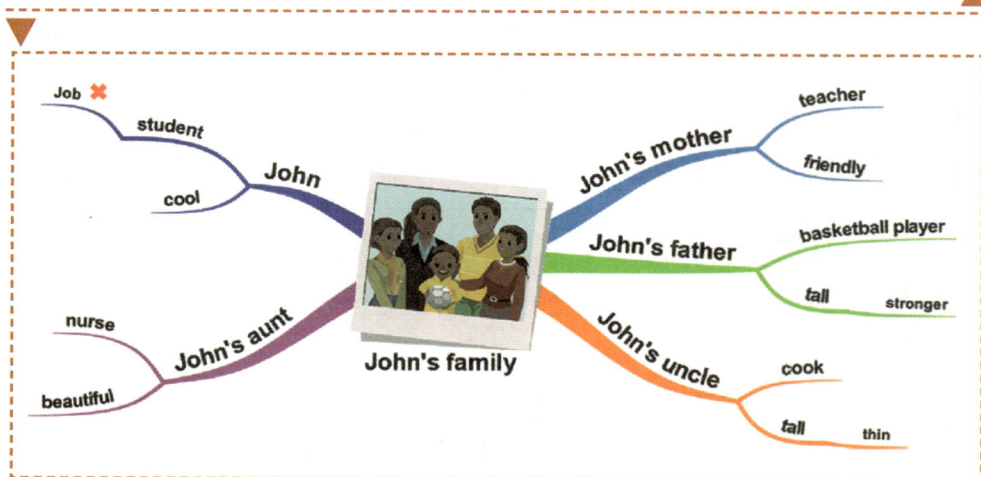

John
- Job ✗
- student
- cool

John's mother
- teacher
- friendly

John's father
- basketball player
- tall
- stronger

John's uncle
- cook
- tall
- thin

John's aunt
- nurse
- beautiful

John's family

小学英语人教版四年级下册

Unit 1 My school

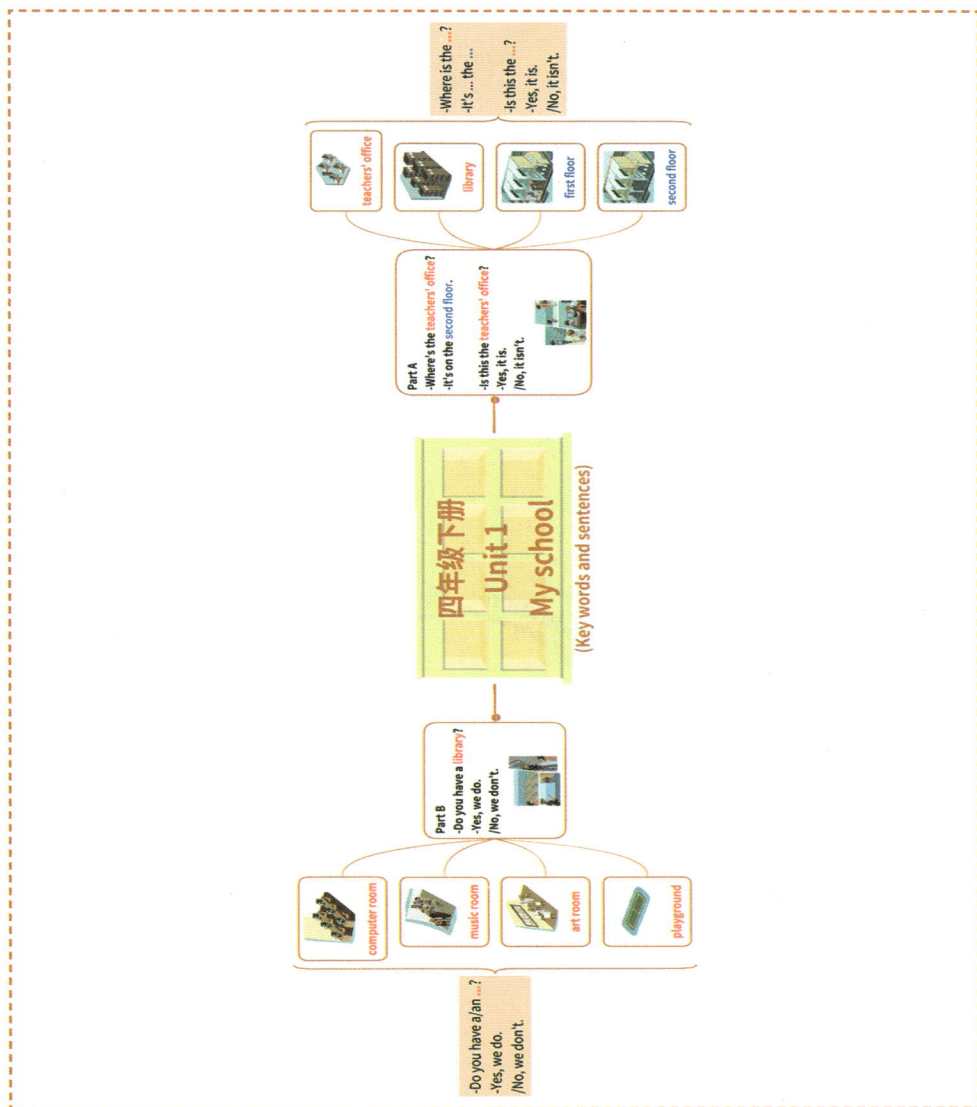

四年级下册 Unit 1 My school
(Key words and sentences)

-Where is the ...?
-It's ... the ...
-Is this the ...?
-Yes, it is.
/No, it isn't.

teachers' office
library
first floor
second floor

Part A
-Where's the teachers' office?
-It's on the second floor.
-Is this the teachers' office?
-Yes, it is.
/No, it isn't.

Part B
-Do you have a library?
-Yes, we do.
/No, we don't.

computer room
music room
art room
playground

-Do you have a/an ...?
-Yes, we do.
/No, we don't.

四年级 下册

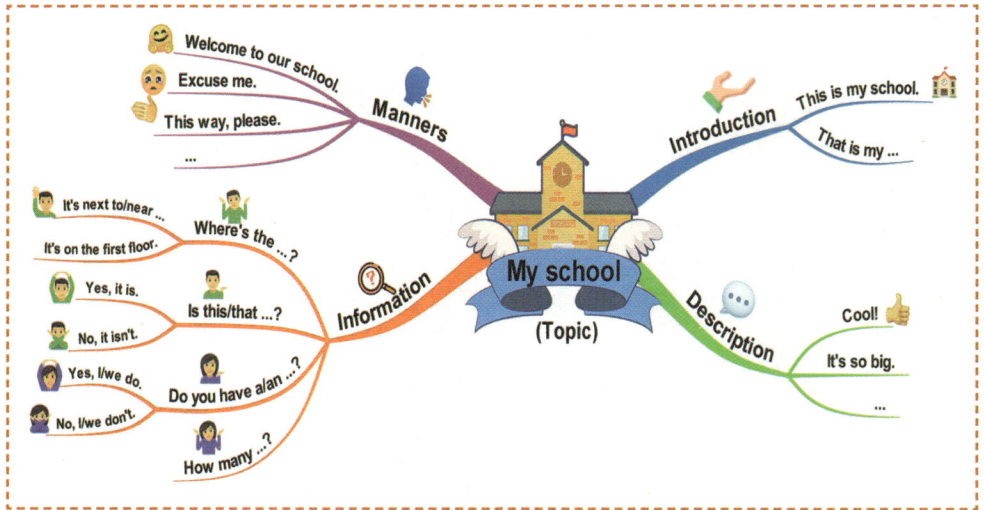

My school (Topic)

Manners
- Welcome to our school.
- Excuse me.
- This way, please.
- ...

Introduction
- This is my school.
- That is my ...

Information
- Where's the ...?
  - It's next to/near ...
  - It's on the first floor.
- Is this/that ...?
  - Yes, it is.
  - No, it isn't.
- Do you have a/an ...?
  - Yes, I/we do.
  - No, I/we don't.
- How many ...?

Description
- Cool!
- It's so big.
- ...

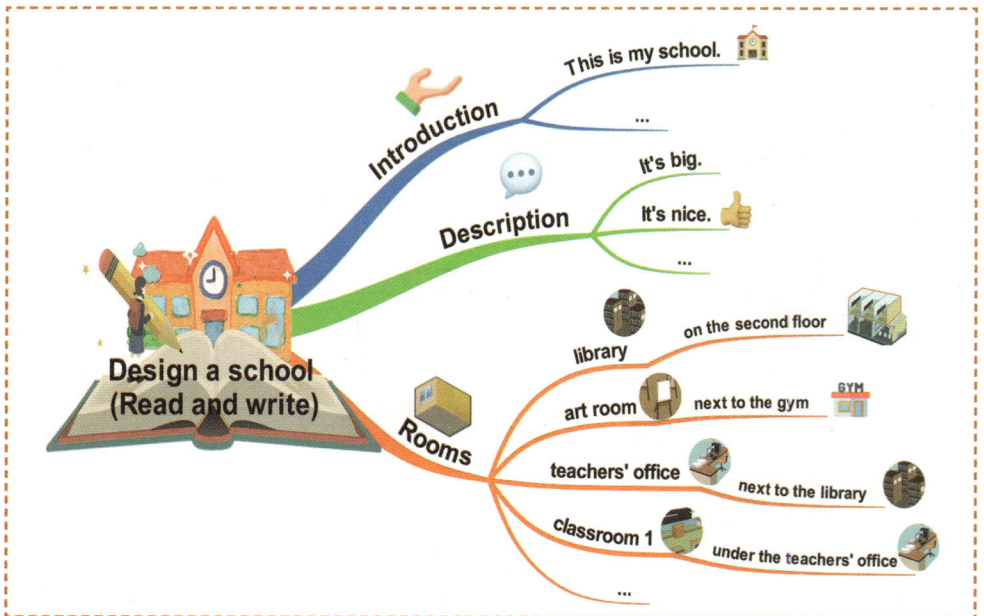

Design a school (Read and write)

Introduction
- This is my school.
- ...

Description
- It's big.
- It's nice.
- ...

Rooms
- library — on the second floor
- art room — next to the gym
- teachers' office — next to the library
- classroom 1 — under the teachers' office
- ...

Unit 2 What time is it?

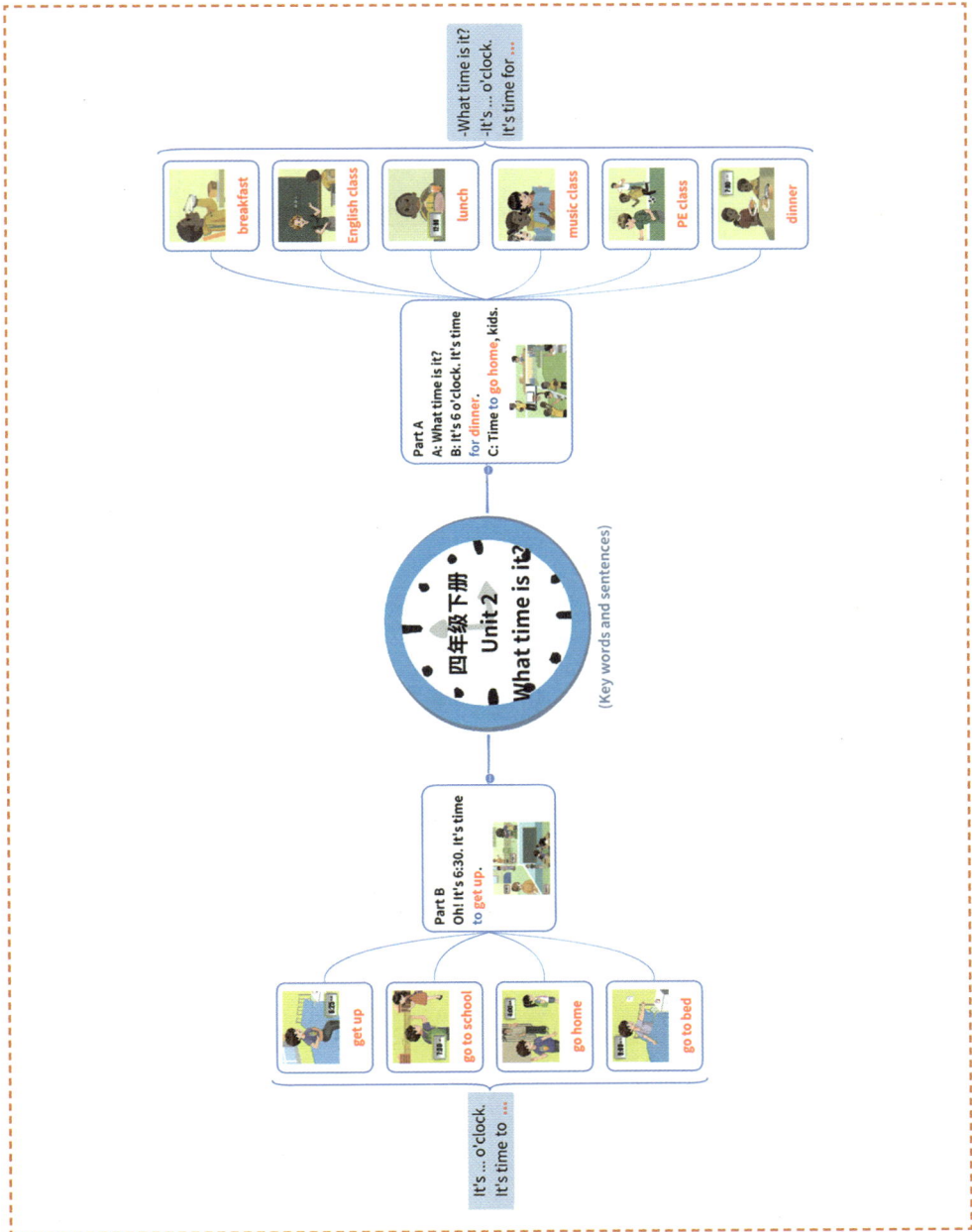

-What time is it?
-It's ... o'clock.
 It's time for ...

breakfast

English class

lunch

music class

PE class

dinner

Part A
A: What time is it?
B: It's 6 o'clock. It's time for dinner.
C: Time to go home, kids.

四年级下册
Unit 2
What time is it?

(Key words and sentences)

Part B
Oh! It's 6:30. It's time to get up.

get up

go to school

go home

go to bed

It's ... o'clock.
It's time to ...

四年级 下册

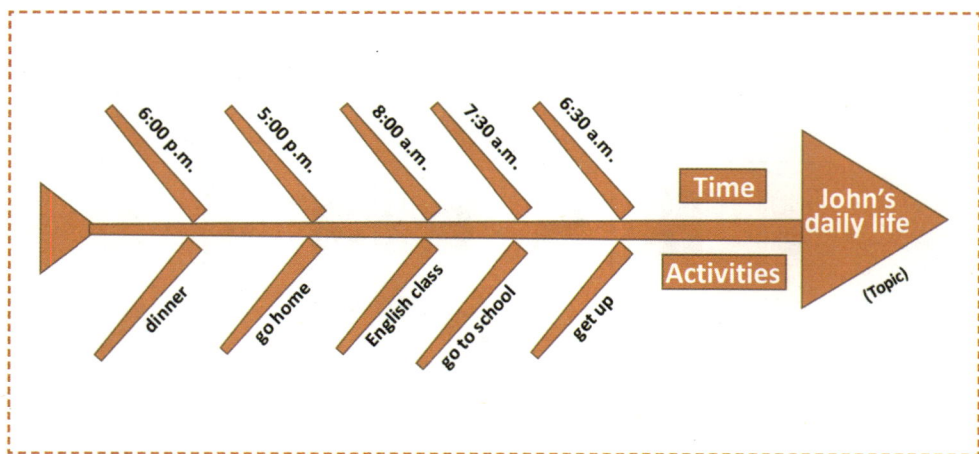

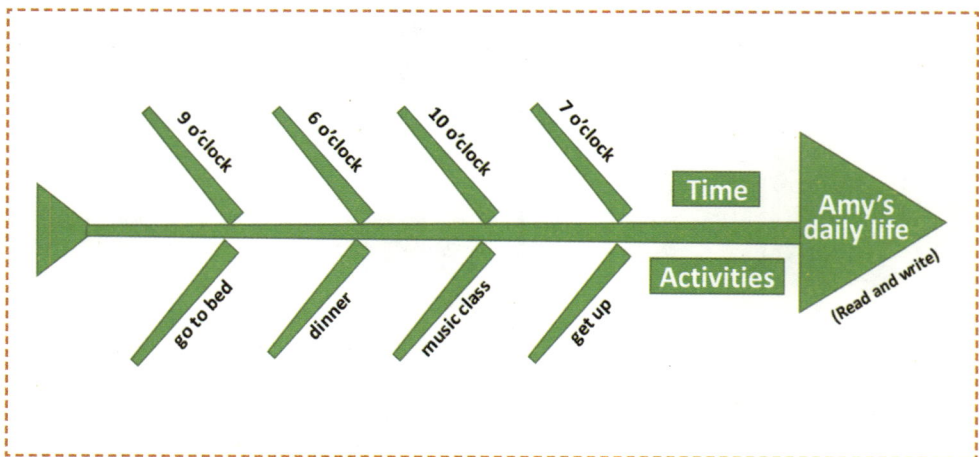

Unit 3 Weather

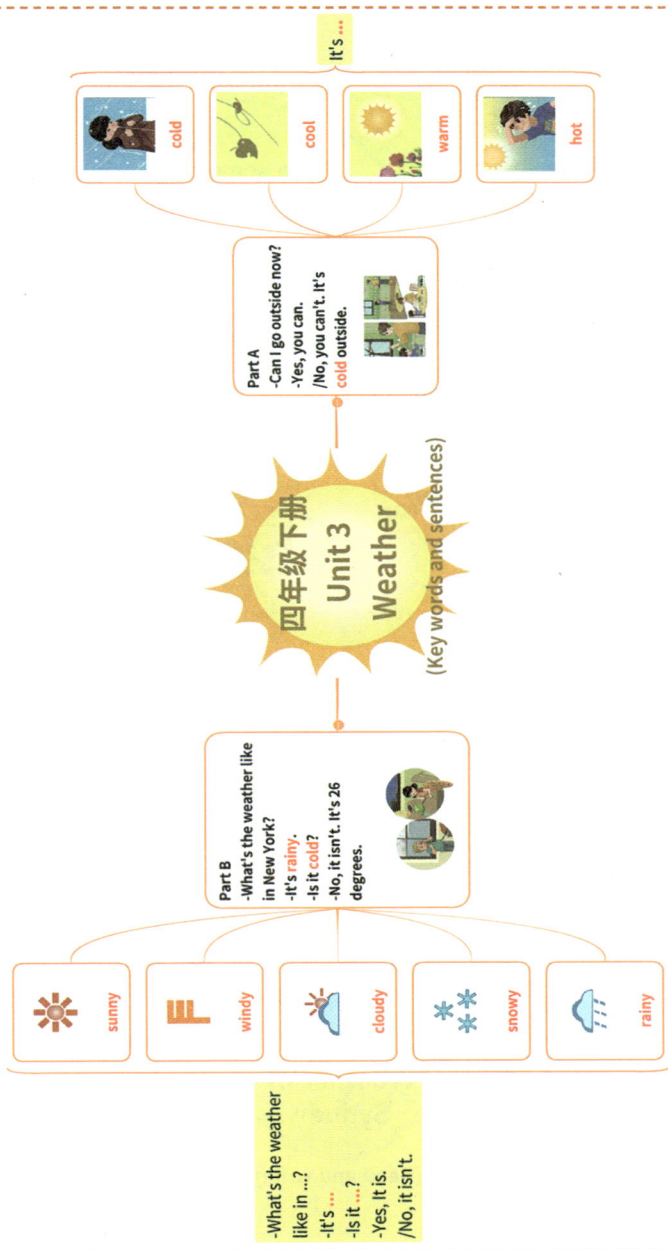

It's ...

cold

cool

warm

hot

Part A
-Can I go outside now?
-Yes, you can.
/No, you can't. It's
cold outside.

四年级下册
**Unit 3
Weather**
(Key words and sentences)

Part B
-What's the weather like
in New York?
-It's rainy.
-Is it cold?
-No, it isn't. It's 26
degrees.

sunny

windy

cloudy

snowy

rainy

-What's the weather
like in ...?
-It's ...
-Is it ...?
-Yes, It is.
/No, it isn't.

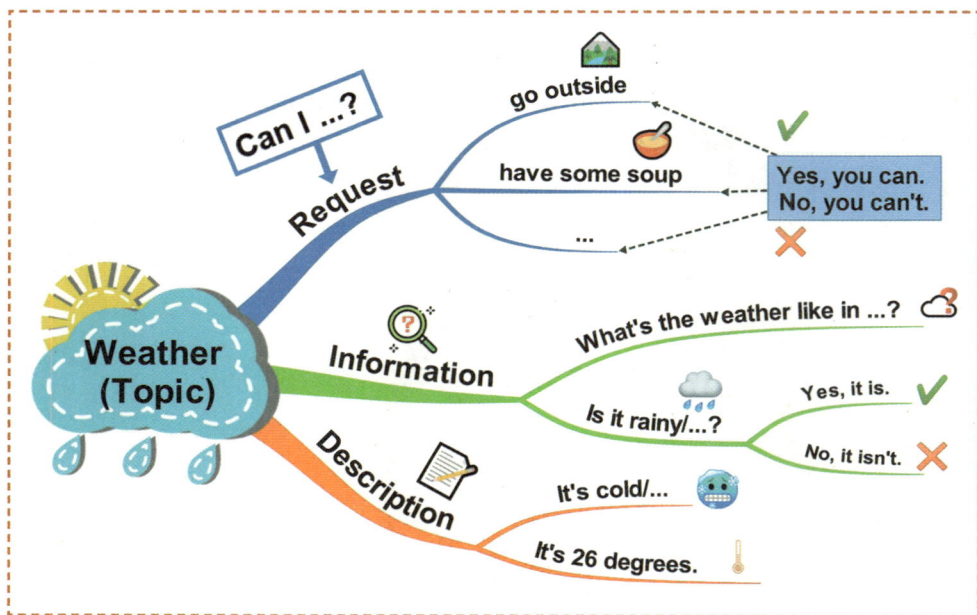

Can I ...?

Request

go outside

have some soup

...

Yes, you can.
No, you can't.

Weather
(Topic)

Information

What's the weather like in ...?

Is it rainy/...?

Yes, it is.

No, it isn't.

Description

It's cold/...

It's 26 degrees.

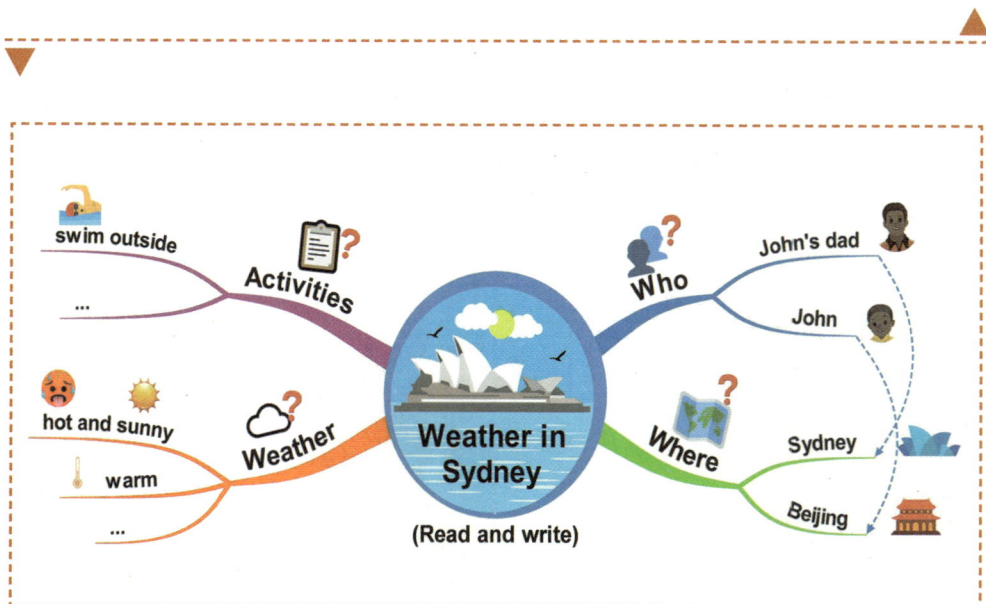

swim outside

...

Activities

hot and sunny

warm

...

Weather

Weather in
Sydney

(Read and write)

Who

John's dad

John

Where

Sydney

Beijing

Unit 4 At the farm

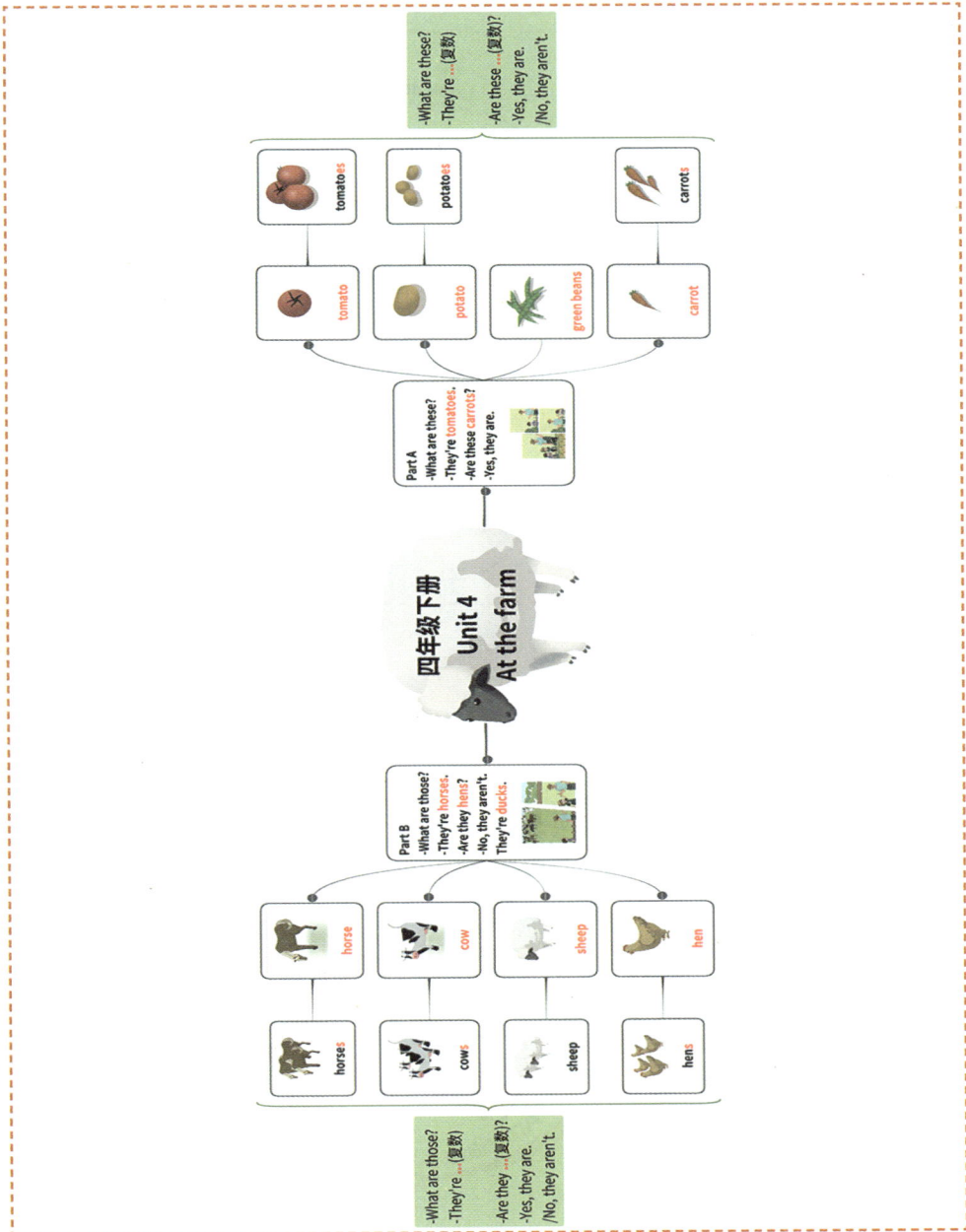

-What are these?
-They're ....(复数).
-Are these ....(复数)?
-Yes, they are.
/No, they aren't.

tomatoes

potatoes

carrots

tomato

potato

green beans

carrot

Part A
-What are these?
-They're tomatoes.
-Are these carrots?
-Yes, they are.

四年级下册
Unit 4
At the farm

Part B
-What are those?
-They're horses.
-Are they hens?
-No, they aren't.
They're ducks.

horse

cow

sheep

hen

horses

cows

sheep

hens

-What are those?
-They're ....(复数).
-Are they ....(复数)?
-Yes, they are.
/No, they aren't.

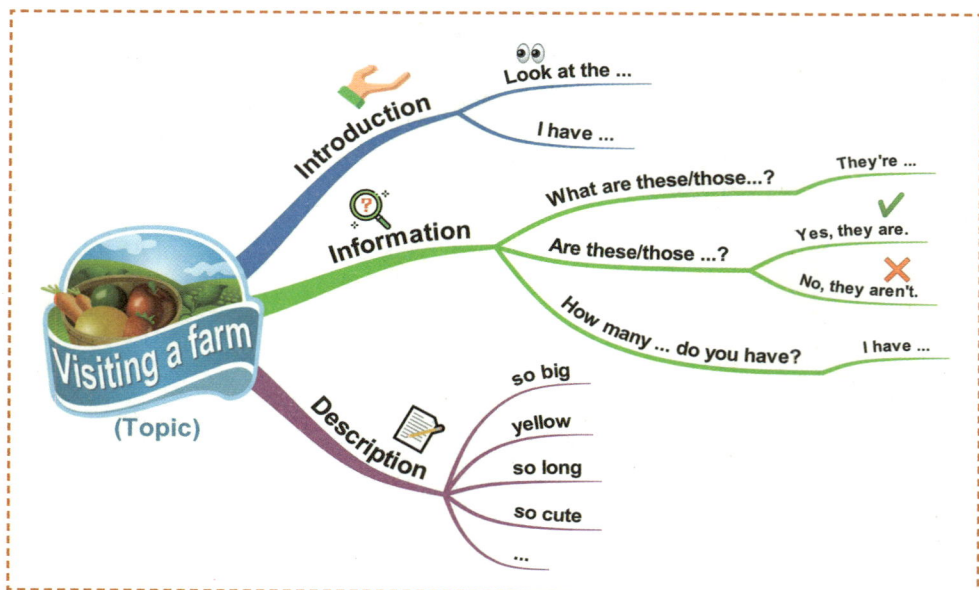

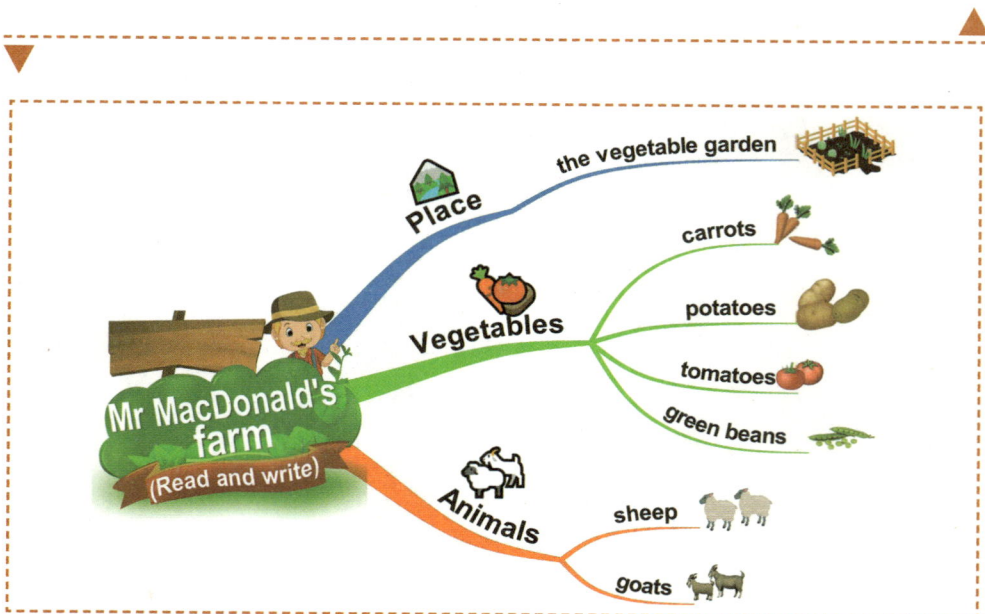

Unit 5 My clothes

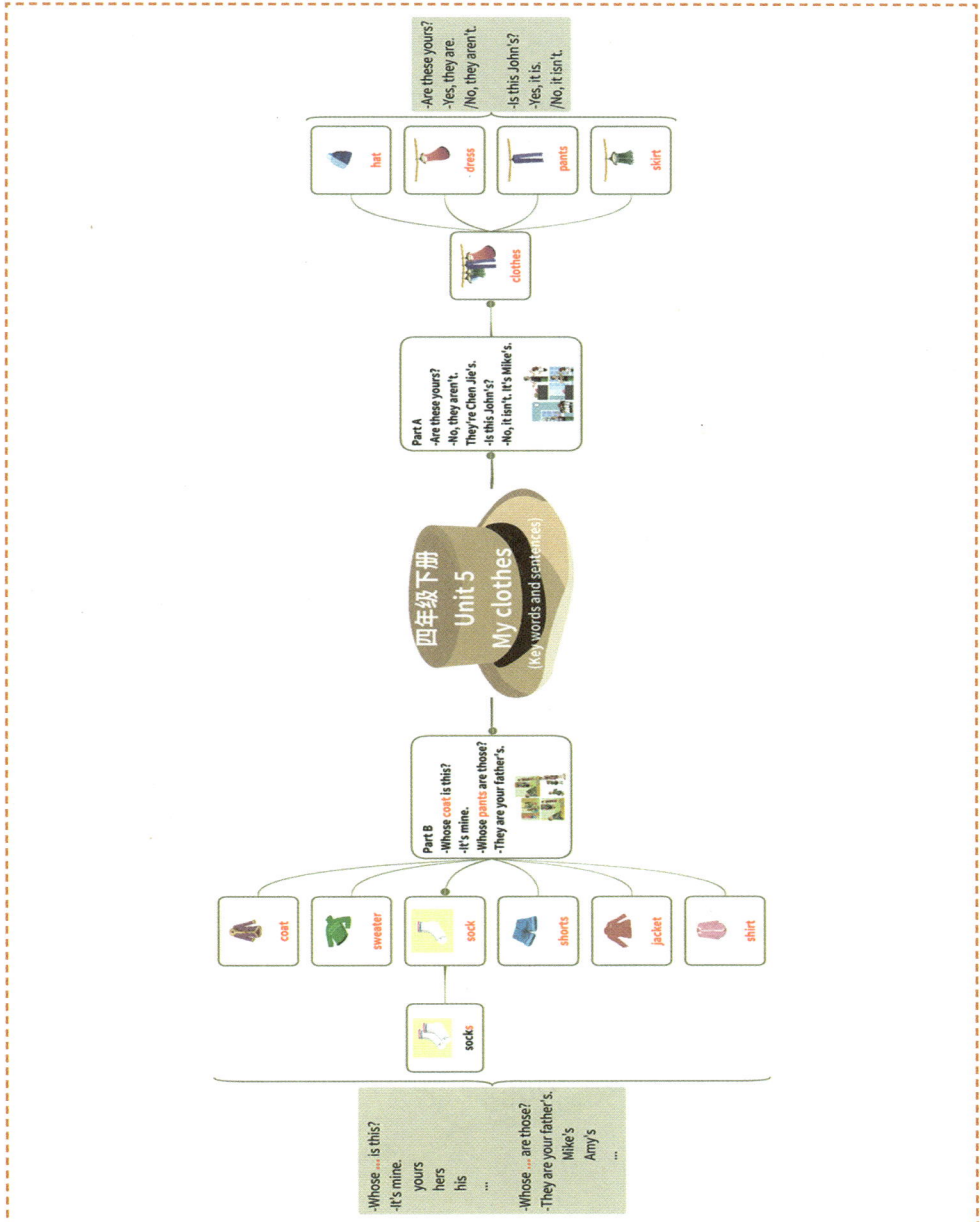

-Are these yours?
-Yes, they are.
/No, they aren't.

-Is this John's?
-Yes, it is.
/No, it isn't.

hat

dress

pants

skirt

clothes

Part A
-Are these yours?
-No, they aren't.
They're Chen Jie's.
-Is this John's?
-No, it isn't. It's Mike's.

四年级下册
Unit 5
My clothes
(Key words and sentences)

Part B
-Whose coat is this?
-It's mine.
-Whose pants are those?
-They are your father's.

coat

sweater

sock

shorts

jacket

shirt

socks

-Whose ... is this?
-It's mine.
  yours
  hers
  his
  ...

-Whose ... are those?
-They are your father's.
  Mike's
  Amy's
  ...

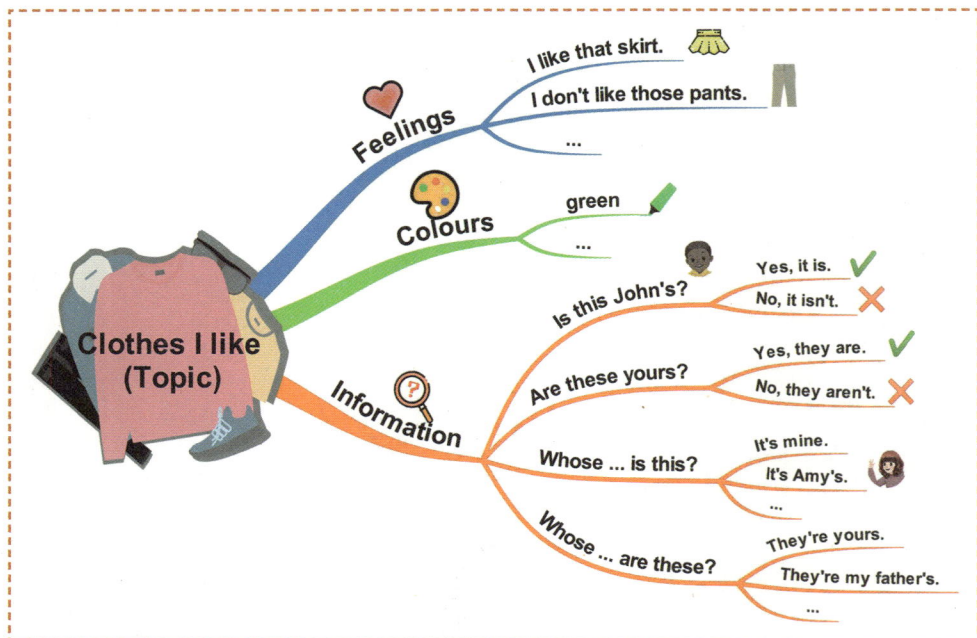

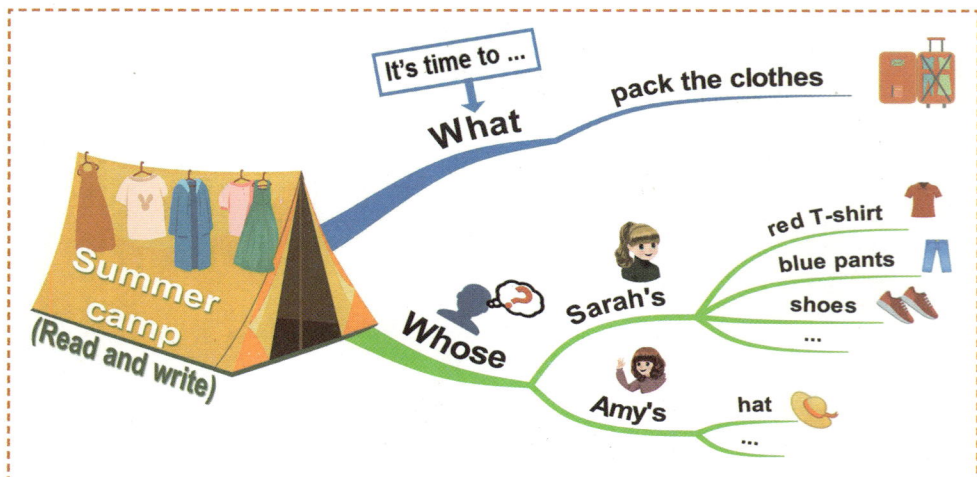

Unit 6 Shopping

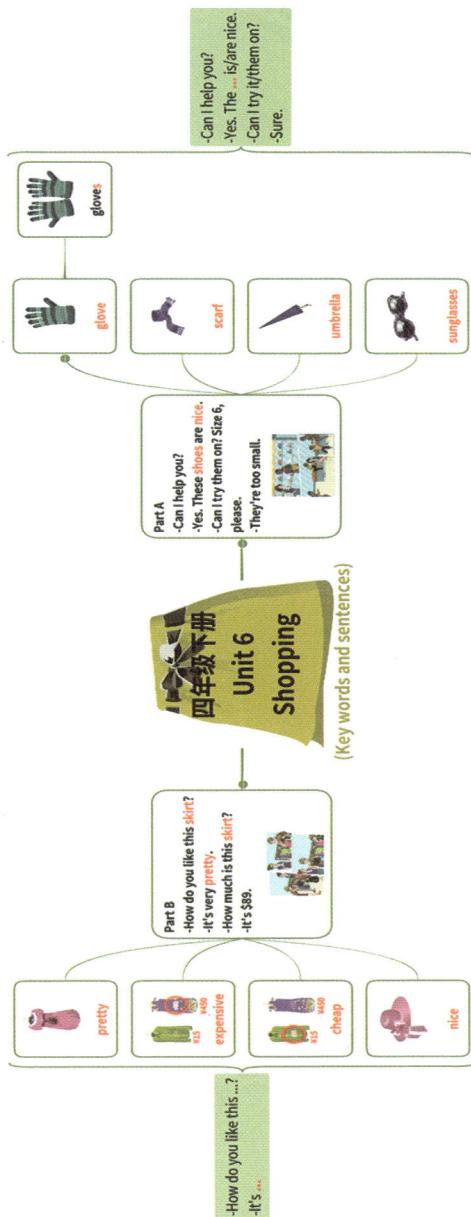

-Can I help you?
-Yes. The ... is/are nice.
-Can I try it/them on?
-Sure.

gloves

glove

scarf

umbrella

sunglasses

Part A
-Can I help you?
-Yes. These shoes are nice.
-Can I try them on? Size 6, please.
-They're too small.

四年级下册
Unit 6
Shopping

(Key words and sentences)

Part B
-How do you like this skirt?
-It's very pretty.
-How much is this skirt?
-It's $89.

pretty

¥450 expensive

¥15 ¥450 cheap

nice

-How do you like this ...?
-It's ...

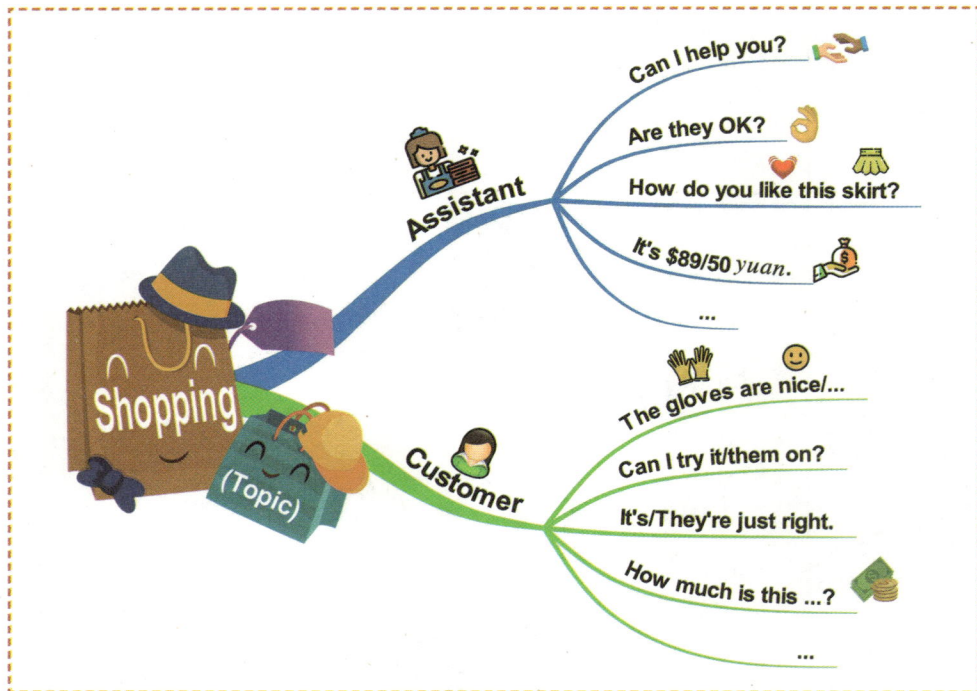

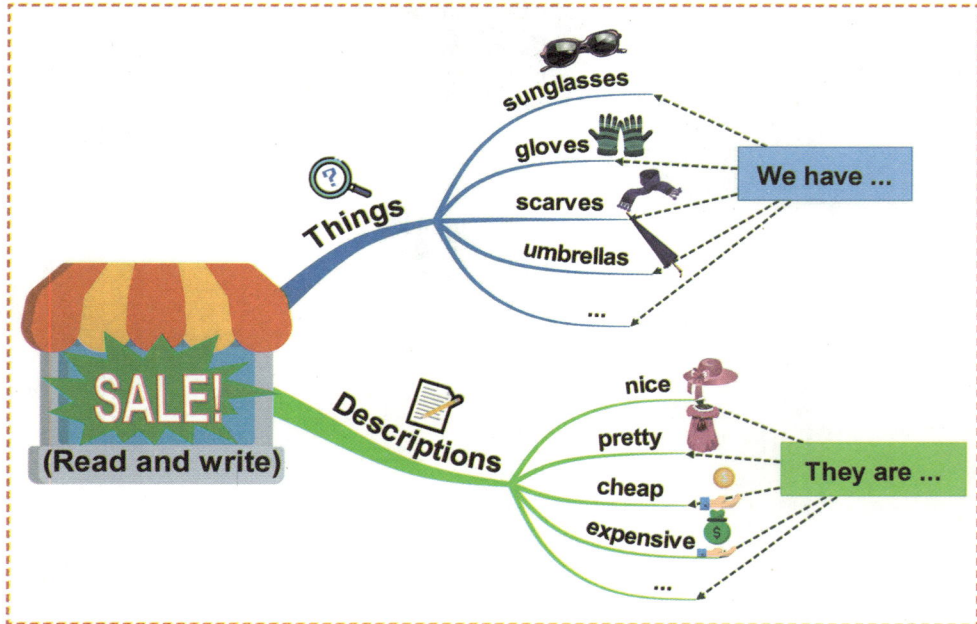

小学英语人教版五年级上册

Unit 1 What's he like?

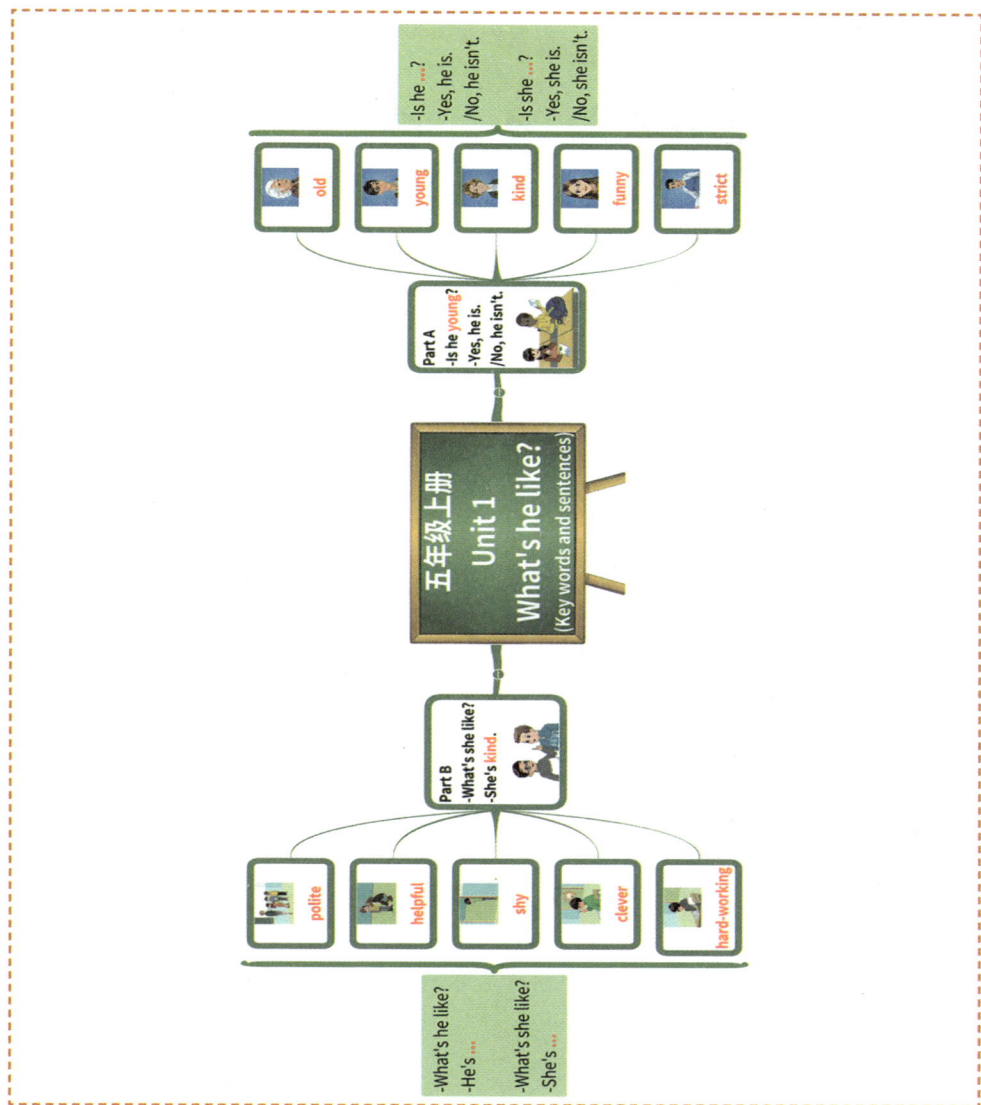

-Is he ...?
-Yes, he is.
/No, he isn't.
-Is she ...?
-Yes, she is.
/No, she isn't.

old   young   kind   funny   strict

Part A
-Is he young?
-Yes, he is.
-No, he isn't.

五年级上册
Unit 1
What's he like?
(Key words and sentences)

Part B
-What's she like?
-She's kind.

polite   helpful   shy   clever   hard-working

-What's he like?
-He's ...
-What's she like?
-She's ...

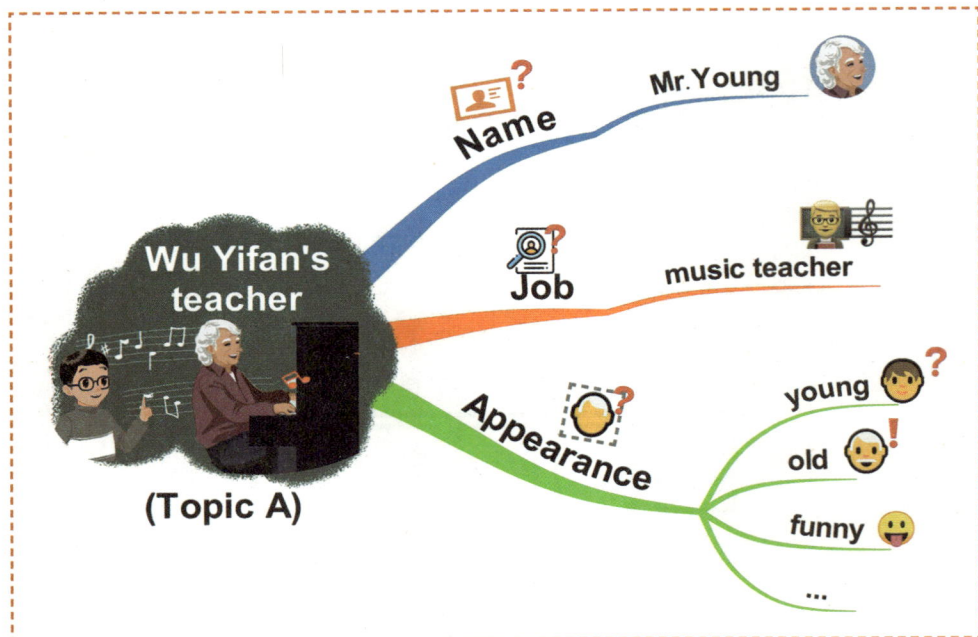

Wu Yifan's teacher

Name — Mr.Young

Job — music teacher

Appearance — young / old / funny / ...

(Topic A)

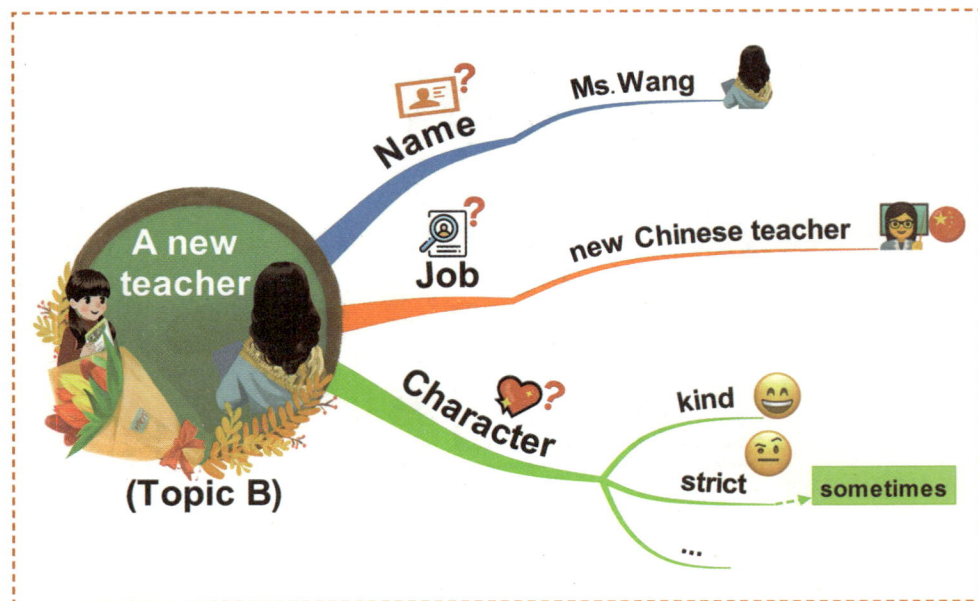

A new teacher

Name — Ms.Wang

Job — new Chinese teacher

Character — kind / strict → sometimes / ...

(Topic B)

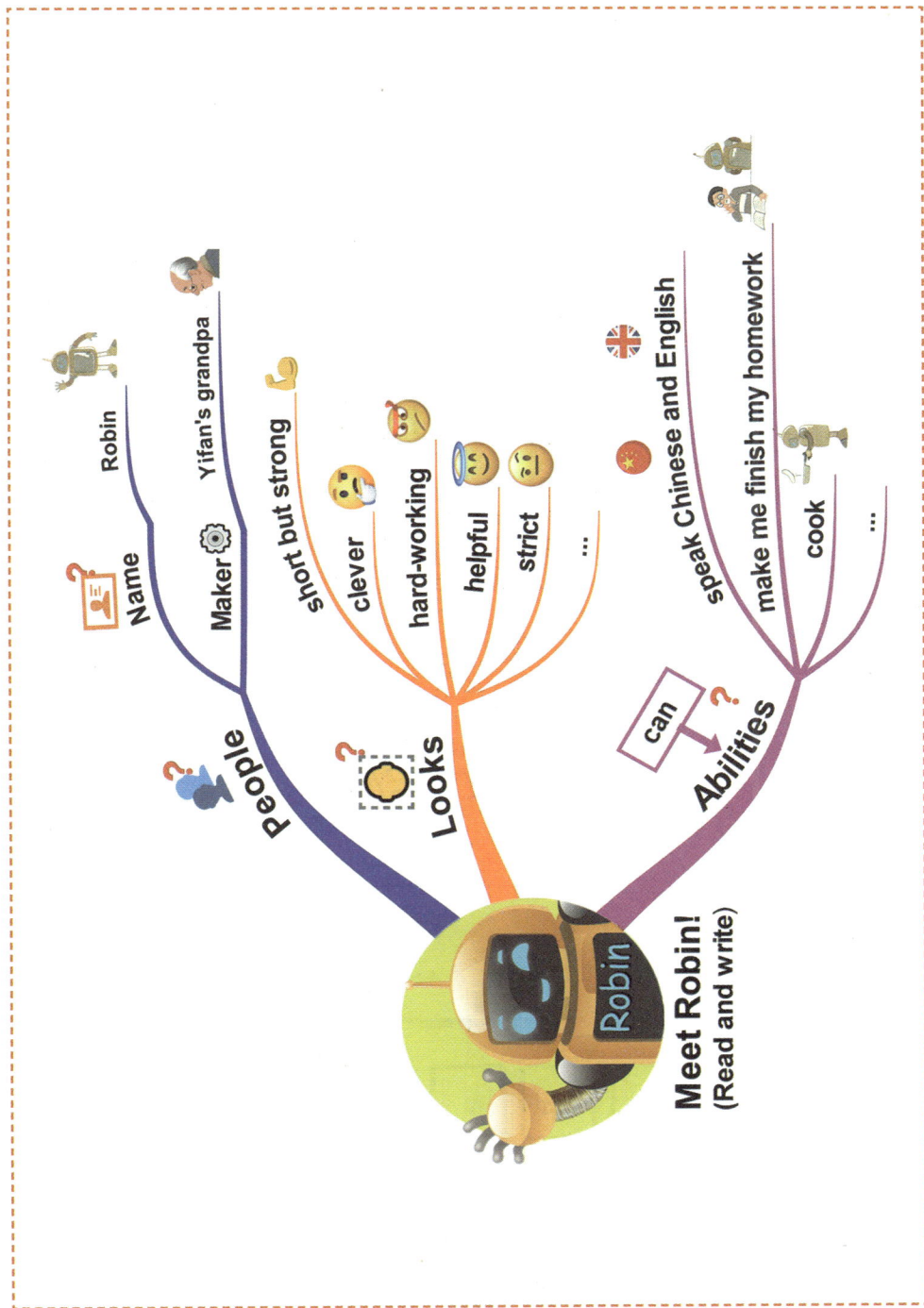

五年级 上册

Meet Robin!
(Read and write)

People
- Name — Robin
- Maker — Yifan's grandpa

Looks
- short but strong
- clever
- hard-working
- helpful
- strict
- ...

Abilities (can)
- speak Chinese and English
- make me finish my homework
- cook
- ...

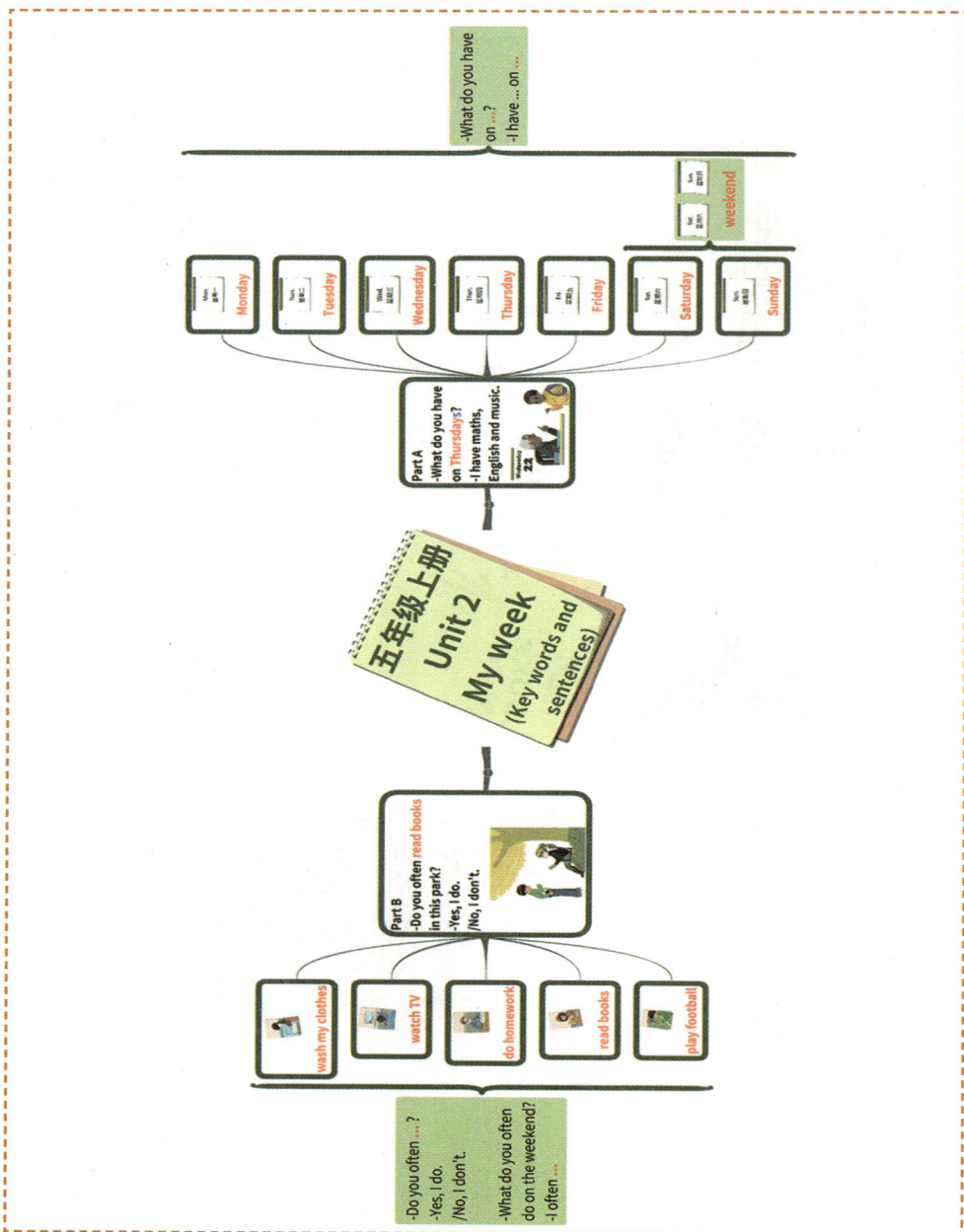

Unit 2 My week

-What do you have
on ... ?
-I have ... on ...

Mon.
星期一
Monday

Tues.
星期二
Tuesday

Wed.
星期三
Wednesday

Thur.
星期四
Thursday

Fri.
星期五
Friday

Sat.
星期六
Saturday

Sun.
星期天
Sunday

Sat.
星期六

Sun.
星期天

weekend

Part A
-What do you have
on Thursdays?
-I have maths,
English and music.

Wednesday
五4

五年级上册
**Unit 2
My week**
(Key words and
sentences)

Part B
-Do you often read books
in this park?
-Yes, I do.
/No, I don't.

wash my clothes

watch TV

do homework

read books

play football

-Do you often ... ?
-Yes, I do.
/No, I don't.

-What do you often
do on the weekend?
-I often ...

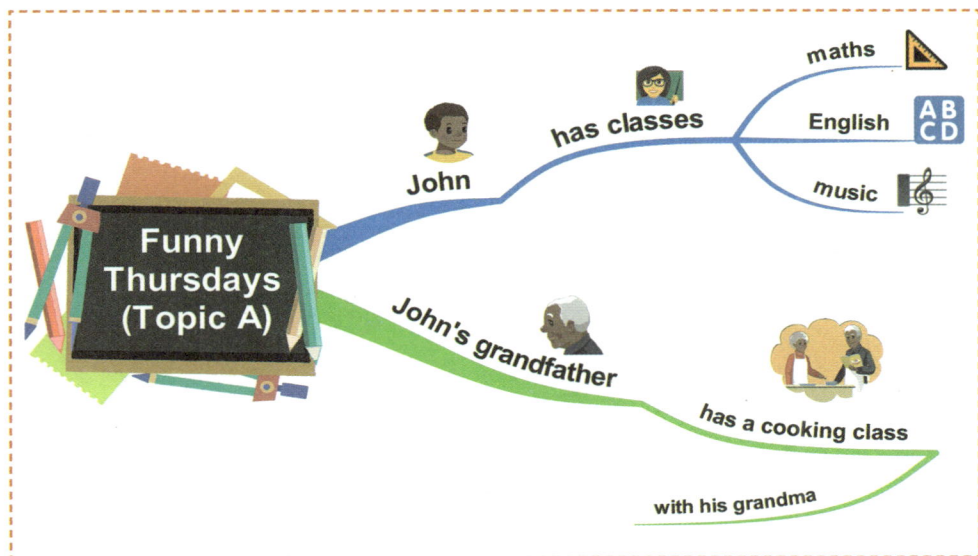

Funny Thursdays (Topic A)

- John — has classes
  - maths
  - English
  - music
- John's grandfather — has a cooking class
  - with his grandma

In a park (Topic B)

- When — Saturday afternoon
- Who
  - Sarah
  - Zhang Peng
- Abilities (can?)
  - read books
  - play football
  - often

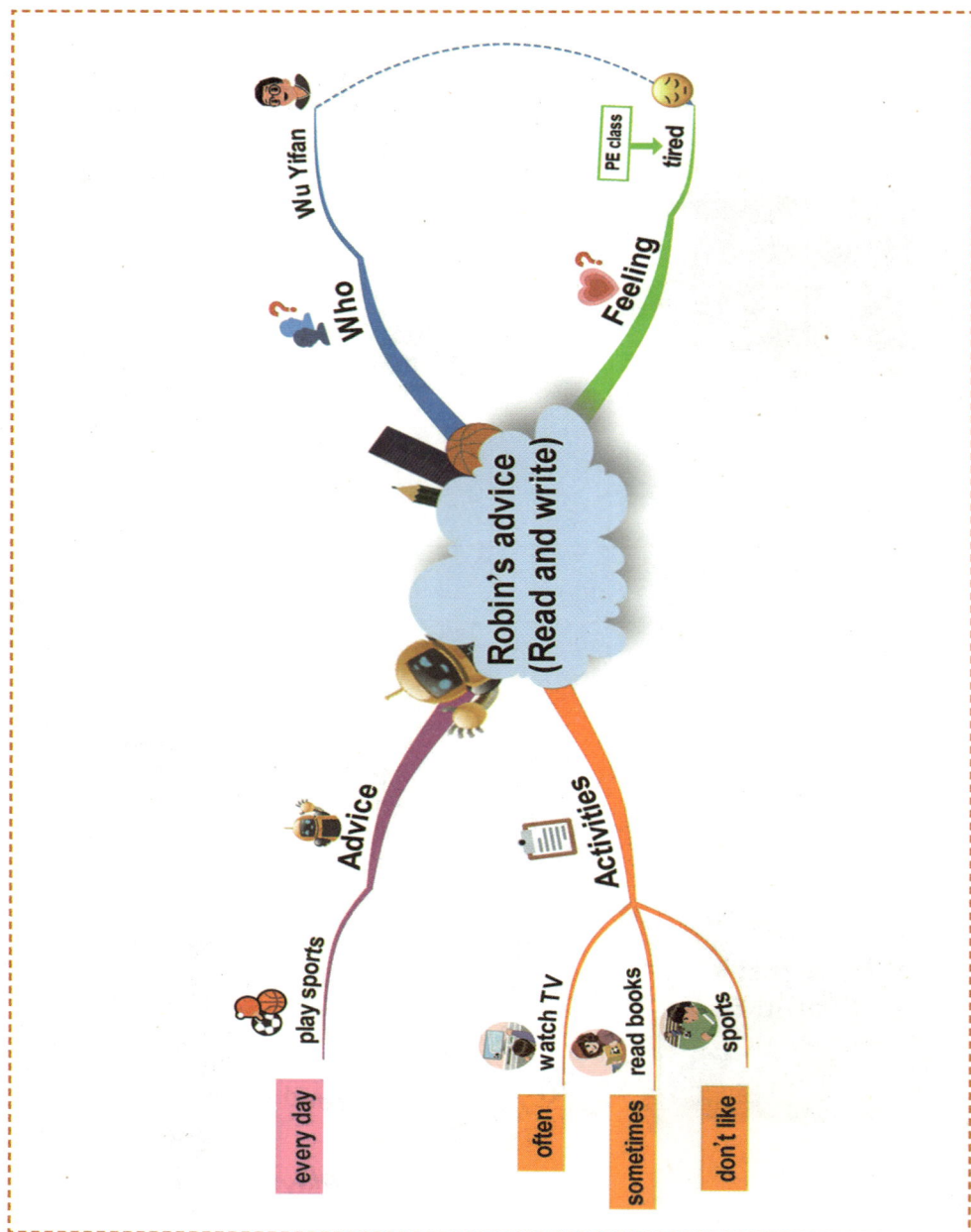

Unit 3 What would you like?

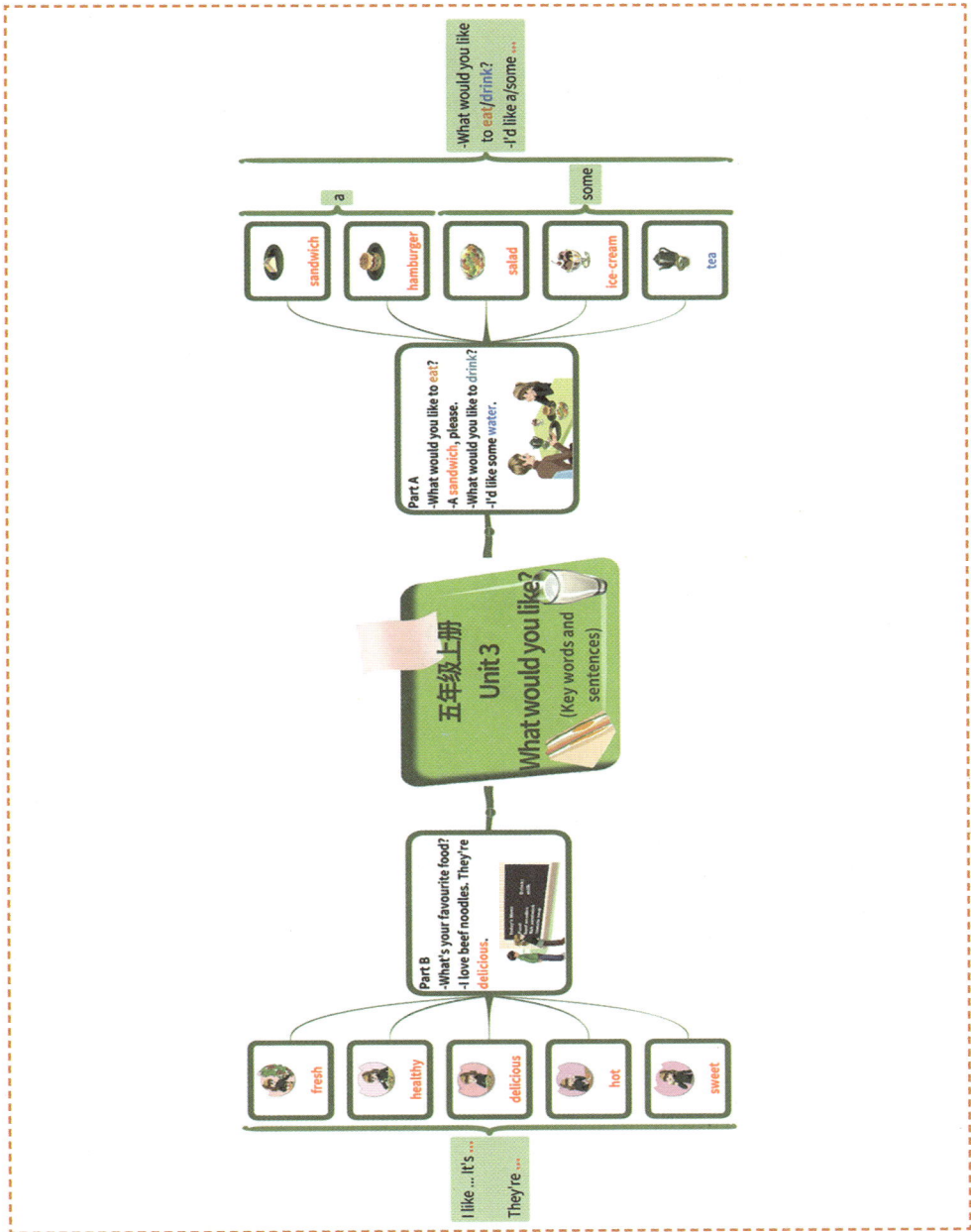

-What would you like
to eat/drink?
-I'd like a/some ···

a

some

sandwich

hamburger

salad

ice-cream

tea

Part A
-What would you like to eat?
-A sandwich, please.
-What would you like to drink some water.
-I'd like some water.

五年级上册
Unit 3
What would you like?
(Key words and sentences)

Part B
-What's your favourite food?
-I love beef noodles. They're delicious.

fresh

healthy

delicious

hot

sweet

I like ··· It's ···
They're ···

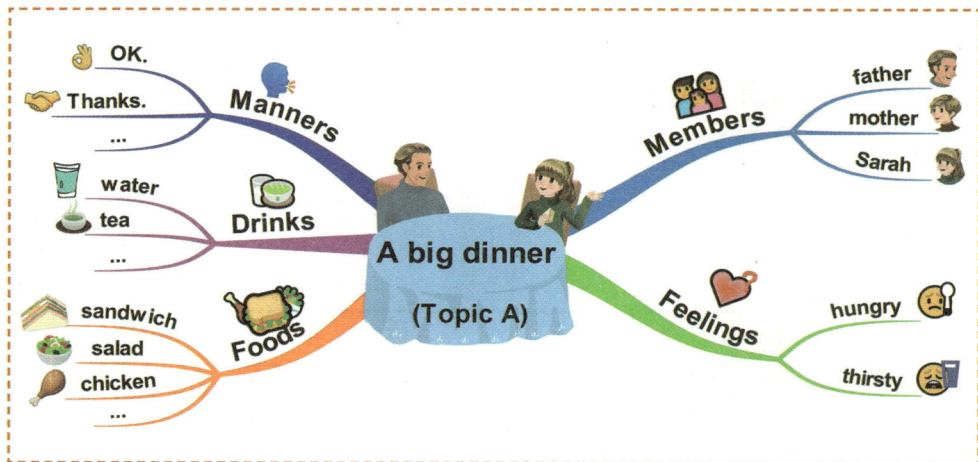

A big dinner
(Topic A)

Manners
- OK.
- Thanks.
- ...

Drinks
- water
- tea
- ...

Foods
- sandwich
- salad
- chicken
- ...

Members
- father
- mother
- Sarah

Feelings
- hungry
- thirsty

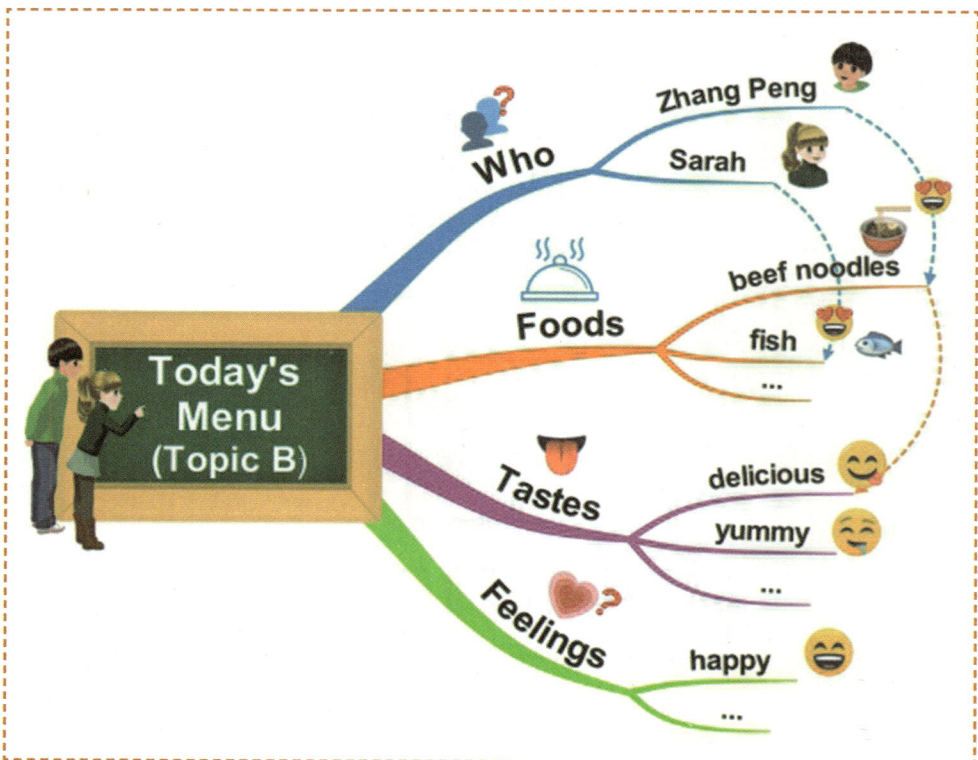

Today's Menu
(Topic B)

Who
- Zhang Peng
- Sarah

Foods
- beef noodles
- fish
- ...

Tastes
- delicious
- yummy
- ...

Feelings
- happy
- ...

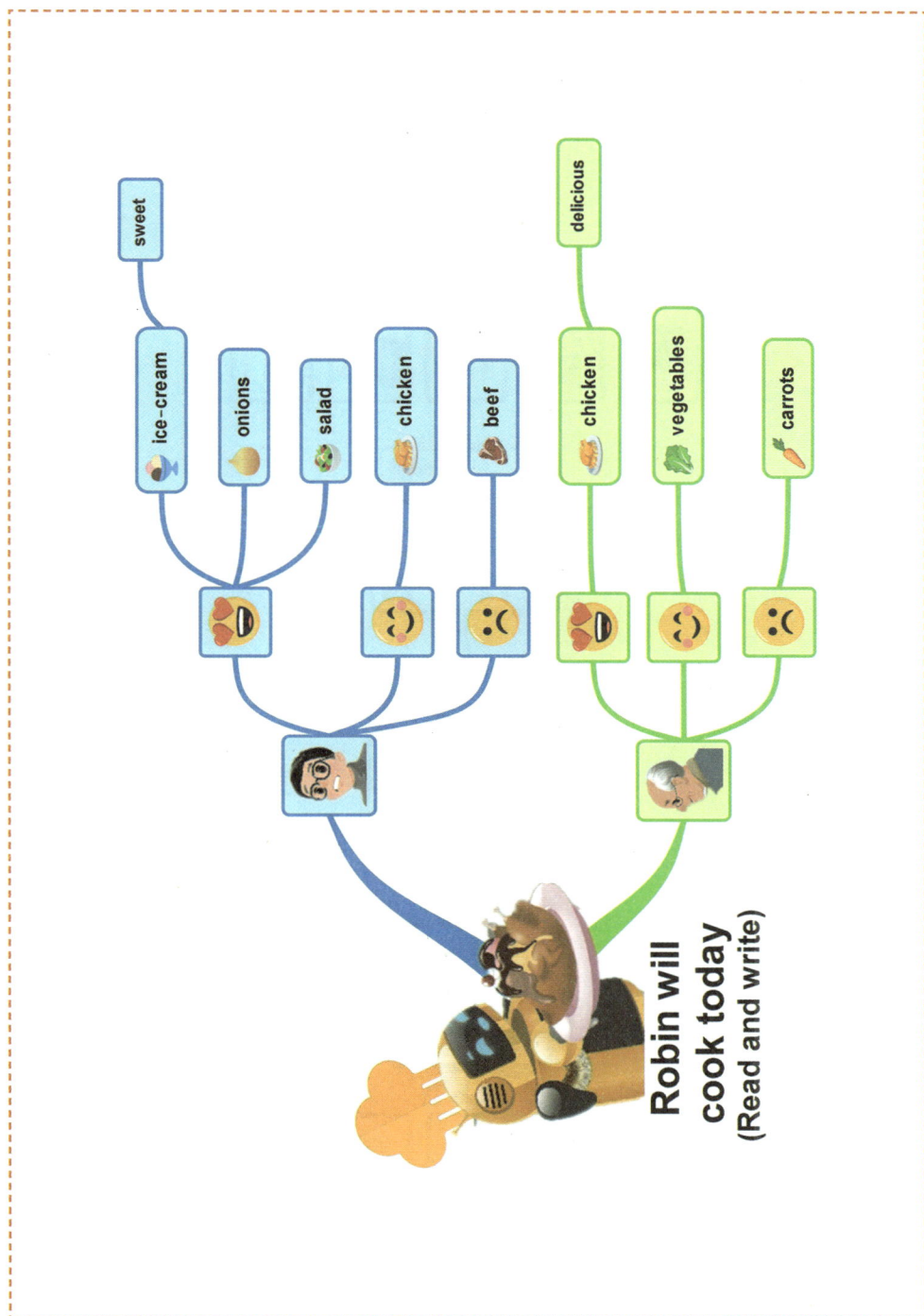

sweet

ice-cream
onions
salad
chicken
beef

delicious

chicken
vegetables
carrots

Robin will
cook today
(Read and write)

Unit 4 What can you do?

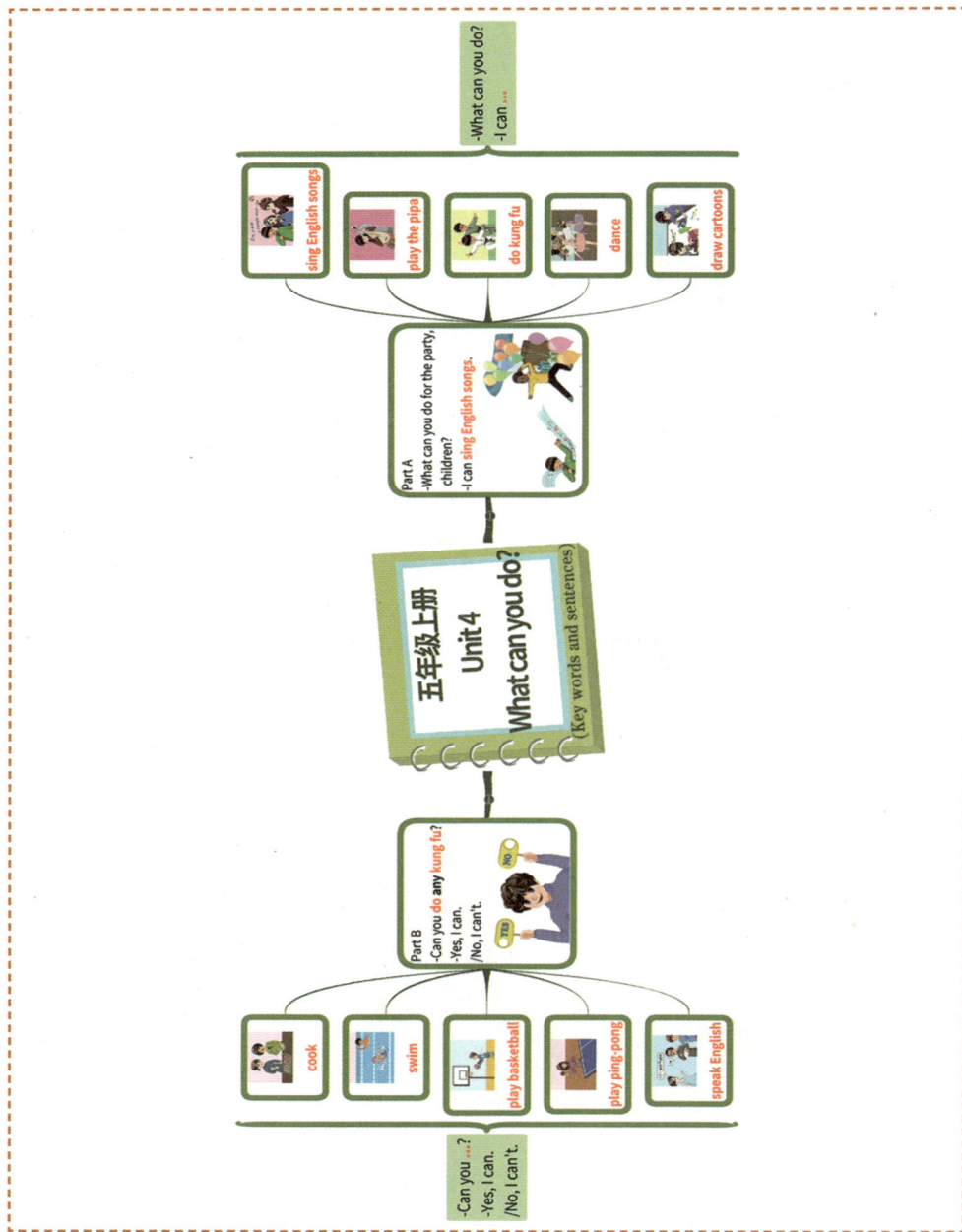

-What can you do?
-I can ...

sing English songs

play the pipa

do kung fu

dance

draw cartoons

Part A
-What can you do for the party, children?
-I can sing English songs.

五年级上册
Unit 4
What can you do?
(Key words and sentences)

Part B
-Can you do any kung fu?
-Yes, I can.
/No, I can't.

cook

swim

play basketball

play ping-pong

speak English

-Can you ...?
-Yes, I can.
/No, I can't.

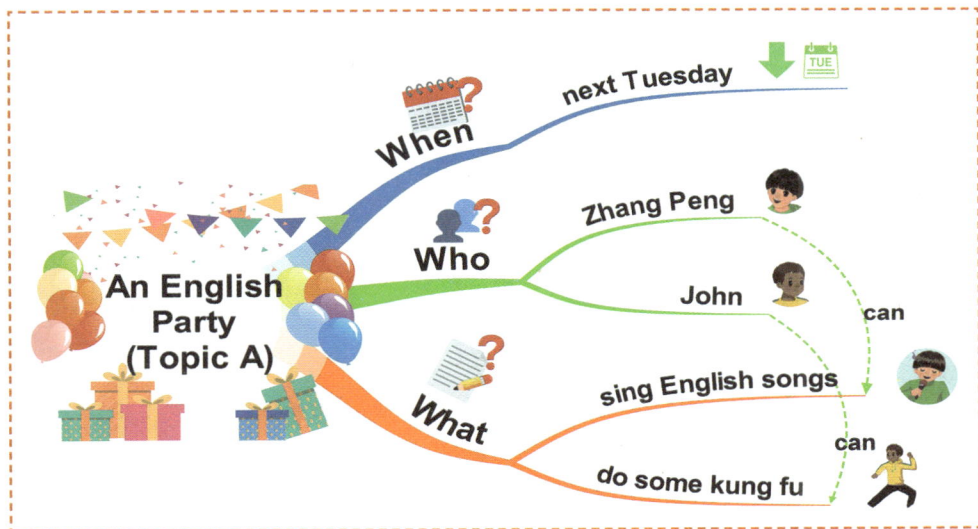

An English Party (Topic A)

When — next Tuesday

Who — Zhang Peng — John — can

What — sing English songs — do some kung fu — can

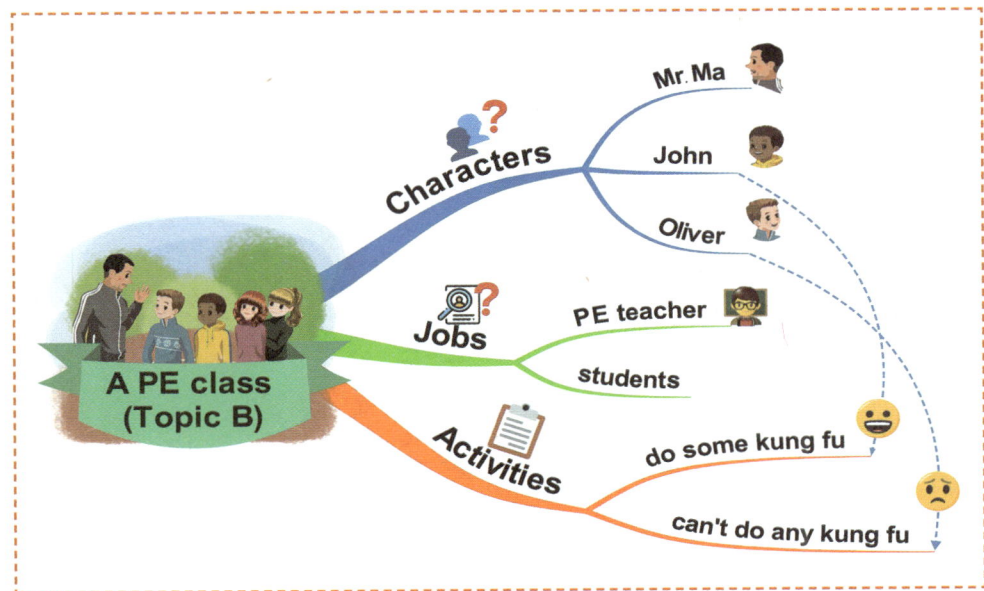

A PE class (Topic B)

Characters — Mr. Ma — John — Oliver

Jobs — PE teacher — students

Activities — do some kung fu — can't do any kung fu

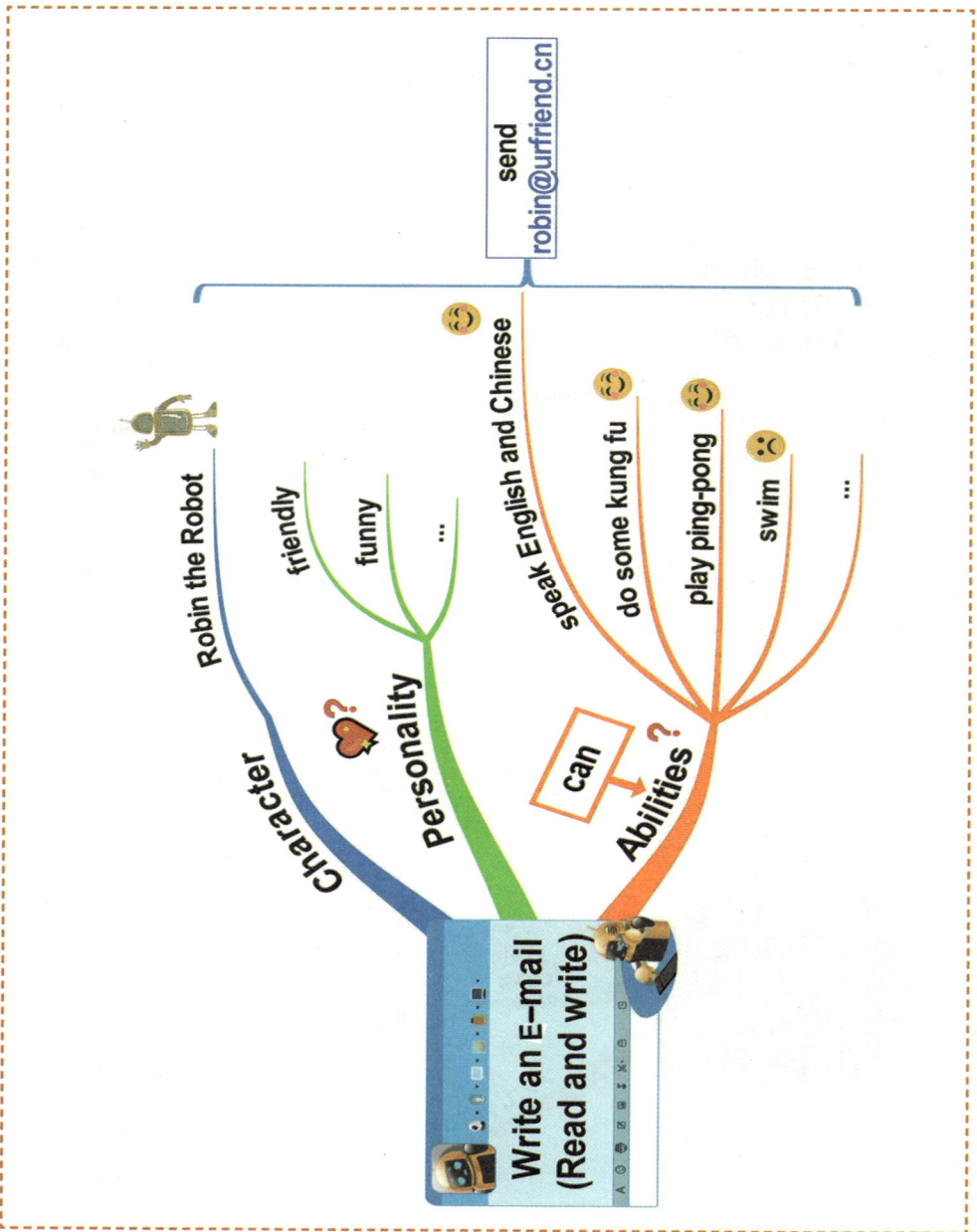

send
robin@urfriend.cn

Robin the Robot

Character

Personality
friendly
funny
...

can → Abilities?
speak English and Chinese
do some kung fu
play ping-pong
swim
...

Write an E-mail
(Read and write)

Unit 5 There is a big bed

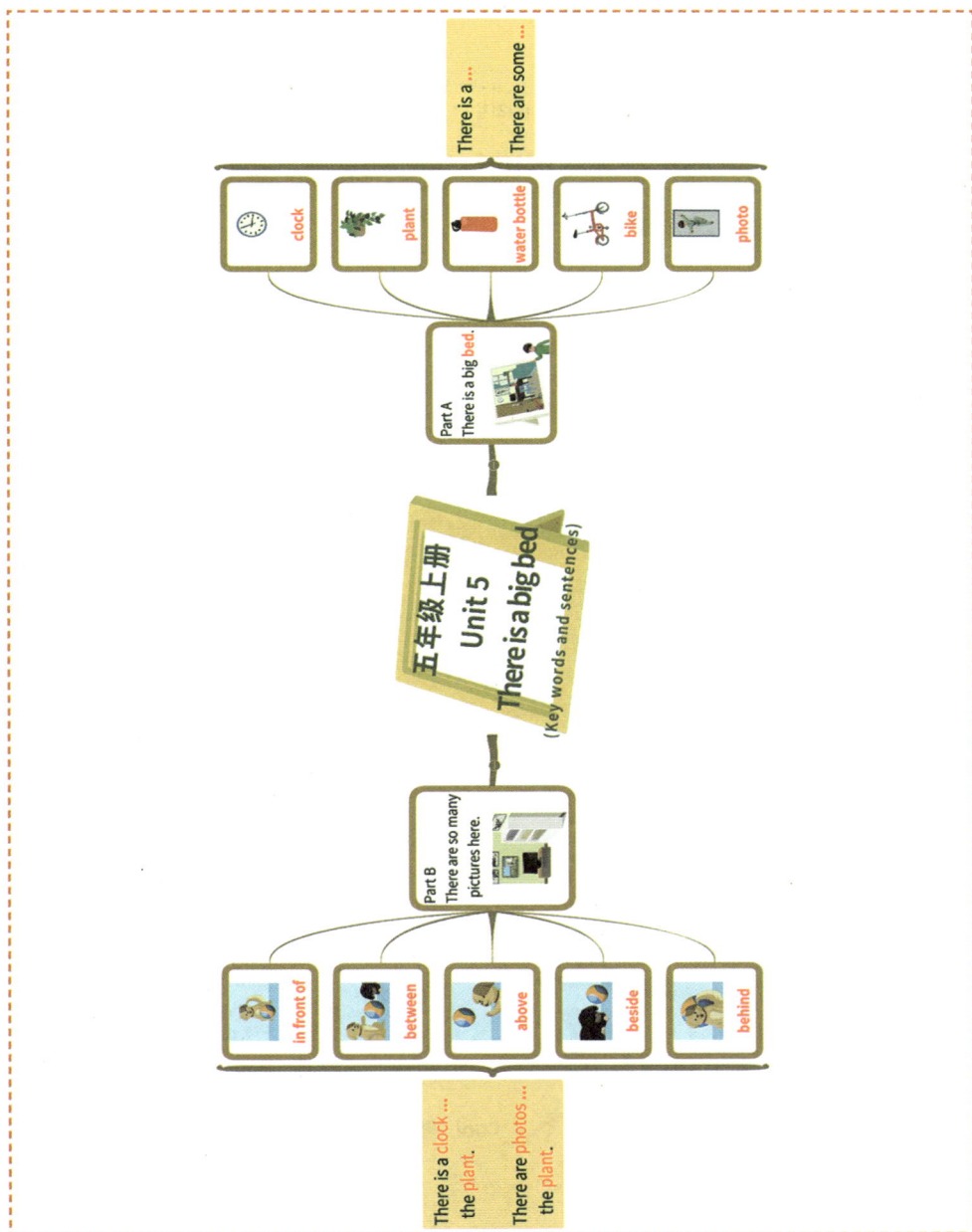

There is a ....
There are some ....

clock

plant

water bottle

bike

photo

Part A
There is a big bed.

五年级上册
Unit 5
There is a big bed
(Key words and sentences)

Part B
There are so many pictures here.

in front of

between

above

beside

behind

There is a clock ....
the plant.
There are photos ....
the plant.

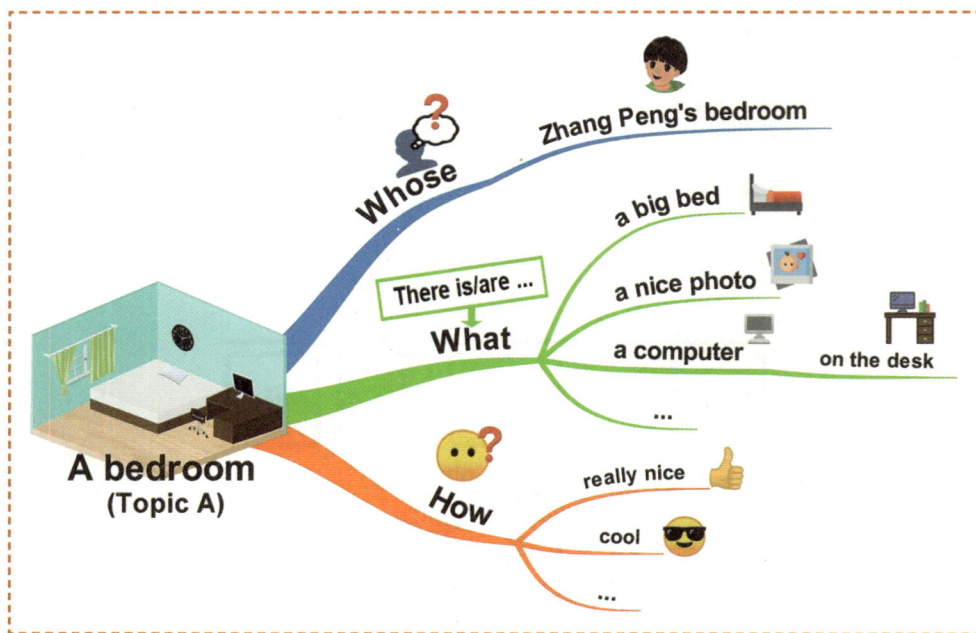

A bedroom
(Topic A)

Whose — Zhang Peng's bedroom

There is/are ...
What
- a big bed
- a nice photo
- a computer — on the desk
- ...

How
- really nice
- cool
- ...

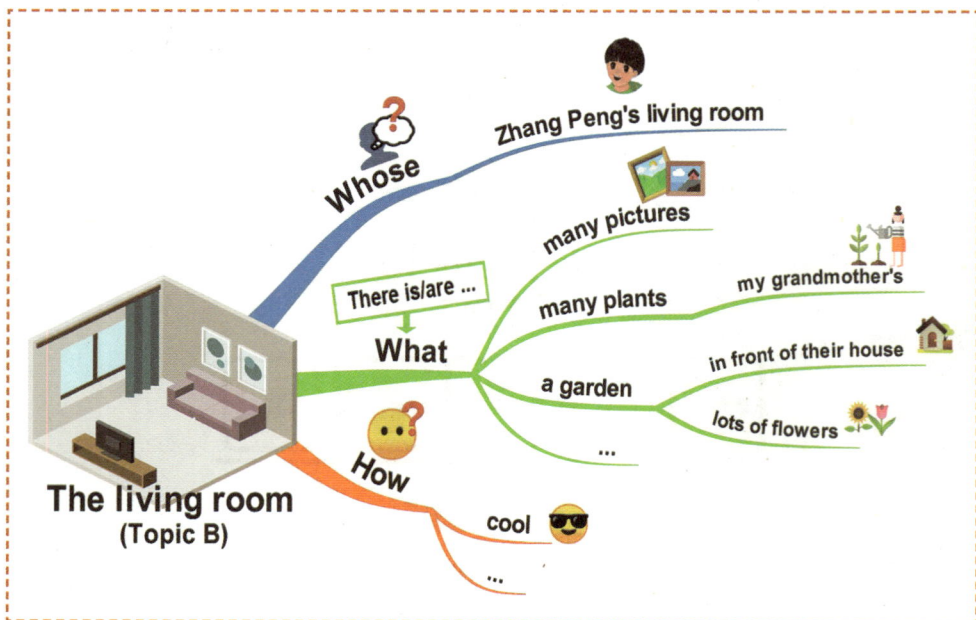

The living room
(Topic B)

Whose — Zhang Peng's living room

There is/are ...
What
- many pictures
- many plants — my grandmother's
- a garden — in front of their house / lots of flowers
- ...

How
- cool
- ...

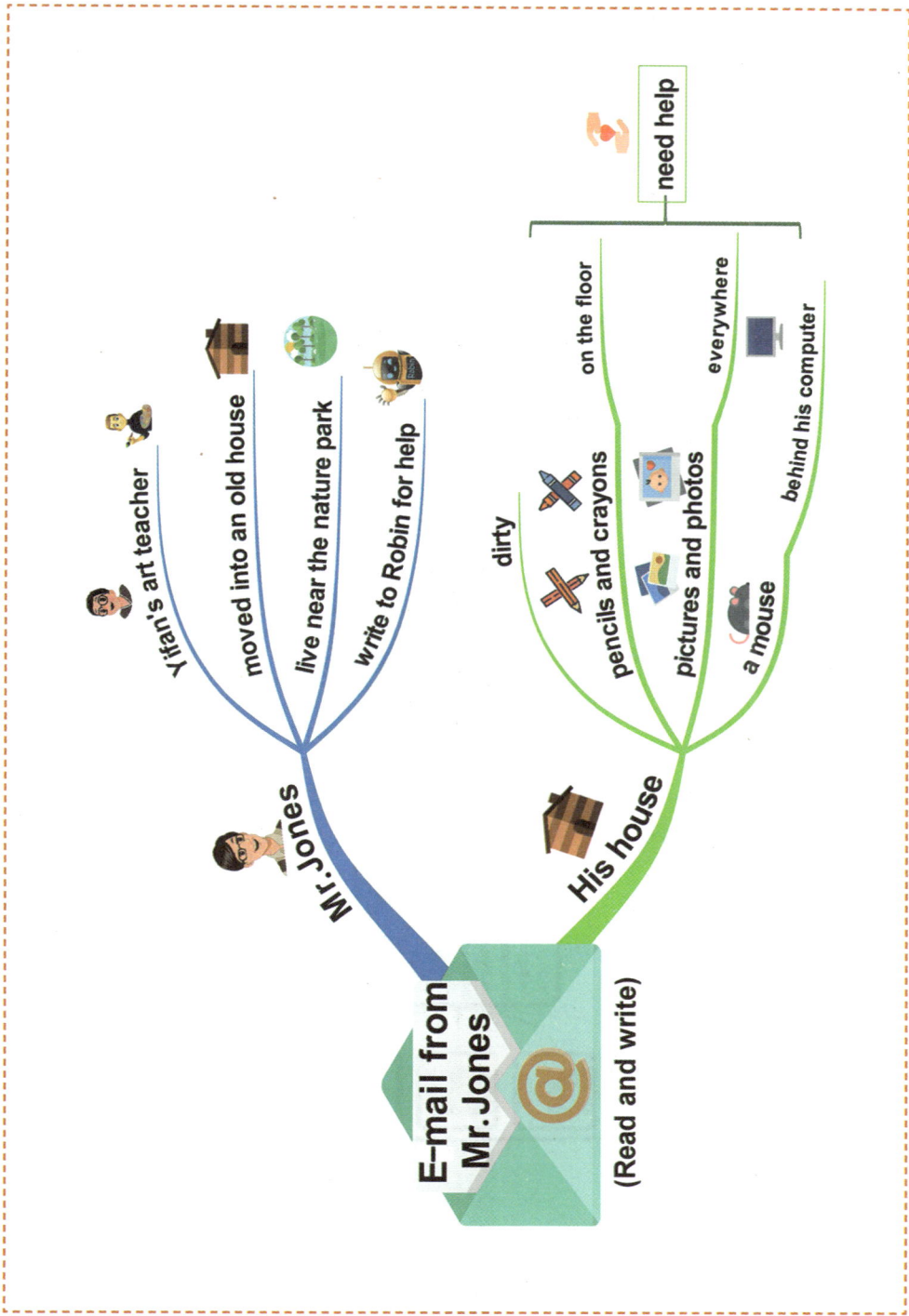

E-mail from Mr. Jones
(Read and write)

Mr. Jones
- Yifan's art teacher
- moved into an old house
- live near the nature park
- write to Robin for help

His house
- dirty
- pencils and crayons
- pictures and photos
- a mouse
- on the floor
- everywhere
- behind his computer

need help

Unit 6　In a nature park

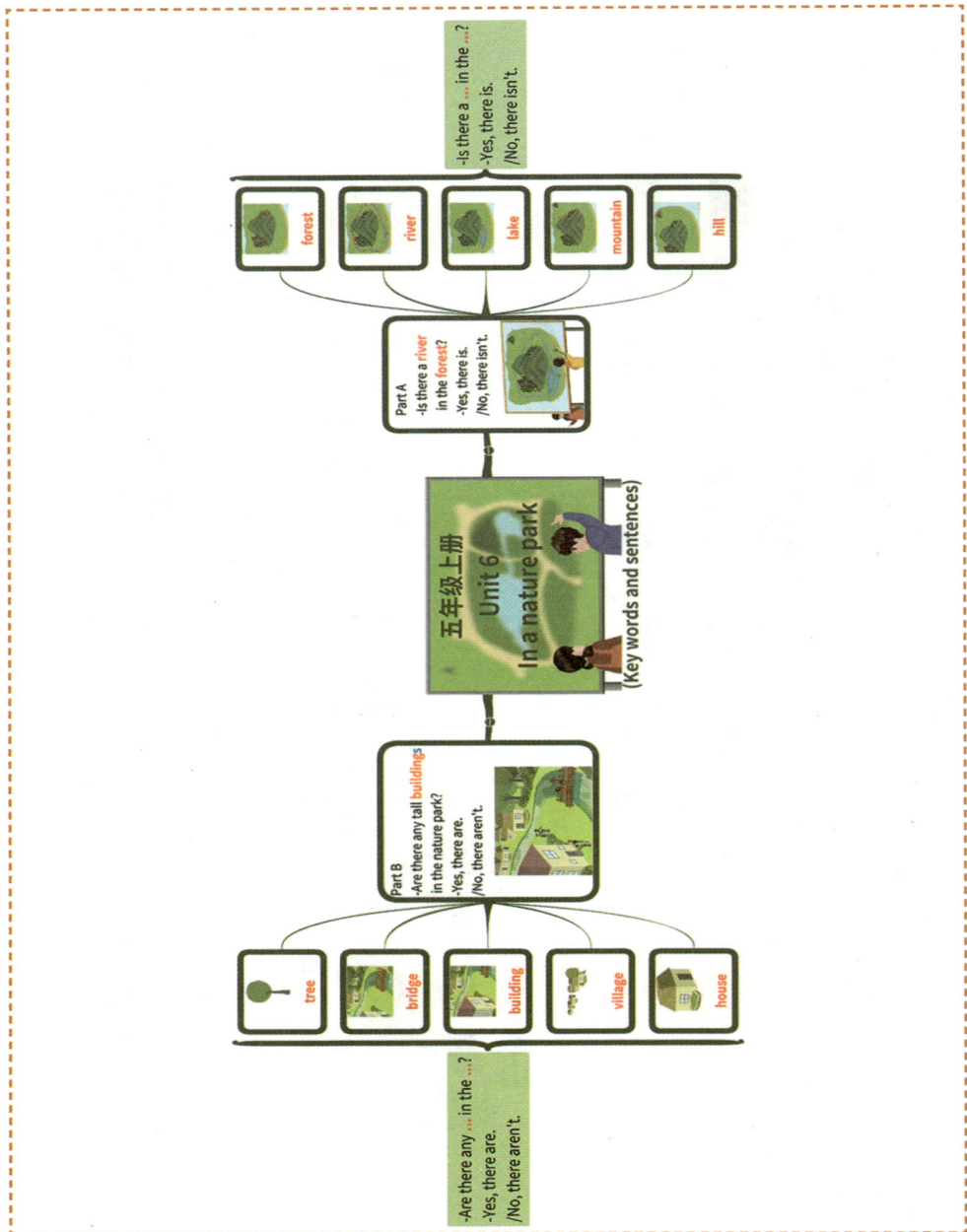

-Is there a ... in the ...?
-Yes, there is.
/No, there isn't.

forest

river

lake

mountain

hill

Part A
-Is there a river in the forest?
-Yes, there is.
/No, there isn't.

五年级上册
Unit 6
In a nature park
(Key words and sentences)

Part B
-Are there any tall buildings in the nature park?
-Yes, there are.
/No, there aren't.

tree

bridge

building

village

house

-Are there any ... in the ...?
-Yes, there are.
/No, there aren't.

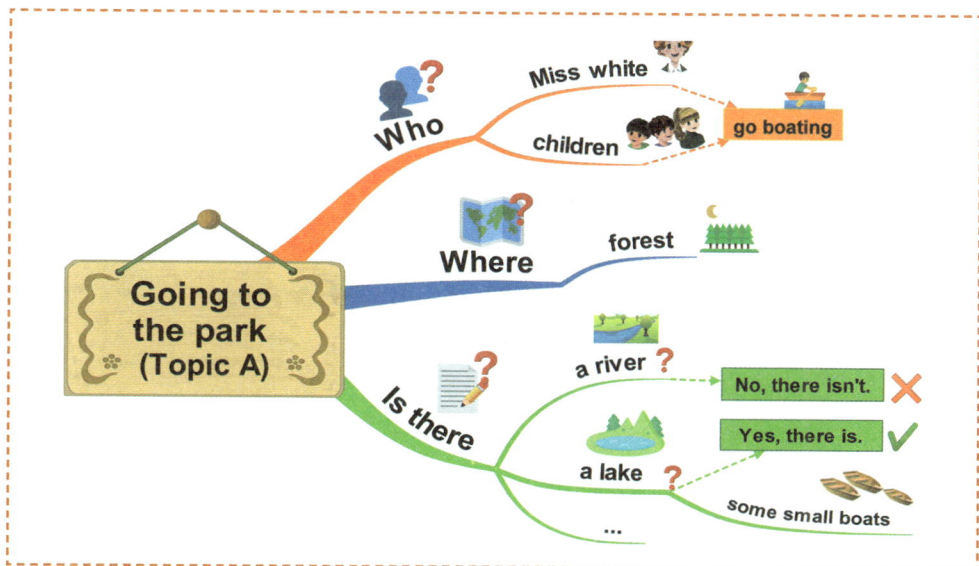

Going to the park (Topic A)

Who — Miss white

children → go boating

Where — forest

Is there — a river ? — No, there isn't. ✗

a lake ? — Yes, there is. ✓ → some small boats

...

五年级 上册

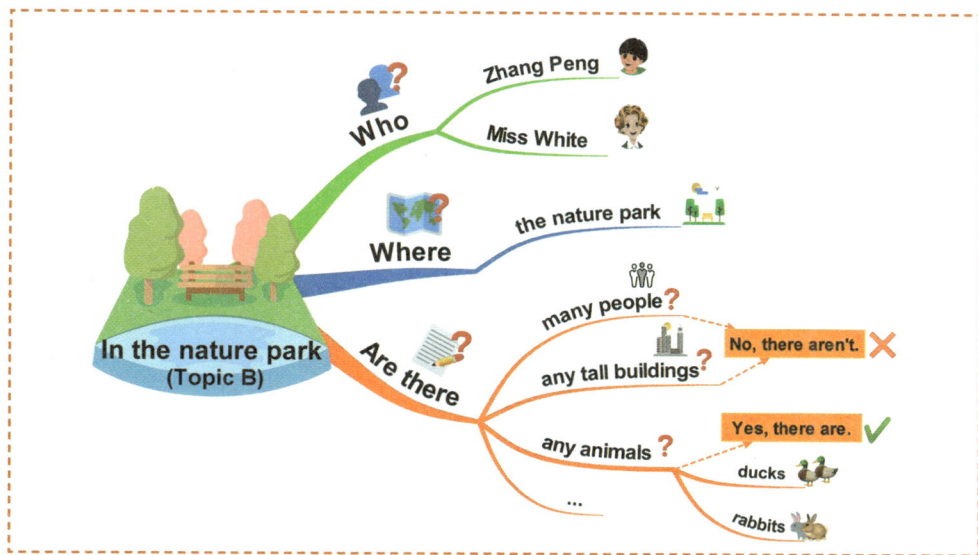

In the nature park (Topic B)

Who — Zhang Peng

Miss White

Where — the nature park

Are there — many people ?

any tall buildings ? — No, there aren't. ✗

any animals ? — Yes, there are. ✓ — ducks

... — rabbits

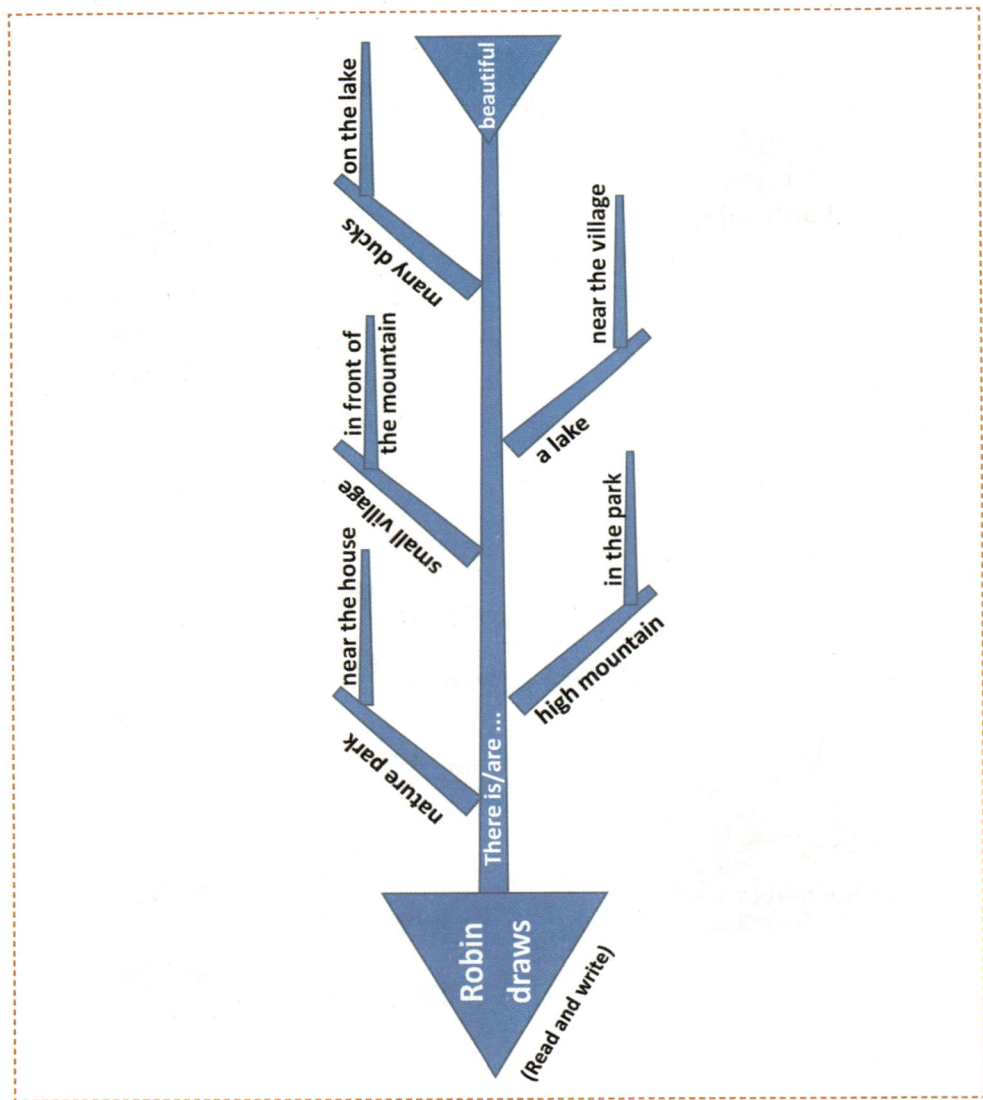

beautiful

on the lake

many ducks

near the village

in front of
the mountain

a lake

small village

near the house

in the park

nature park

high mountain

There is/are ...

Robin
draws

(Read and write)

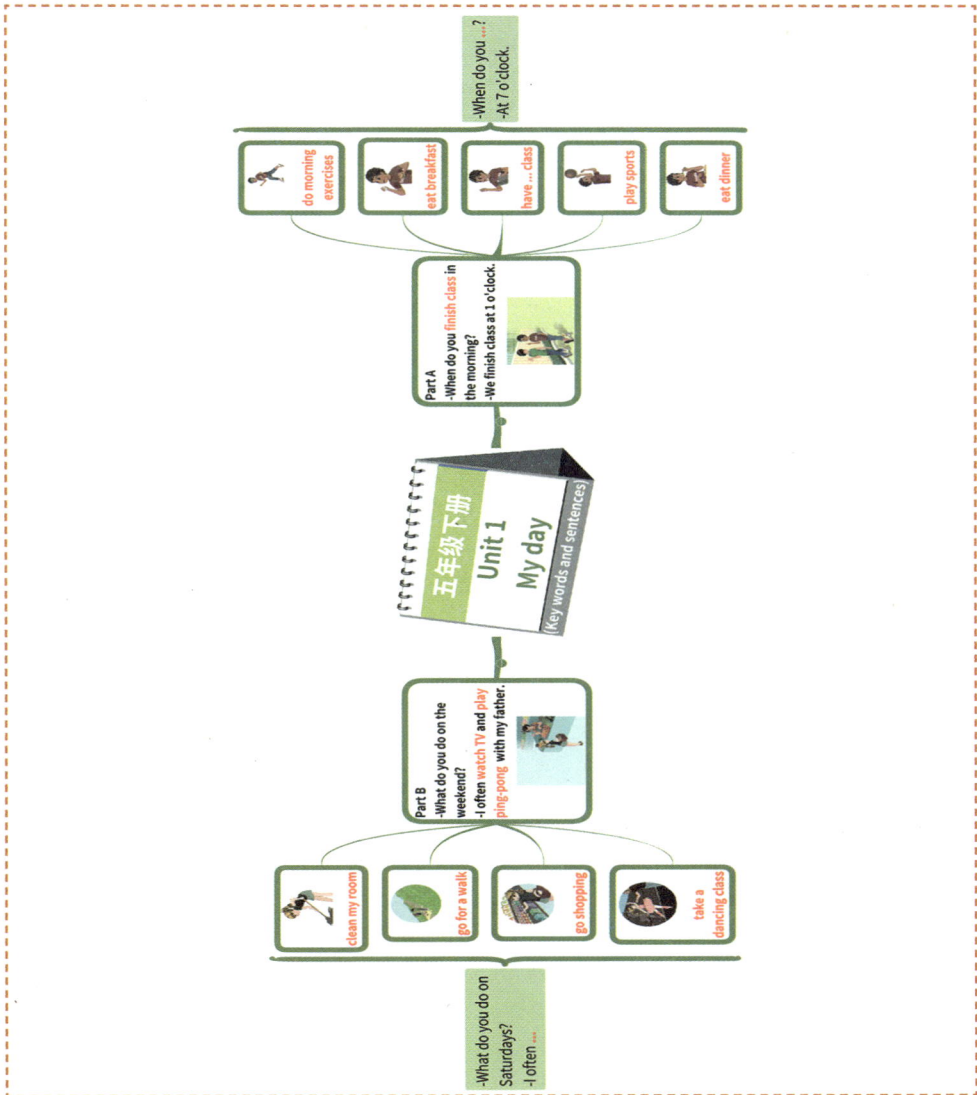

小学英语人教版五年级下册

Unit 1 My day

-When do you ...?
-At 7 o'clock.

do morning exercises

eat breakfast

have ... class

play sports

eat dinner

Part A
-When do you finish class in the morning?
-We finish class at 1 o'clock.

五年级下册
Unit 1
My day
(Key words and sentences)

Part B
-What do you do on the weekend?
-I often watch TV and play ping-pong with my father.

clean my room

go for a walk

go shopping

take a dancing class

-What do you do on Saturdays?
-I often ....

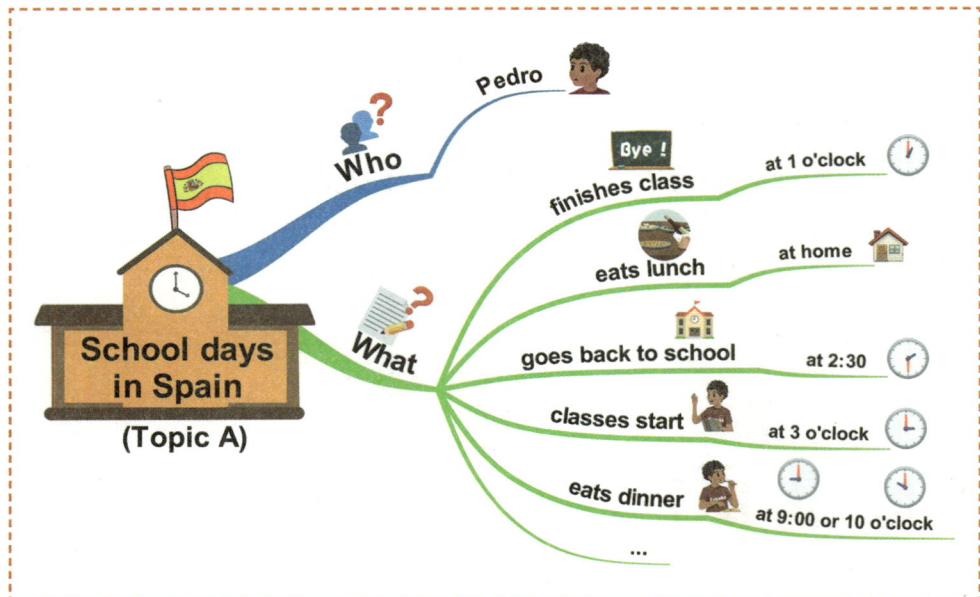

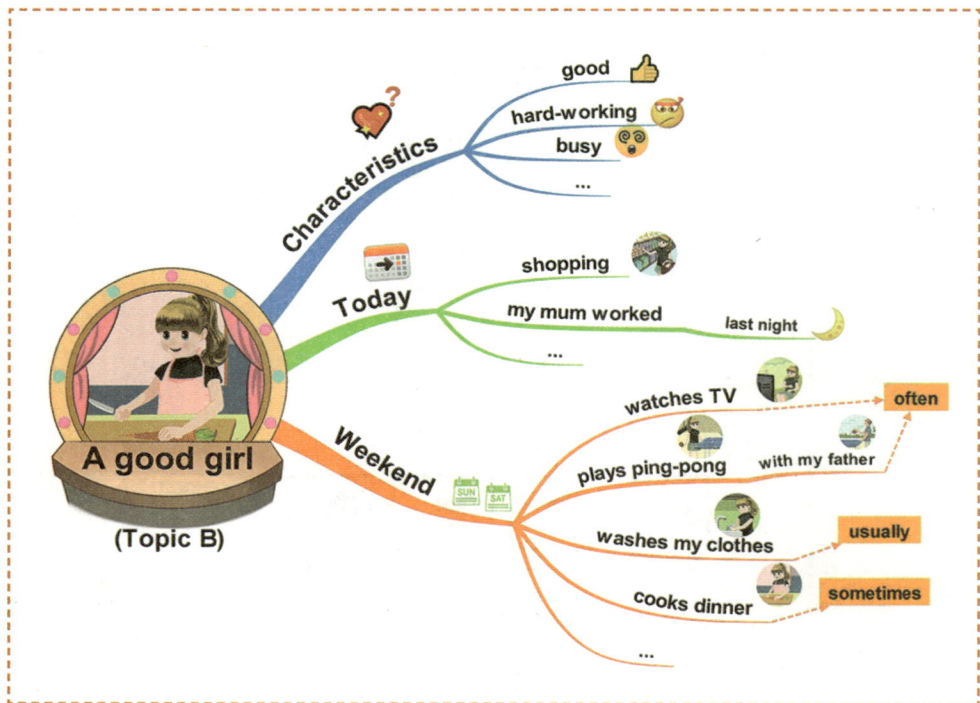

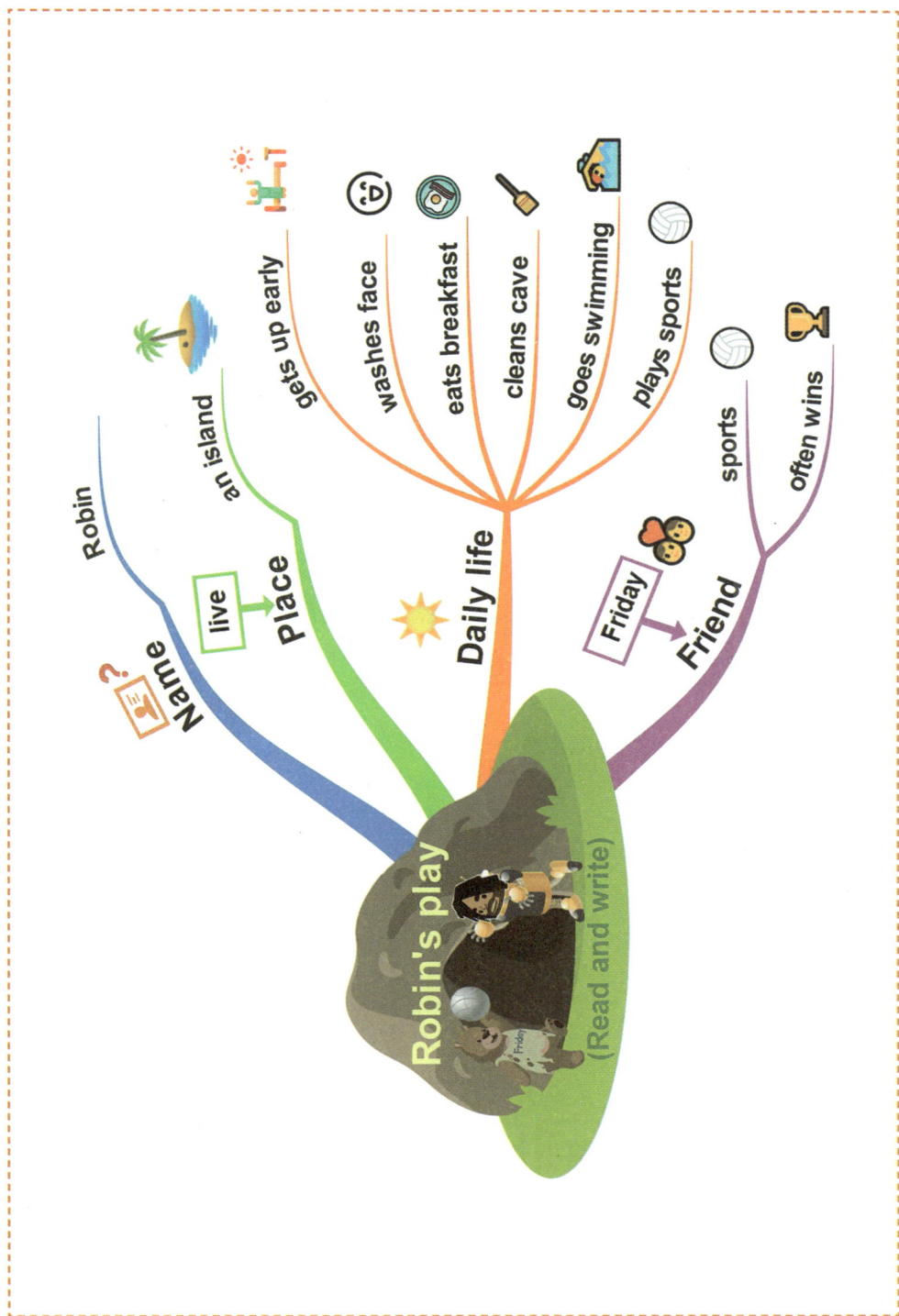

Robin's play
(Read and write)

Name
- Robin

Place — live
- an island

Daily life
- gets up early
- washes face
- eats breakfast
- cleans cave
- goes swimming
- plays sports

Friend — Friday
- sports
- often wins

五年级 下册

Unit 2 My favourite season

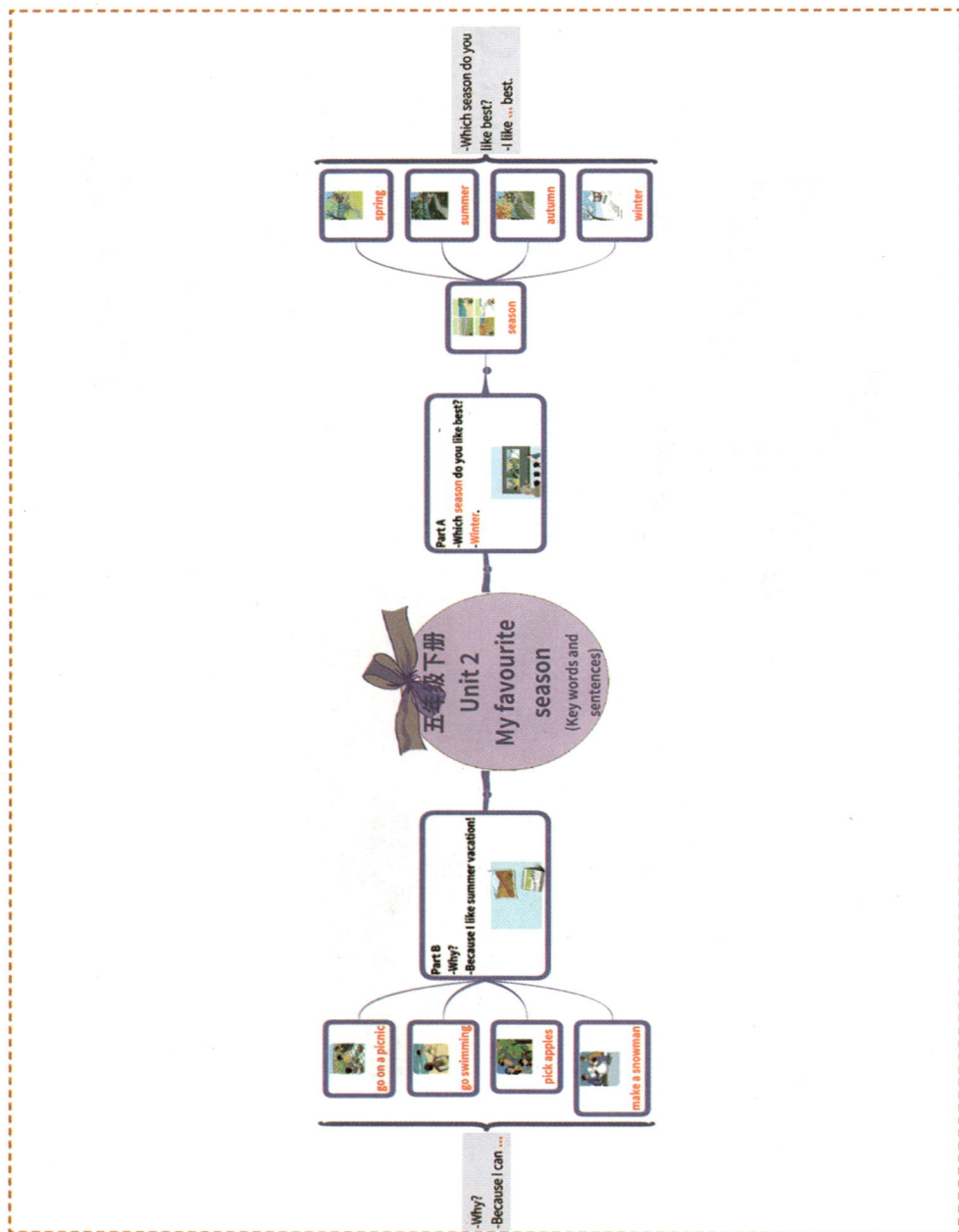

- Which season do you like best?
- I like ... best.

spring summer autumn winter

season

Part A
- Which season do you like best?
- Winter.

五年级下册
Unit 2
My favourite season
(Key words and sentences)

Part B
- Why?
- Because I like summer vacation!

go on a picnic go swimming pick apples make a snowman

- Why?
- Because I can ...

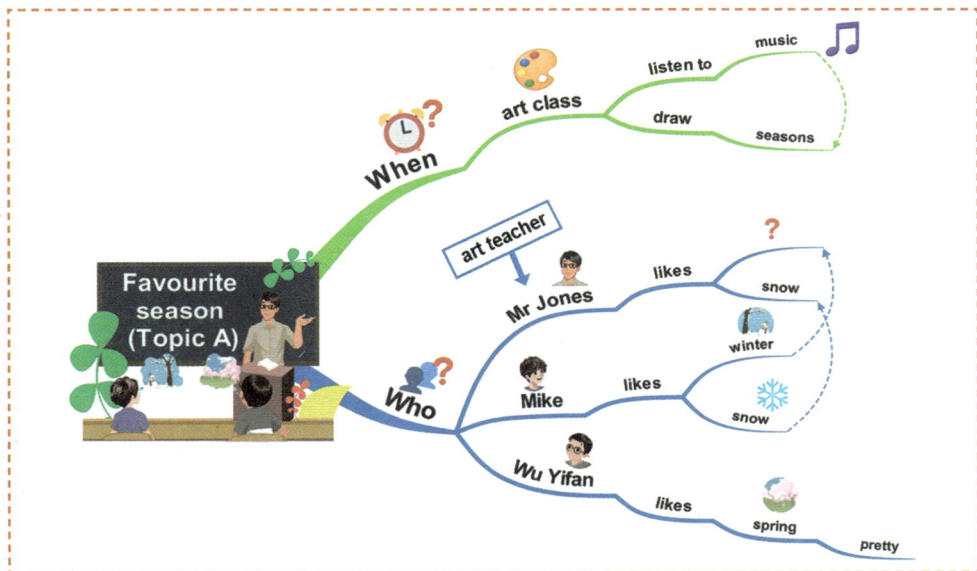

Favourite season (Topic A)

When — art class — listen to — music

draw — seasons

Who — art teacher → Mr Jones — likes — ? — snow — winter

Mike — likes — snow

Wu Yifan — likes — spring — pretty

五年级 下册

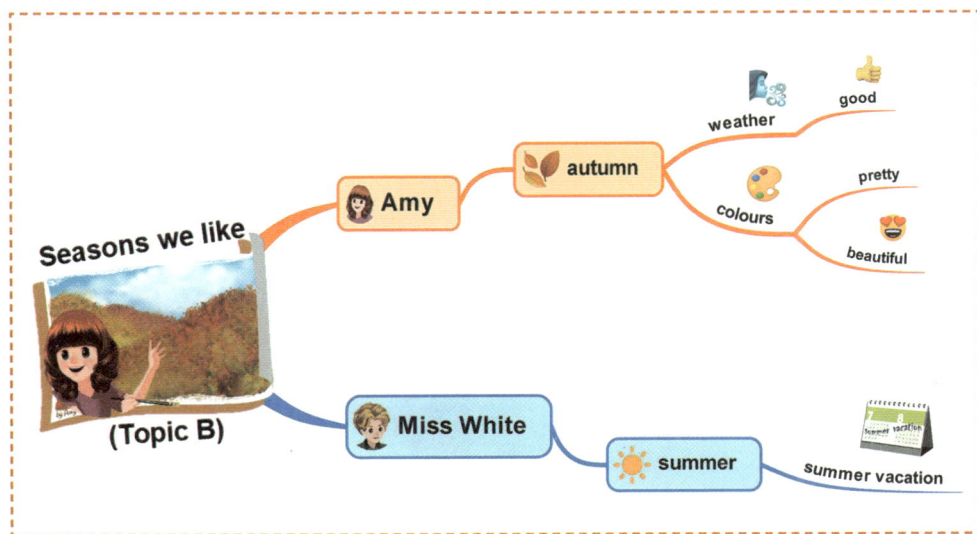

Seasons we like (Topic B)

Amy — autumn — weather — good

colours — pretty — beautiful

Miss White — summer — summer vacation

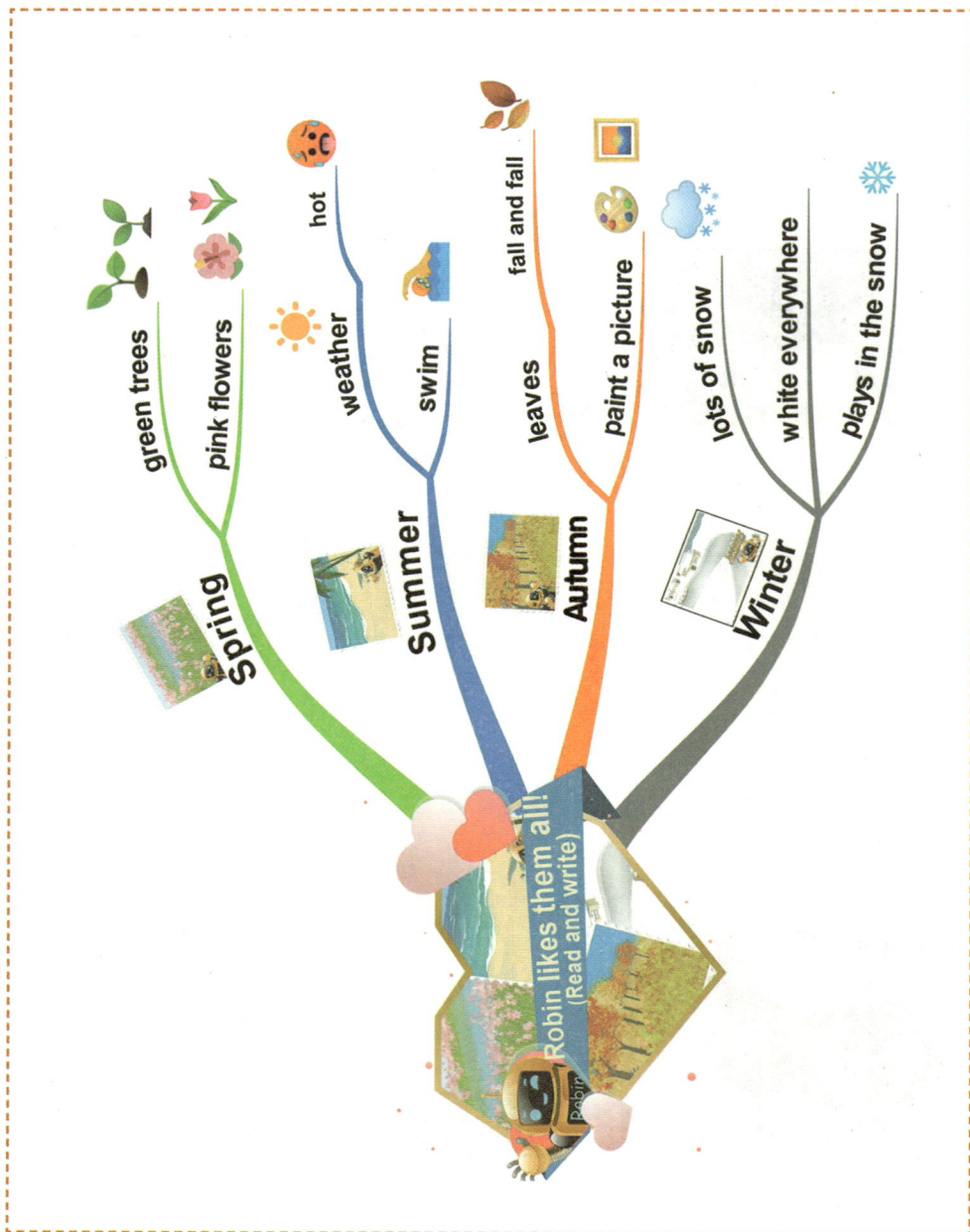

green trees

pink flowers

hot

weather

swim

fall and fall

leaves

paint a picture

lots of snow

white everywhere

plays in the snow

Spring

Summer

Autumn

Winter

Robin likes them all!
(Read and write)

Unit 3 My school calendar

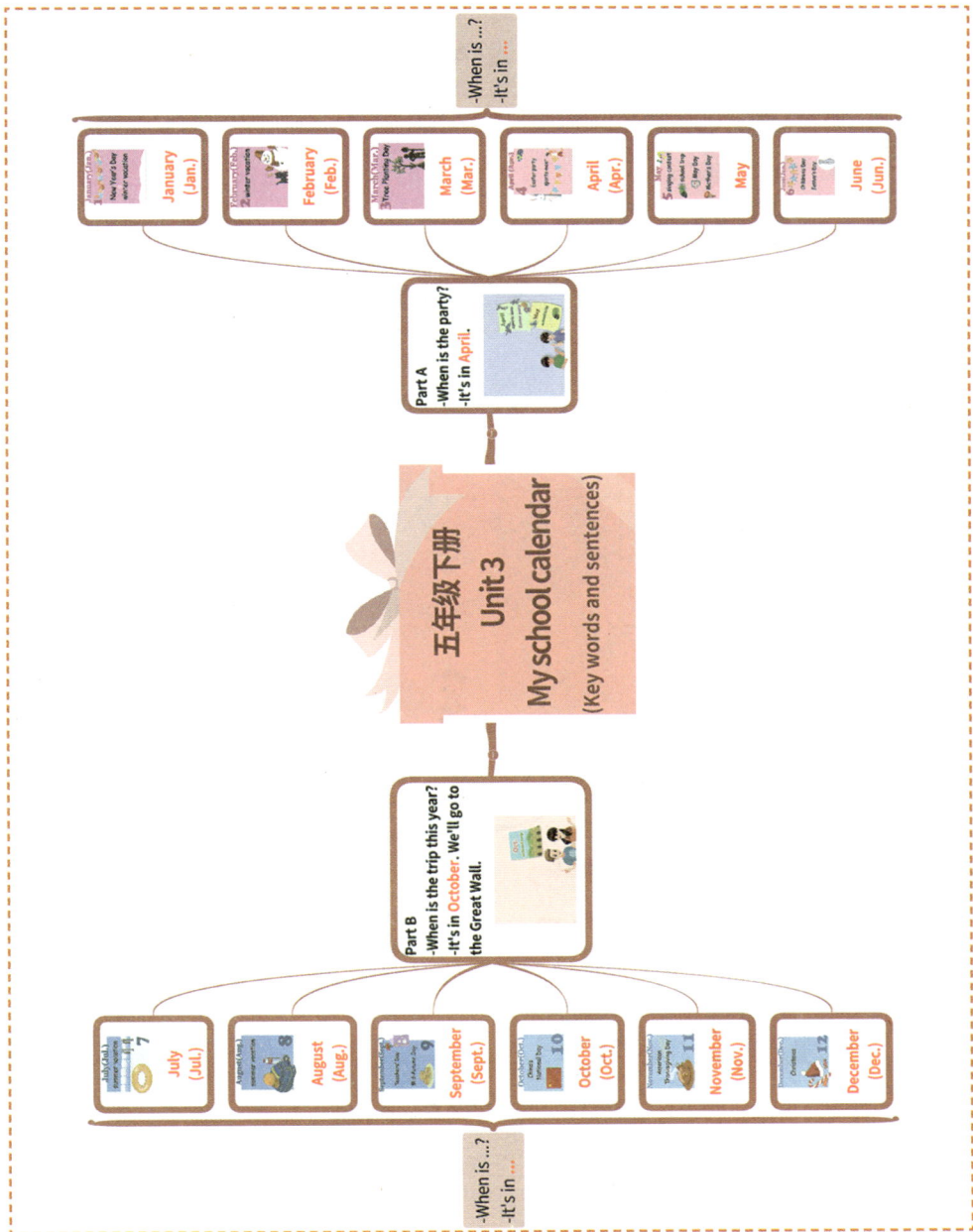

-When is ...?
-It's in ....

January
(Jan.)

New Year's Day
winter vacation

February
(Feb.)

winter vacation

March
(Mar.)

Tree Planting Day

April
(Apr.)

Easter party
sports meet

May
(May.)

singing contest
Bike Day
Mother's Day

June
(Jun.)

Children's Day

Part A
-When is the party?
-It's in April.

五年级下册
Unit 3
My school calendar
(Key words and sentences)

Part B
-When is the trip this year?
-It's in October. We'll go to
the Great Wall.

July
(Jul.)

August
(Aug.)

September
(Sept.)

Teacher's Day
Mid-Autumn Day

October
(Oct.)

China
National Day

November
(Nov.)

International Day
Thanksgiving Day

December
(Dec.)

Christmas

-When is ...?
-It's in ....

五
年
级
下
册

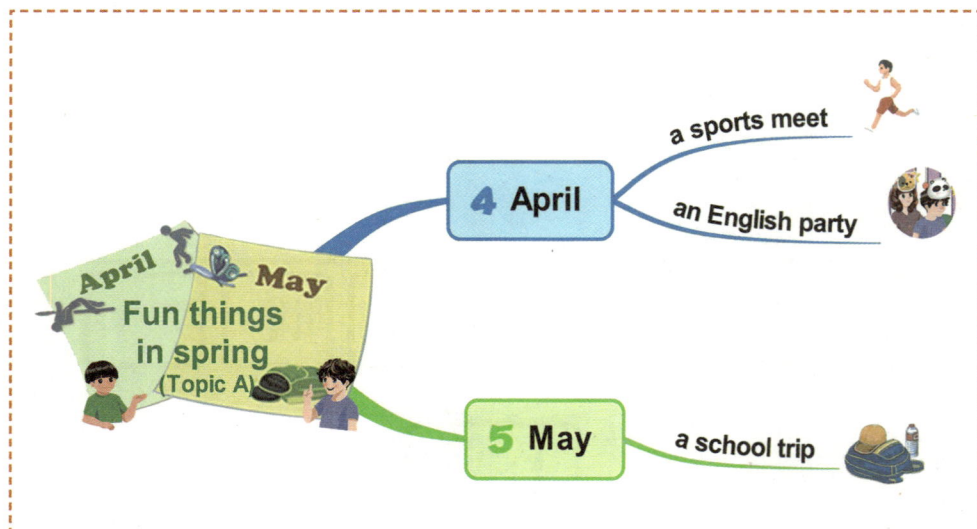

April May
Fun things in spring
(Topic A)

4 April
a sports meet
an English party

5 May
a school trip

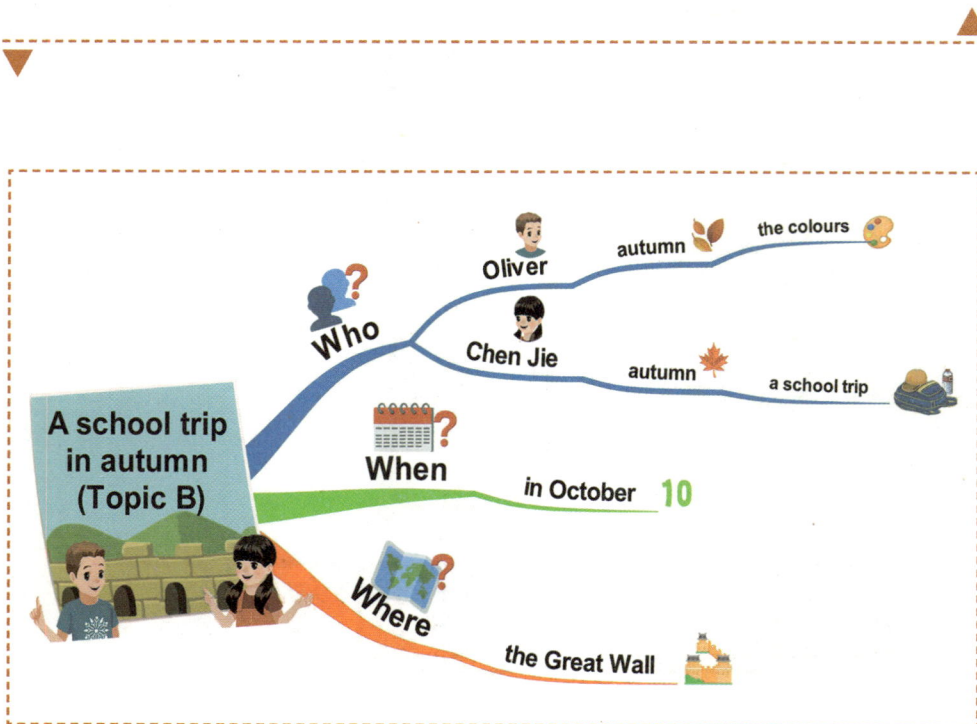

A school trip in autumn
(Topic B)

Who

Oliver — autumn — the colours

Chen Jie — autumn — a school trip

When — in October 10

Where — the Great Wall

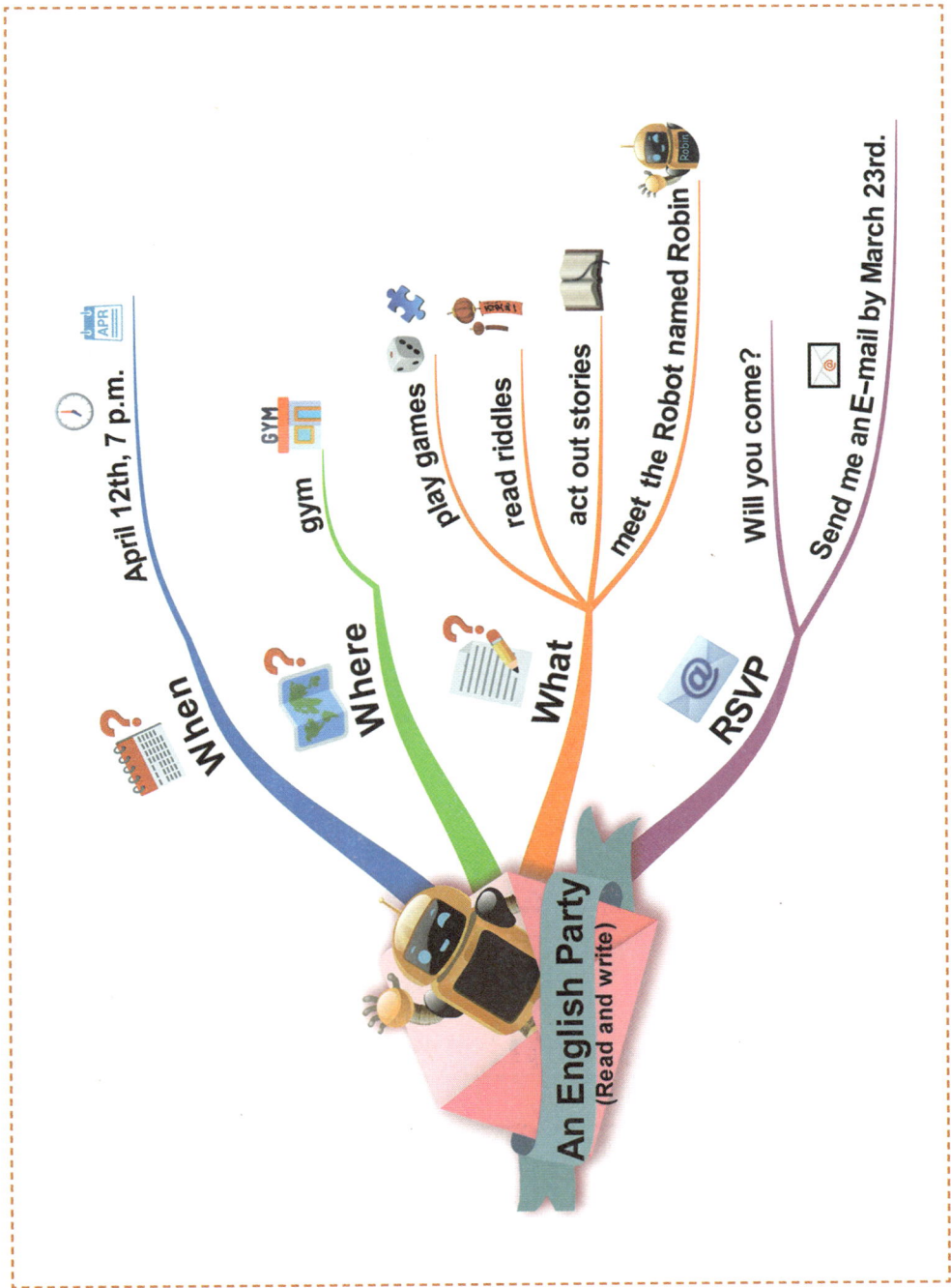

An English Party
(Read and write)

When — April 12th, 7 p.m.

Where — gym

What — play games / read riddles / act out stories / meet the Robot named Robin

RSVP — Will you come? / Send me an E-mail by March 23rd.

五年级 下册

Unit 4 When is the art show?

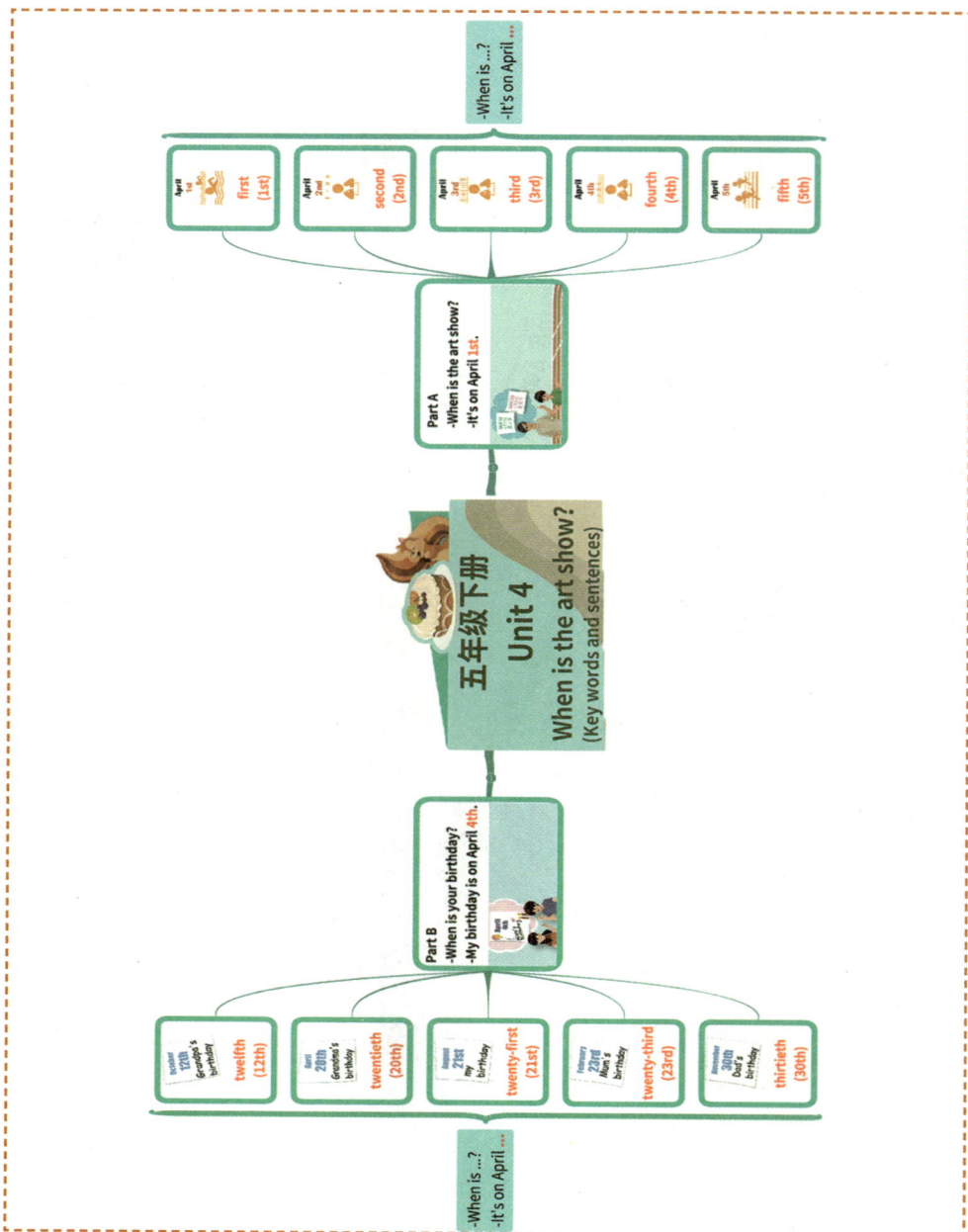

-When is ...?
-It's on April ...

| April 1st first (1st) | April 2nd second (2nd) | April 3rd third (3rd) | April 4th fourth (4th) | April 5th fifth (5th) |

Part A
-When is the art show?
-It's on April 1st.

五年级下册
Unit 4
When is the art show?
(Key words and sentences)

Part B
-When is your birthday?
-My birthday is on April 4th.

| twelfth 12th Grandpa's birthday | twentieth 20th Grandma's birthday | twenty-first 21st my birthday | twenty-third 23rd Mum's birthday | thirtieth 30th Dad's birthday |

-When is ...?
-It's on April ...

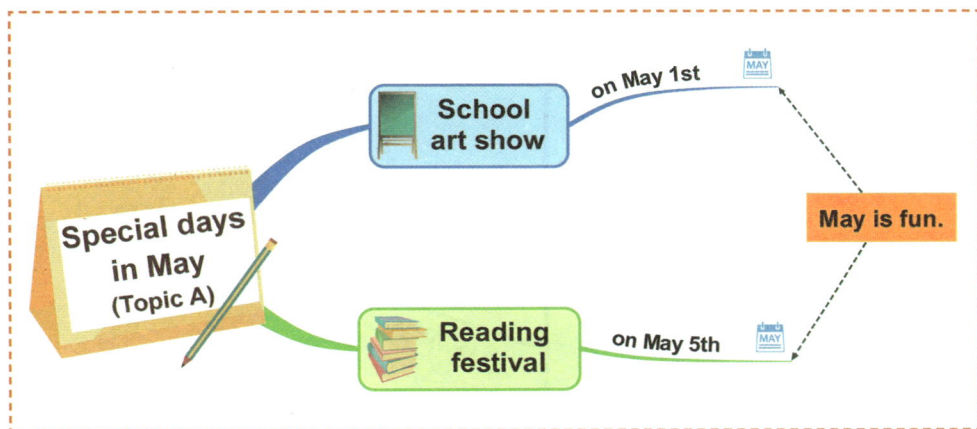

School art show — on May 1st

Special days in May (Topic A)

Reading festival — on May 5th

May is fun.

五年级 下册

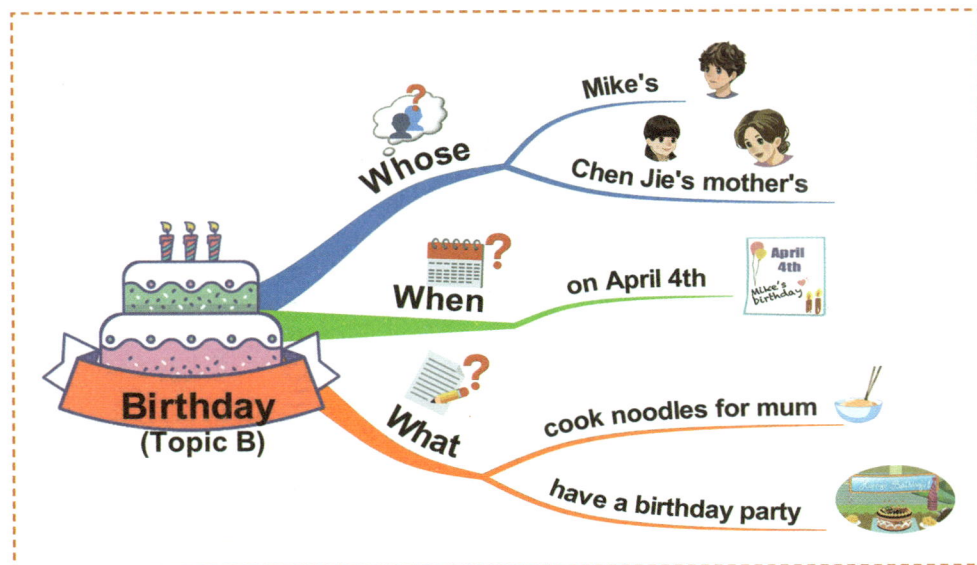

Whose — Mike's / Chen Jie's mother's

When — on April 4th

Birthday (Topic B)

What — cook noodles for mum / have a birthday party

Two new kittens

April 15th
two new kittens
pink
young
can't see

April 26th
eyes are open
blue

April 21st
six days old
make noises
hungry
white fur
cute

May 3rd
walk
play with Robin

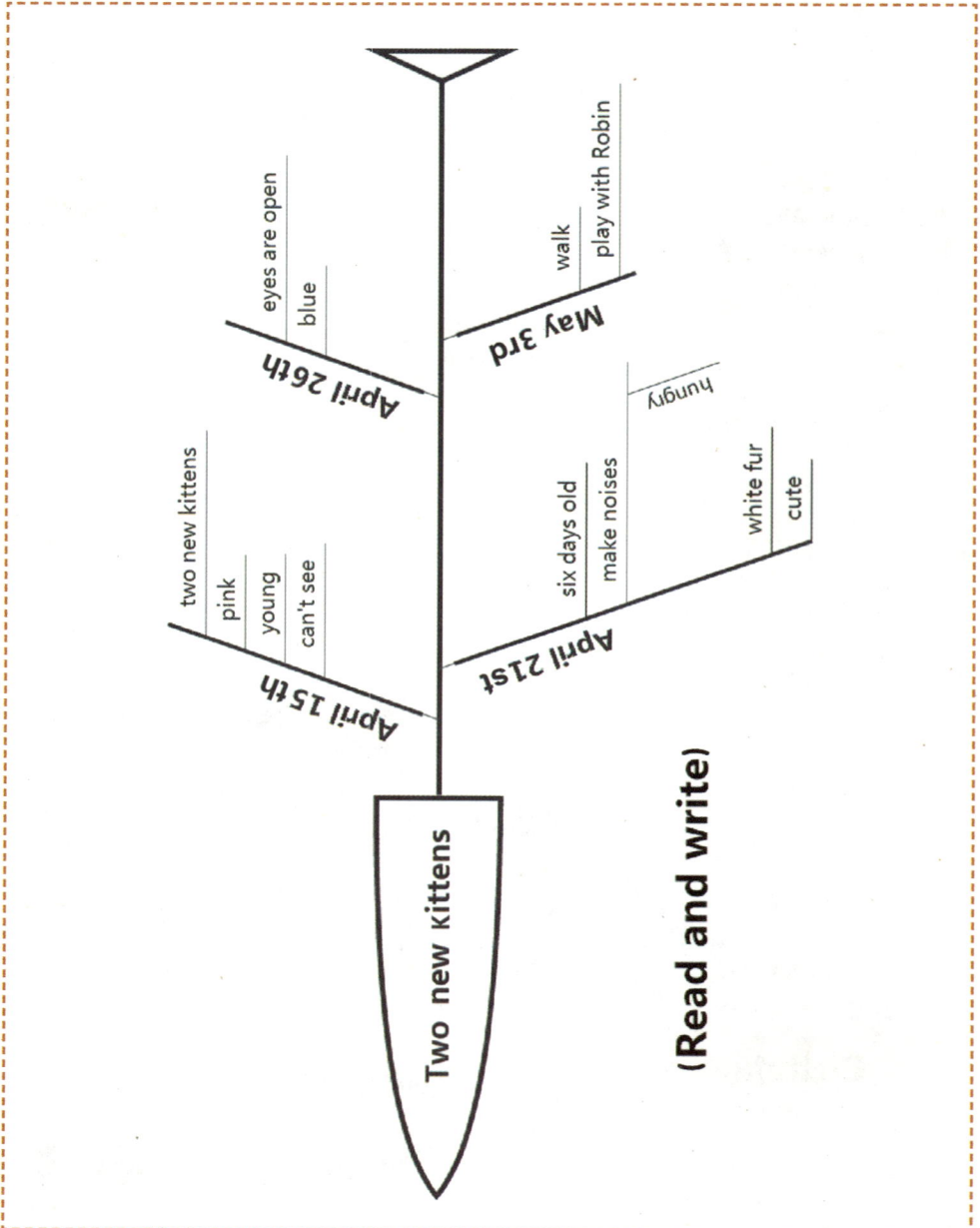

(Read and write)

Unit 5 Whose dog is it?

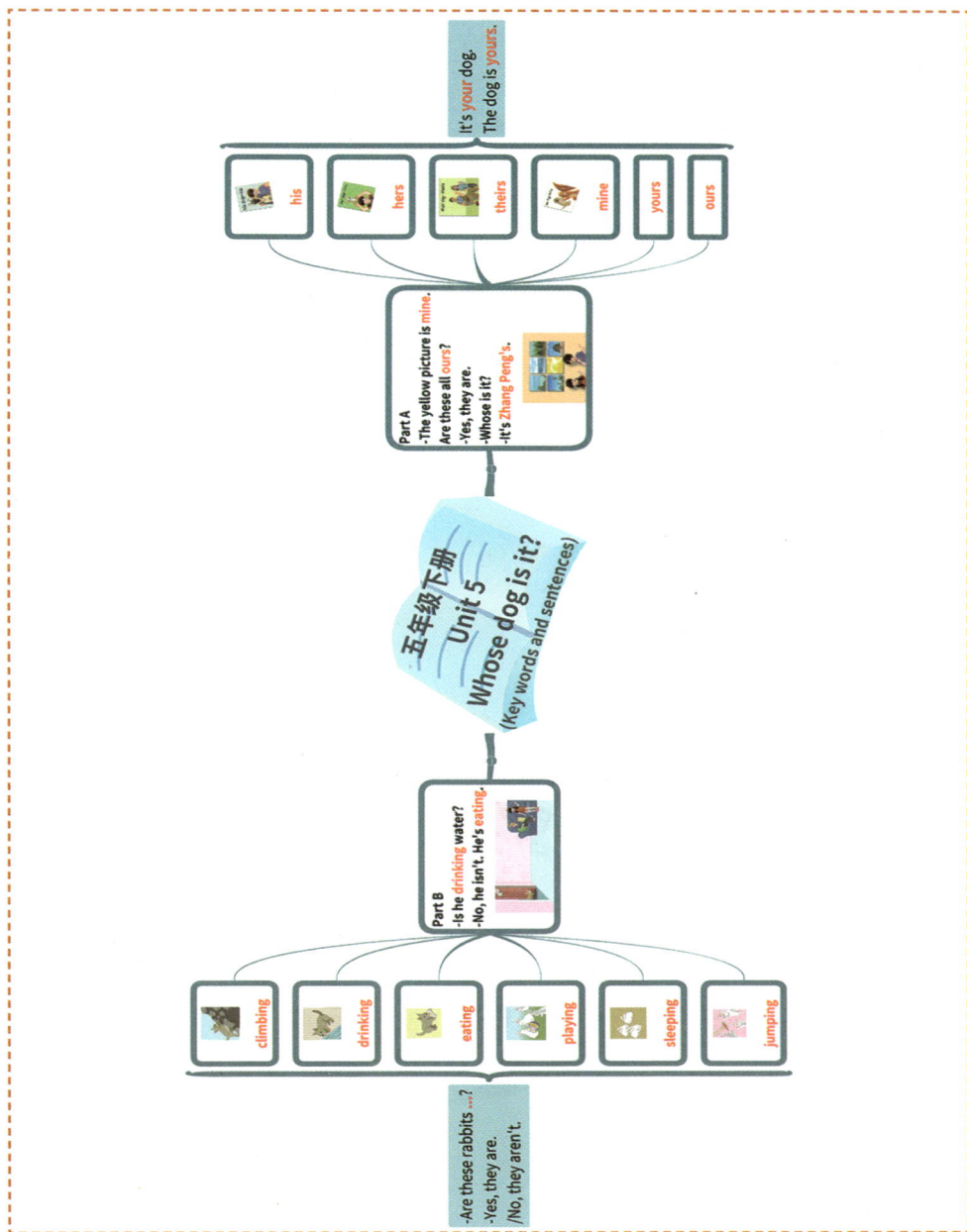

It's your dog.
The dog is yours.

his
hers
theirs
mine
yours
ours

Part A
-The yellow picture is mine.
-Are these all ours?
-Yes, they are.
-Whose is it?
-It's Zhang Peng's.

五年级下册
Unit 5
Whose dog is it?
(Key words and sentences)

Part B
-Is he drinking water?
-No, he isn't. He's eating.

climbing
drinking
eating
playing
sleeping
jumping

-Are these rabbits ...?
-Yes, they are.
/No, they aren't.

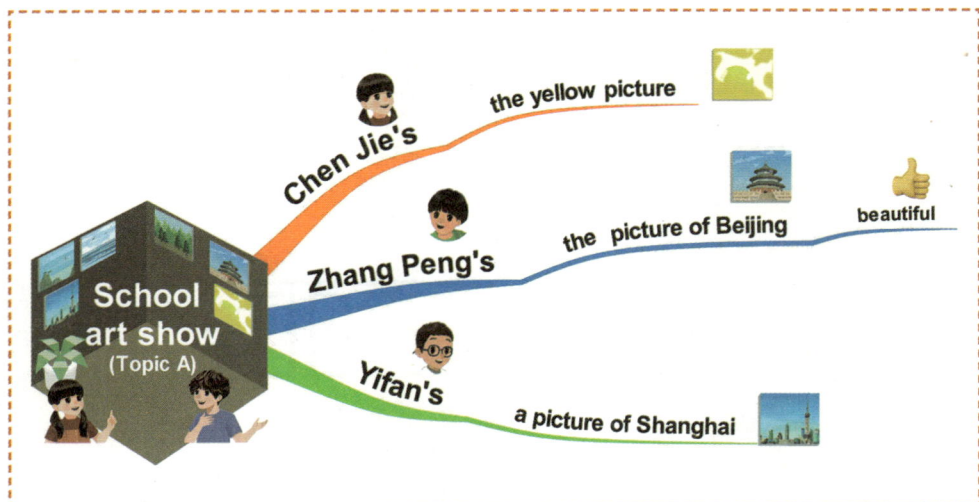

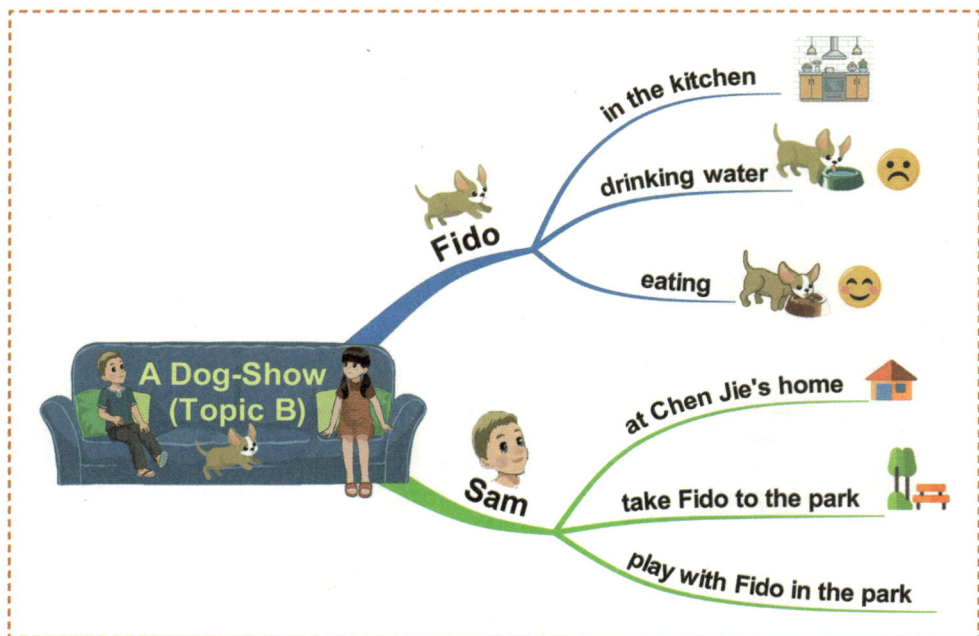

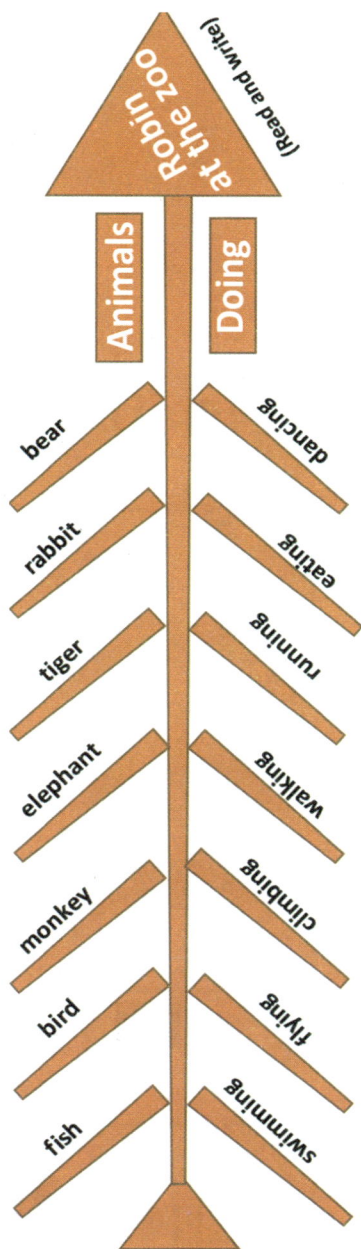

五年级 下册

Unit 6 Work quietly!

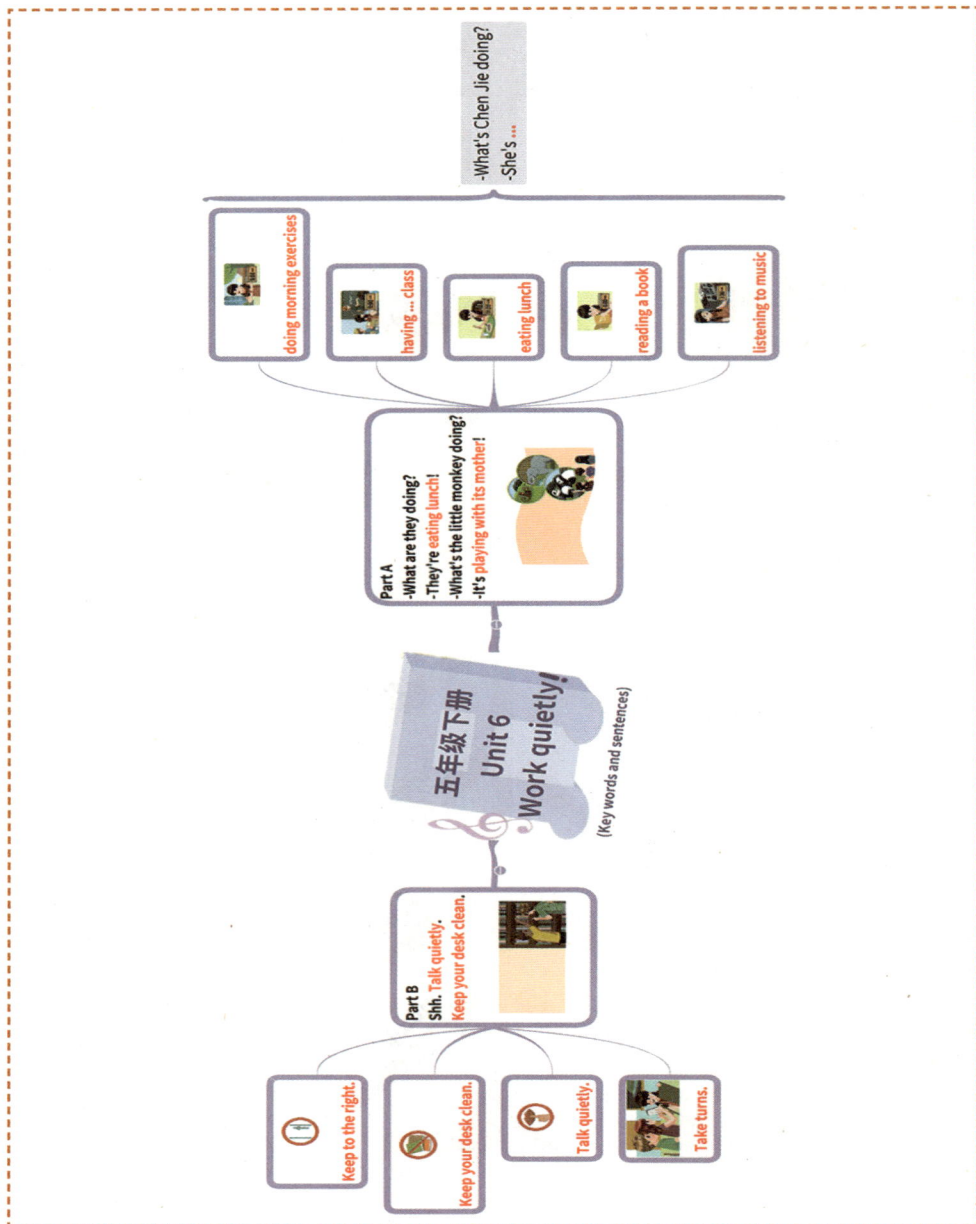

-What's Chen Jie doing?
-She's ...

doing morning exercises

having ... class

eating lunch

reading a book

listening to music

Part A
-What are they doing?
-They're eating lunch!
-What's the little monkey doing?
-It's playing with its mother!

五年级下册
Unit 6
Work quietly!

(Key words and sentences)

Part B
Shh. Talk quietly.
Keep your desk clean.

Keep to the right.

Keep your desk clean.

Talk quietly.

Take turns.

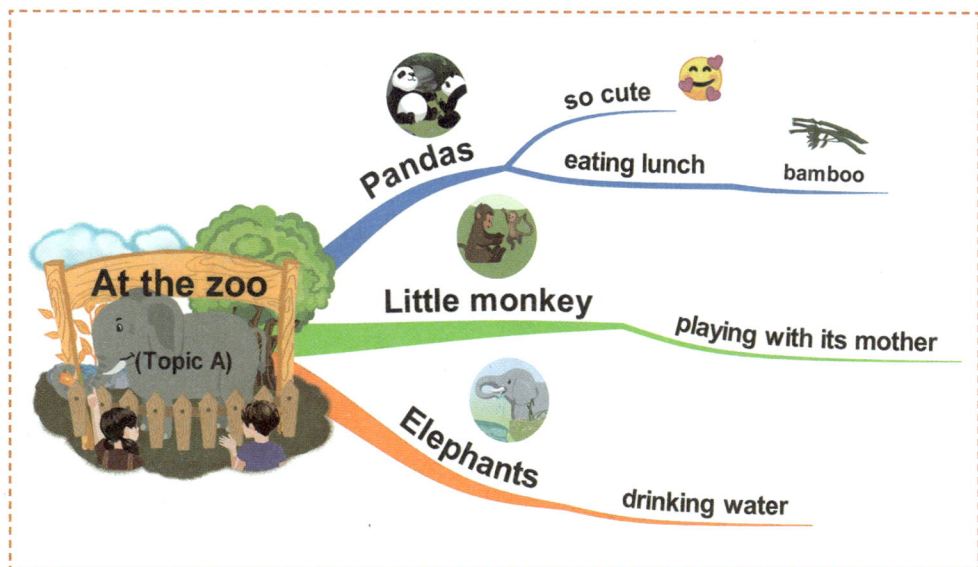

At the zoo (Topic A)

Pandas — so cute — eating lunch — bamboo

Little monkey — playing with its mother

Elephants — drinking water

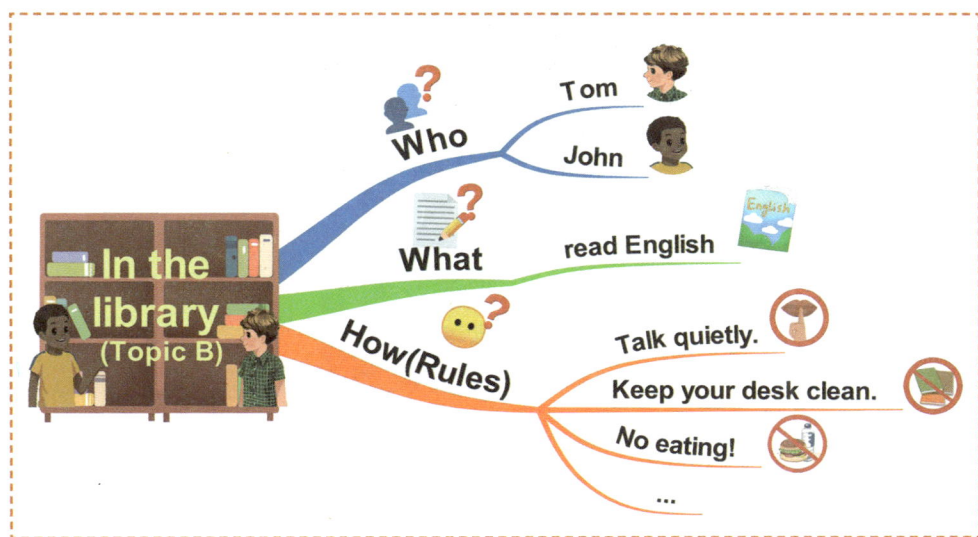

In the library (Topic B)

Who — Tom — John

What — read English

How (Rules) — Talk quietly. — Keep your desk clean. — No eating! — ...

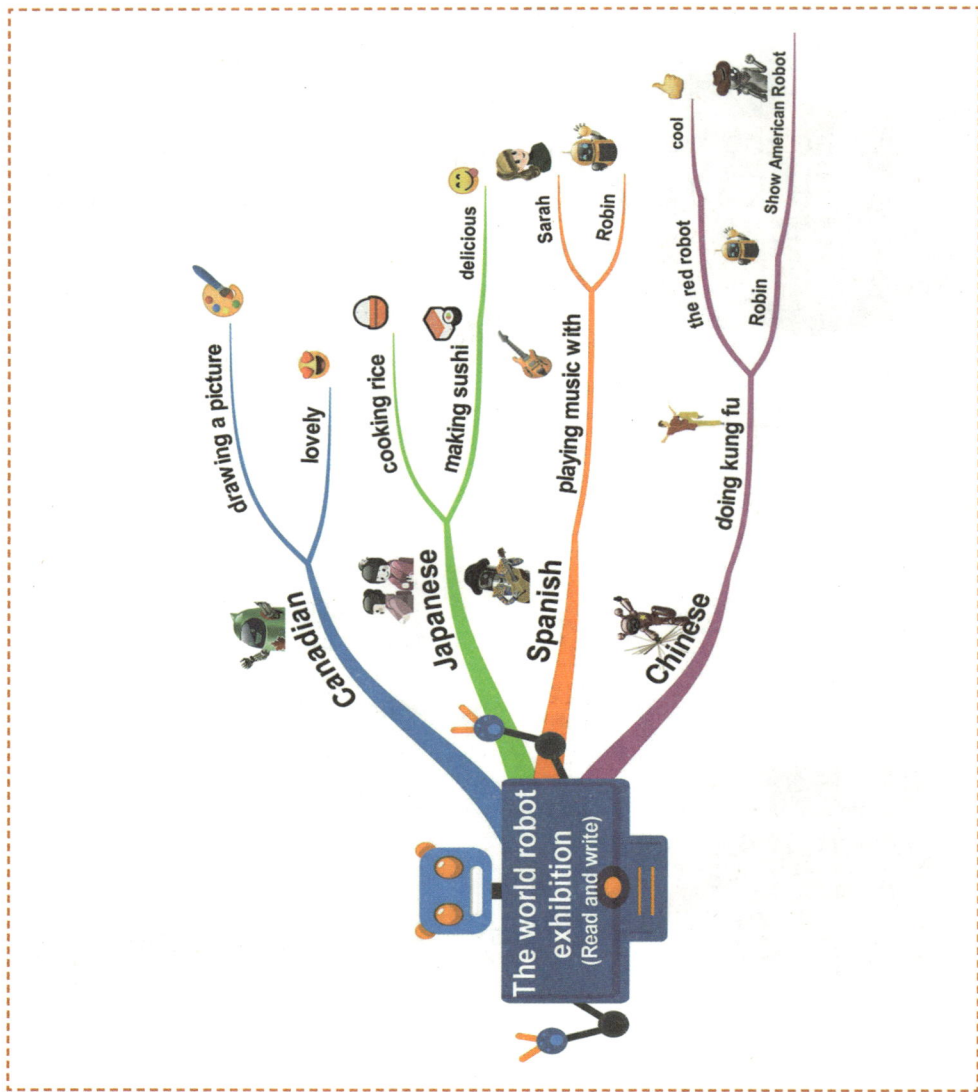

The world robot exhibition (Read and write)

- Canadian
  - drawing a picture
  - lovely
- Japanese
  - cooking rice
  - making sushi
  - delicious
- Spanish
  - playing music with
  - Sarah
  - Robin
- Chinese
  - doing kung fu
  - the red robot
  - cool
  - Robin
  - Show American Robot

小学英语人教版六年级上册

Unit 1 How can I get there?

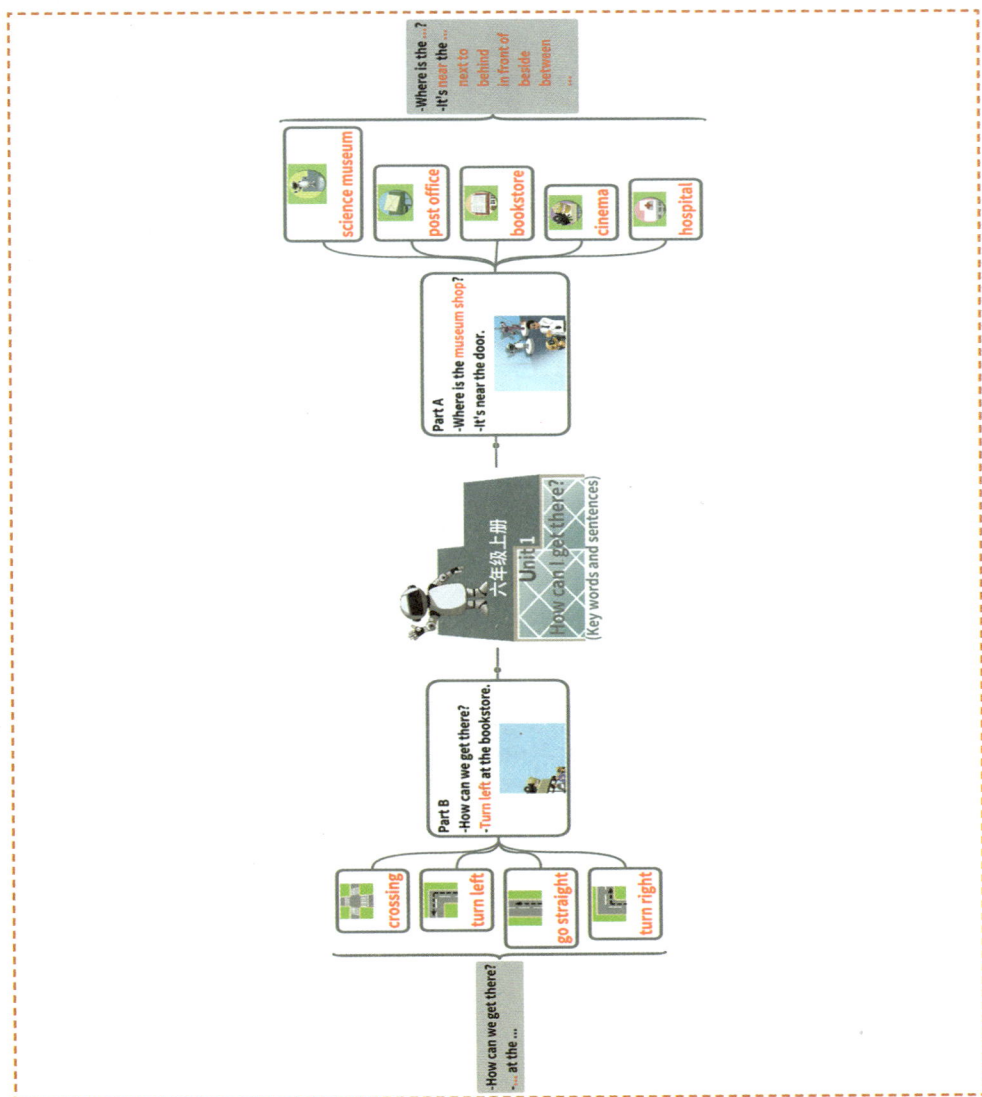

- Where is the ...?
- It's near the ...
  next to
  behind
  in front of
  beside
  between
  ...

science museum
post office
bookstore
cinema
hospital

Part A
- Where is the museum shop?
- It's near the door.

六年级上册
Unit 1
How can I get there?
(Key words and sentences)

Part B
- How can we get there?
- Turn left at the bookstore.

crossing
turn left
go straight
turn right

- How can we get there?
- ... at the ...

六年级 上册

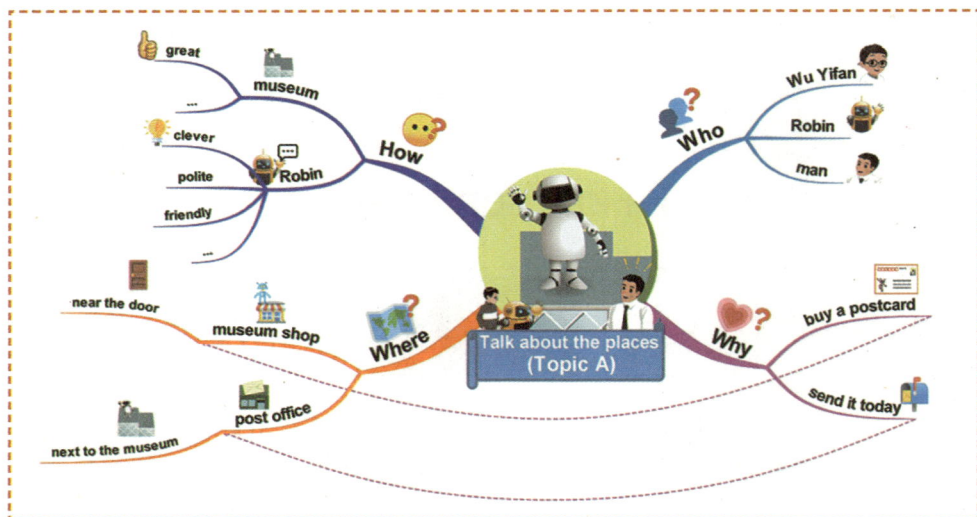

Topic A

great — museum
clever — polite — friendly — Robin
How
Who — Wu Yifan / Robin / man
Talk about the places (Topic A)
near the door — museum shop — Where
next to the museum — post office
Why — buy a postcard / send it today

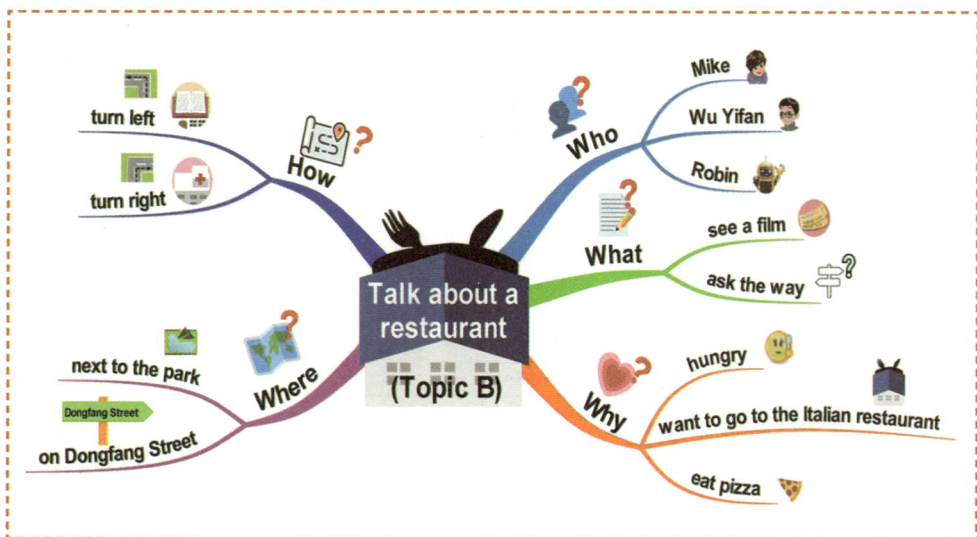

turn left — turn right — How
Who — Mike / Wu Yifan / Robin
What — see a film / ask the way
Talk about a restaurant (Topic B)
next to the park — on Dongfang Street — Where
Dongfang Street
Why — hungry / want to go to the Italian restaurant / eat pizza

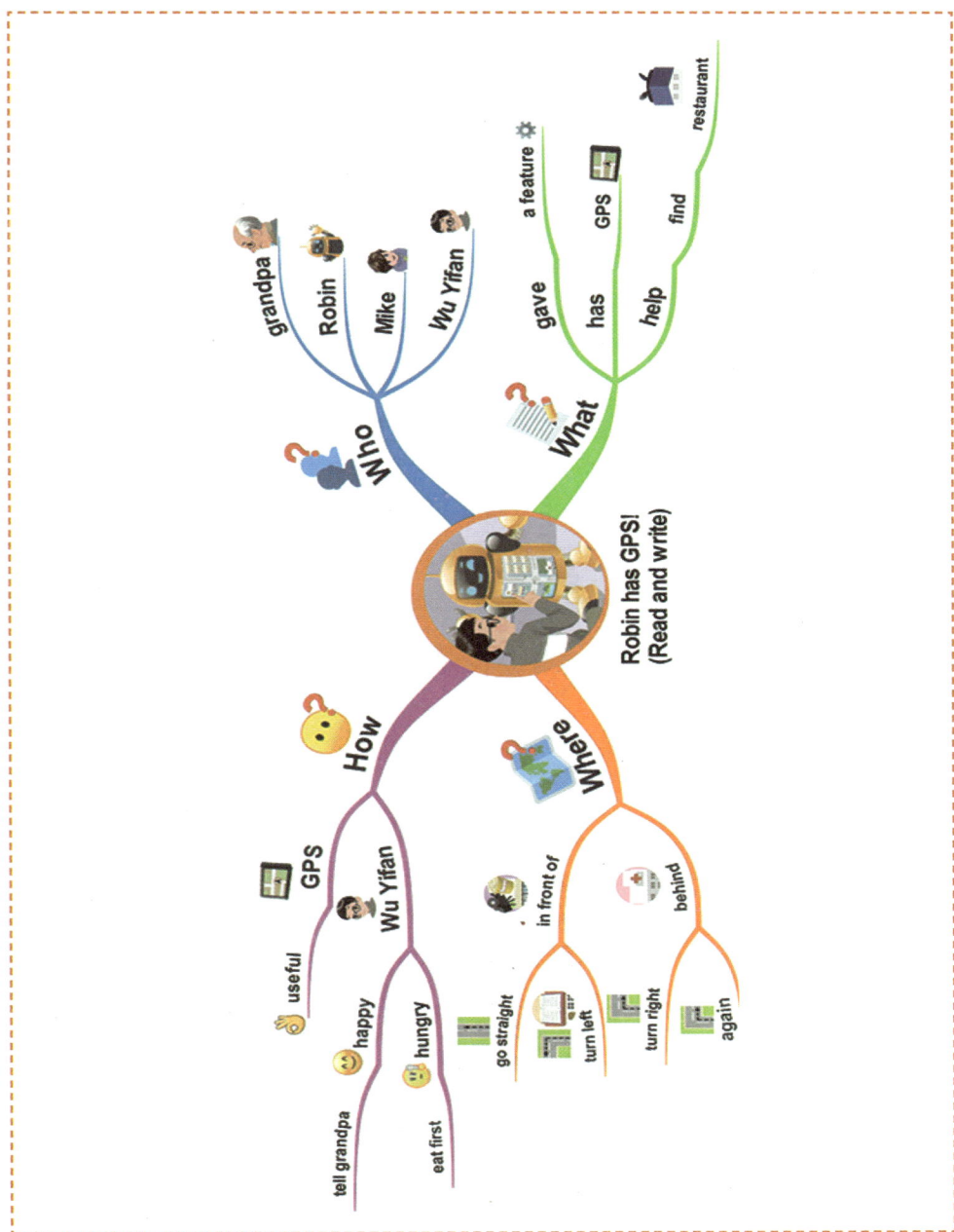

Robin has GPS!
(Read and write)

Who
- grandpa
- Robin
- Mike
- Wu Yifan

What
- gave
- has — GPS
- help — find — restaurant
  - a feature

How
- GPS — useful
- Wu Yifan
  - happy — tell grandpa
  - hungry — eat first

Where
- in front of
  - go straight
  - turn left
- behind
  - turn right
  - again

六年级 上册

Unit 2 Ways to go to school

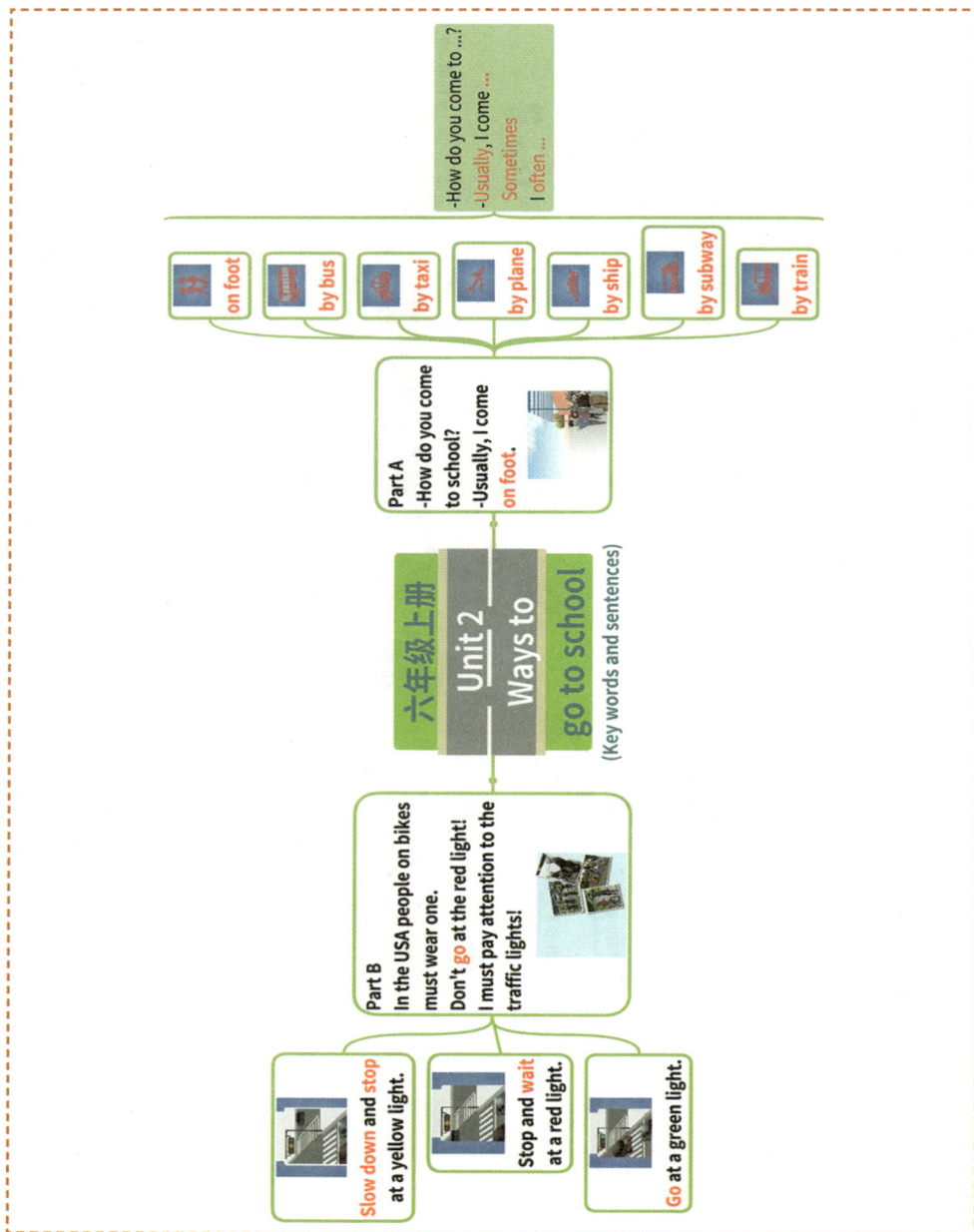

-How do you come to ...?
-Usually, I come ...
Sometimes I often ...

on foot

by bus

by taxi

by plane

by ship

by subway

by train

Part A
-How do you come to school?
-Usually, I come on foot.

六年级上册
Unit 2
Ways to go to school
(Key words and sentences)

Part B
In the USA people on bikes must wear one.
Don't go at the red light!
I must pay attention to the traffic lights!

Slow down and stop at a yellow light.

Stop and wait at a red light.

Go at a green light.

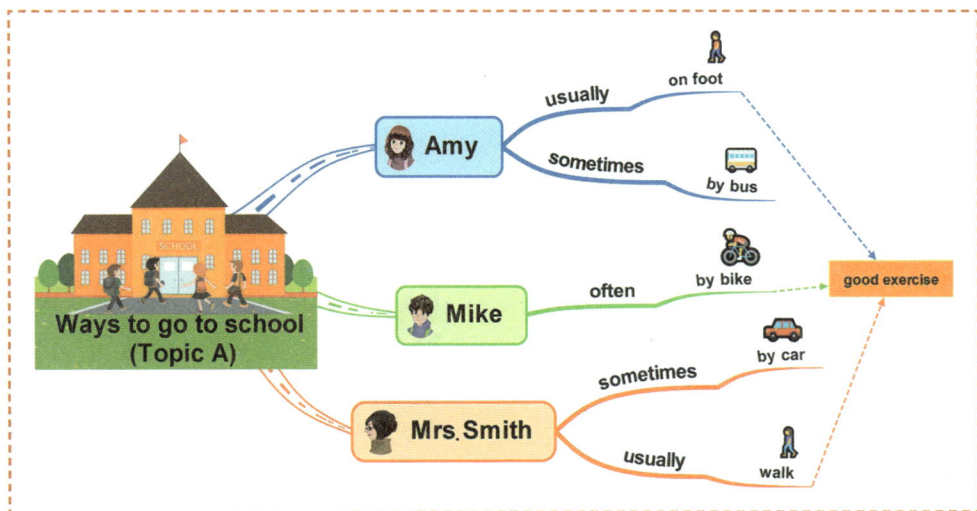

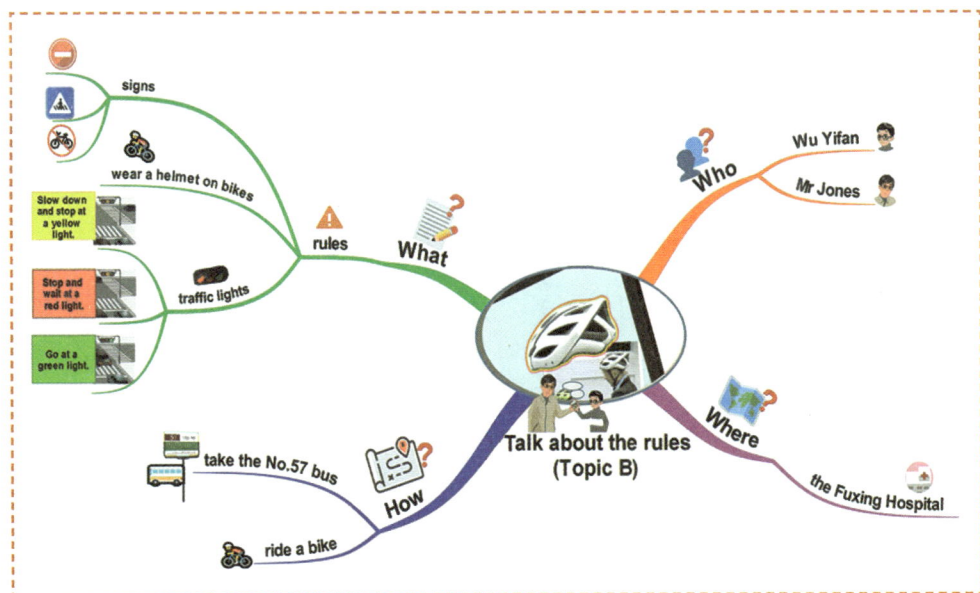

六年级 上册

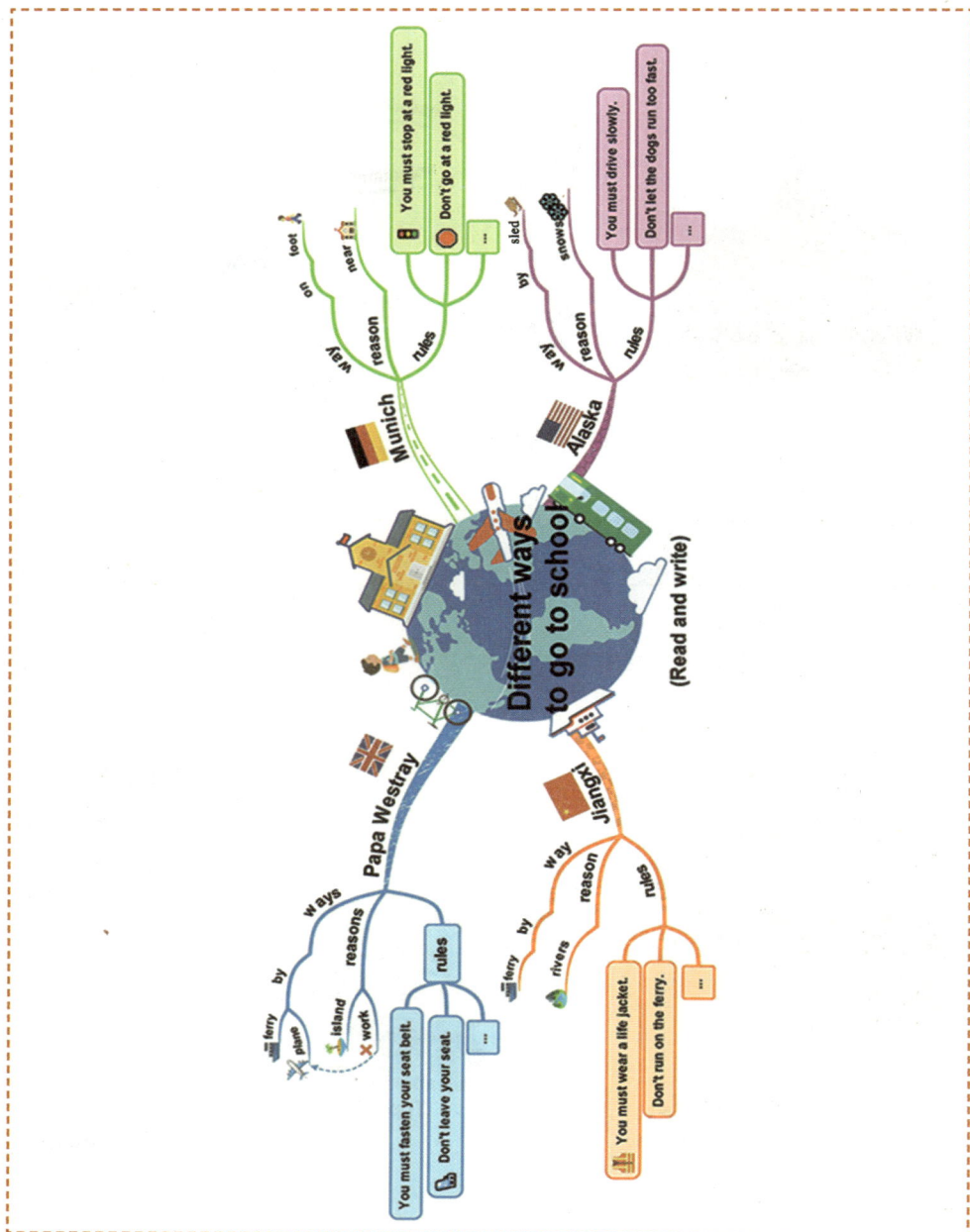

Different ways
to go to school
(Read and write)

Munich
way — on foot
reason — near
rules — You must stop at a red light.
Don't go at a red light.
...

Alaska
way — by sled
reason — snows
rules — You must drive slowly.
Don't let the dogs run too fast.
...

Papa Westray
ways — by ferry, plane
reasons — island, work
rules — You must fasten your seat belt.
Don't leave your seat.
...

Jiangxi
way — by ferry
reason — rivers
rules — You must wear a life jacket.
Don't run on the ferry.
...

Unit 3 My weekend plan

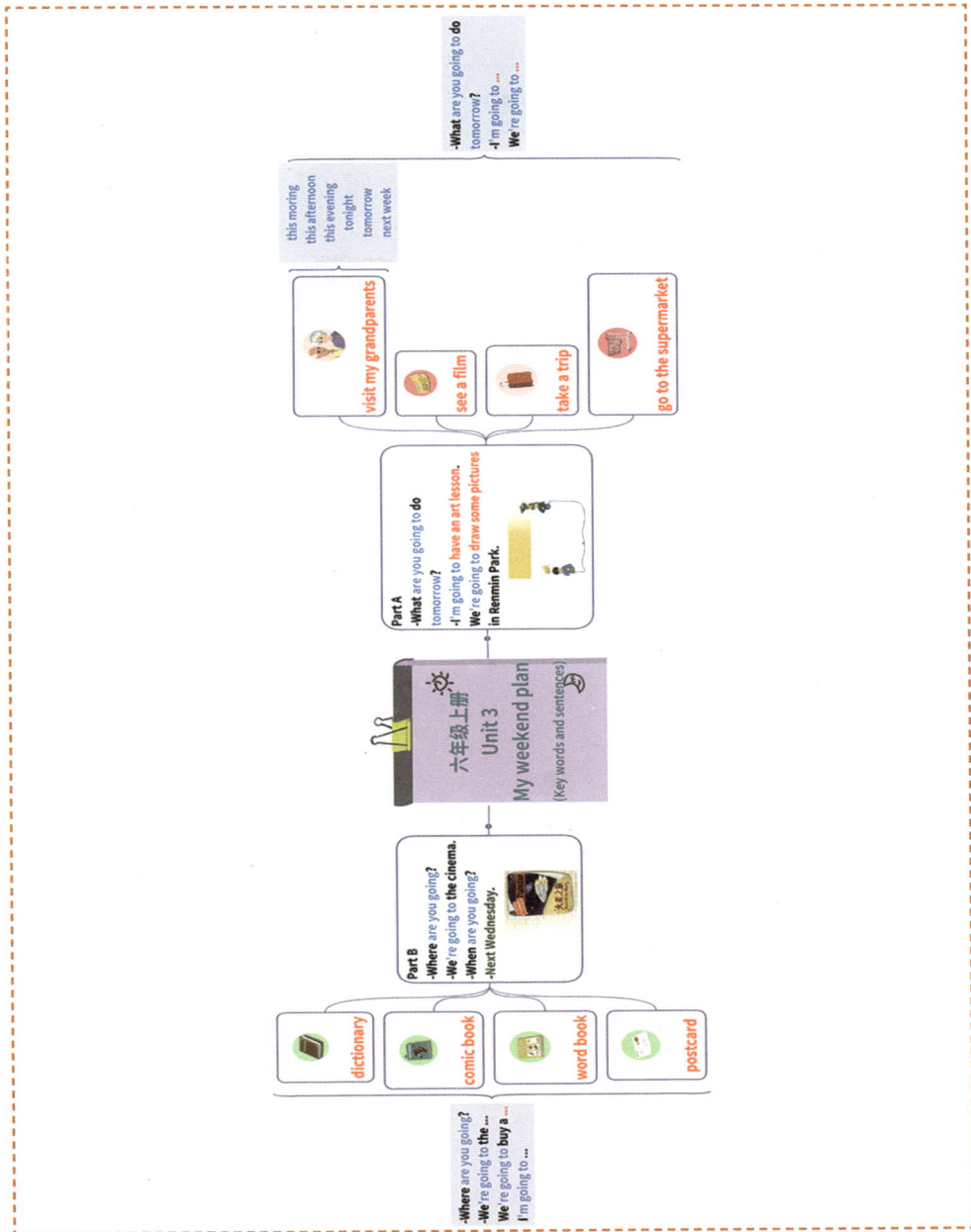

-**What are you going to do tomorrow?**
-**I'm going to …**
We're going to …

this moring
this afternoon
this evening
tonight
tomorrow
next week

visit my grandparents

see a film

take a trip

go to the supermarket

Part A
-**What are you going to do tomorrow?**
-**I'm going to have an art lesson.**
We're going to draw some pictures in Renmin Park.

六年级 上册
Unit 3
My weekend plan
(Keywords and sentences)

Part B
-**Where are you going?**
-**We're going to the cinema.**
-**When are you going?**
-**Next Wednesday.**

dictionary

comic book

word book

postcard

-**Where are you going?**
-**We're going to the …**
-**We're going to buy a …**
-**I'm going to …**

六年级 上册

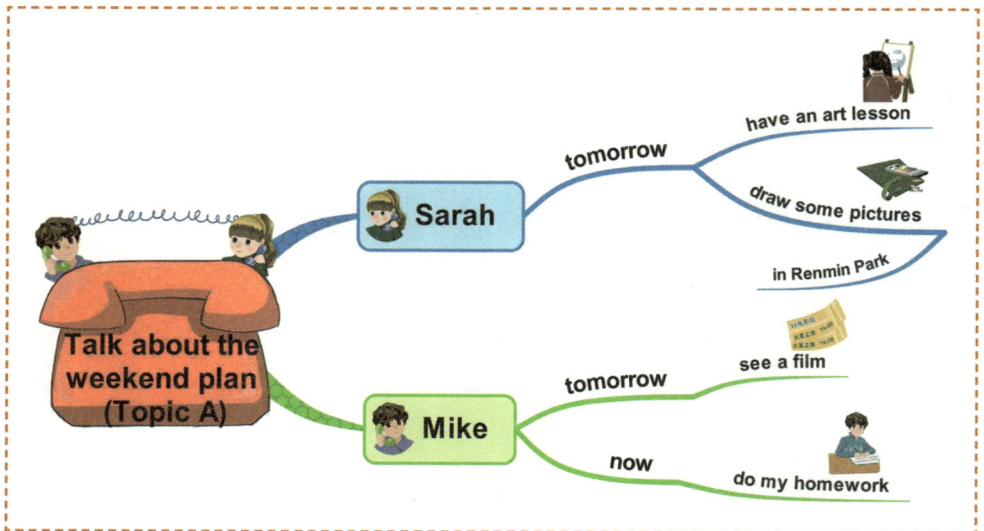

Talk about the weekend plan (Topic A)

Sarah — tomorrow — have an art lesson
draw some pictures
in Renmin Park

Mike — tomorrow — see a film
now — do my homework

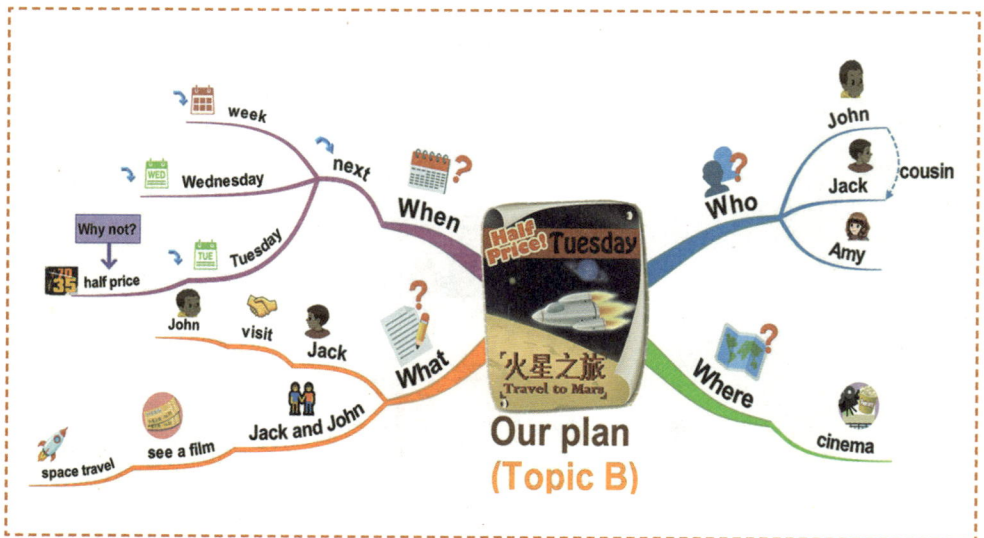

When — next — week
Wednesday
Tuesday — half price — Why not?

What — John — visit — Jack
Jack and John — see a film — space travel

Our plan (Topic B)
Half Price! Tuesday
火星之旅 Travel to Mars

Who — John
Jack — cousin
Amy

Where — cinema

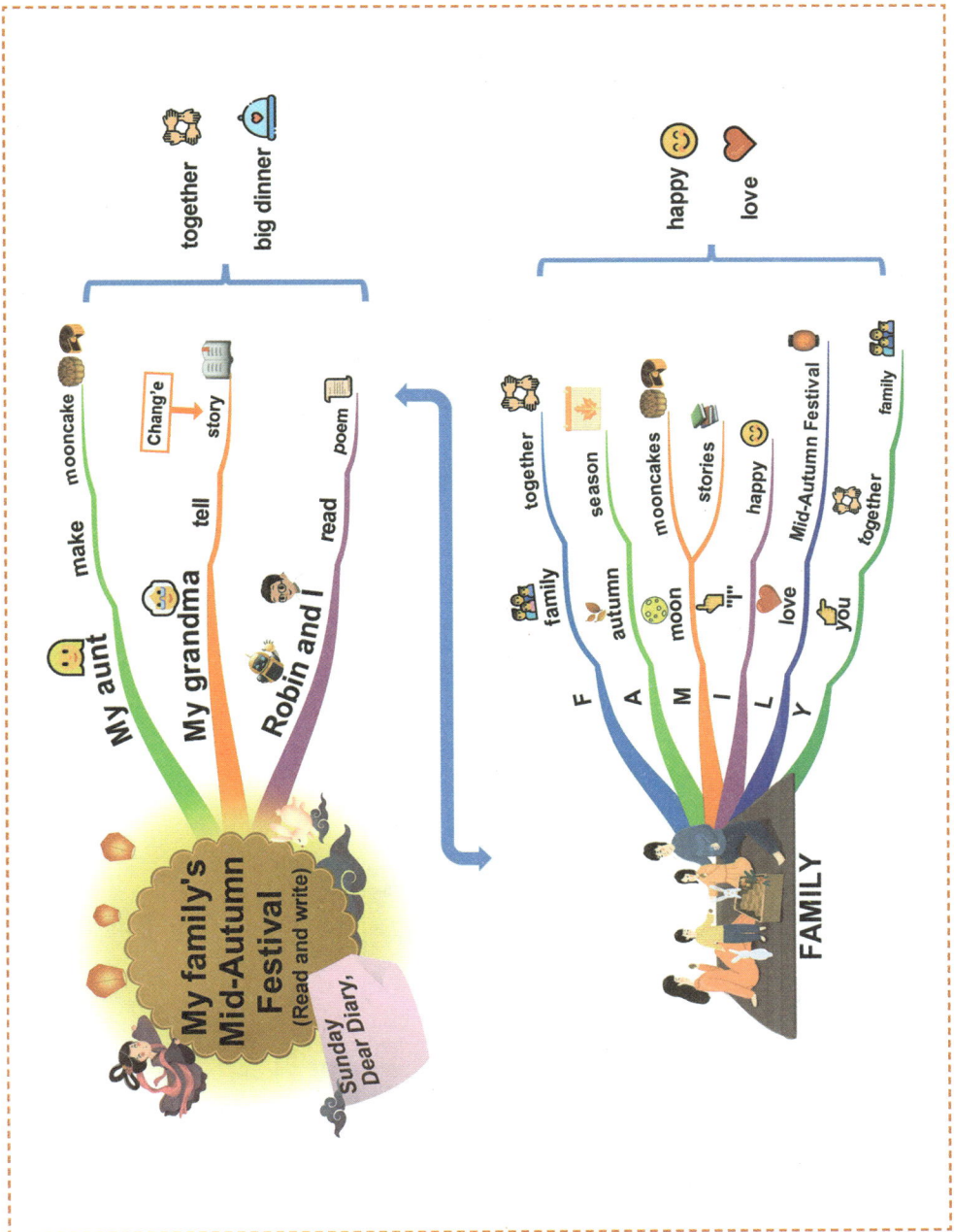

together
big dinner

happy
love

mooncake
make
My aunt

Chang'e → story
tell
My grandma

poem
read
Robin and I

My family's
Mid-Autumn
Festival
(Read and write)

Sunday,
Dear Diary,

together
family
F

season
autumn
A

mooncakes
moon
M

stories
""
I

happy
love
L

Mid-Autumn Festival
you
Y

together
family

FAMILY

六年级 上册

Unit 4 I have a pen pal

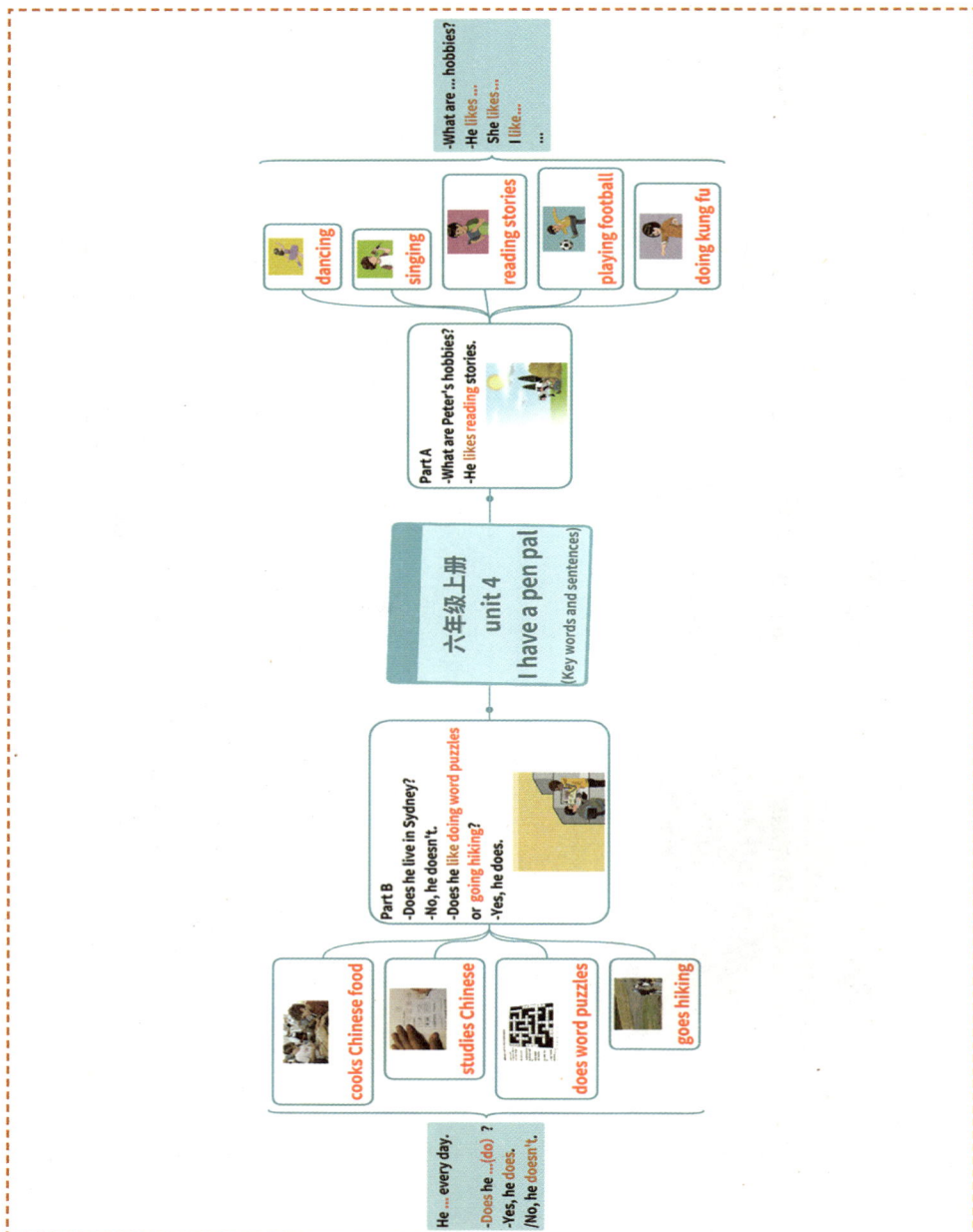

六年级上册 unit 4 I have a pen pal (Key words and sentences)

Part A
-What are Peter's hobbies?
-He likes reading stories.

- dancing
- singing
- reading stories
- playing football
- doing kung fu

-What are ... hobbies?
-He likes ...
She likes ...
I like ...
...

Part B
-Does he live in Sydney?
-No, he doesn't.
-Does he like doing word puzzles or going hiking?
-Yes, he does.

- cooks Chinese food
- studies Chinese
- does word puzzles
- goes hiking

He ... every day.
-Does he ...(do) ?
-Yes, he does.
/No, he doesn't.

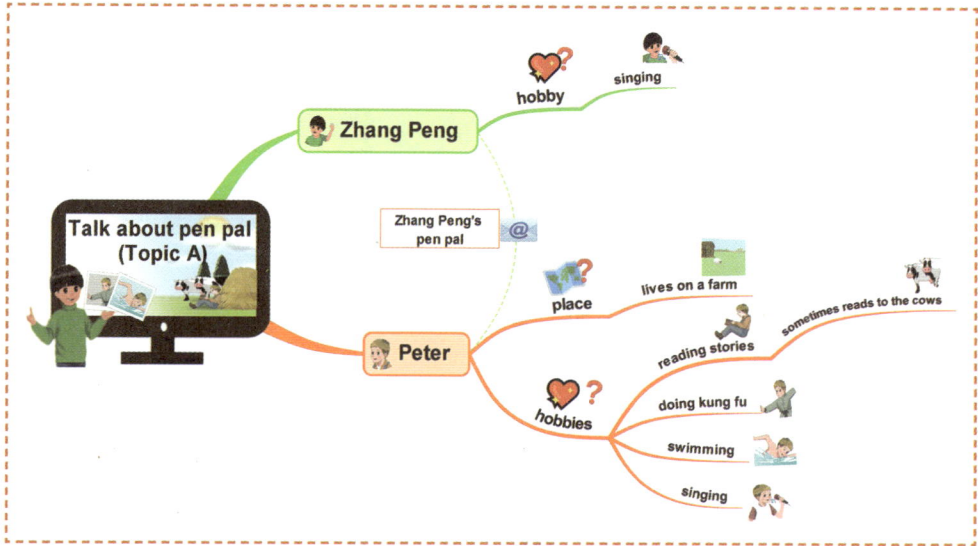

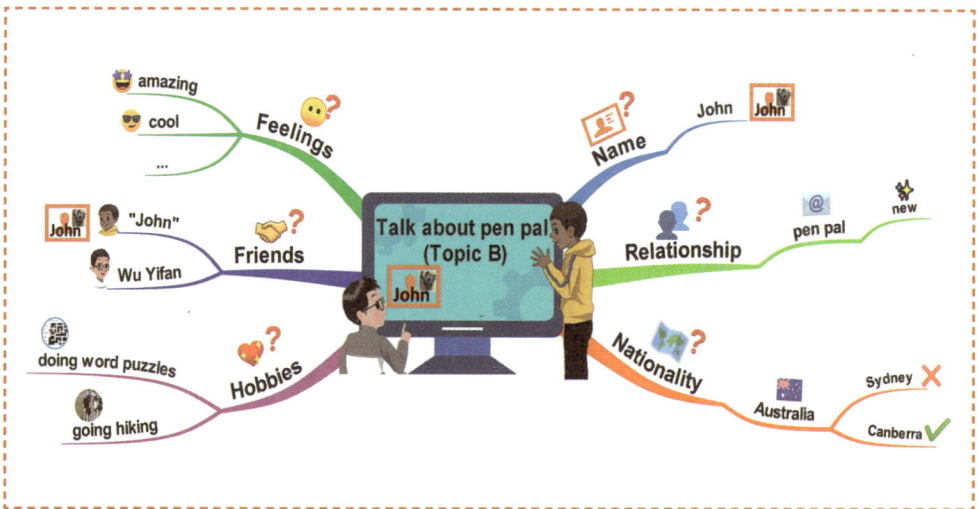

六 年 级 上 册

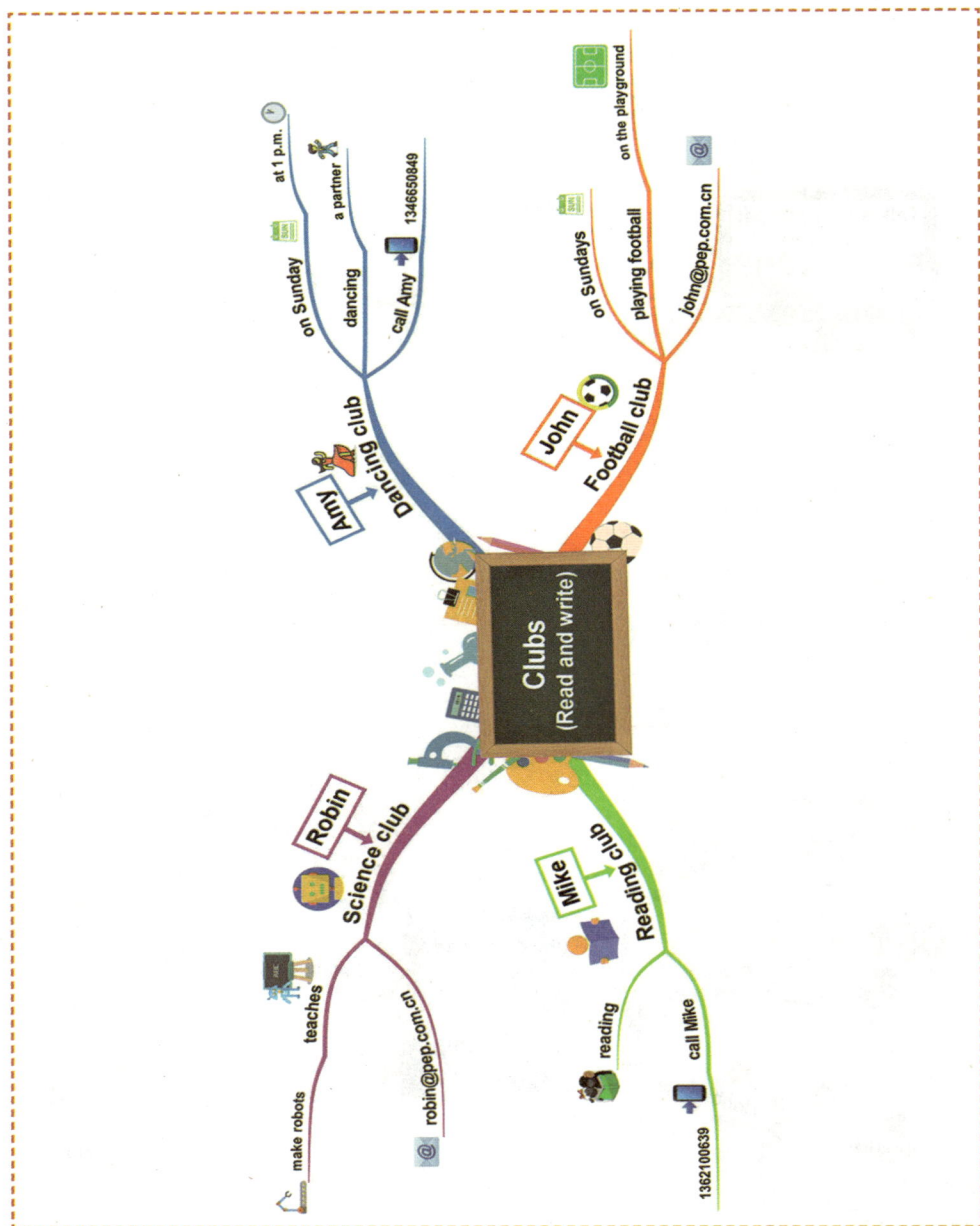

Clubs
(Read and write)

Amy → Dancing club
- on Sunday — at 1 p.m.
- dancing — a partner
- call Amy — 1346650849

John → Football club
- on Sundays — on the playground
- playing football
- john@pep.com.cn

Robin → Science club
- teaches — make robots
- robin@pep.com.cn

Mike → Reading club
- reading
- call Mike — 1362100639

Unit 5 What does he do?

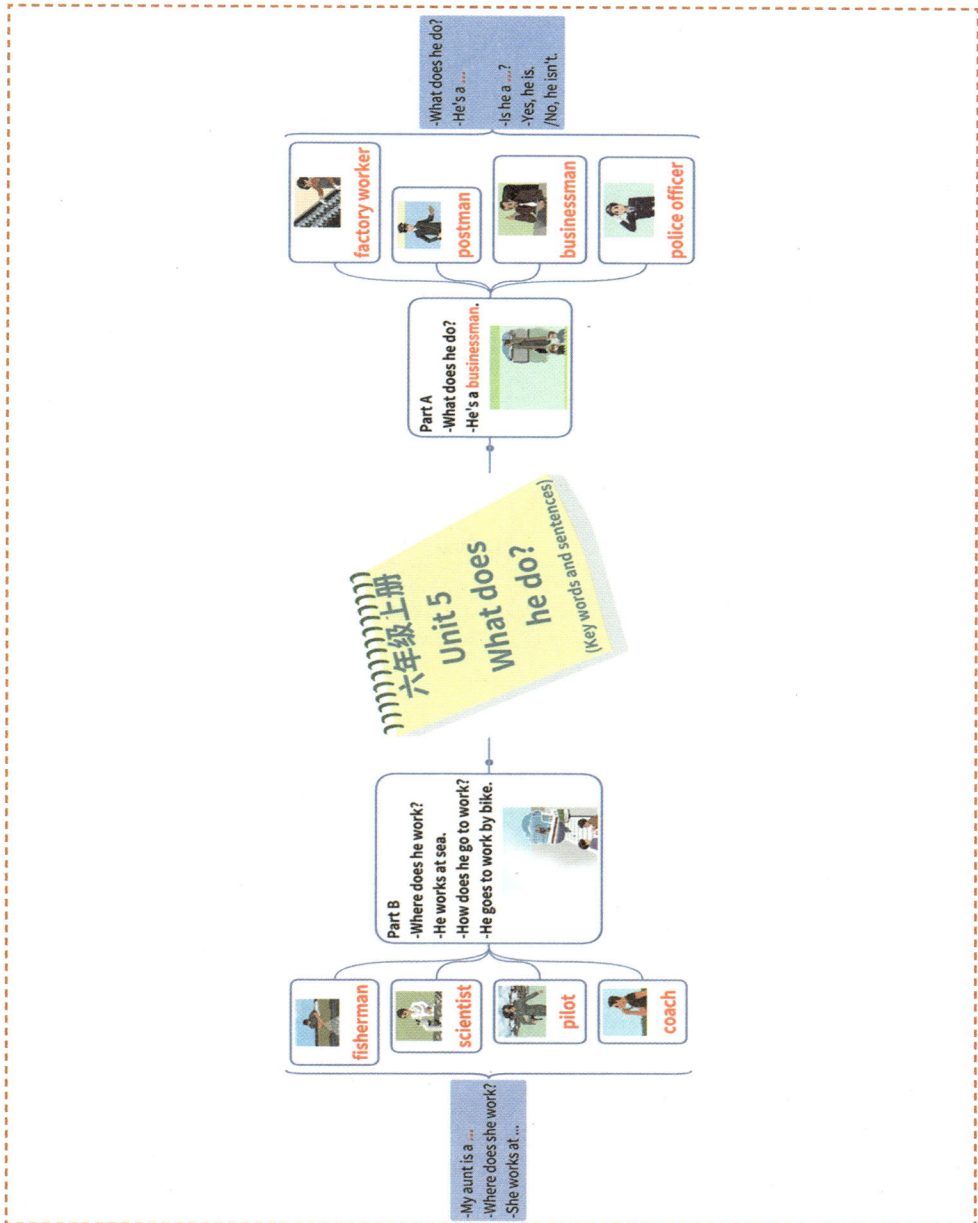

-What does he do?
-He's a ...
-Is he a ...?
-Yes, he is.
/No, he isn't.

factory worker

postman

businessman

police officer

Part A
-What does he do?
-He's a businessman.

六年级上册
Unit 5
What does he do?
(Key words and sentences)

Part B
-Where does he work?
-He works at sea.
-How does he go to work?
-He goes to work by bike.

fisherman

scientist

pilot

coach

-My aunt is a ...
-Where does she work?
-She works at ...

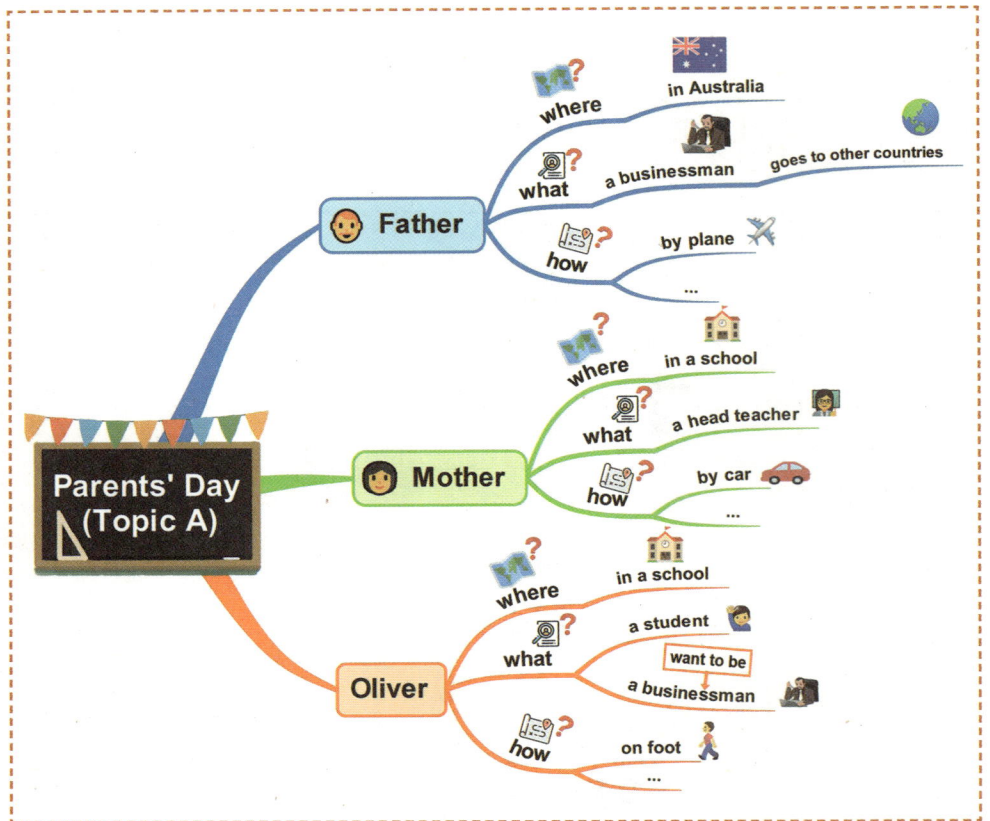

Parents' Day (Topic A)

Father
- where — in Australia
- what — a businessman — goes to other countries
- how — by plane — ...

Mother
- where — in a school
- what — a head teacher
- how — by car — ...

Oliver
- where — in a school
- what — a student — want to be a businessman
- how — on foot — ...

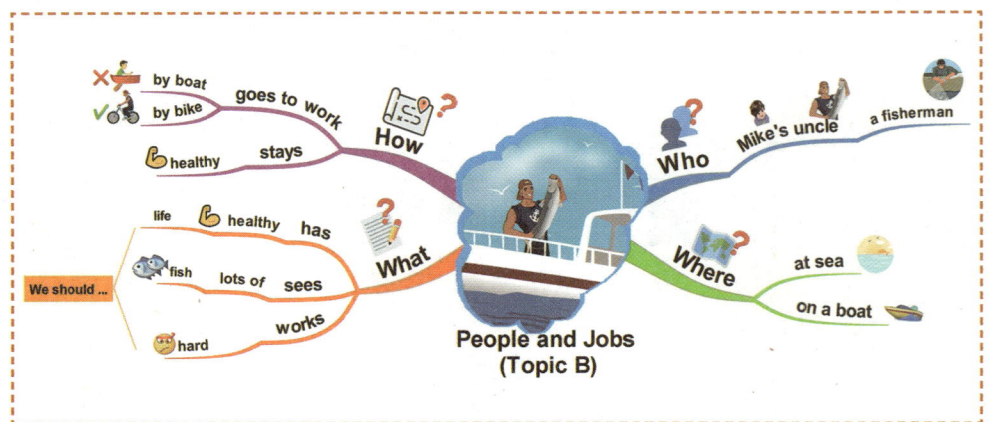

People and Jobs (Topic B)

How
- goes to work — by boat ✗ / by bike ✓
- stays — healthy

What
- has — healthy life
- sees — lots of fish
- works — hard
- We should ...

Who
- Mike's uncle — a fisherman

Where
- at sea
- on a boat

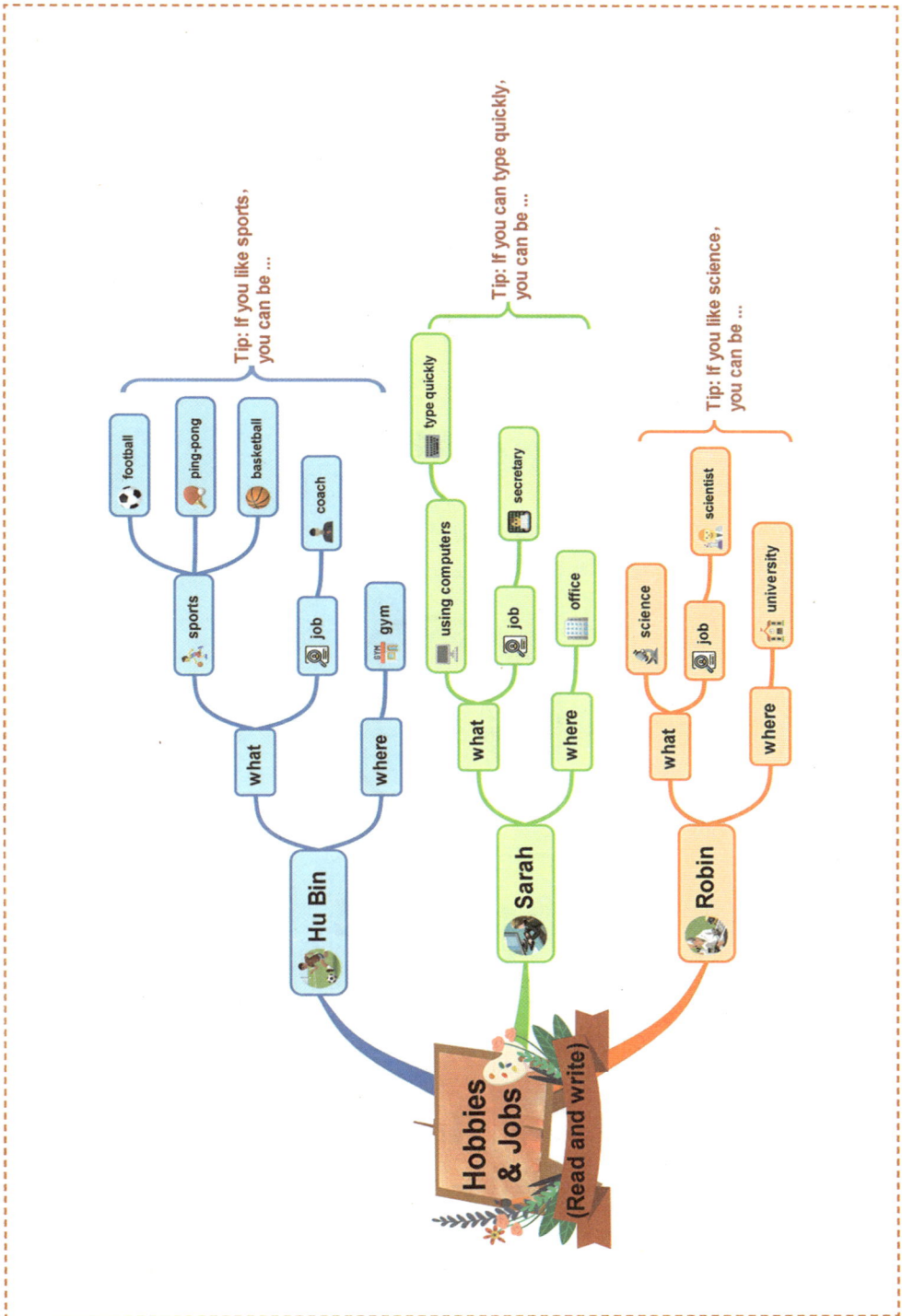

Unit 6 How do you feel?

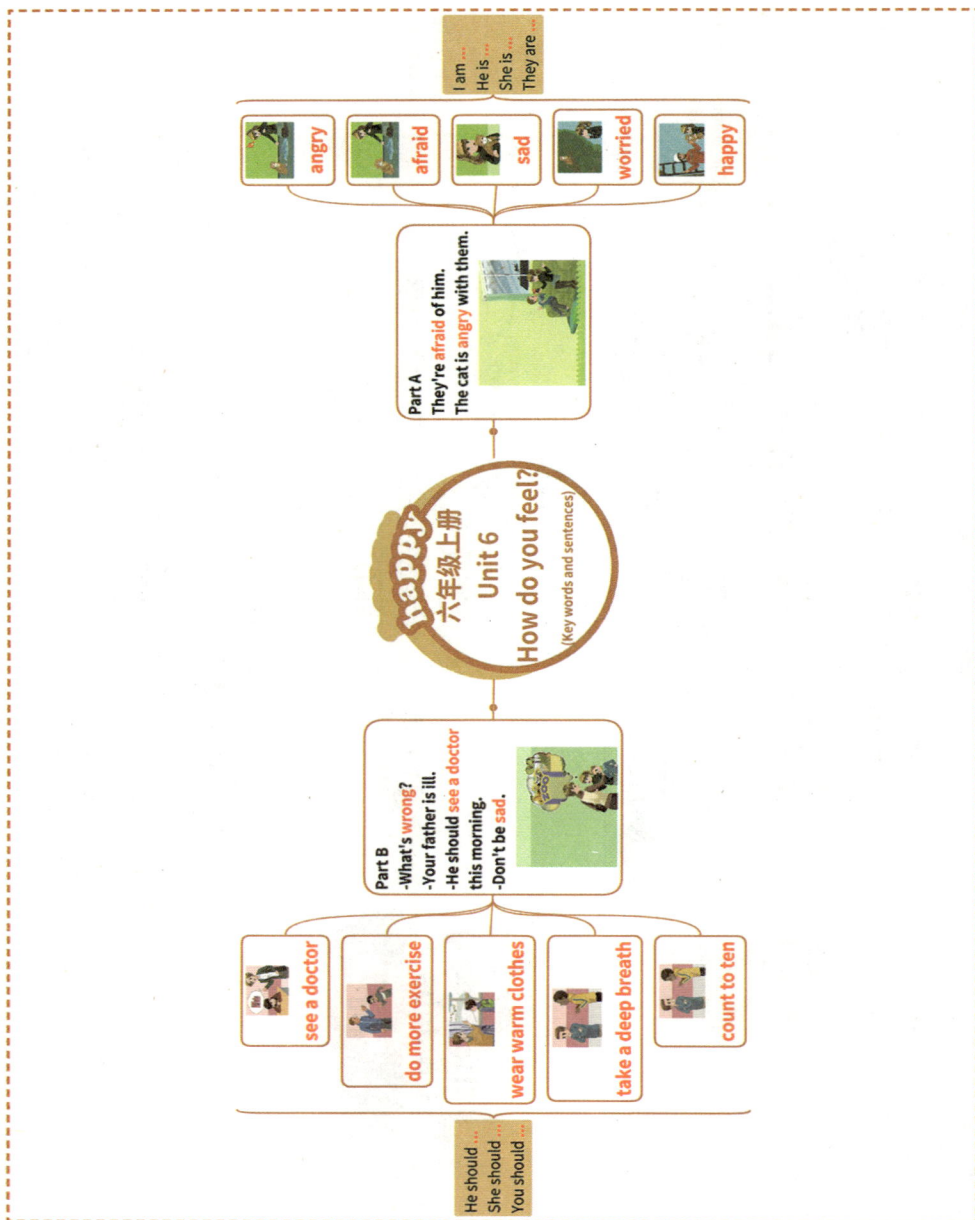

I am ...
He is ...
She is ...
They are ...

angry afraid sad worried happy

Part A
They're afraid of him.
The cat is angry with them.

happy
六年级上册
Unit 6
How do you feel?
(Key words and sentences)

Part B
-What's wrong?
-Your father is ill.
-He should see a doctor this morning.
-Don't be sad.

see a doctor do more exercise wear warm clothes take a deep breath count to ten

He should ...
She should ...
You should ...

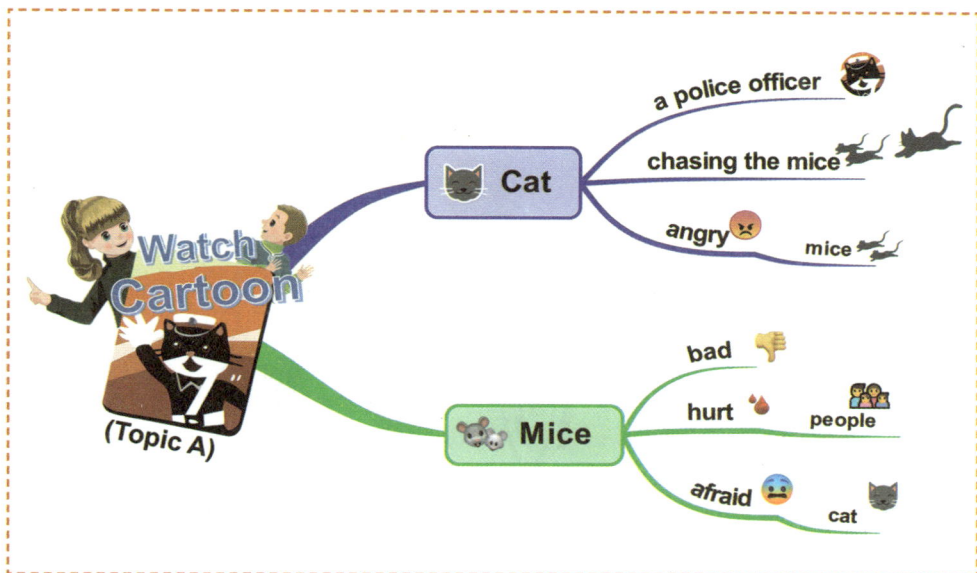

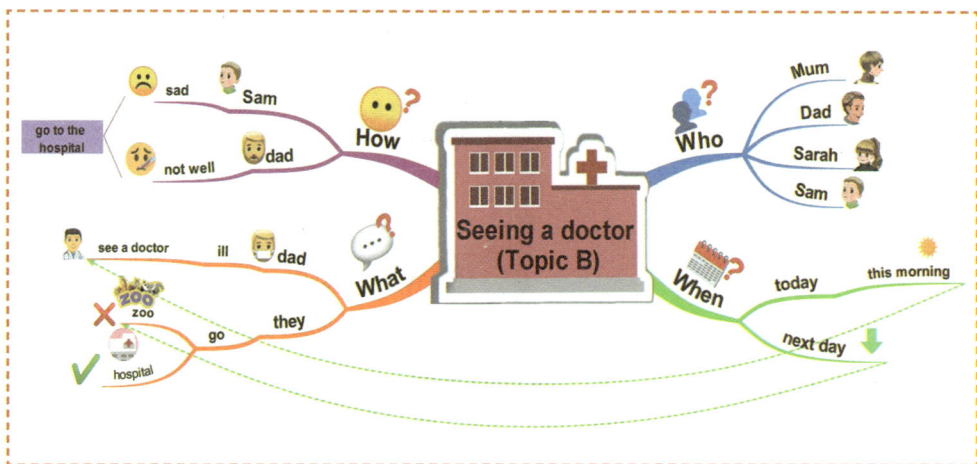

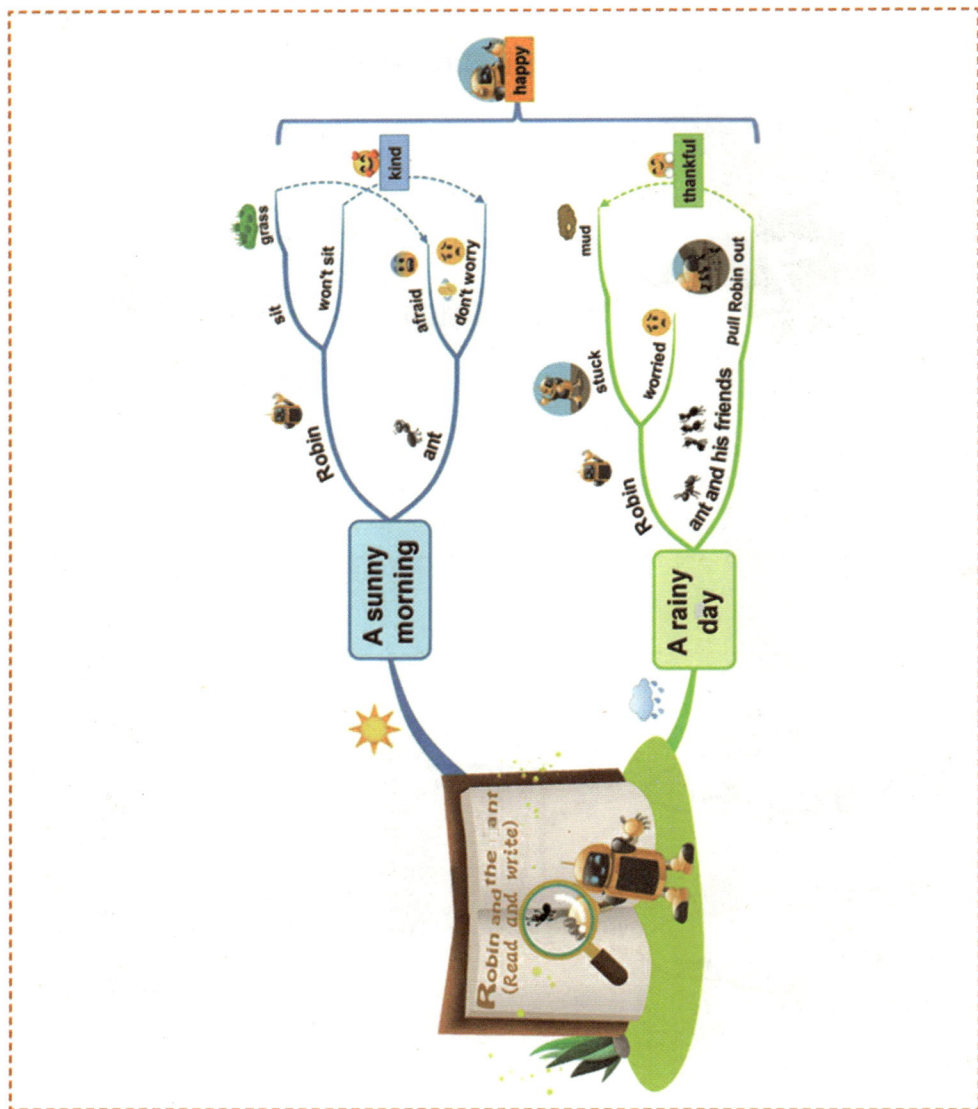

小学英语人教版六年级下册

Unit 1 How tall are you?

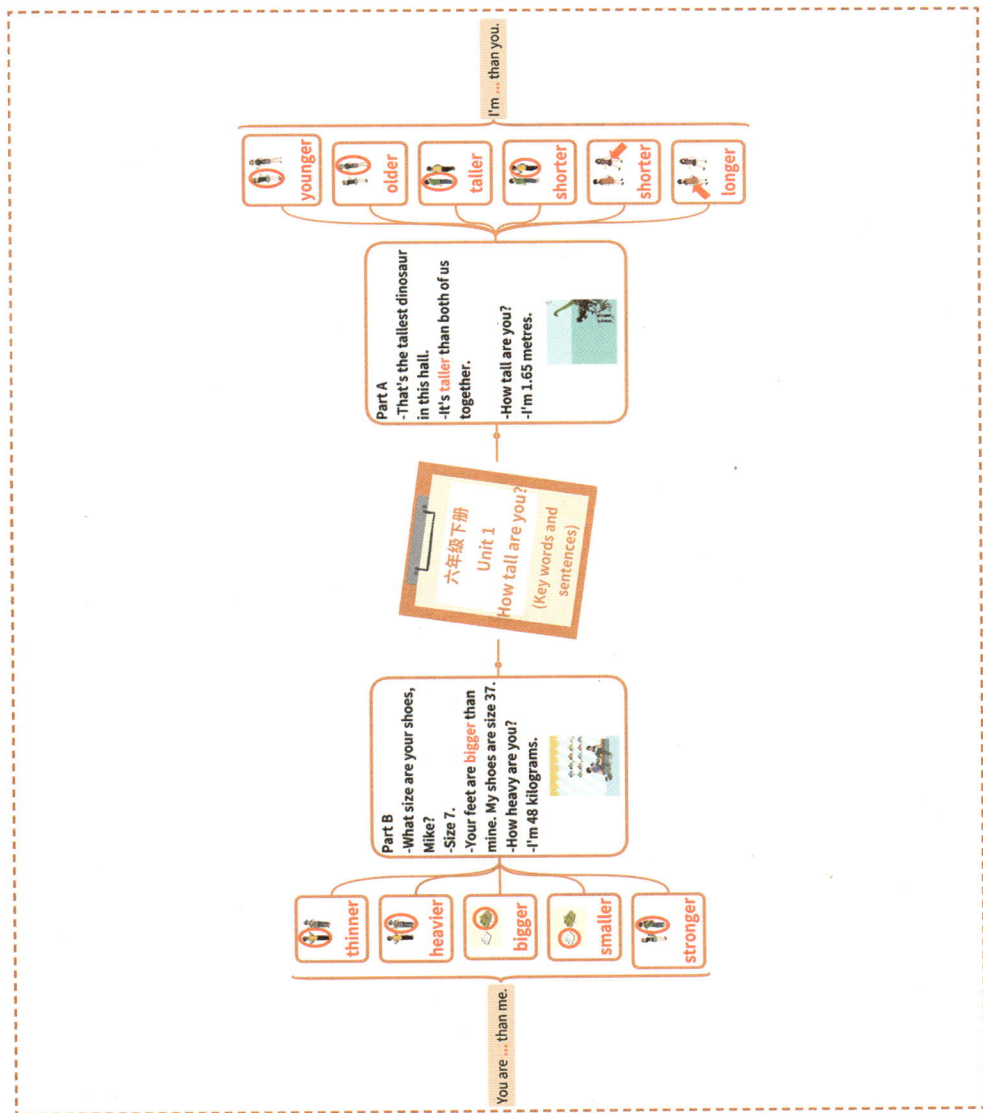

六年级 下册

I'm .... than you.

younger · older · taller · shorter · shorter · longer

Part A
-That's the tallest dinosaur in this hall.
-It's taller than both of us together.

-How tall are you?
-I'm 1.65 metres.

六年级下册
Unit 1
How tall are you?
(Key words and sentences)

Part B
-What size are your shoes, Mike?
-Size 7.
-Your feet are bigger than mine. My shoes are size 37.
-How heavy are you?
-I'm 48 kilograms.

thinner · heavier · bigger · smaller · stronger

You are ... than me.

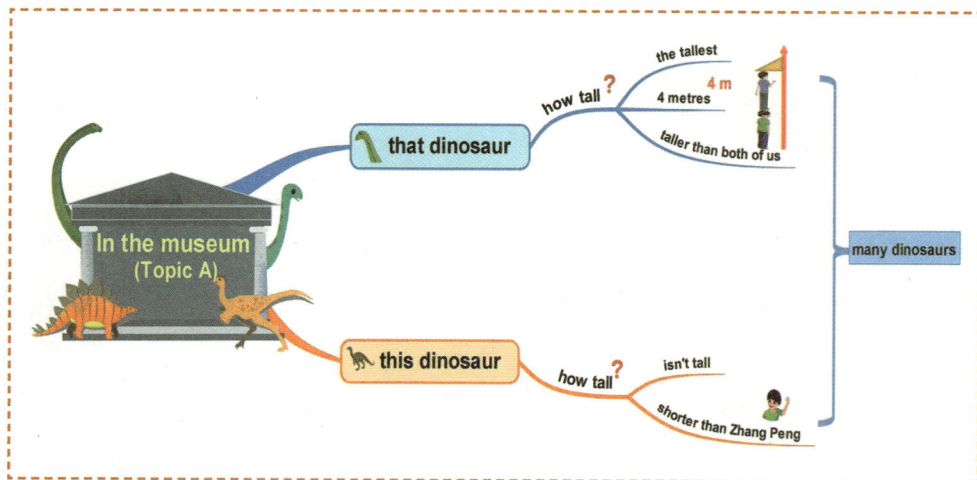

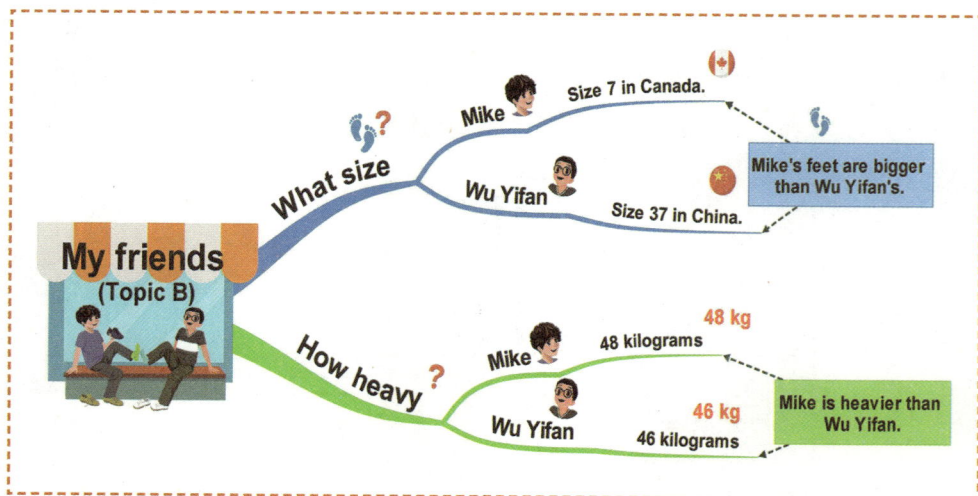

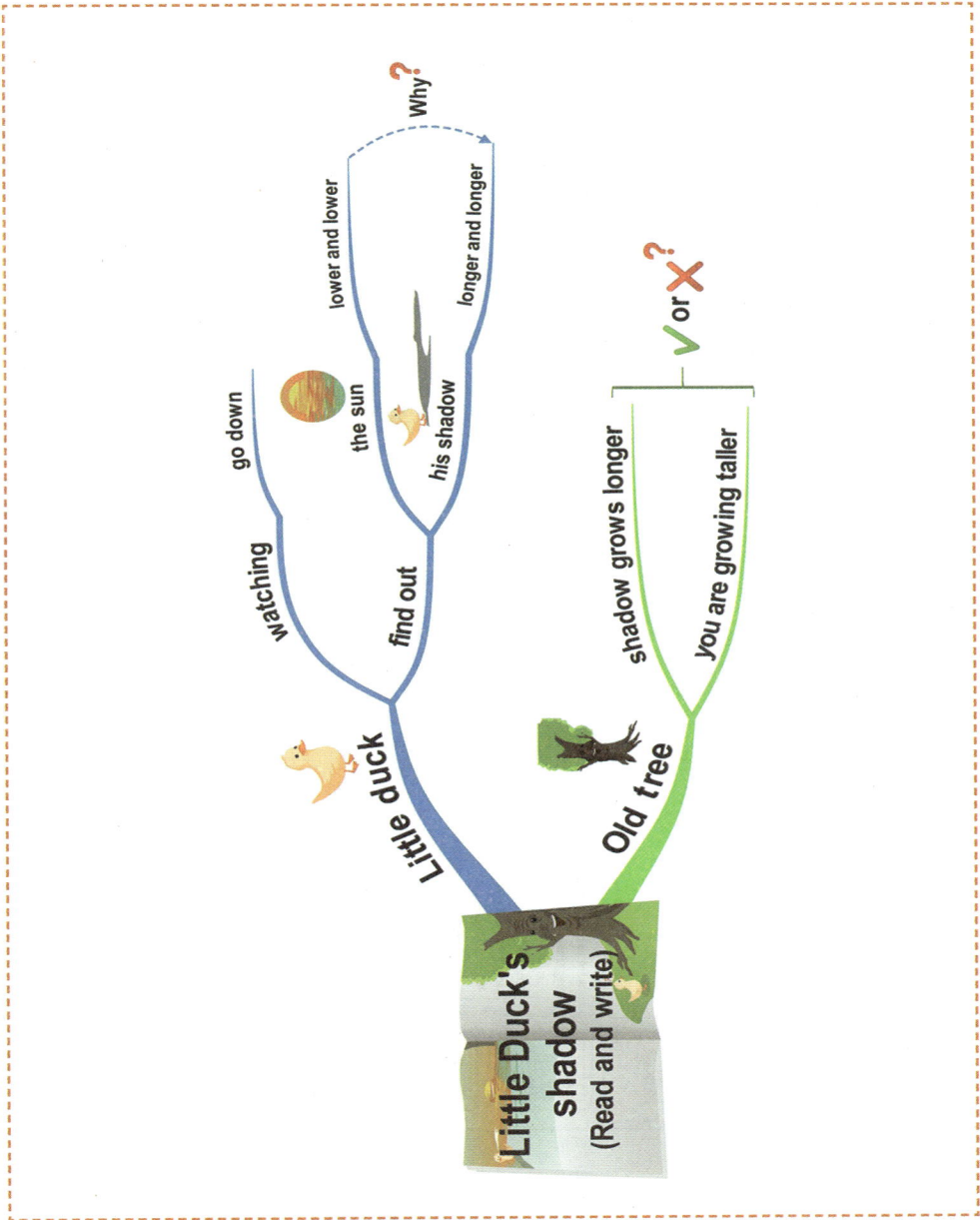

Why?

lower and lower

longer and longer

go down

the sun

his shadow

watching

find out

√ or ✗?

shadow grows longer

you are growing taller

Little duck

Old tree

Little Duck's shadow
(Read and write)

六年级　下册

Unit 2 Last weekend

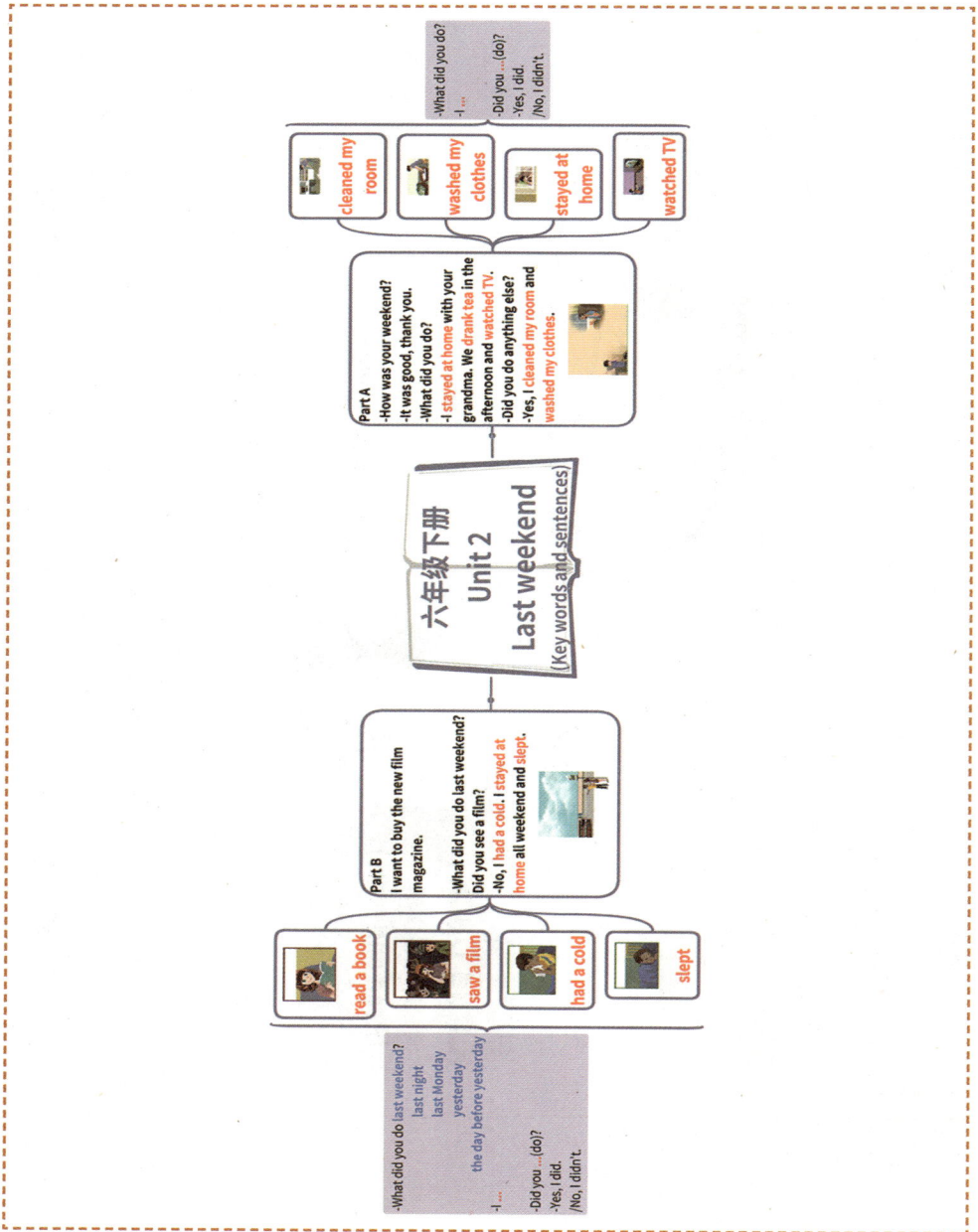

六年级下册
Unit 2
Last weekend
(Key words and sentences)

Part A
-How was your weekend?
-It was good, thank you.
-What did you do?
-I stayed at home with your grandma. We drank tea in the afternoon and watched TV.
-Did you do anything else?
-Yes, I cleaned my room and washed my clothes.

cleaned my room

washed my clothes

stayed at home

watched TV

-What did you do?
-I ...
-Did you ...(do)?
-Yes, I did.
/No, I didn't.

Part B
I want to buy the new film magazine.
-What did you do last weekend? Did you see a film?
-No, I had a cold. I stayed at home all weekend and slept.

read a book

saw a film

had a cold

slept

-What did you do last weekend?
last night
last Monday
yesterday
the day before yesterday
-I ...
-Did you ...(do)?
-Yes, I did.
/No, I didn't.

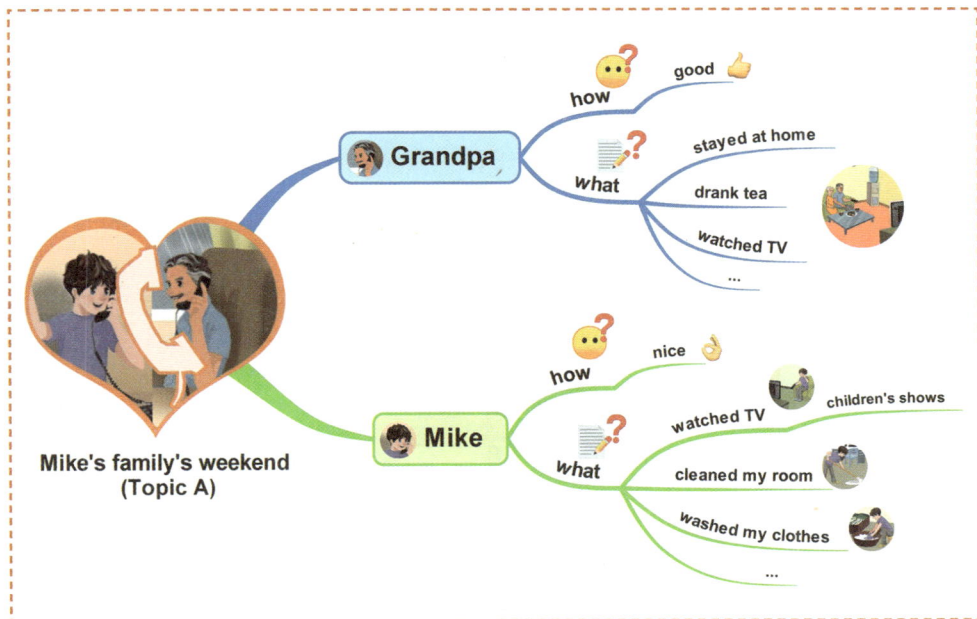

Mike's family's weekend
(Topic A)

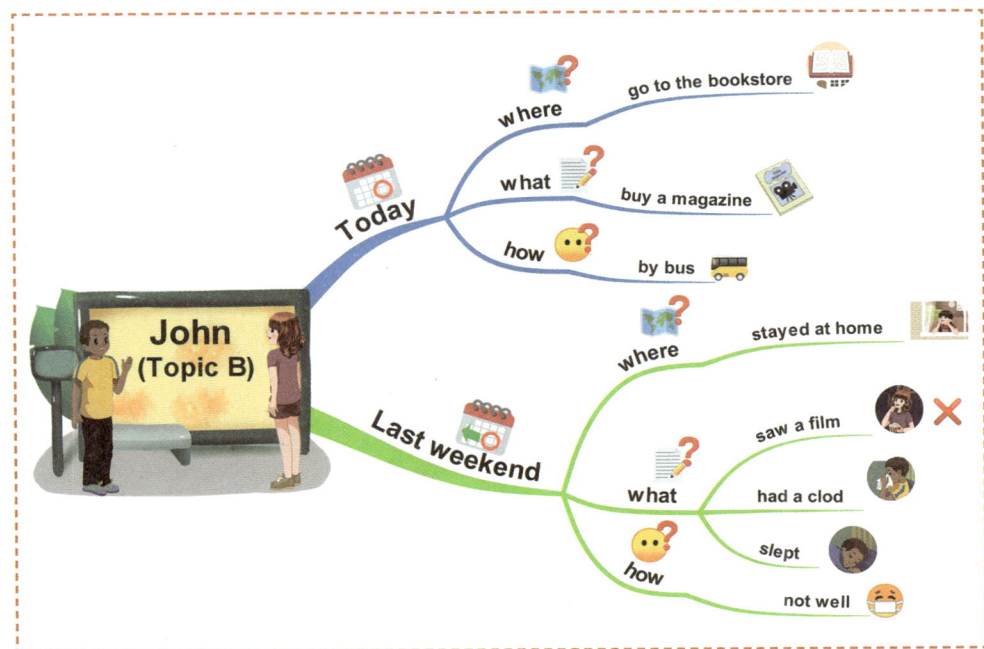

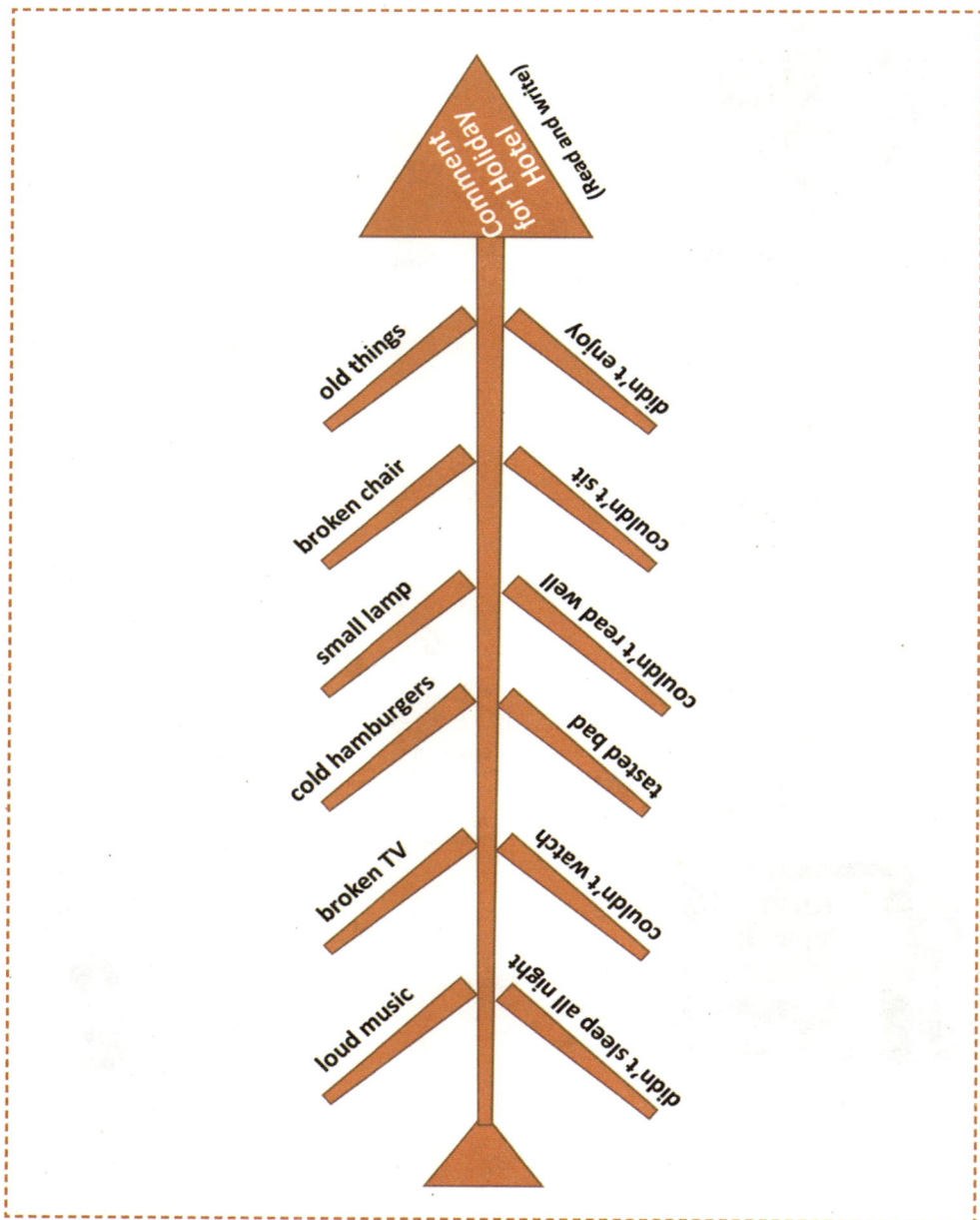

Comment for Holiday for Hotel (Read and write)

old things — didn't enjoy
broken chair — couldn't sit
small lamp — couldn't read well
cold hamburgers — tasted bad
broken TV — couldn't watch
loud music — didn't sleep all night

Unit 3 Where did you go?

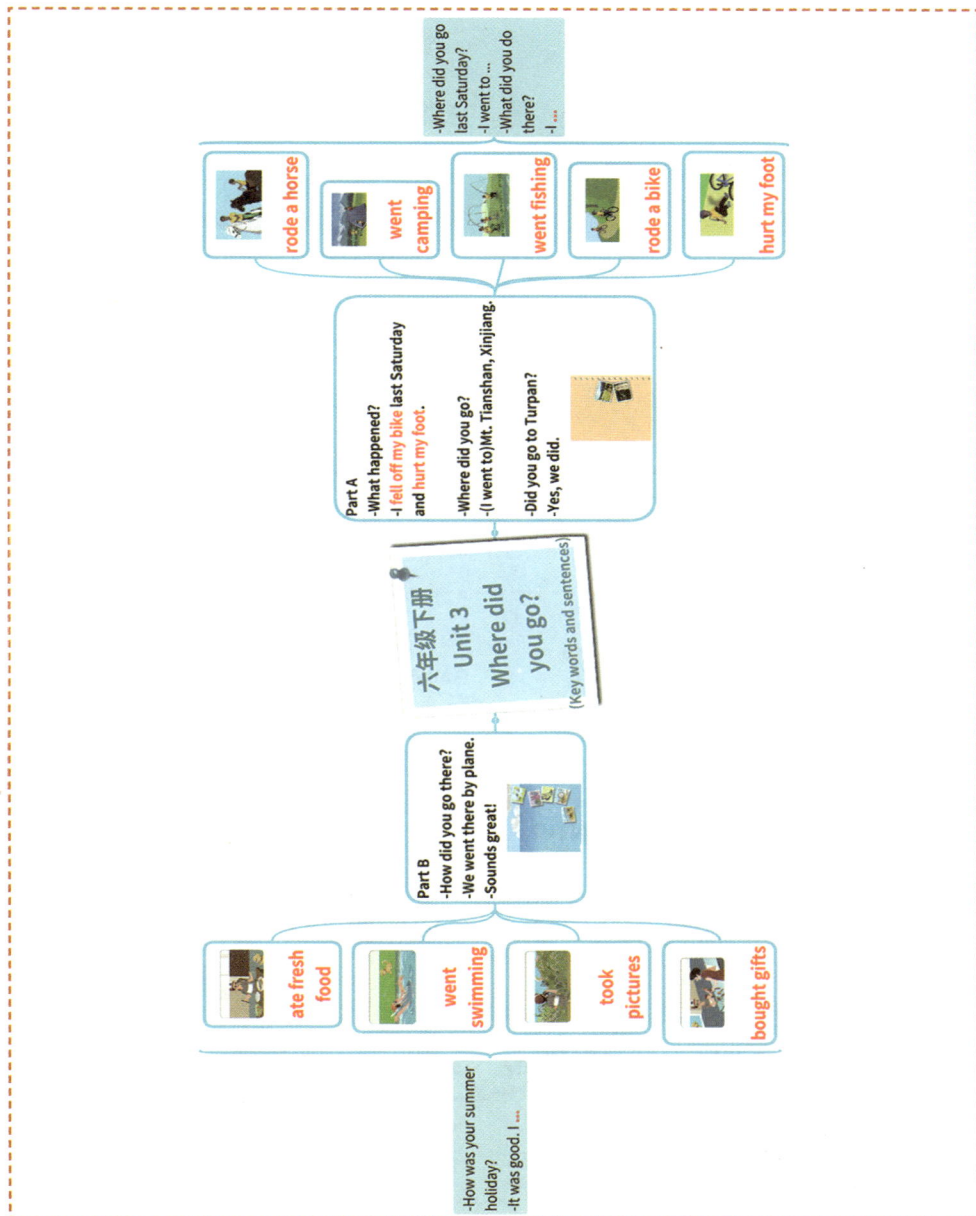

-Where did you go
last Saturday?
-I went to ...
-What did you do
there?
-I ...

rode a horse

went camping

went fishing

rode a bike

hurt my foot

Part A
-What happened?
-I fell off my bike last Saturday
and hurt my foot.
-Where did you go?
-(I went to)Mt. Tianshan, Xinjiang.
-Did you go to Turpan?
-Yes, we did.

六年级下册
Unit 3
Where did
you go?
(Key words and sentences)

Part B
-How did you go there?
-We went there by plane.
-Sounds great!

ate fresh food

went swimming

took pictures

bought gifts

-How was your summer
holiday?
-It was good. I ...

六年级

下册

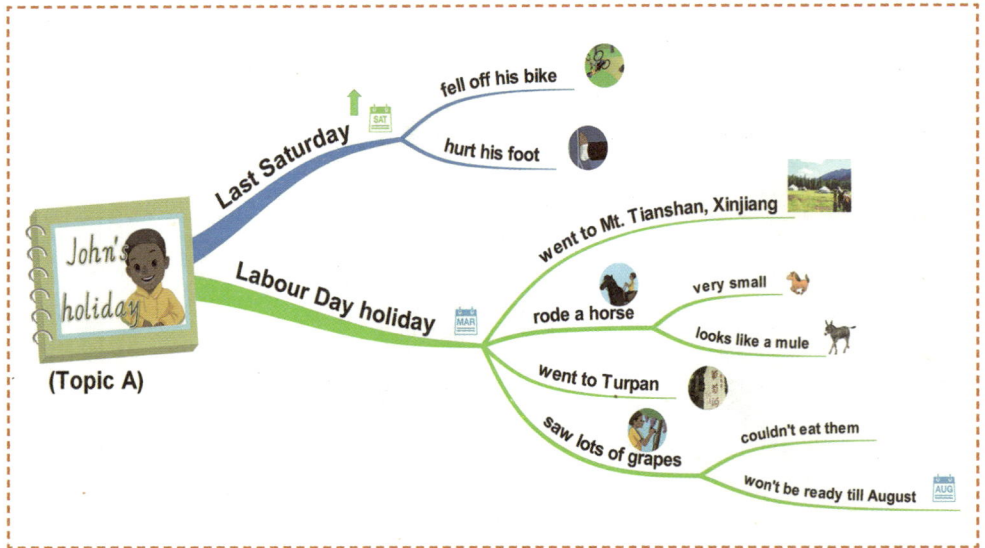

(Topic A)

Last Saturday
- fell off his bike
- hurt his foot

Labour Day holiday
- went to Mt. Tianshan, Xinjiang
- rode a horse
  - very small
  - looks like a mule
- went to Turpan
- saw lots of grapes
  - couldn't eat them
  - won't be ready till August

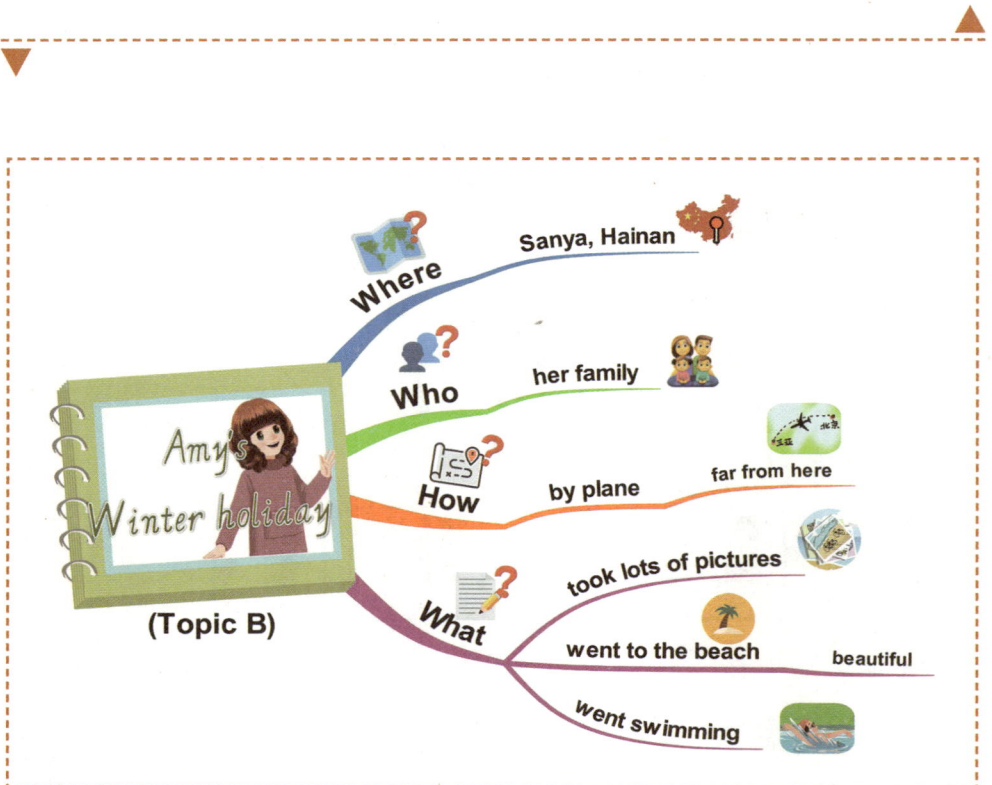

(Topic B)

Amy's Winter holiday

Where — Sanya, Hainan

Who — her family

How — by plane — far from here

What
- took lots of pictures
- went to the beach — beautiful
- went swimming

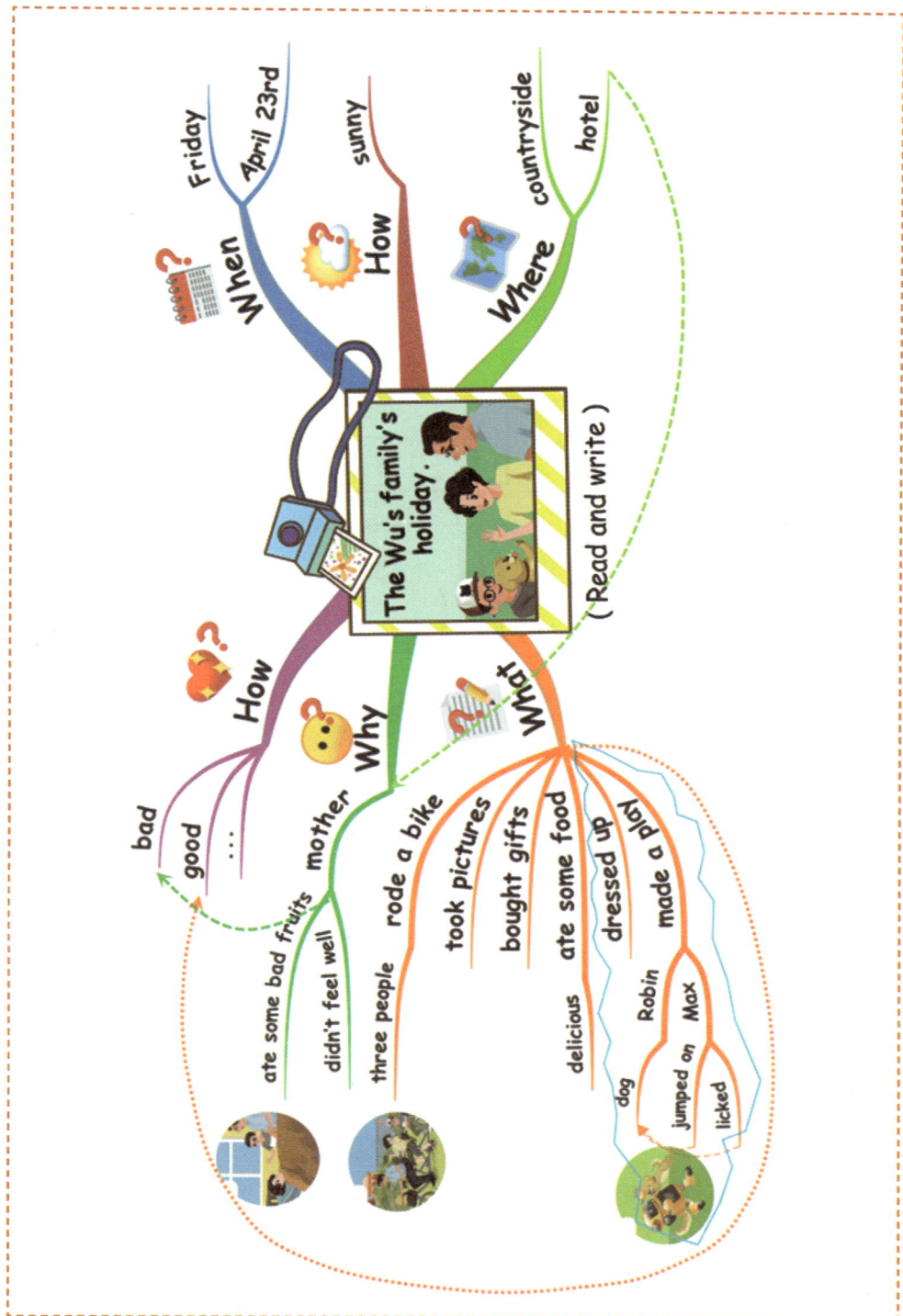

六年级 下册

The Wu's family's holiday.

(Read and write)

When
- Friday
- April 23rd

How
- sunny

Where
- countryside
- hotel

How
- bad
- good
- ...

Why
- ate some bad fruits
- didn't feel well
- mother
- three people

What
- rode a bike
- took pictures
- bought gifts
- ate some food
  - delicious
- dressed up
  - dog
  - Robin
  - Max
    - jumped on
    - licked
- made a play

Unit 4 Then and now

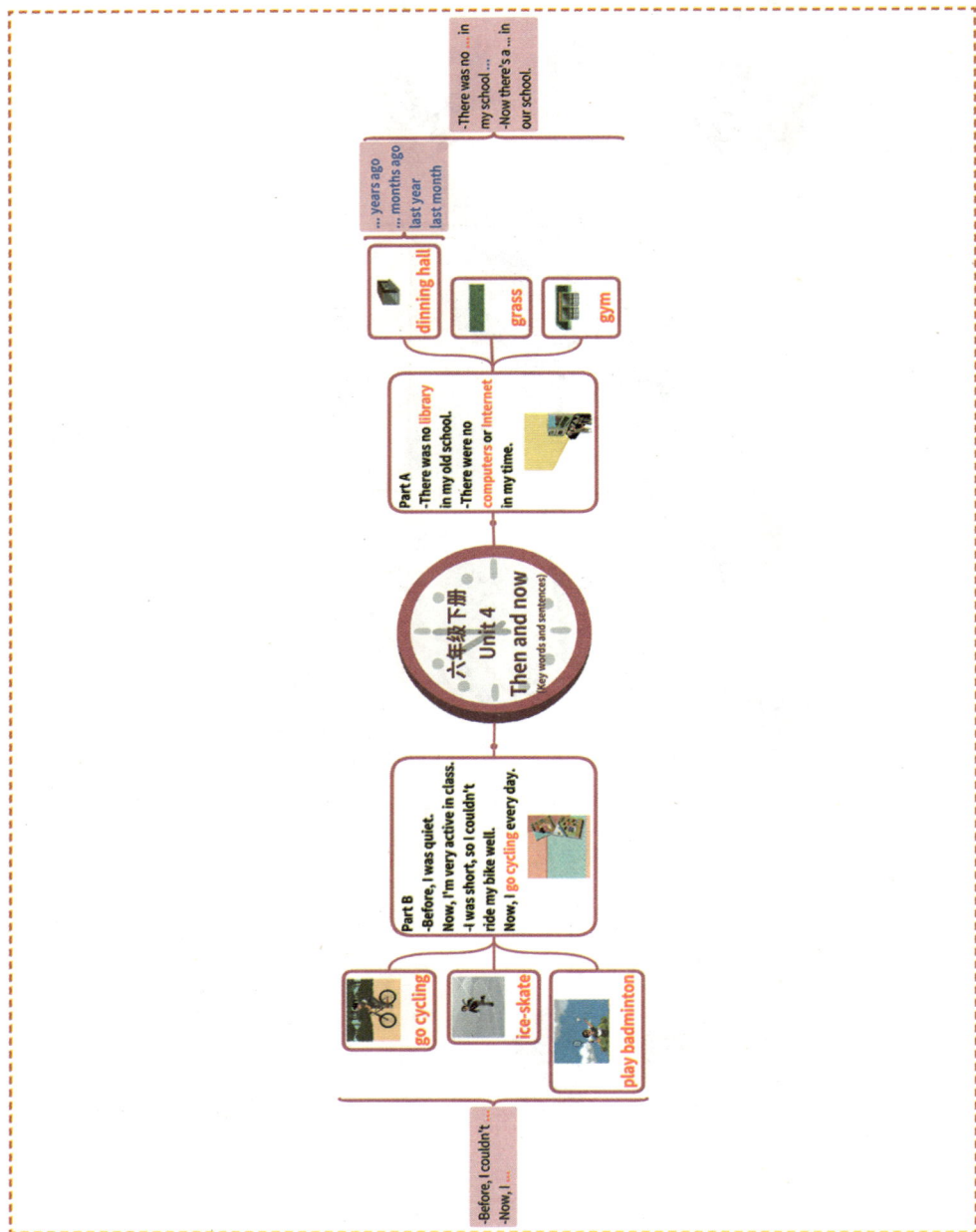

-There was no ... in my school. ...
-Now there's a ... in our school.

... years ago
... months ago
last year
last month

dinning hall

grass

gym

Part A
-There was no library in my old school.
-There were no computers or Internet in my time.

六年级下册
Unit 4
Then and now
(Key words and sentences)

Part B
-Before, I was quiet. Now, I'm very active in class.
-I was short, so I couldn't ride my bike well. Now, I go cycling every day.

go cycling

ice-skate

play badminton

-Before, I couldn't ...
-Now, I ...

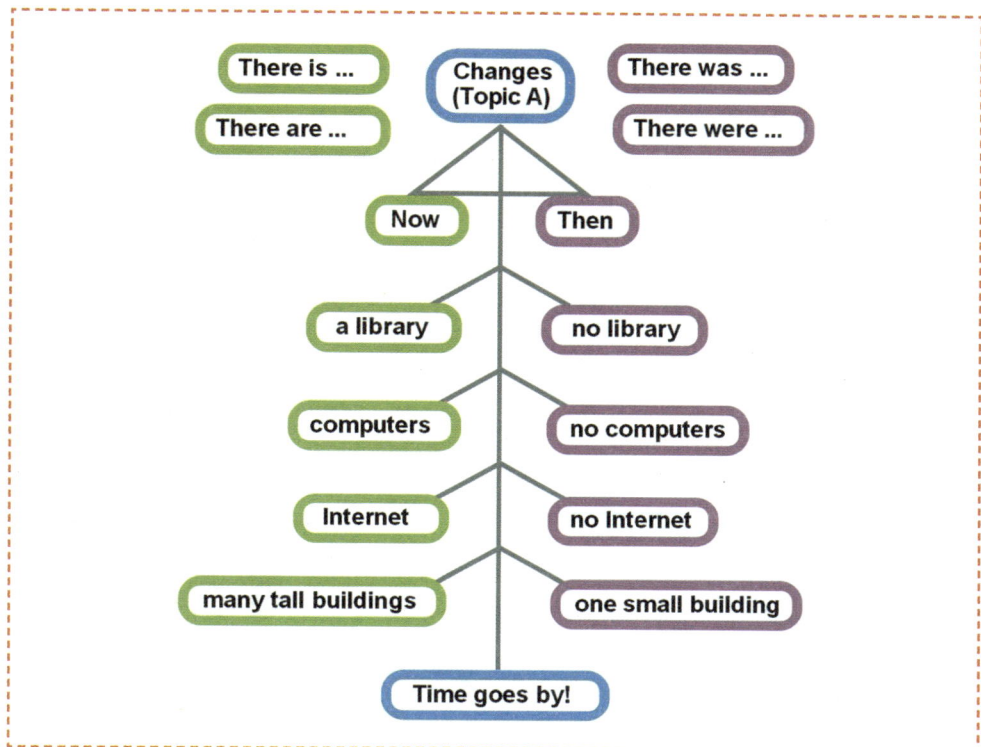

There is ...

There are ...

Changes (Topic A)

There was ...

There were ...

Now

Then

a library — no library

computers — no computers

Internet — no Internet

many tall buildings — one small building

Time goes by!

六年级 下册 »

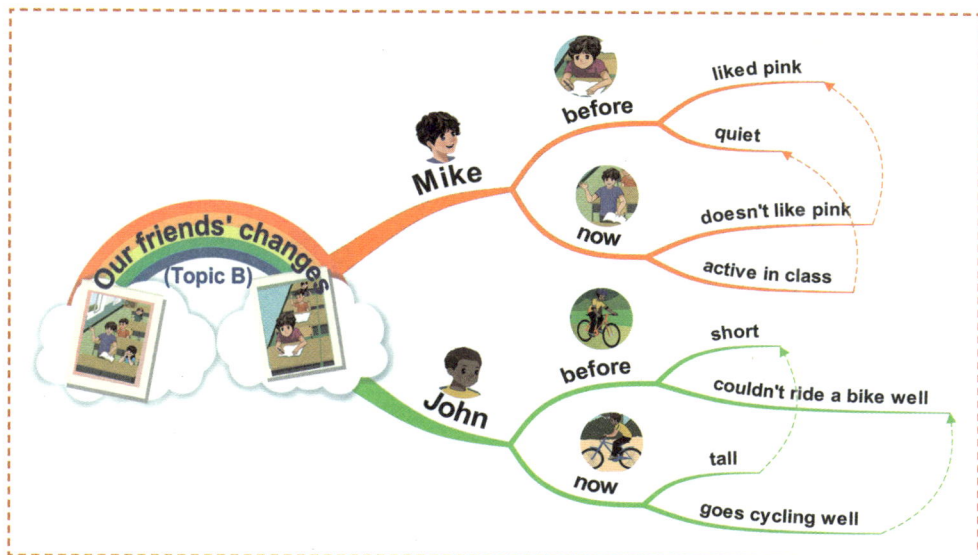

Our friends' changes (Topic B)

Mike

before — liked pink / quiet

now — doesn't like pink / active in class

John

before — short / couldn't ride a bike well

now — tall / goes cycling well

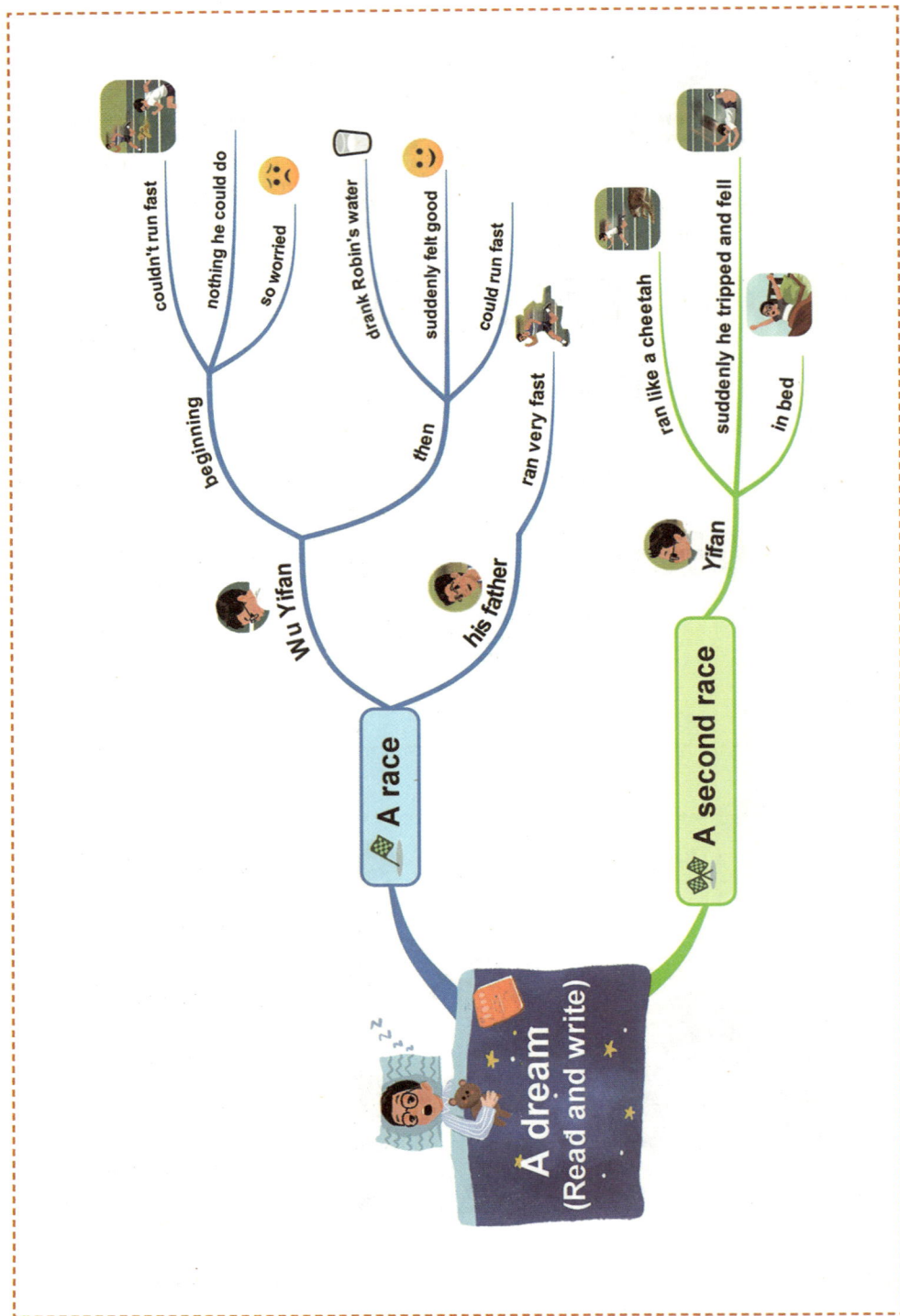

couldn't run fast

nothing he could do

so worried

drank Robin's water

suddenly felt good

could run fast

ran very fast

ran like a cheetah

suddenly he tripped and fell

in bed

beginning

then

Wu Yifan

his father

Yifan

A race

A second race

A dream
(Read and write)

附 思维导图参考教材①

PEP 三年级上册

PEP 三年级下册

PEP 四年级上册

PEP 四年级下册

PEP 五年级上册

PEP 五年级下册

PEP 六年级上册

PEP 六年级下册

① 《义务教育教科书英语（三年级起点）》，人民教育出版社，三至六年级。

Library rules

How can I get there?

My plan

In a park

Birthday party

My favourite pet

Ways to go to …

My pen pal

illness and health

My favourite food

My favourite season

Tree Planting Day

My family's hobbies

Making friends

Last weekend

My room

A helpful boy/girl

My day

My dream

My week

My teacher

National Day

五年级下
五年级上

六年级上

六年级下

写作思维导图

小学英语人教版五年级上册

Unit 1 What's he like?

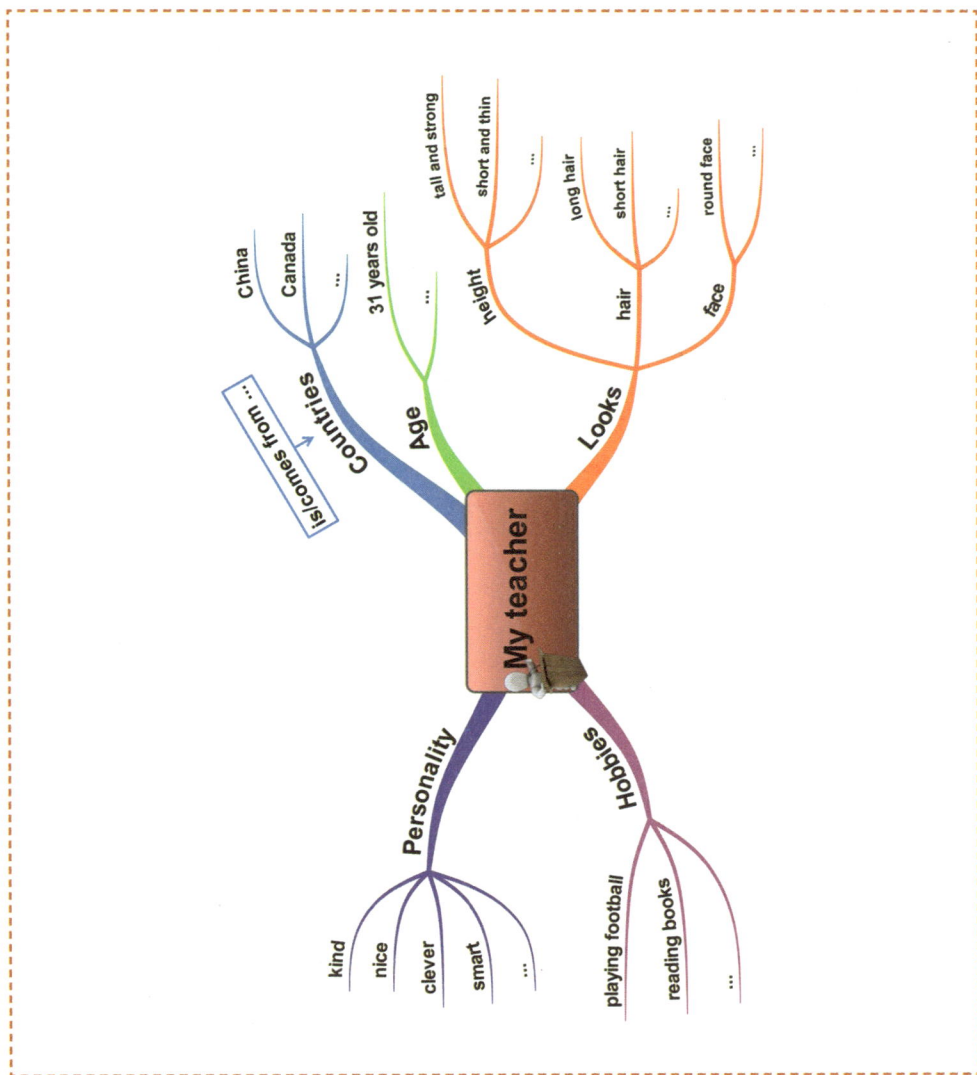

Unit 2 My week

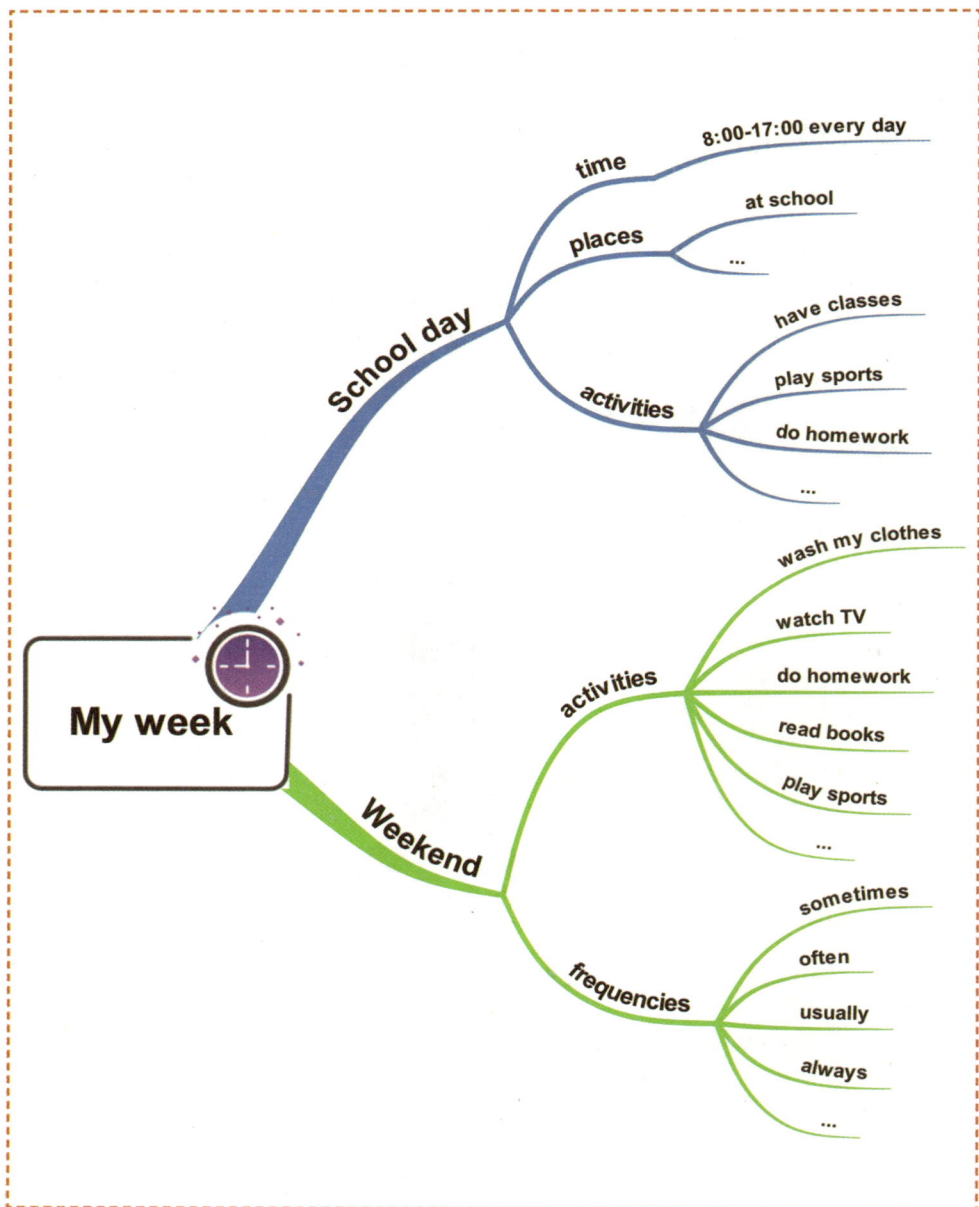

- **My week**
  - **School day**
    - **time**
      - 8:00-17:00 every day
    - **places**
      - at school
      - ...
    - **activities**
      - have classes
      - play sports
      - do homework
      - ...
  - **Weekend**
    - **activities**
      - wash my clothes
      - watch TV
      - do homework
      - read books
      - play sports
      - ...
    - **frequencies**
      - sometimes
      - often
      - usually
      - always
      - ...

Unit 3 What would you like?

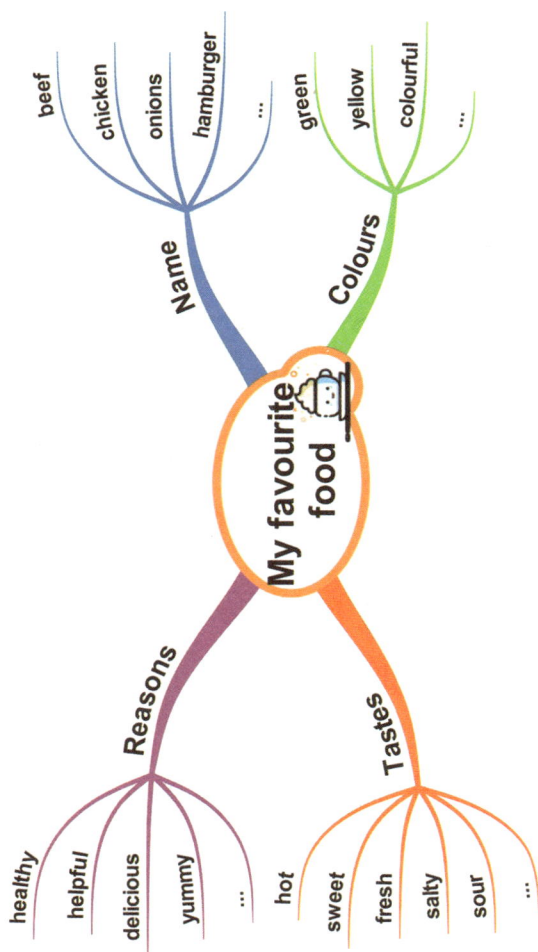

Unit 4 What can you do?

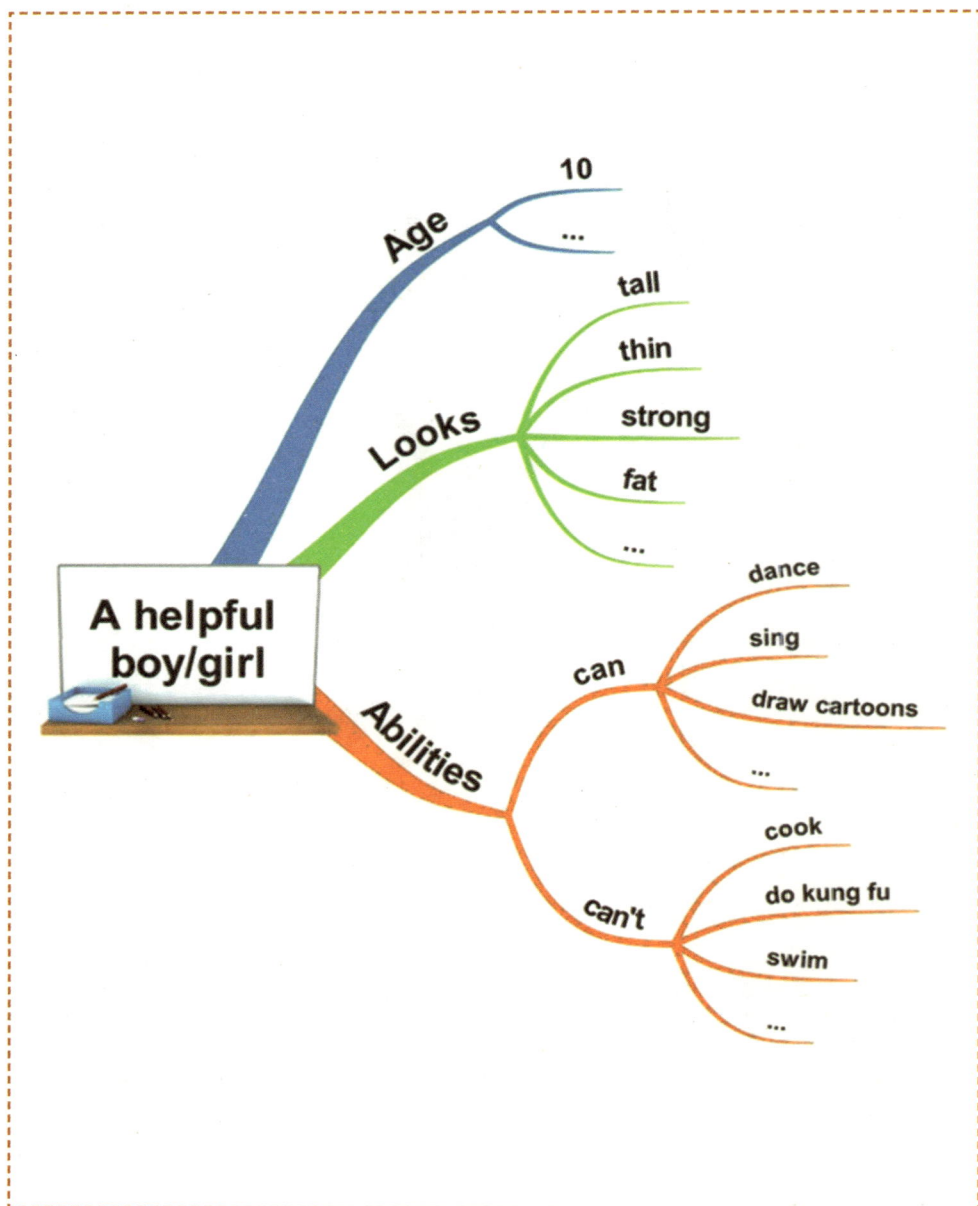

Age
10
...

Looks
tall
thin
strong
fat
...

A helpful boy/girl

Abilities

can
dance
sing
draw cartoons
...

can't
cook
do kung fu
swim
...

Unit 5 There is a big bed

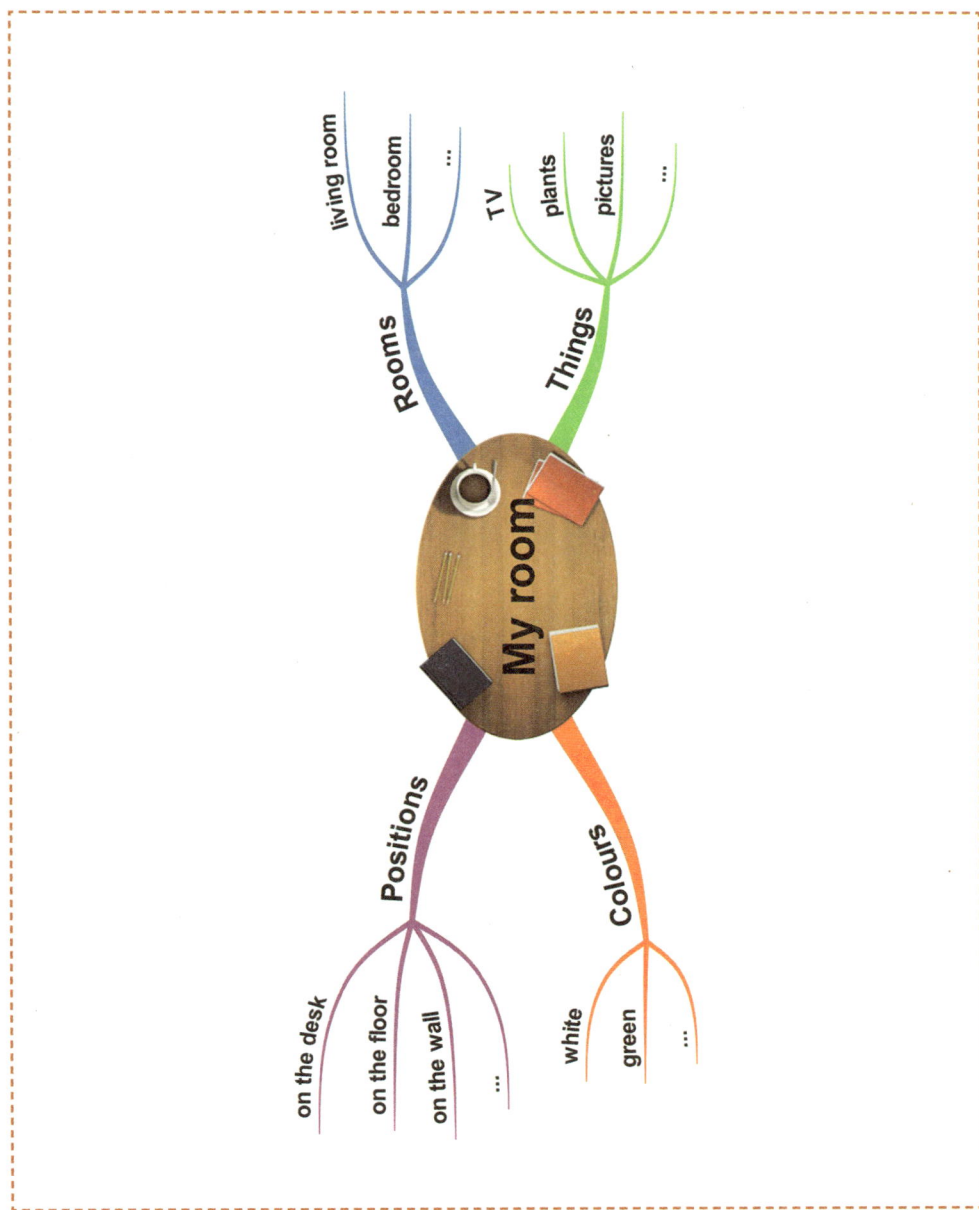

Unit 6 In a nature park

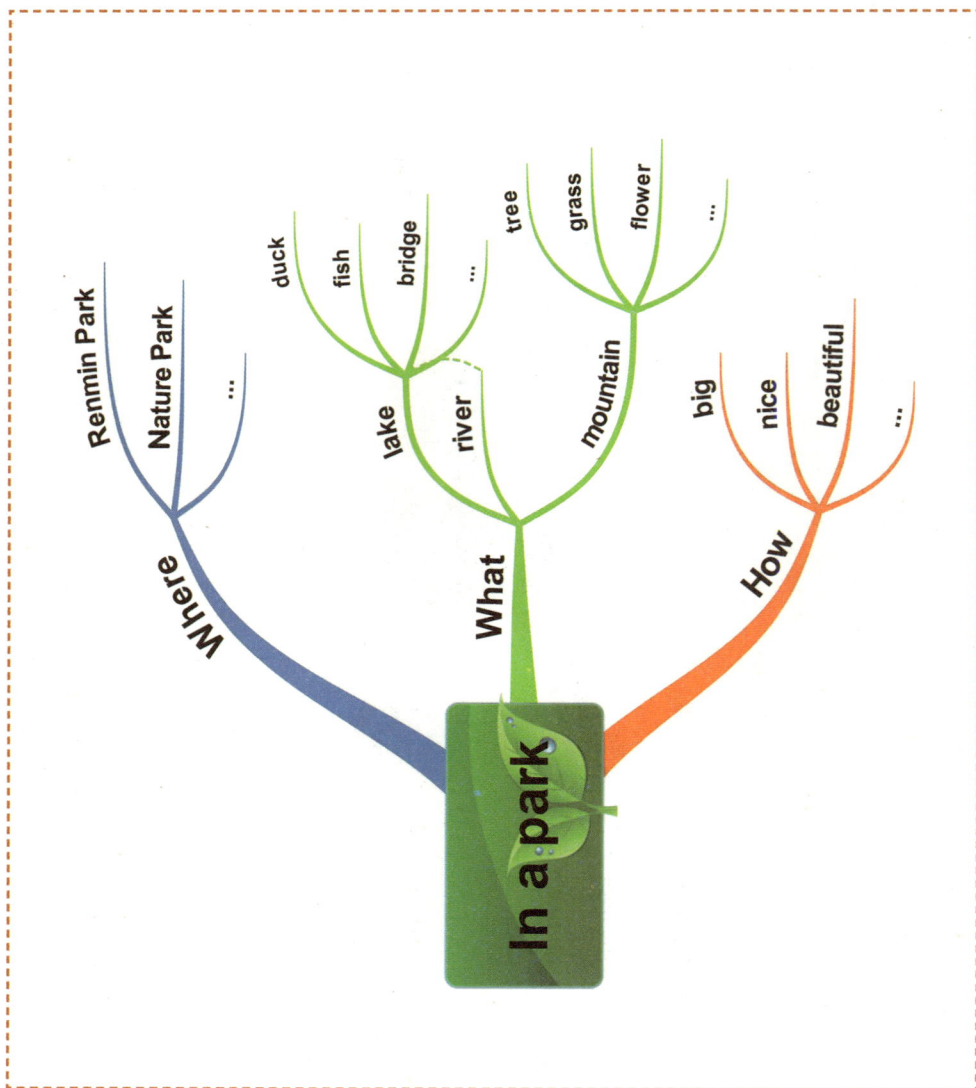

小学英语人教版五年级下册

Unit 1 My day

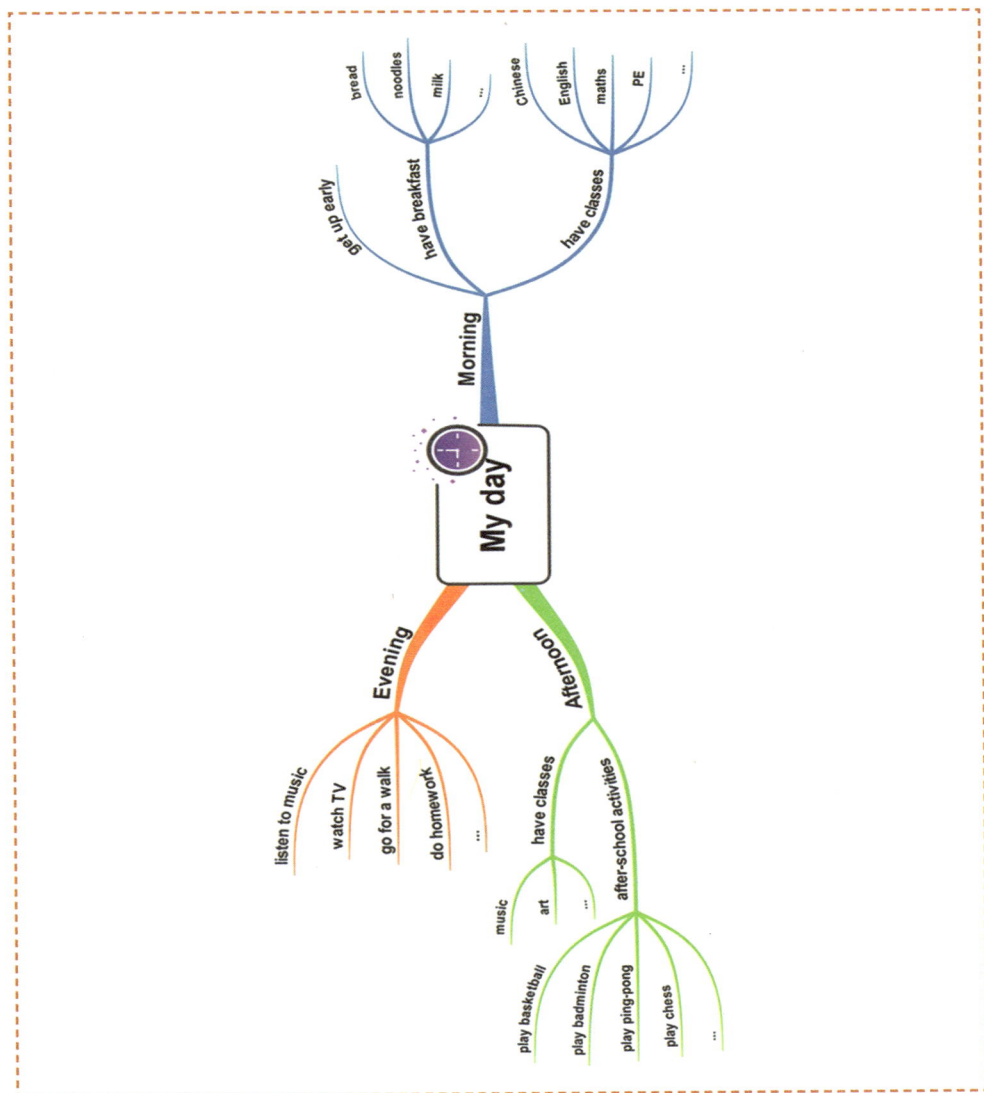

Unit 2 My favourite season

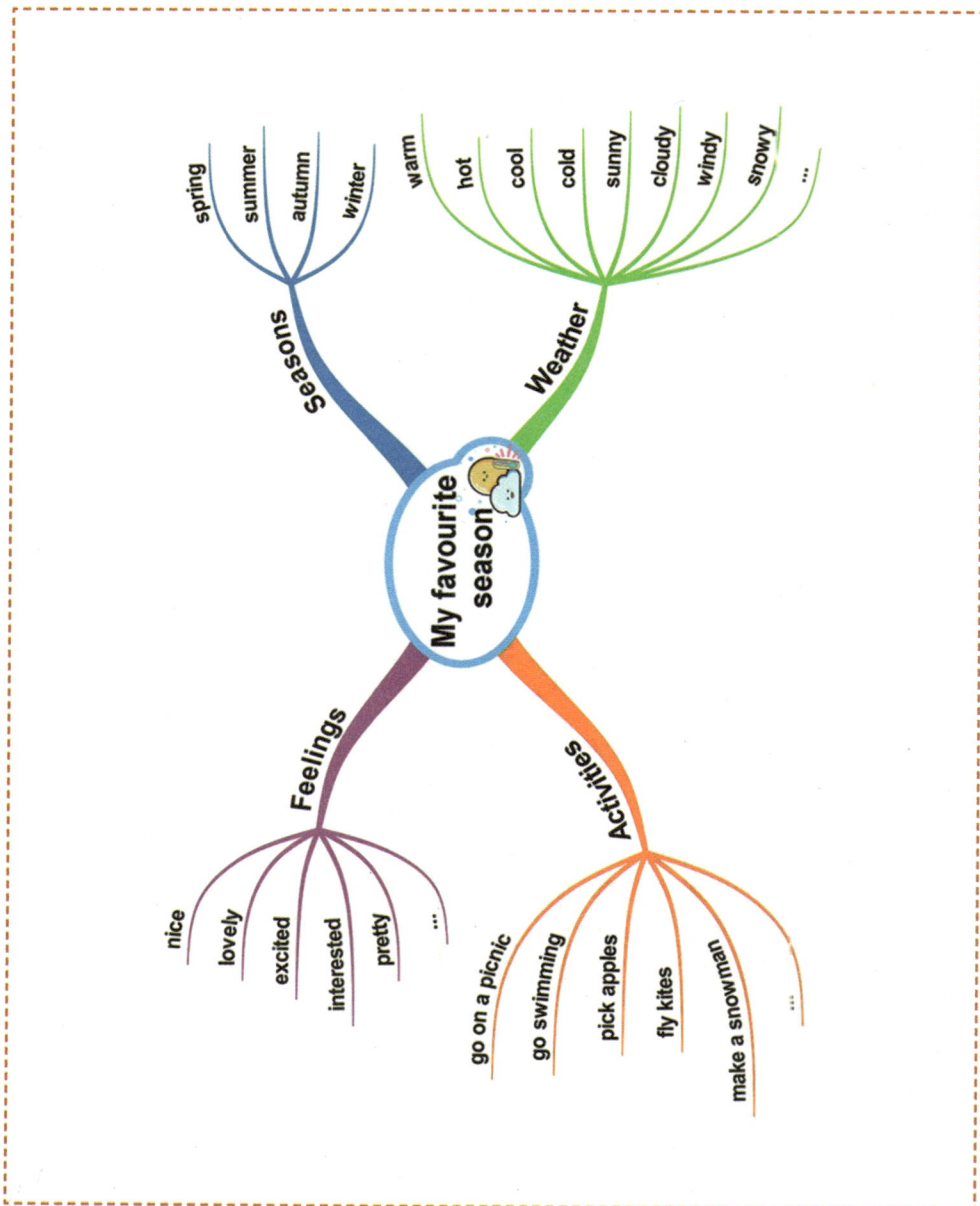

My favourite season

Seasons
- spring
- summer
- autumn
- winter

Weather
- warm
- hot
- cool
- cold
- sunny
- cloudy
- windy
- snowy
- ...

Feelings
- nice
- lovely
- excited
- interested
- pretty
- ...

Activities
- go on a picnic
- go swimming
- pick apples
- fly kites
- make a snowman
- ...

Unit 3 My school calendar

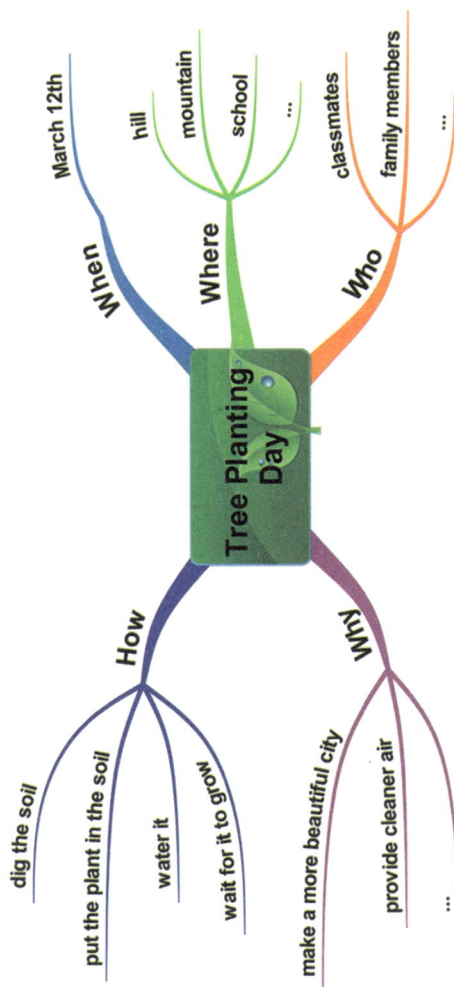

When — March 12th

Where — hill / mountain / school / ...

Who — classmates / family members / ...

Tree Planting Day

How — dig the soil / put the plant in the soil / water it / wait for it to grow

Why — make a more beautiful city / provide cleaner air / ...

五年级 下册

Unit 4 When is the art show?

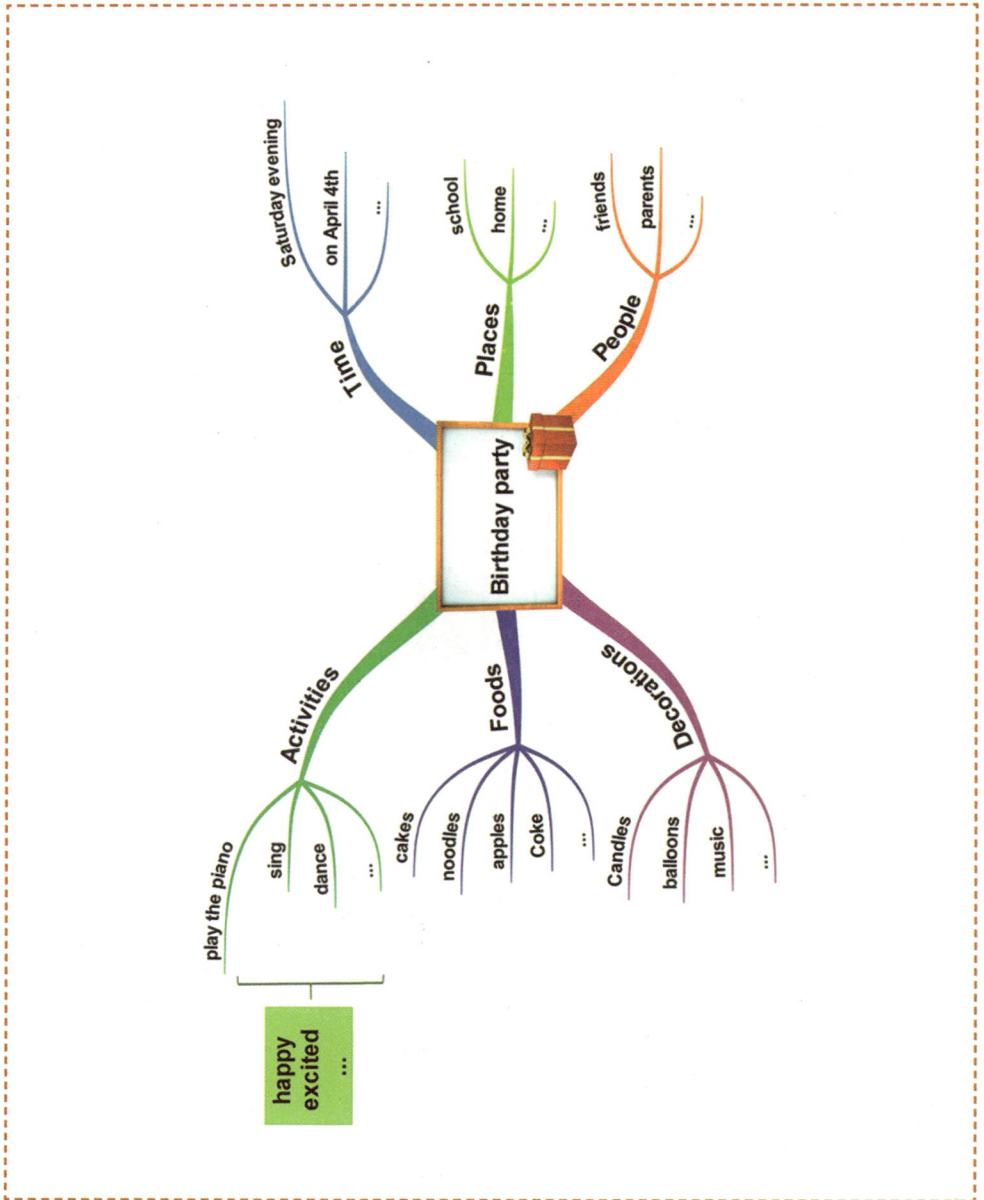

A mind map with **Birthday party** at the center, branching into:

- **Time**: Saturday evening, on April 4th, ...
- **Places**: school, home, ...
- **People**: friends, parents, ...
- **Activities**: play the piano, sing, dance, ... → happy, excited, ...
- **Foods**: cakes, noodles, apples, Coke, ...
- **Decorations**: Candles, balloons, music, ...

Unit 5 Whose dog is it?

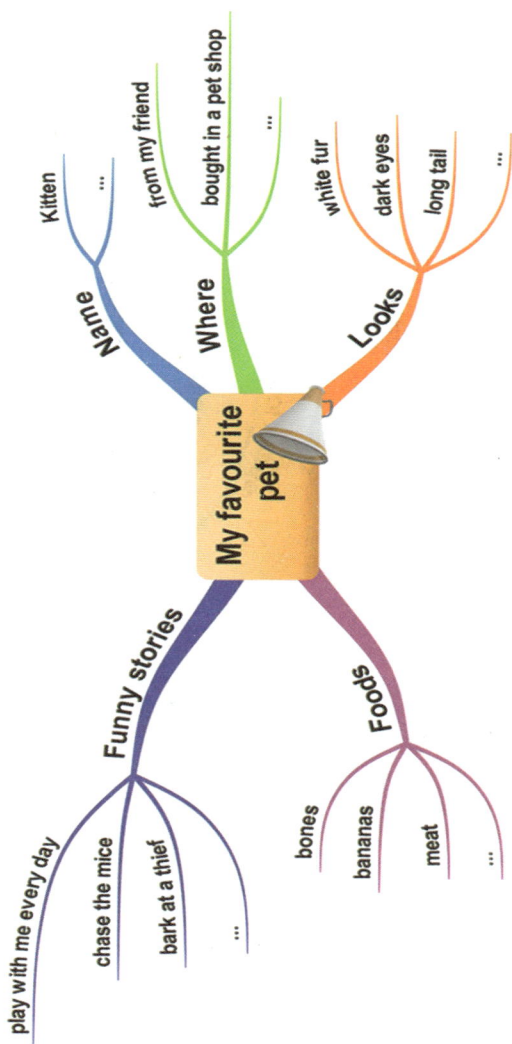

My favourite pet

Name
- Kitten
- ...

Where
- from my friend
- bought in a pet shop
- ...

Looks
- white fur
- dark eyes
- long tail
- ...

Funny stories
- play with me every day
- chase the mice
- bark at a thief
- ...

Foods
- bones
- bananas
- meat
- ...

Unit 6 Work quietly!

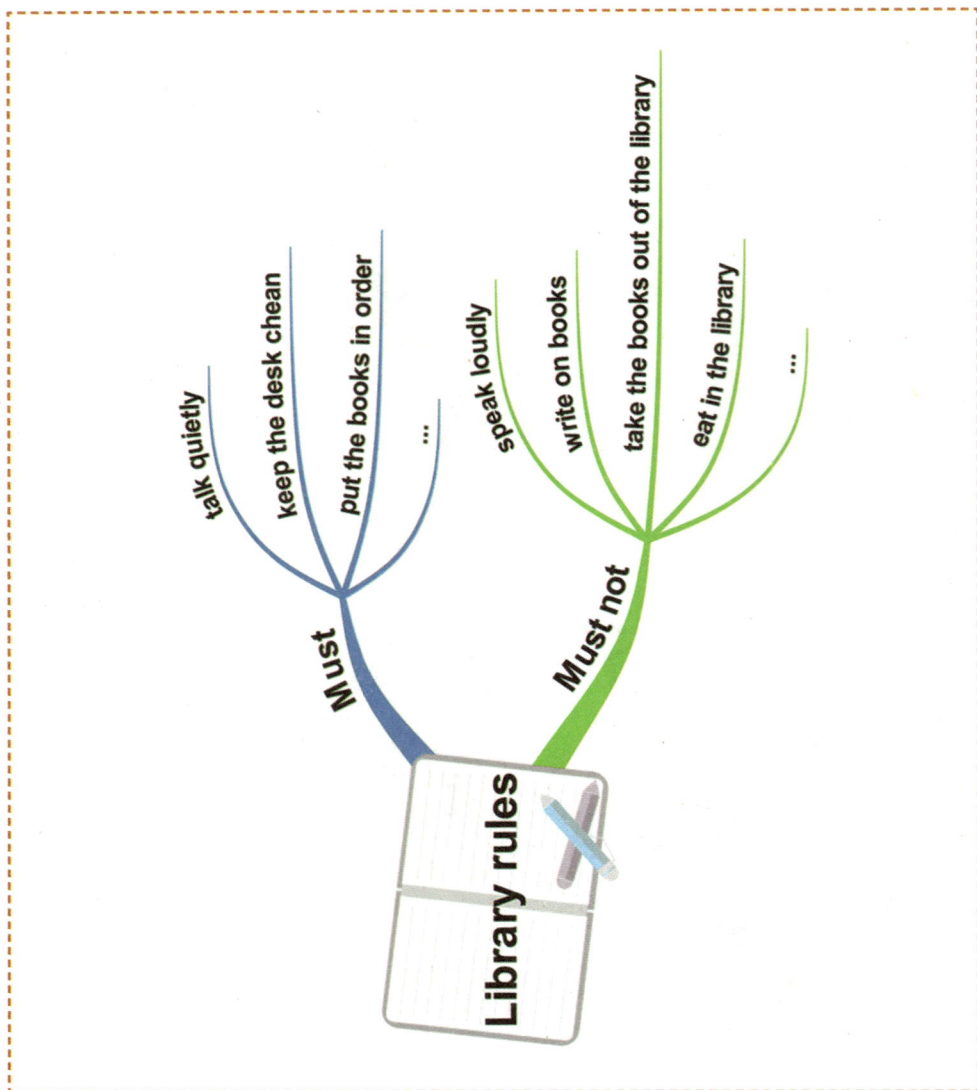

talk quietly

keep the desk chean

put the books in order

...

Must

speak loudly

write on books

take the books out of the library

eat in the library

...

Must not

Library rules

小学英语人教版六年级上册

Unit 1 How can I get there?

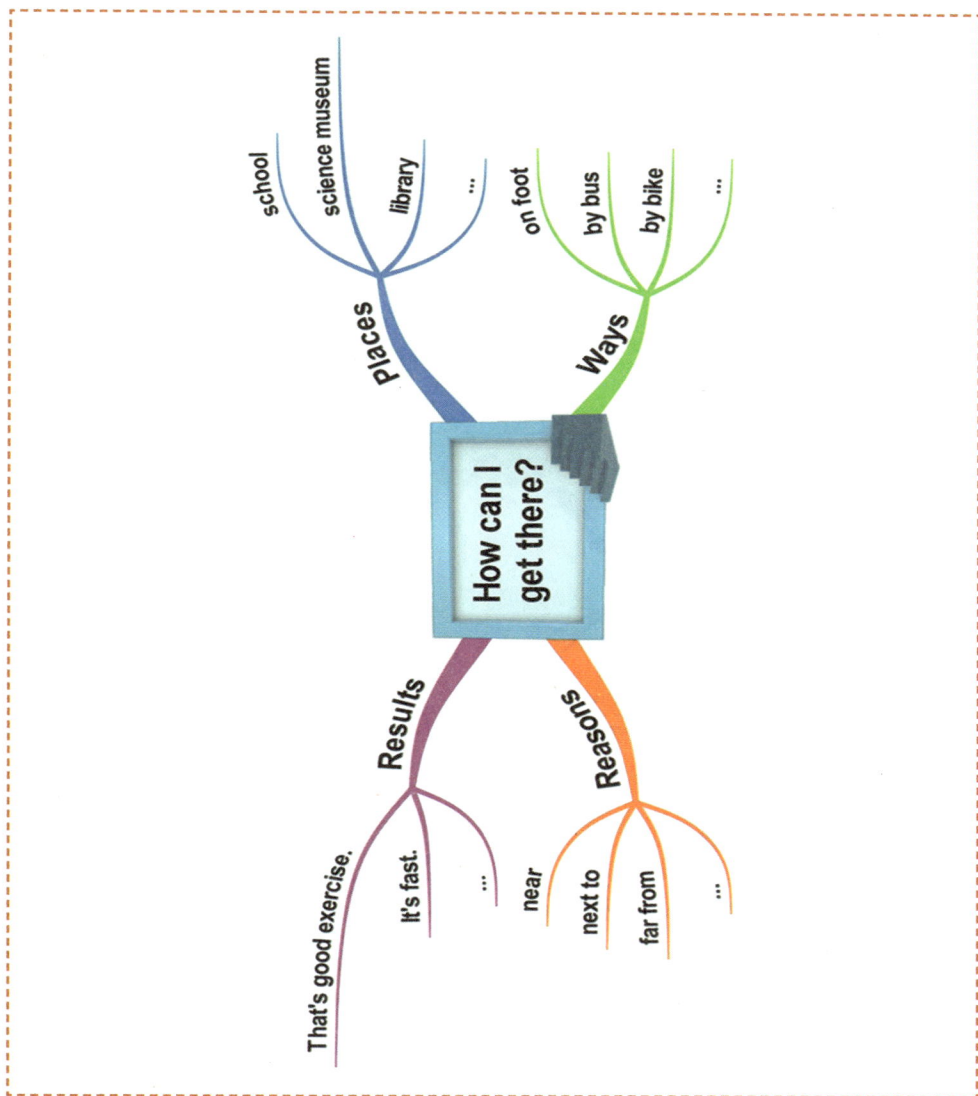

Places
- school
- science museum
- library
- ...

Ways
- on foot
- by bus
- by bike
- ...

How can I get there?

Results
- That's good exercise.
- It's fast.
- ...

Reasons
- near
- next to
- far from
- ...

Unit 2 Ways to go to school

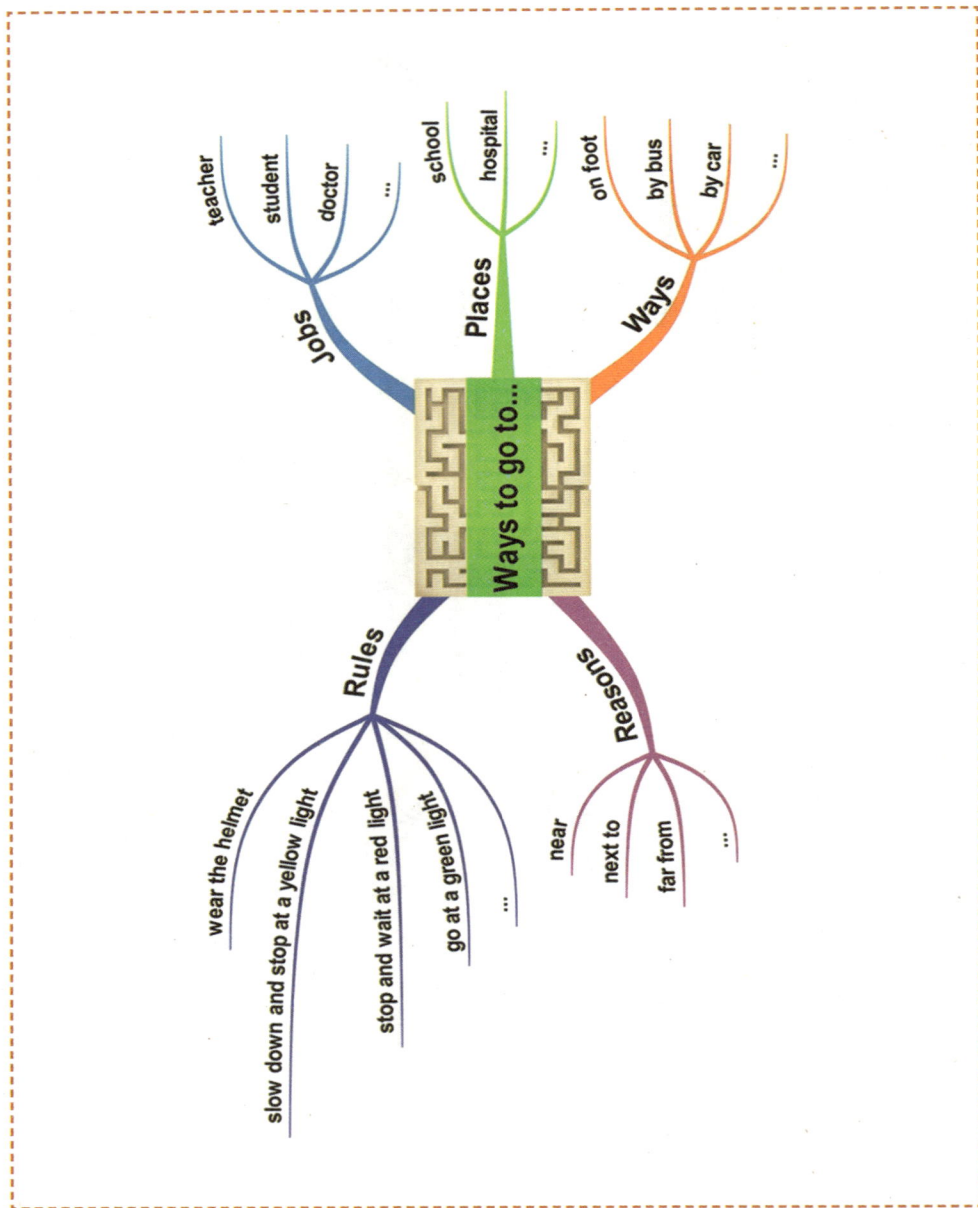

teacher
student
doctor
...

school
hospital
...

on foot
by bus
by car
...

Jobs

Places

Ways

Ways to go to...

Rules

Reasons

wear the helmet
slow down and stop at a yellow light
stop and wait at a red light
go at a green light
...

near
next to
far from
...

Unit 3 My weekend plan

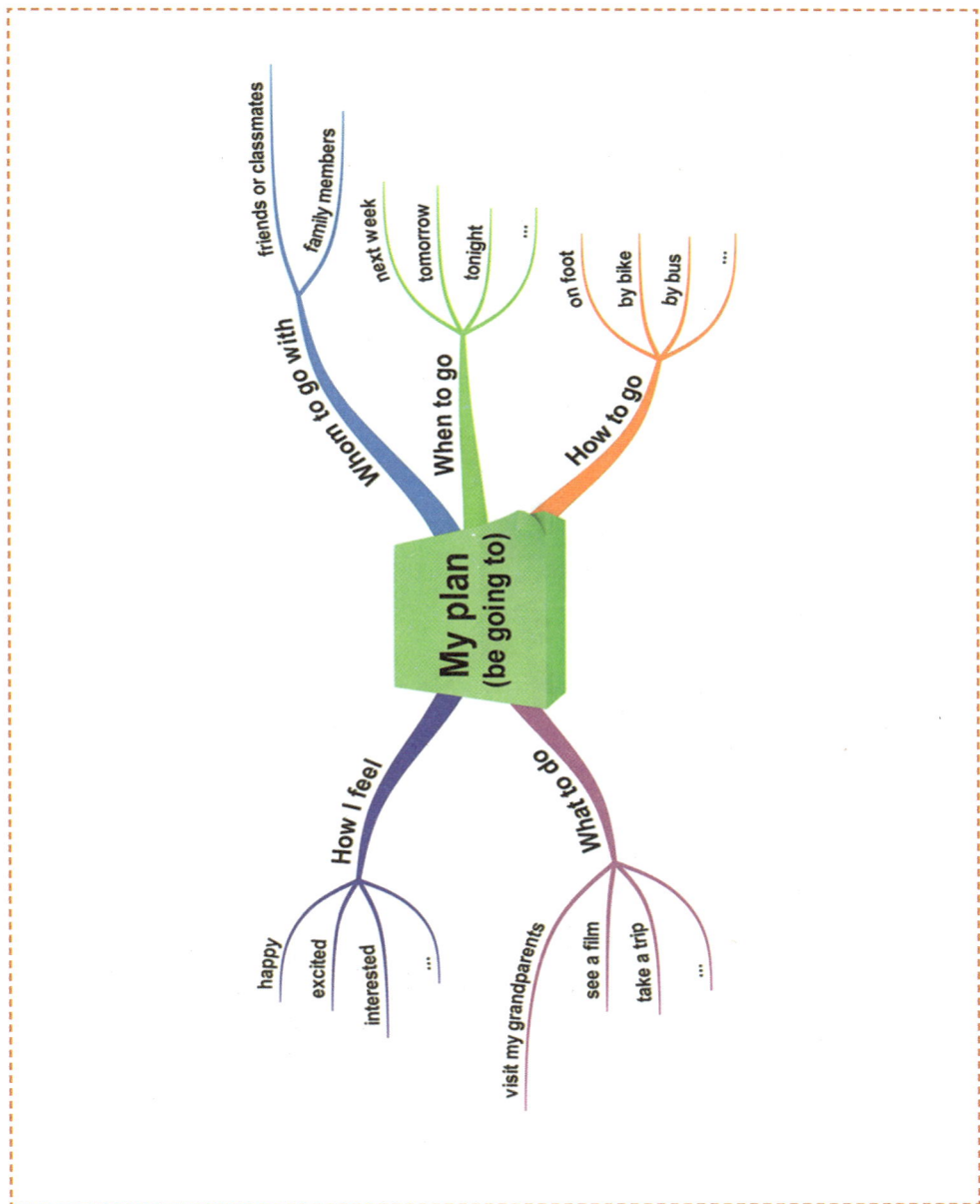

Unit 4 I have a pen pal

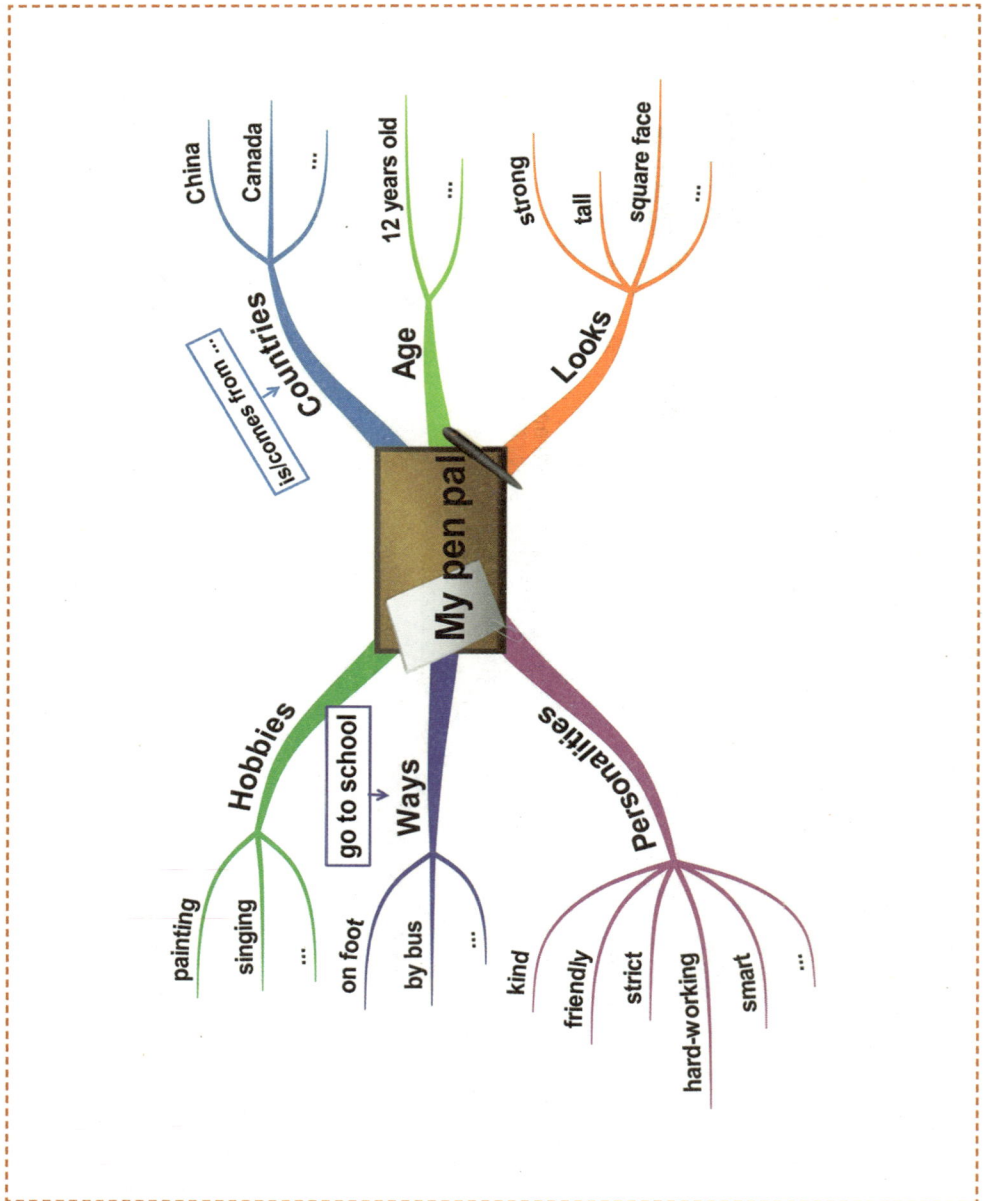

Unit 5 What does he do?

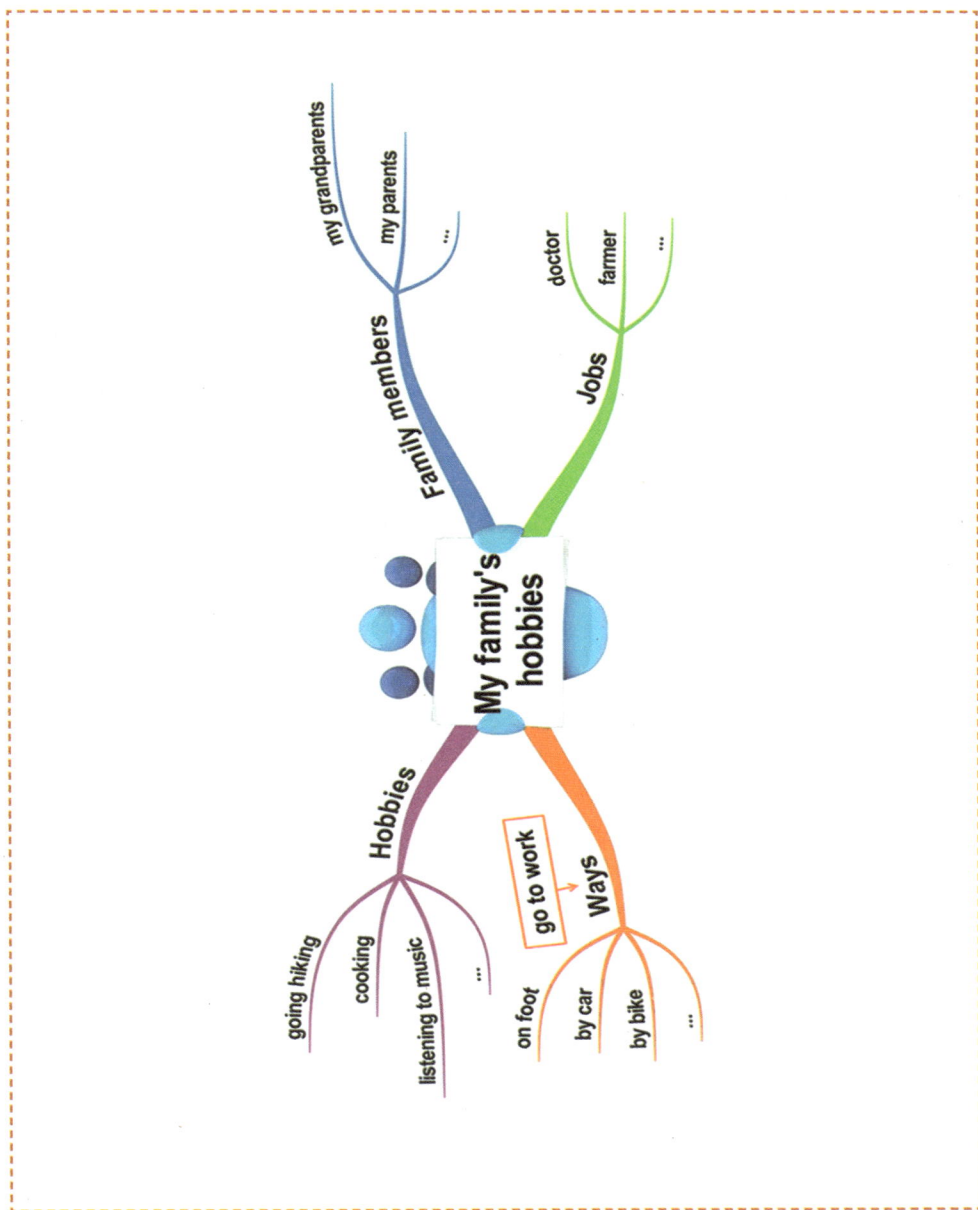

My family's hobbies

Family members
- my grandparents
- my parents
- ...

Jobs
- doctor
- farmer
- ...

Hobbies
- going hiking
- cooking
- listening to music
- ...

Ways — go to work
- on foot
- by car
- by bike
- ...

Unit 6 How do you feel?

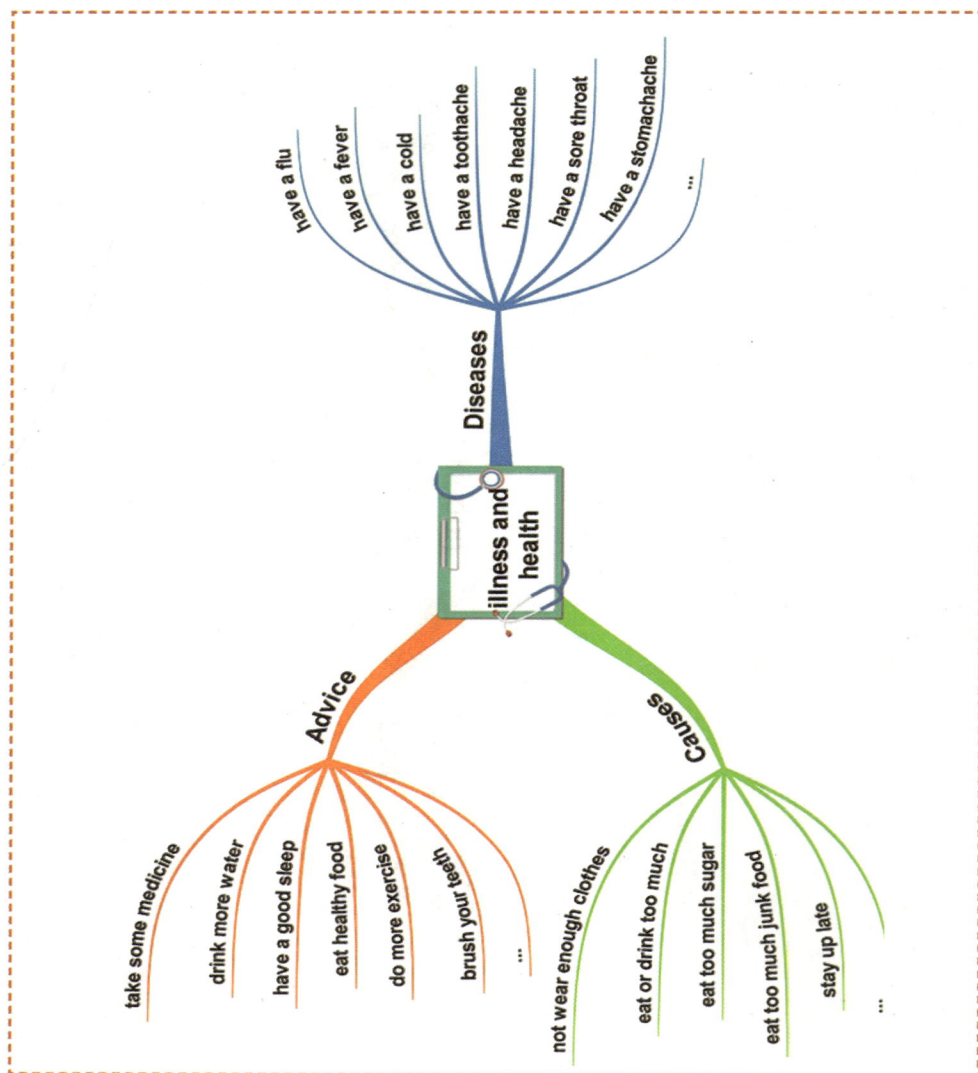

Diseases
- have a flu
- have a fever
- have a cold
- have a toothache
- have a headache
- have a sore throat
- have a stomachache
- ...

illness and health

Advice
- take some medicine
- drink more water
- have a good sleep
- eat healthy food
- do more exercise
- brush your teeth
- ...

Causes
- not wear enough clothes
- eat or drink too much
- eat too much sugar
- eat too much junk food
- stay up late
- ...

小学英语人教版六年级下册

Unit 1 How tall are you?

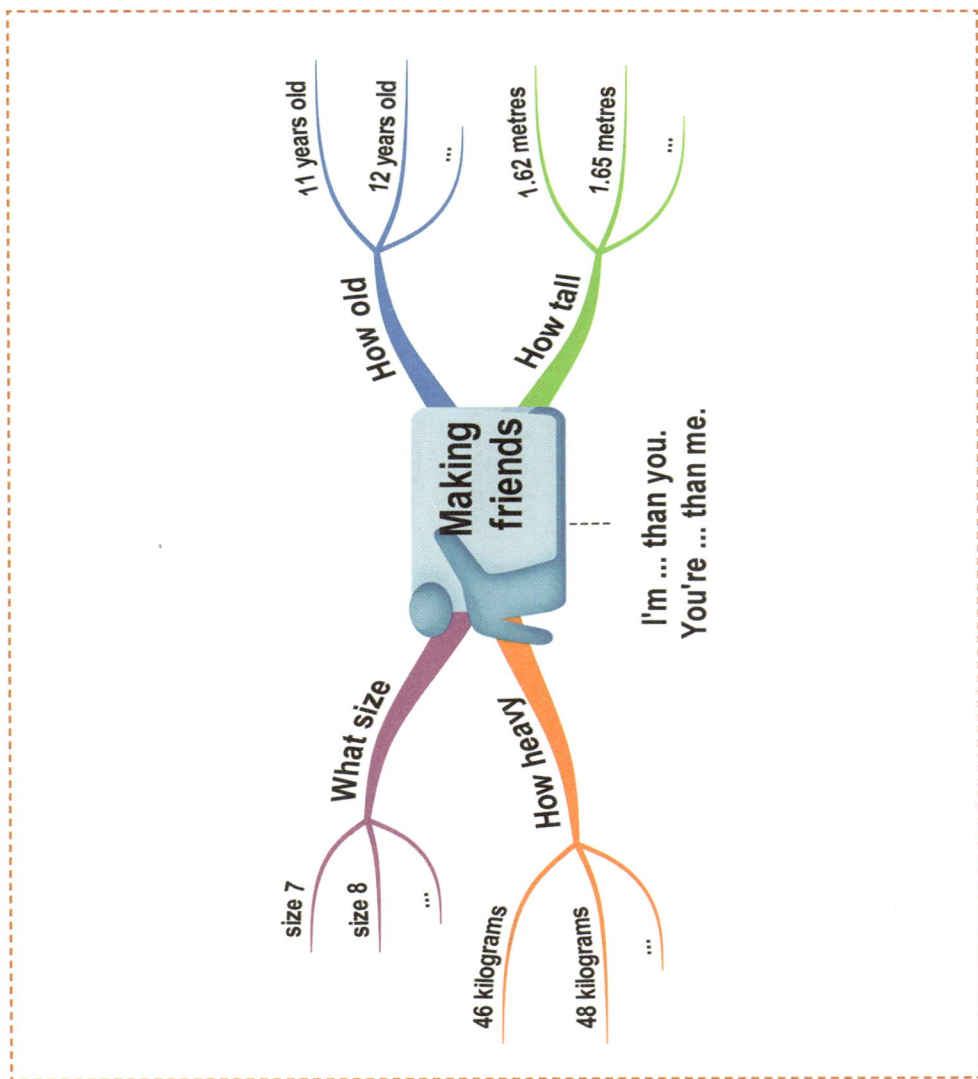

11 years old

12 years old

...

1.62 metres

1.65 metres

...

How old

How tall

Making friends

I'm ... than you.
You're ... than me.

What size

How heavy

size 7

size 8

...

46 kilograms

48 kilograms

...

Unit 2 Last weekend

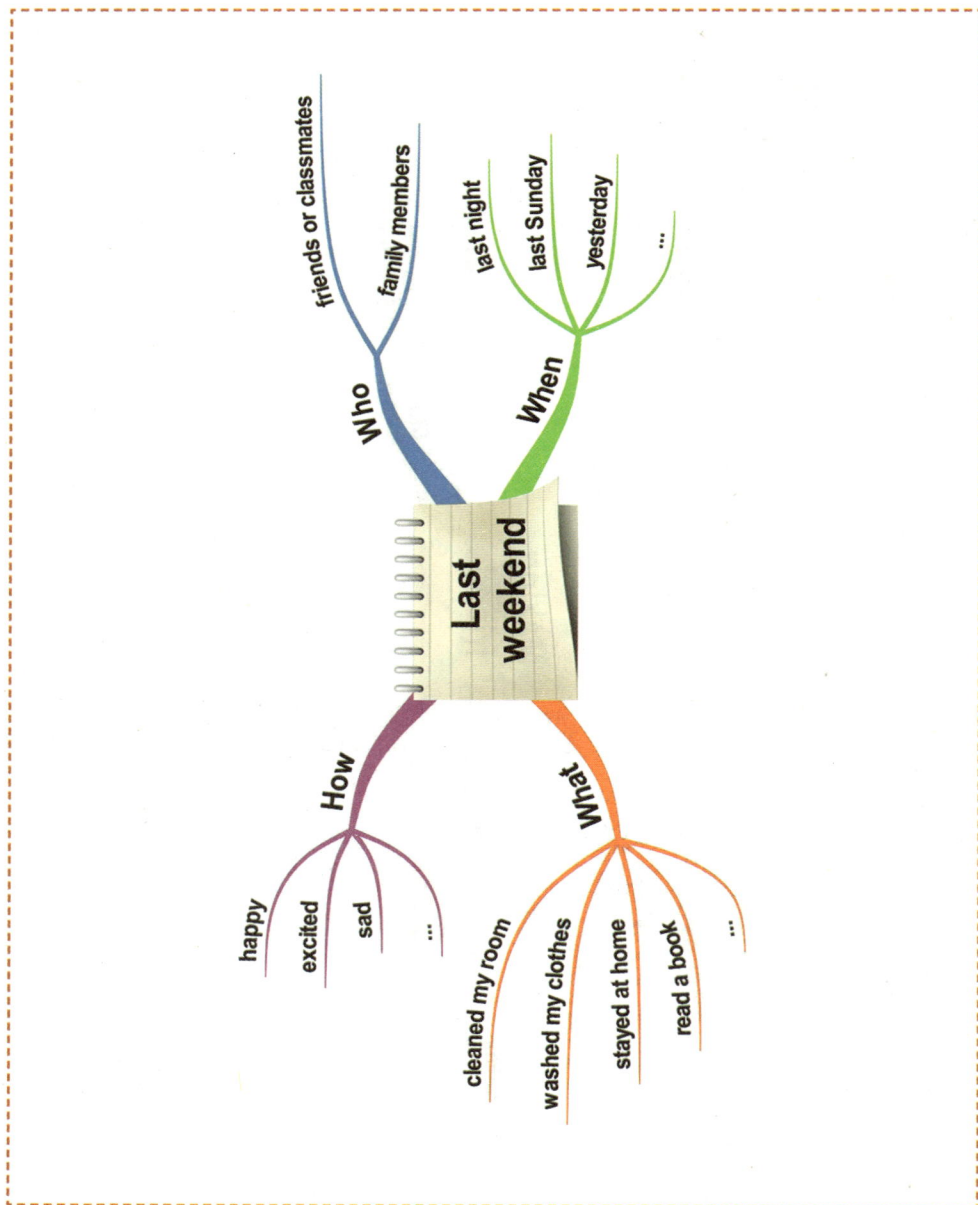

Unit 3 Where did you go?

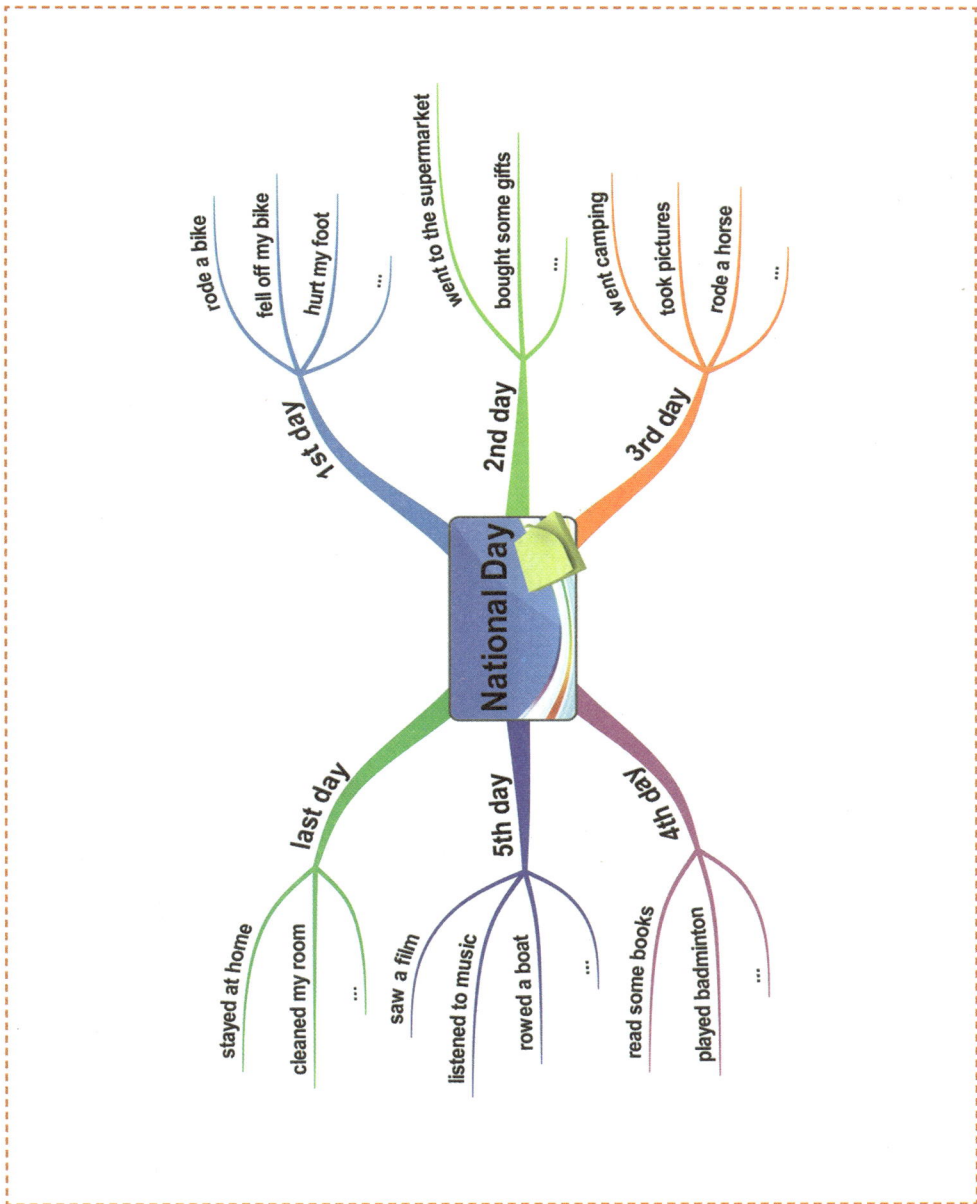

rode a bike

fell off my bike

hurt my foot

...

went to the supermarket

bought some gifts

...

went camping

took pictures

rode a horse

...

1st day

2nd day

3rd day

National Day

last day

5th day

4th day

stayed at home

cleaned my room

...

saw a film

listened to music

rowed a boat

...

read some books

played badminton

...

Unit 4 Then and now

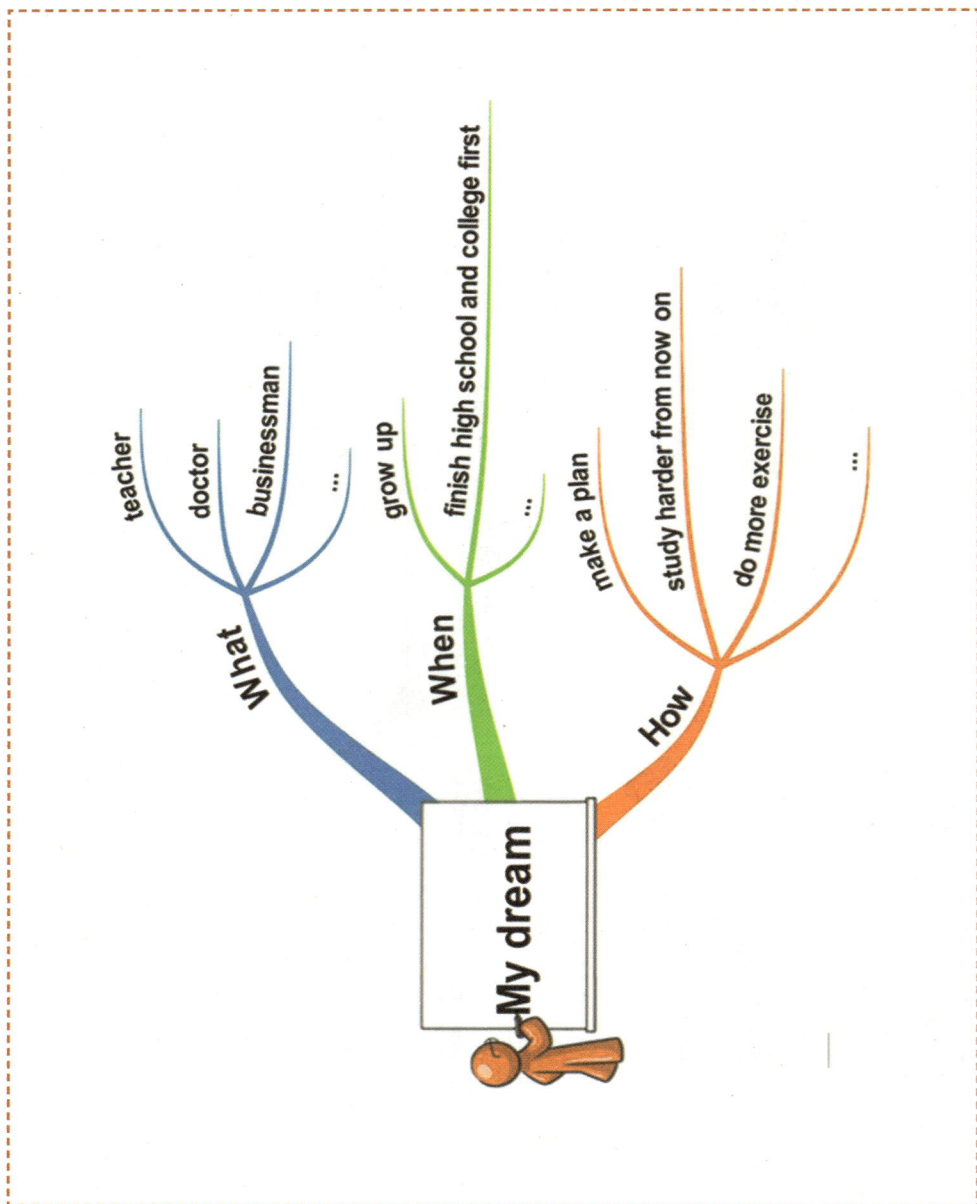

现在
进行时

一般
将来时

一般
现在时

代词

名词

一般
过去时

介词

形容词、
副词的
比较等级

数词

冠词

语法思维导图

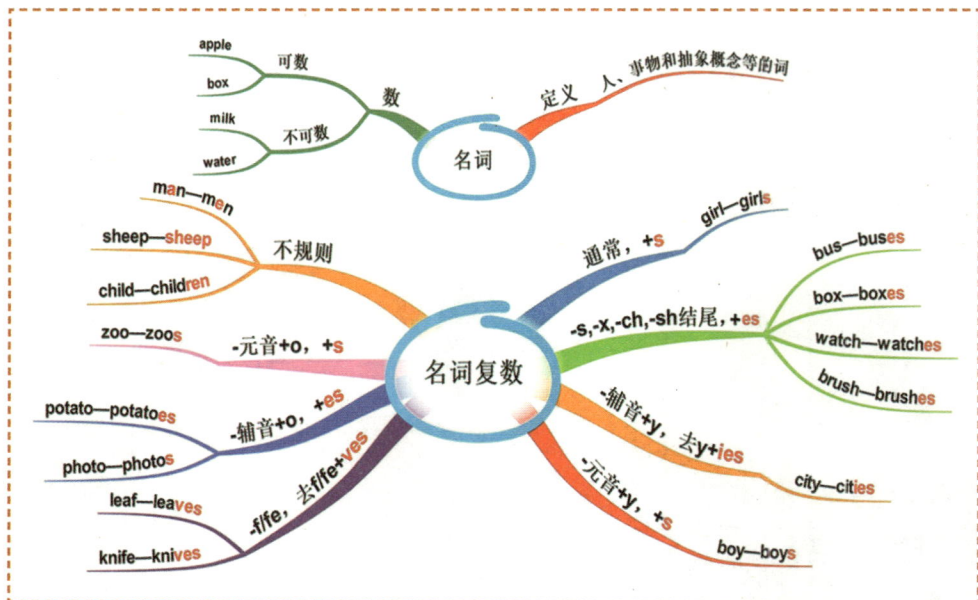

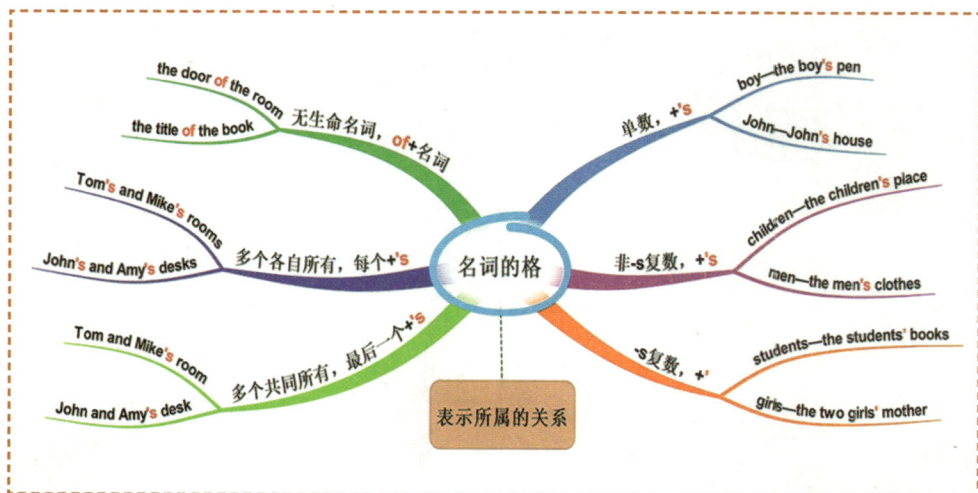

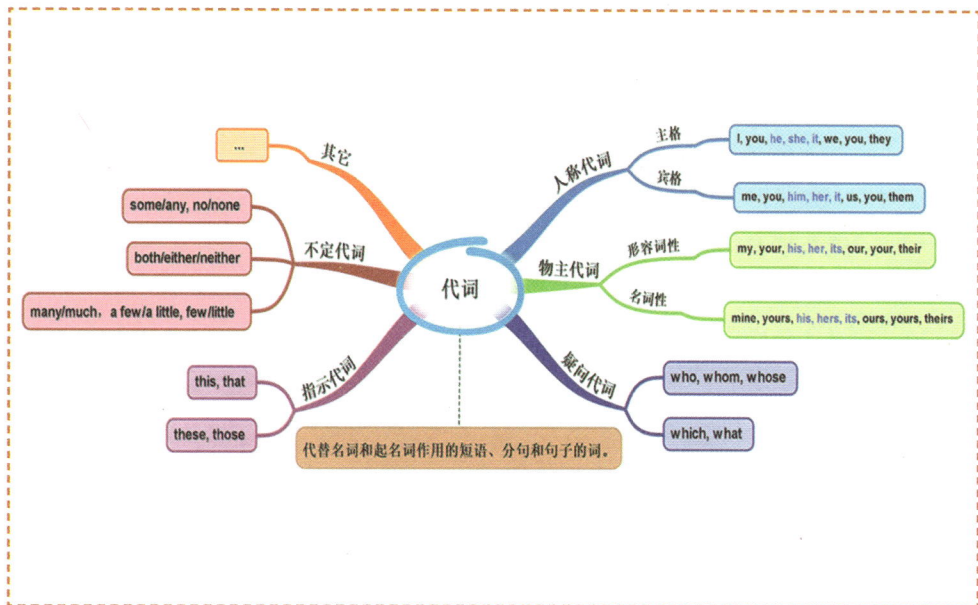

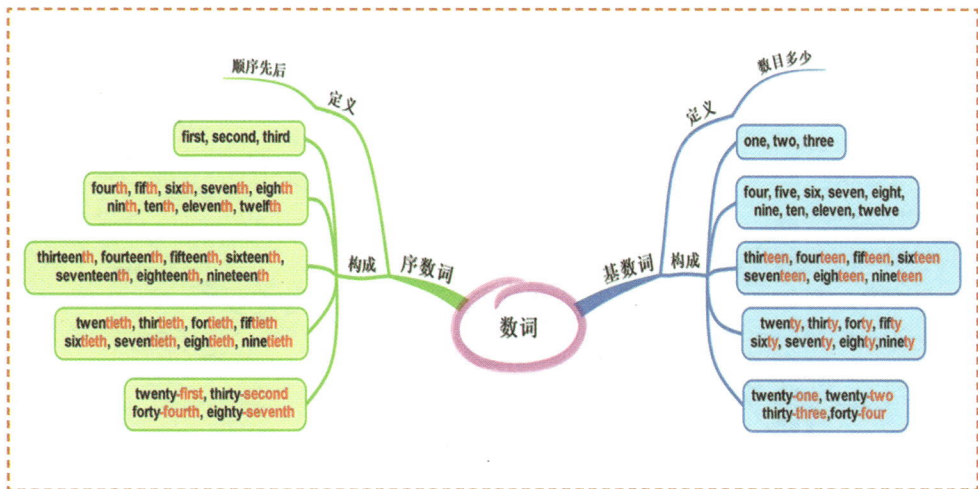

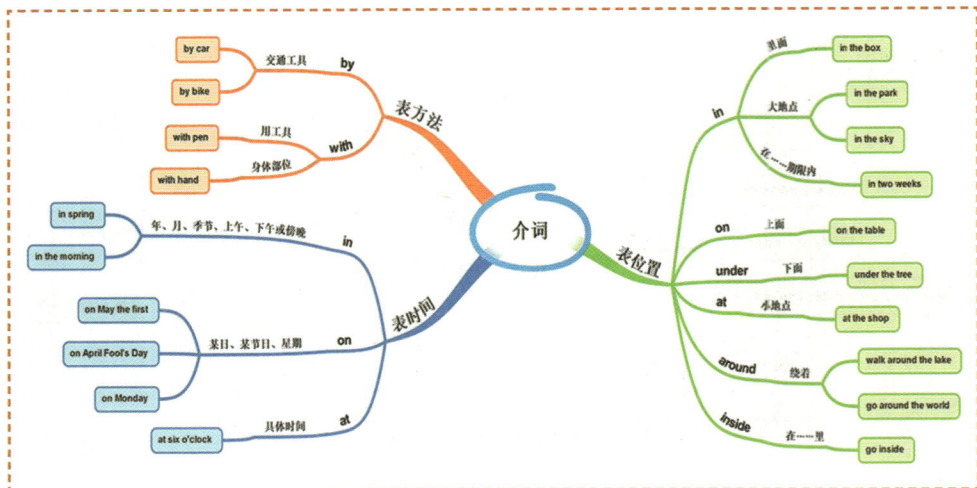

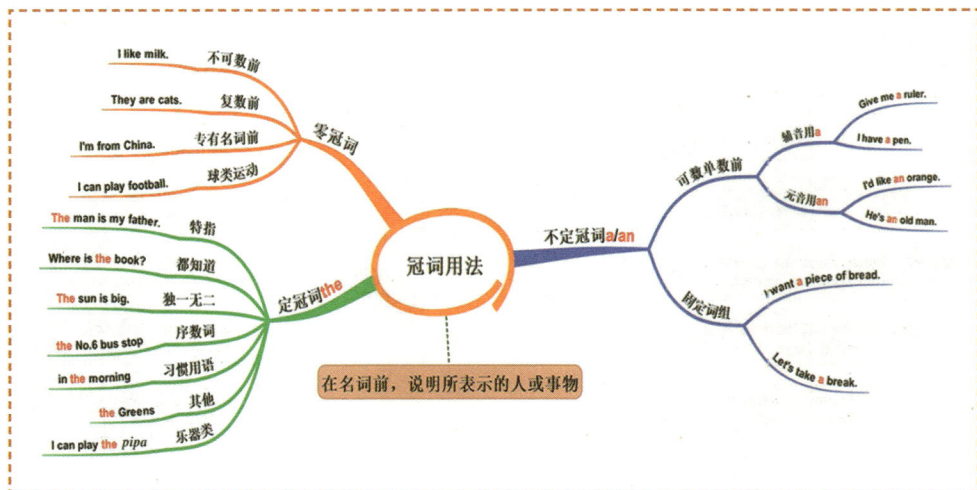

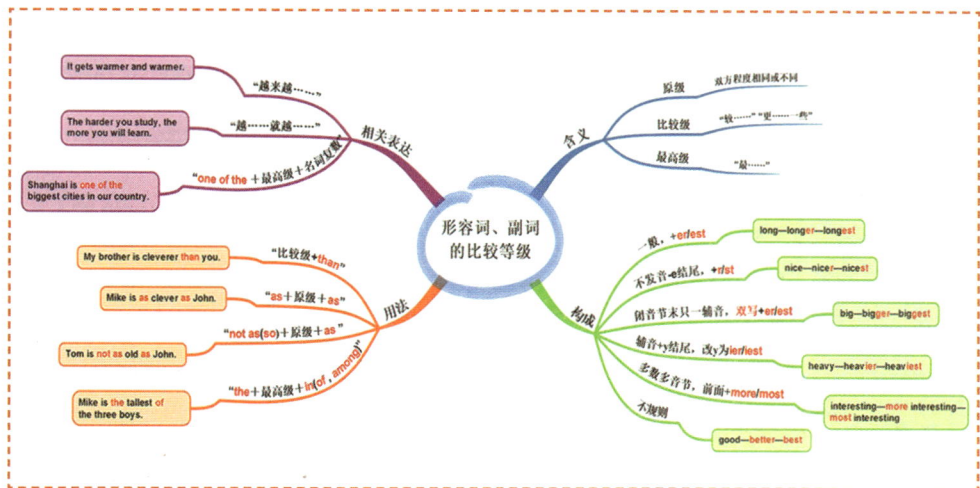

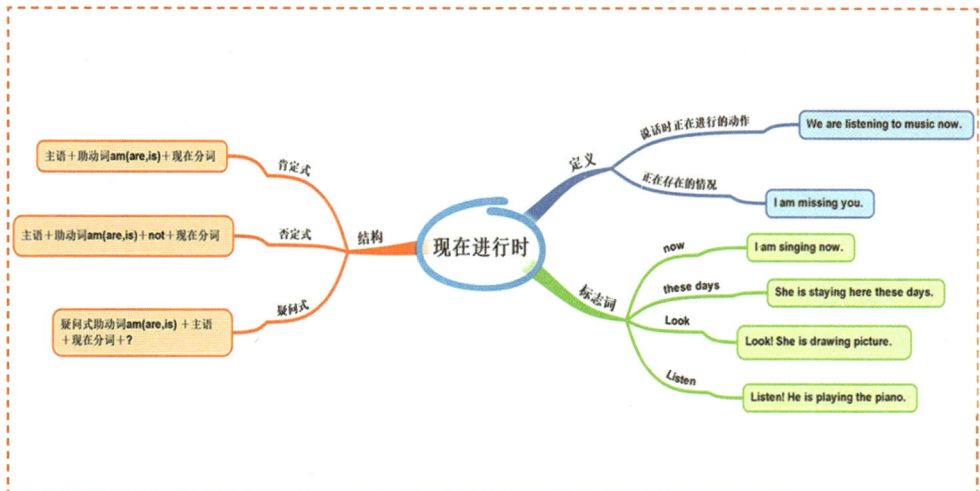

语法思维导图 >>

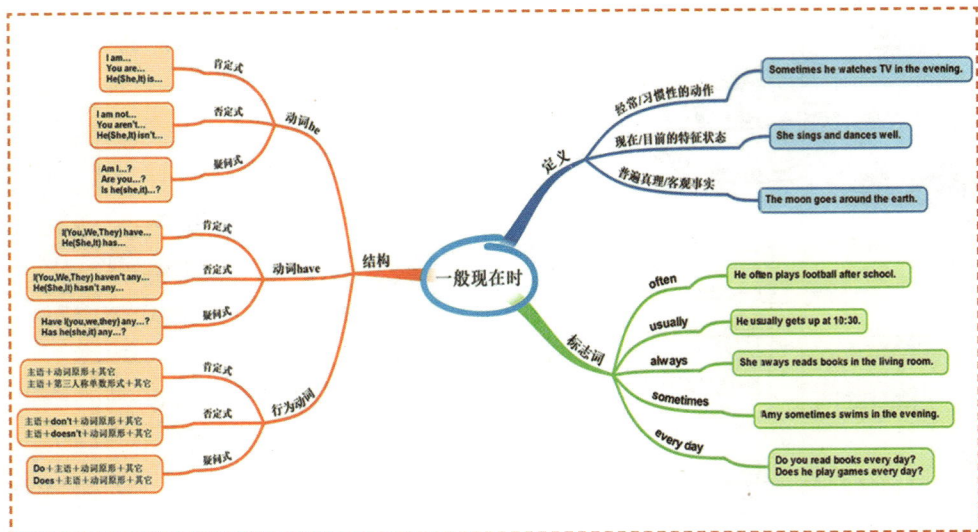

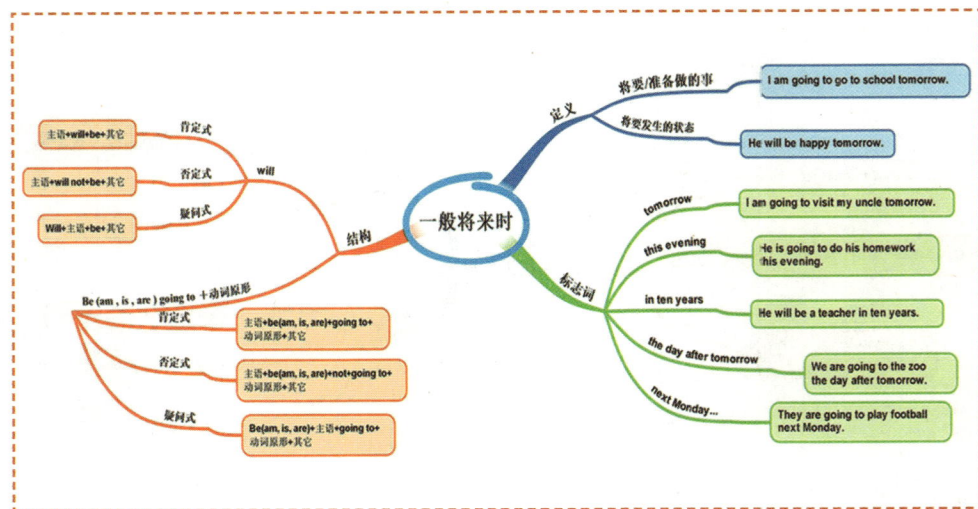

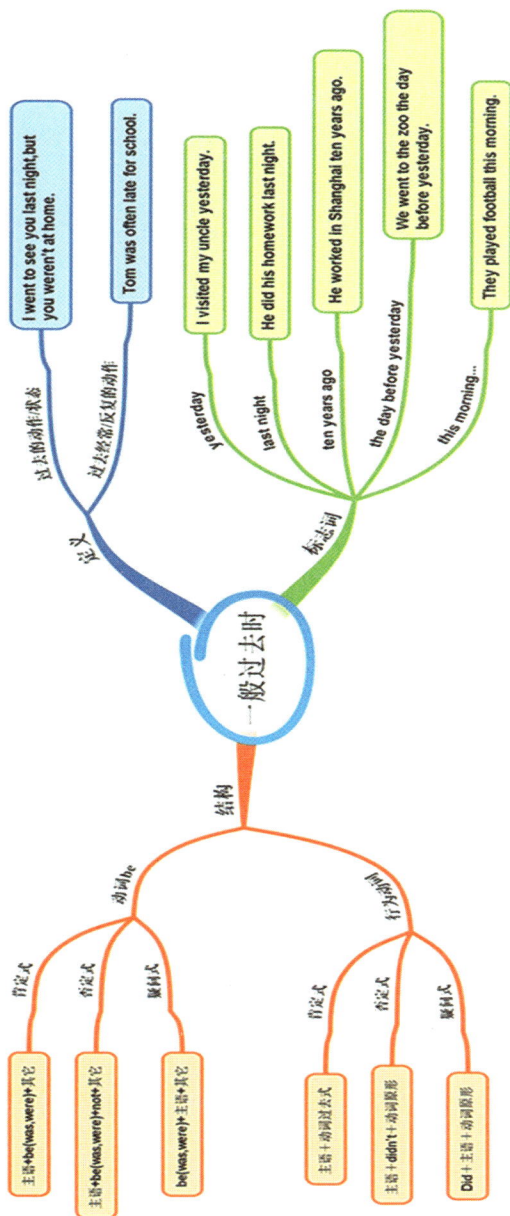

一般过去时

定义
- 过去的动作/状态
  - I went to see you last night,but you weren't at home.
- 过去经常/反复的动作
  - Tom was often late for school.

标志词
- yesterday
  - I visited my uncle yesterday.
- last night
  - He did his homework last night.
- ten years ago
  - He worked in Shanghai ten years ago.
- the day before yesterday
  - We went to the zoo the day before yesterday.
- this morning...
  - They played football this morning.

结构
- 动词be
  - 肯定式
    - 主语+be(was,were)+其它
  - 否定式
    - 主语+be(was,were)+not+其它
  - 疑问式
    - be(was,were)+主语+其它
- 行为动词
  - 肯定式
    - 主语+动词过去式
  - 否定式
    - 主语+didn't+动词原形
  - 疑问式
    - Did+主语+动词原形

语法思维导图

下 篇
思维导图绘制方法

万丈高楼平地起，学习思维导图也是一样的。我们一线教师为了减少在实际操作中犯各种各样的错误，掌握一些简单的、正确的规则和技巧是非常必要的。本章将从专业术语、核心要素、绘制规则、绘制步骤进行阐述。

一、思维导图的专业术语

为了更好地绘制一幅思维导图，以本人的自我介绍（如下图）为例来说明几个思维导图的专业术语，它们是：中心主题、主节点、父节点、子节点、主分支和子分支。

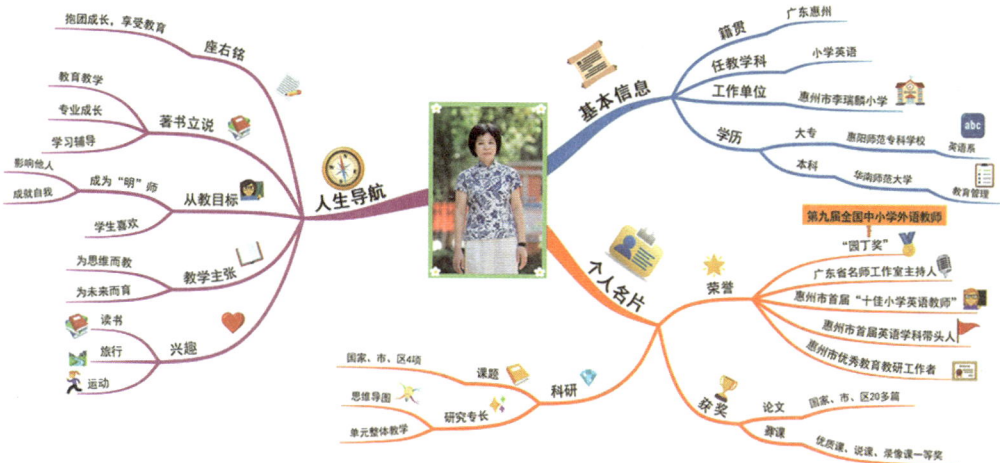

自我介绍的思维导图

中心主题：位于思维导图的最中心，它可以是图像或文字，是一幅思维导图中最明显、最核心的部分。 由于本图是用来自我介绍的，所以用了我的照片表示中心主题。中心主题也可以用文字来表示，可以写成"韩丽萍的自我介绍"。

主节点：直接隶属于中心主题的下一级节点，也是整个思维导图的一级节点。图中包含"基本信息""个人名片"和"人生导航"3个主节点。

父节点和子节点：处于相邻层级的相连的两个节点构成父子关系。如图中"籍贯"是"基本信息"的子节点，"基本信息"是"籍贯"的父节点。

主分支：也称为一级分支，直接隶属于中心主题的节点及其节点的子节点构成的分支。图中包含了"基本信息""个人名片"和"人生导航"3个主分支。

子分支：隶属于某个非中心节点的分支都可以称为该节点的子分支。图中"从教目标"所在的分支就是"人生导航"。①

二、思维导图的核心要素

一幅完整的思维导图，包含六大方面的核心要素。它们分别是：心——中心图，线——线条，词——关键词，图——图像，色——颜色，构——结构。在绘制过程中，我们要严格遵守思维导图的核心绘制法则，灵活运用六大核心要素，从而建立有效的思维秩序和逻辑结构。②

三、思维导图绘制的规则

东尼·博赞在书中给出的思维导图的绘制规则是这样的：

（1）从白纸的中心开始画，周围要留出空白。

（2）用一幅图像或图画表达中心思想。

（3）绘图时尽可能使用多种颜色。

（4）连接中心图像和主要分支，然后再连接主要分支和二级分支，接着再连接二级分支和三级分支，依次类推。

（5）用美丽的曲线连接，永远不要使用直线连接。

（6）每条线上注明一个关键词。

（7）尽可能多地使用图形。

这些规则被广为接受，但不足之处在于没有清晰地说明为什么要这么做，以及哪些是必须遵守的，哪些是可以调整的。根据在实践中的运用与体会，我们分别从纸张、关键词、图像（图标）、线条、颜色和顺序做更进一层的细化阐述。

（一）纸张使用规则

1. 使用完全空白，没有网格线、小图案或颜色的纸张

在绘制思维导图时，要使用完全空白，没有网格线、小图案或颜色的纸张。因为使用带有网格线的纸，格子线与思维导图的线条相互交错，会对思维本身产

---

① 赵国庆.别说你懂思维导图［M］.北京：人民邮电出版社，2015.

② 刘艳.看完就用的思维导图［M］.北京：中信出版集团，2018.

生干扰（如下图）。

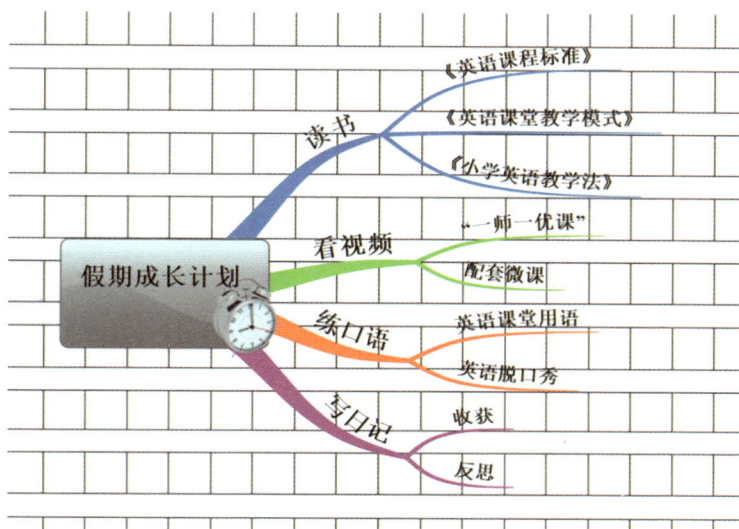

带格子的纸会给思维导图本身带来干扰

而使用带有小图案或颜色的纸张，因为它们本身就具有图案和色彩，同样会对思维本身产生干扰（如下图）。

带有小图案或颜色的纸张给思维导图本身带来干扰

2. 视主分支数量决定纸张的摆放

若思维导图内容较多（主分支数大于或等于4条时），建议将白纸横放，将中心主题置于白纸的中心位置（如下图）。

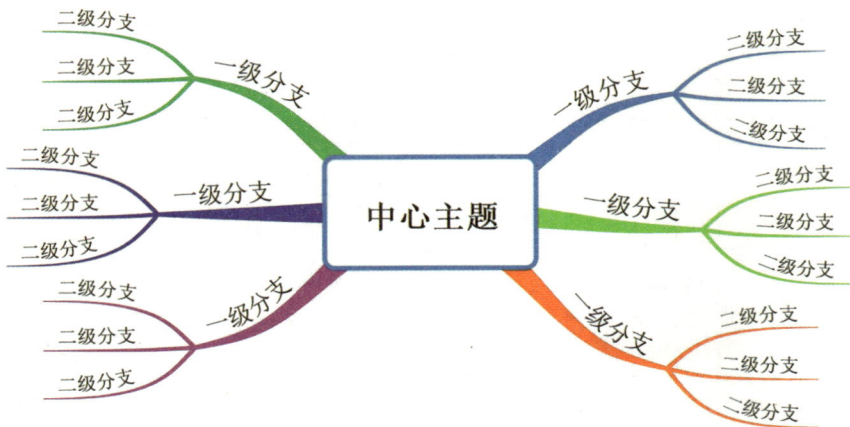

白纸横放示例

若思维导图的主分支不多（小于或等于3条时），建议将白纸竖放，将中心主题置于白纸的中部偏左的位置（如下图）。

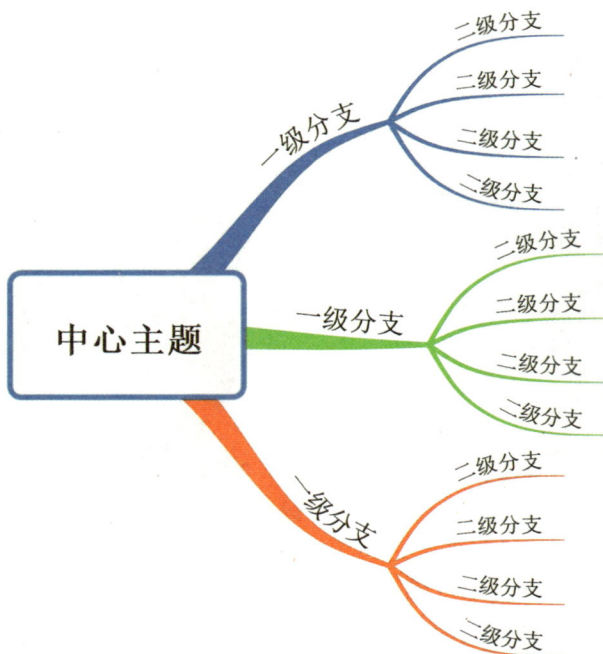

白纸竖放示例

（二）关键词使用规则

关键词能够概括文章主旨、揭示文章中心、展示文章脉络、标示句段关系，对于加深内容的理解与记忆有很大的帮助。①

1. 尽量用词而不是短语或句子

关键词的选择一般以名词或动词为主。因为名词、动词不仅是构成意思表达的基本元素，更是强烈可视化的词语，它们能够强化我们对内容的理解和记忆。

2. 一线一词

原则上，一条线上只写一个关键词，即"一线一词"。中文关键词最好在四个字以内，可以是一个字、两个字的词语或四个字的成语；英文的关键词原则上要求只承载一个单词。②

如下两图的对比："in the morning do homework"实际上是包含了"morning" "do" 和 "homework" 三个关键词，"in the evening watch TV and have a big dinner" 包含了"evening" "watch" "TV" "have" 和 "dinner" 五个关键词，同样需要拆分（根据实际教学需要，可以把"do homework" "watch TV" "have dinner" 当作关键词）。

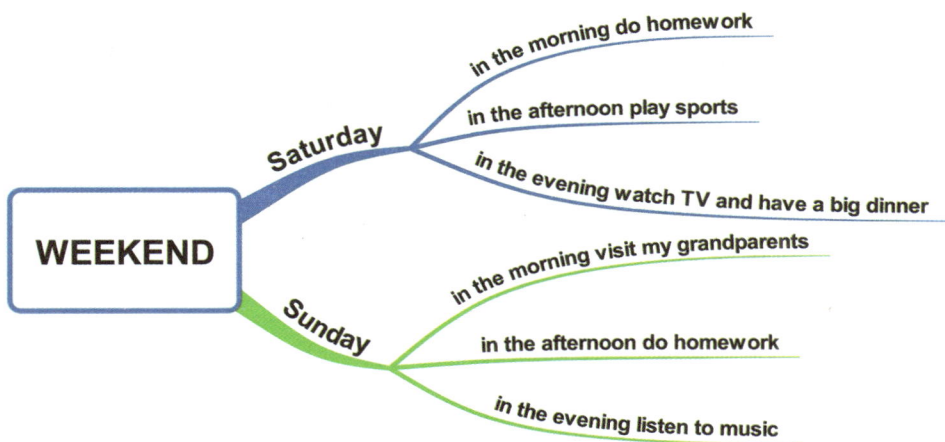

关键词的不当使用

---

① 刘艳.看完就用的思维导图［M］.北京：中信出版集团，2018.

② 刘艳.看完就用的思维导图［M］.北京：中信出版集团，2018.

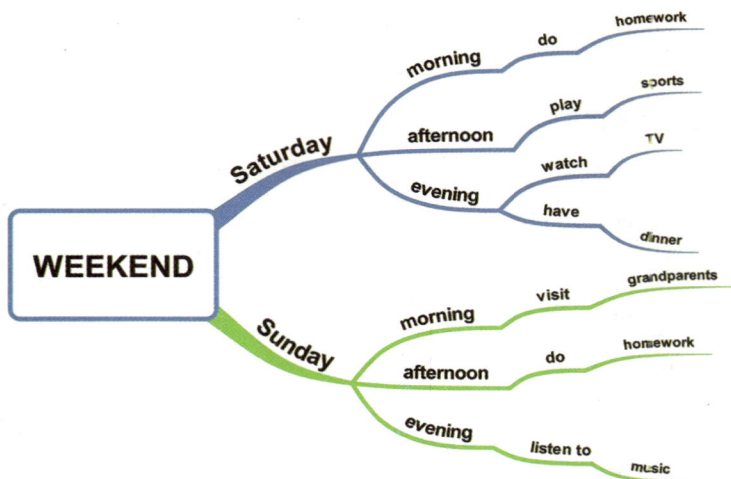

关键词的合理使用

3. 当句子是独立意义单元时，短语或者句子可以做关键词，特别是英文关键词

并不是说关键词绝对不能使用短语或者句子，如果短语或者句子本身就是一个独立意义单元且不可拆分时是可以用短语或句子做关键词的。例如：诗句、格言、特殊用语等是可以做关键词的。[①] 2017年刘艳写的《你一学就会的思维导图》中提到："对于一些特殊情况也要学会特殊对待，一些专有名词、科学术语、书本名称、章节段落名称、特定概念等，如果进行提炼就失去了意义，为了保证思想的正确传递，可以放在一个线条上。"

（三）图像（图标）使用规则

1. 尽量使用中心图像

使用图像（图标）可以吸引人的眼睛和大脑的注意力，可以触发联想、帮助记忆、提高视觉感触力，更好地突出主题。如下图，读者一眼就可以知道这幅思维导图的中心是"水果"。

---

① 赵国庆.别说你懂思维导图［M］.北京：人民邮电出版社，2015.

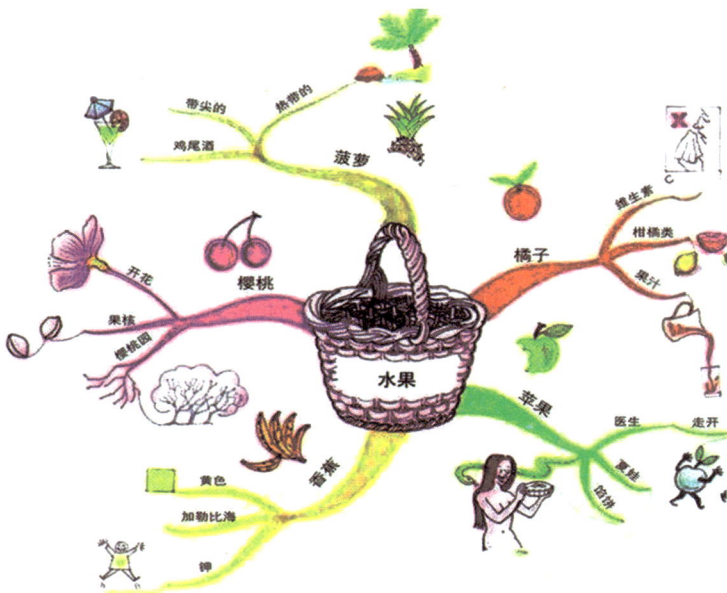

中心图的合理使用

2. 图像（图标）应与要表达的内容紧密相关

图像（图标）的作用是透过图像（图标）的引导，让读者触发联想、发散思维，更好地突出主题中心内容，所以图像（图标）应与要表达的内容紧密相关。

如下图，读者一眼就可以知道这幅思维导图是关于"spring"所包括的月份、节日、活动、天气等内容的。

图像（图标）与中心内容相关

3. 每个分支的图像（图标）大小呈递减模式

图像（图标）起到了画龙点睛的作用，每幅思维导图都是一幅思维作品。每个分支的图像（图标）大小要呈递减模式，即下一层的图像（图标）应该是比上一层的图像（图标）小。

（四）线条使用规则

1. 尽可能使用曲线

使用曲线主要是因为美观。我们前面提到了思维导图应用于教学上的理论之一就是脑科学理论。脑科学研究表明，人的大脑是由亿万个脑细胞组成的。每个细胞中均含有胞体和突起，突起根据形状又可以分为树突和轴突。思维导图的主分支与子分支与大脑神经有着异曲同工之妙，二者不仅"形似"，而且"神似"。

2. 线条由粗到细，线条的长度与线上的关键词等长

线条由粗到细的目的：一是突出主题；二是美观。线条的长度尽量与线上关键词的长度相当，这样可以让思维导图更加紧凑和美观（如下图）。这里还要特别提醒的是除中心主题的线条要粗些，有重要信息的地方线条也可适当加粗一些。

从粗到细的线条

3. 不同分支之间可以建立相互呼应的关系

在绘制思维导图时，如果不同分支之间存在一定的关联则可以采用箭头建立

关系（如下图）。

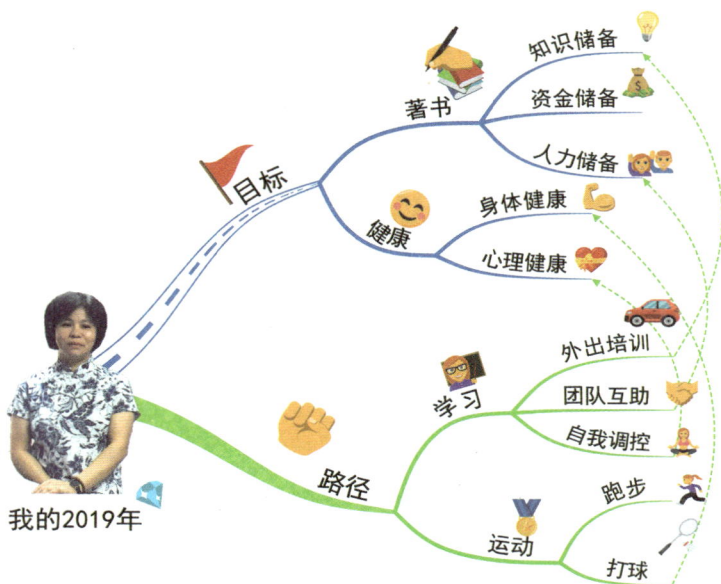

箭头的使用

（五）颜色使用规则

色彩是加强记忆和提高创造力最有用的工具之一。在绘制思维导图时，尽可能一个分支采用一个主色调，而不是一个层次一个主色调（如下面两图对比）。

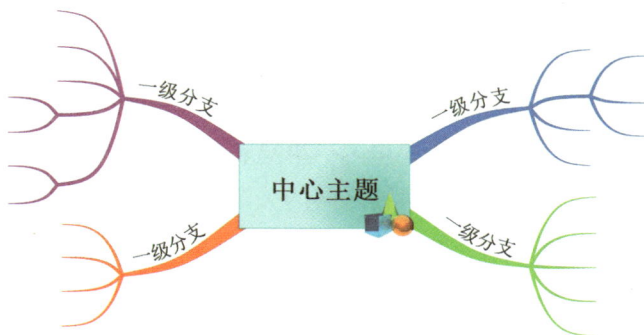

正确案例：一个分支一个主色调

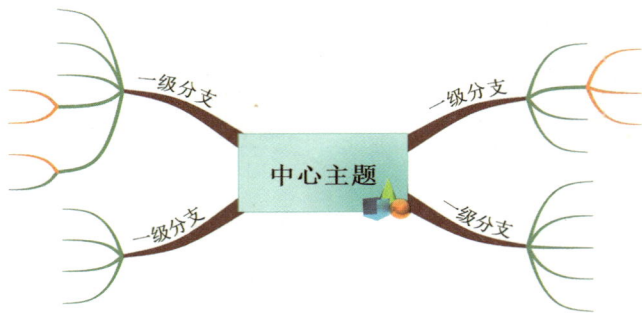

不当案例：一个层次一个主色调

（六）顺序规则

不管是读思维导图还是绘制思维导图都是建议从纸张的右上角45°开始，按照顺时针的方向到左上角结束。统一顺序规则，这既方便初学者找到绘图捷径，有规可依，又让第一次阅读思维导图的读者知道从哪里开始，有序可循。

四、思维导图绘制的步骤

1. 俯览全貌，聚焦主题（中心）

思维导图绘制的首要策略，就是先对素材做全面了解然后聚焦主题（中心）。主题（中心）具有牵引性，帮助导出图中各个分支。它可以是标题、事件、事物、核心观点，甚至是态度与情感。

2. 找准关键词，构思分支

思维导图最大的特色之一就是通过找出关键词所代表的图像，它能更清晰地透过图像的引导，在脑海中还原出文章重点。而左脑的最大专长就是分析事物并做出判断，抽丝剥茧找出不同事物之间的关系。因此，我们通过找准关键词，对关键词进行构思，选择恰当的图形、图像、符号来阐释分支意义，多用一些视觉、听觉、嗅觉、味觉等元素，使大脑更容易理解与记忆。

3. 扩展层次，延伸分支

思维导图的分层通常是放射式层次，越重要的内容越靠近中心，由内向外逐渐扩展。一般情况下从中心分支延伸出来的分支不要超过7个（大脑短时记忆一次能记住7个信息片段），因为主干越多越不利于记忆，而且理解起来也很困难。

4.巧画连线，拓展联想

连线是思维导图的重要组成部分，连接关键词和图标之间应该是生动的、富有创意的曲线，而不是直线。因为曲线就像我们大脑神经系统的脉络一样，它更符合自然，具有美的元素。每条连线都要与前一条连线的末端衔接起来，并从中心向外扩散。否则，思维就会出现断层，记忆与联想也随之出现断层。

5.图标色彩，增强视觉

图标和色彩是思维导图调用大脑各个部分功能的重要技巧。图标，即画简单的图形来表意，把个体领悟到的内容和丰富的思想感情用简笔画的形式画出来。色彩，是各种形式思想最主要的刺激物，它可以表示线性联系之外的关联，红色或色彩边框等可以起到突出重点的作用。一般建议使用三种以上的色彩。

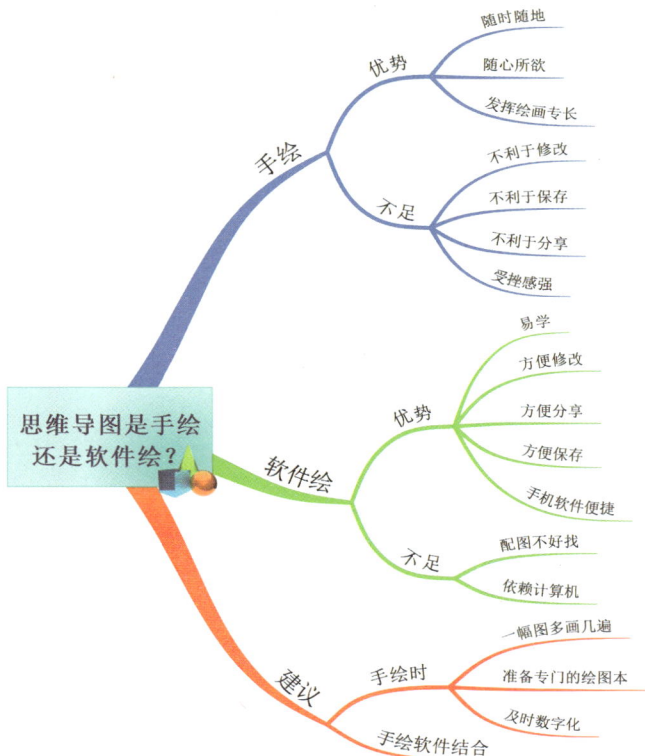

手绘制作思维导图与软件制作思维导图的比较①

---

① 赵国庆.别说你懂思维导图［M］.北京：人民邮电出版社，2015.

　　如上图，随着信息技术的发展，思维导图的软件开发越来越多了。对于用手绘好还是软件绘制好人们各有己见，众说纷纭。早期的思维导图基本上都是手绘的多，但随着信息技术的发展，目前针对绘制思维导图的设计特点而开发的软件越来越多了，如：iMindMap、XMind、MindMapEditor、 MindManager、Inspiration、FreeMind、 Personalbrain、MindGenius、Kidspiration、MindMaster、百度脑图、万彩脑图大师等。其中Kidspiration是专门为儿童学习量身定做的，它在界面设计和图画库内容上充分考虑了儿童的认知特点， 配备了英文语音提示，适合小学生学习英语时使用。XMind还提供了手机App版。不管哪种方法，只要能完美地表达中心主题就行了，事实上经常是两者交替地使用。

望着即将成书的稿子，我百感交集。虽然窗外已是炎炎的夏日，虽然朋友们大都已在旅行的途中，但我的内心仍然很平静，因为我享受着成稿带来的快乐。

自2013年主持课题"思维导图在小学英语教学中的应用研究与实践"以来，我与课题组成员用了两年时间完成了研究工作，用了一年的时间去应用和验证，并于2016年课题获得了惠州市第九届教育科研成果一等奖。同年，我荣幸成为广东省名师工作室主持人。四年来，依托工作室我把研究成果由实验学校扩大到惠州市各县区，伴随着工作室承担全国各地的跟岗任务，研究的成果也相继扩大到西藏林芝、广东湛江、潮州、梅州、汕头、汕尾、清远、肇庆、揭阳、韶关等地，反响热烈。

"纸上得来终觉浅，绝知此事要躬行"，在整个课题研究与应用推广的七年过程中，我与课题组成员通过理论学习、专题讲座、研讨课、示范课、送课下乡等形式不断地检验课题研究成果的可操作性与实用性。同时应惠州学院外国语学院、各县区进修学校以及兄弟学校的邀请先后做了60多场关于思维导图应用于小学英语教学中的讲座，指导了20多名教师在各级赛课中获得一等奖，这些都为本书的编写积累了丰富的素材。在成书之时我也深深地体会到以下几点。

一、要做有生命力的课题

我们从狭义上常说：问题即是课题。课题"思维导图在小学英语教学中的应用研究与实践"就是基于过去我们的英语课堂以教师为主，学生被动学习，造成学习兴趣不浓，学习效果不佳的困境而提出的。如何通过优化课堂教学策略来发展学生的发散思维，从而培养学生自主学习的能力无疑是本课题提出的基础。这些年，我们把课题的研究成果回归应用于一线课堂教学，并广泛地推广应用验证，可以说，其所到之处皆为赞之、学之和用之。这让我深刻地认识到只有把一线教学中遇到的问题上升为课题研究，然后把研究的成果反馈于一线教学实践并对教学改革有促进作用的课题才是有生命力的课题。

二、独行速，众行远

"事非经过不知难"，从开始有写书的想法，到如今书稿即将付梓，从对书的内容的界定到内容的编排，还有涉及出版书的经费等等，其间经历了许多的不易，个中甘苦不一一罗列。最重要的是书中每一幅思维导图从对文本内容的阅读到小组讨论得出的初图，再到电脑的绘制，最后到校对，无不凝聚了全体编委的心血和集体智慧。这里要特别感谢两位电脑高手，一位是来自广东省惠州东湖双语学校的董智慧老师，另一位是来自广东省惠东县新安小学的叶思通老师，每一期的思维导图绘制培训他们都让老师们满载而归，对书中每一幅思维导图的绘制做到精益求精。这里再次让我领悟到团队的重要性。感谢一直陪伴我前行的伙伴们。

三、千点万点不如高人一点

我的专业成长得到很多高人的指点，这是我人生最宝贵的财富。在思维导图应用于课堂教学的研讨课例中，我们的课例得到了北京师范大学外文学院程晓堂和王蔷两位教授的亲临点评。课题在申报、开题、实施、结题等环节中我得到了十余年来亦师亦友的惠城区教育局教研员李军荣老师的指导，是他七年来持续为我提供实施的平台！在课题研究成果的应用推广过程中，我得到了惠州市教育科学研究院陈绍安副院长（现任广东省惠州市华罗庚中学校长）的支持与帮助，是他为我搭建了与全市中小学校教育一线的桥梁，让思维导图的研究成果绽放光彩！

写到这里，书稿算是匆匆完成了，心中感动、感谢、感恩！在此，对所有帮助过我的领导、专家、导师和同行们表示深深的谢意。

本书的编写参考和吸收了许多专家的研究成果，凡是引用的均已在参考文献中罗列，感谢这些前辈们的贡献。同时特别鸣谢三名书系编辑部对我们整个撰写过程的指导与帮助。由于本人学识尚浅，书中一定还有很多遗漏、不当甚至错误之处，还望广大读者匡谬赐正。

韩丽萍
2020年8月于惠州